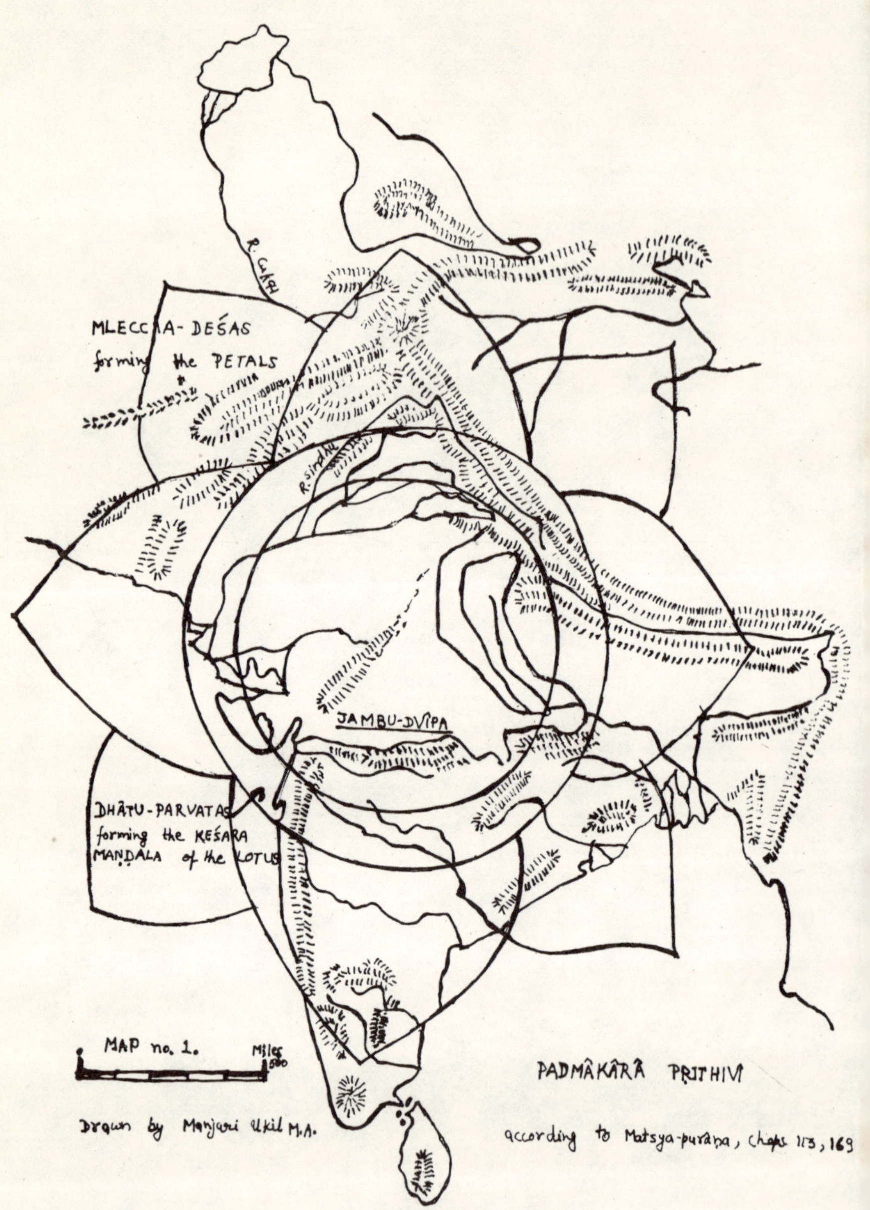
MLECCHA-DEŚAS
forming the PETALS
R. Sindhu
JAMBU-DVĪPA
DHĀTU-PARVATAS
forming the KEŚARA
MAṆḌALA of the LOTUS
MAP no. 1.
Miles 500
Drawn by Manjari Ukil M.A.
PADMÂKÂRÂ PṚTHIVI
according to Matsya-purāṇa, Chaps. 113, 169

Foreign Influence on Indian Culture

(from c. 600 B.C. to 320 A.D.)

Manjari Ukil

Originals

Delhi-110052

Published by
Originals
(an imprint of Low Price Publications)
A-6, Nimri Commercial Centre,
Near Ashok Vihar Phase-IV, Delhi-110052
Phones: 27302453
e-mail: lpp@nde.vsnl.net.in
visit us at: www.lppindia.com

First Published 2006

ISBN 81-88629-60-X

Printed at
D K Fine Art Press P Ltd.
Delhi-110052

PRINTED IN INDIA

Dedicated to

Baba and Ma

with the best wishes and love

and

To my beloved husband Shantanu Ukil

under whose inspiration after my marriage

I completed my studies,

without him it would not have been completed.

I am grateful to him

Bukuma

Manjari Ukil

Preface

In his inimitable style in the poem "***He Mor Chitta***" (O My Mind) Gurudev Rabindranath Tagore has said that in this vast sea of humanity of India have mingled so many races from far and wide,

"In this land of India, on the shore of vast humanity

We know not whence, and at whose call, these myriad stream of men

Have come rushing forth impetuously to lose themselves in this sea.

Aryan and non-Aryan, Dravidian and Chinese, Scythian, Hun, Pathan and Moghul, all, have merged into one body".

(Translated by late Indira Devi Chowdhurani, Visva-Bharati Quarterly, Vol. VI, 1929).

In this book I have dealt with certain aspects of culture of ancient India from c. 600 B.C. to 320 A.D. The complex nature of Indian culture makes it impossible to trace the traits left by the foreigners in that remote past. In a diverse and culturally rich country like India of the ancient times there remains very little difference between civilization and culture.

The cultural life of a nation consists of social behaviour of its inhabitants manifested in their typical customs and usages, it's spiritual emancipation enriched by the advancement of ethics, philosophy religion, it's aesthetic experiences and technical abilities expressed through the medium of fine arts and other aspects of higher pursuit s of intellectual life. I have examined in some detail and traces that the westerners left upon three major aspects of Indian culture, viz., social life, fine arts and religion.

When I started my study several years ago, on this subject, I had thought to make an attempt to trace the history of how India enriched her culture as a result of the contacts with the foreigners, who came over and over again and made India their home. So I had the title of my work as "Foreign Influence of Indian Culture". But as gradually my work progressed, I realised that the topic was too ambitious and its scope was too wide as it would have meant to trace the influence of all the foreign tribes on all the aspects of Indian culture, which would not have been possible for me to do justice in a few years time. Consequently, I limited my studies to the western influences on some aspects of ancient Indian culture to make of the study more precise.

I have planned the work in the following manner: First, the period of the study has been defined. I have chose this period as it witnessed the succession of foreign invasions and immirgation from the West and those people had brought with them completely new and different traditions of social institutions, techniques in fine arts and theistic ideas. India finds herself faced to difficult situations as the invaders had many uncommon cultural traits than hers. How India adjusted to their culture as circumstances necessitated is a highly fascinating history. It relates how the indigenous and the foreign tribes tried to solve the first clashes of inconsistency which later on subsided down to give way to co-operation and mutual understanding. This happy co-ordination is one of the chief virtues of Indian civilization.

References in literature about India's contact with the West in this period have come down to us. It was in this epoch that the Indians absorbed in spiritual thinking, saw the incursions of the sophisticated Persians from Achaemenid Iran, the proud and energetic Greeks and Bactrians, the more savage yet remarkably adaptable Scythio-Parthians and the versatile Kushans in the heart of their motherland. It was in this period that we find India becoming conscious about lands beyond her boundary and her horizon stretching out towards the West.

I have given a brief political outline as a background of the whole picture. In the following sections I have dealt with the land and the sea-routes to and from the west to India, as those routes were followed in those ages. I have based my discussion of routes on contemporary sources, chiefly Indian.

In the second chapter I have discussed the available Indian literary sources for the purpose. How and in what sense the term *Mleccha* (meaning a foreigner) has been used in the contemporary Indian literature is discussed in an independent section of this chapter. Some of the Indian tribes who had settled in the ages preceding in the bordering regions had been actually influenced deeply by the foreign contacts in this period and were branded as *Mlecchas*. They contributed considerably in enriching Indian culture. So I have included several of them for my study.

In the third chapter, the western impacts on ancient India's social system have been included. The reason for presenting a study of social life first is that, before an external influence is felt on any other spheres of culture of a land, society in general faces its impacts first of all, and it is more susceptible to new things while other aspects of culture are rather conservative.

The Indian society is comprised of many institutions and systems, such as, the distinction of the castes, the various *saṃskāras* (customs) which the people followed and common ways of life. The foreign impact is rather obvious on some of those social institutions while on the others it is not quite clear. I have taken into account only those aspects of social life on which the alien traits are somewhat pronounced.

After causing certain changes or renovations in the society, the newly arrived forces find their way to the realm of fine arts. They rejuvenate the visual and plastic expression and add new innovations to the sphere of music, dance and drama. They add new varieties to the already existing set-motifs of the minor arts, refresh the stereo-typed skill of the traditional artists, artisans and craftsmen. In the fourth chapter, I have presented a study of all these influences in the realm of fine arts. It is a seizing history of how the new-comers made themselves and their skill prominent through the chisel and brushes of the native artists and artisans.

The foreign impacts take longest time to react on the sphere of religious life of a people. It seems that the human mind is more conservative in his theistic dogmas and anything that is new or blended with an exotic colouring is accepted only after a prolonged, time-tested persistence. Religion is the last to yield before a fresh surge of foreign ideas. Society may accept new ways in it's everyday life, that is, the styles may change in dress and costume, new dishes may be added to the culinary art, and acceptance of new modes and mediums of expression in it's feelings in fine arts becomes obvious, yet it adheres to it's philosophical and religious beliefs of hoary past. For India of the past as has been said that art was the "hand-maid of religion"; any adjustment and inter-change of ideas in the realm of religion is bound to tint her artistic expressions too.

The fifth and the last chapter of the book deals with the study of the western influences of the religious beliefs of India. I have discussed the possible influence on the Brahmanical religion in a more detailed manner. In separate sections, I have dealt with the various prominent sects that flourished during this period. The *Mahāyāna* Buddhism has been left out from this study as it's main development does not come in the period and it is commonly accepted that Jainism got hardly influenced by any external doctrine.

During this period of study general disturbances and calamities fell over the land. One can easily imagine that the successive foreign invasions of the Achaemenid Iranians, Hellenistic Greeks and specially of the Bactrian Greeks, the barbarious Schythio-Parthians and the Kushans aroused a feeling of insecurity in the mind of the common people. It was heightened up by the bitter strife in between the followers of Gautama Buddha, Mahavira and the orthodox adheres of the earlier Vedic tradition. It seems, that in this period when the political sky of India was clouded with transitional uncertainties, the common people, irrespective of their faiths, viz. Vedic, Buddhist or Jaina, greeted any government that provided a shelter to them, e.g., be it Indo-Hellenistic, Scythian or Kushan, be the ruler a man with cosmopolitan outlooks, a devout Buddhist or a *Brāhmaṇa*, a *Kshatriya*, even a *Vrātya*.

It is only natural, that some humanitarian authorities, took the leading role and tried to create a happy harmony amongst the diverse centrifugal forces. Fortunately enough some of the great kings of this period—Aśoka, Menander, Kanishka and Rudradaman were personalities of this rank. Indeed, the contemporary agriculturists, business guilds, artists, artisans, doctors, astrologers, priests, officials, clerks, literati—all belonging to the commoner's class had welcomed the golden rule of these kings which did not make any difference between the races, the castes and faiths. It appears from the literary references that the followers of the Gautama Buddha were somewhat more liberal in accepting the foreigners into their fold. But as their contribution towards culture was indiscriminately utilized by the Hindus, Buddhists and Jainas alike no classification has been made to define Brahmanical culture or Buddhist culture. Hence no distinction has been made either to describe a picture of a Hindu society or a Buddhist society, and Brahmanical art and Buddhist art. The archaeological remains of this period are mostly Buddhistic, and it had cast a profound influence on the Hindu art and architecture of the period that followed. Therefore what the Buddhists accepted from the foreigners was adopted and applied by the Hindus.

The subject is very fascinating. This book is not in any way conclusive. It is just an attempt to present a picture of the cultural interaction of an age of the history of our land when it came in contact with the others. The brief account that has been given is atleast sufficient to show how receptive and full of vitality our people of these age were. This could be just an opening for a fuller study of all the aspects of India's culture. For a comprehensive study of this nature it is absolutely imperative to know many classical languages like Old Persian, Hebrew, Greek, Latin etc., and I have contended myself only with the English translations. Though some of these aspects have been studied by other great scholars, I have tried to present a little more complete picture of the various aspects in this book and at many places I have suggested some new interpretations.

While conscious of my limitations I submit this book with the words of

Śrīmadbhāgavāta Gītā:

"Karmaṇye-vādhikāraste..."

Santiniketan
September, 1964

Manjari Ukil

Foreword

It is difficult to write about an author and her work with detachment and dispassion if one's past remains inseparably intertwined with her personality, as is natural if the author happens to be one's mother. Keeping this constraint firmly in view, we attempt a foreword here with a certain amount of trepidation.

In an age when political boundaries apart, almost all other mutually exclusive barriers are fast giving way to an emerging global composite culture, it is immensely interesting to look back and glean information, as much as possible, about a hoary past of cultural cross-fertilization of ideas and methods that had taken place on the land that is known as physical Indian subcontinent. This is an area of academic investigation that enjoys ever increasing relevance even after the passage of more than 2,500 years since the days when the people of this land had experienced cultural intercourse with their immediate western and north-western neighbours from south-west and central Asia. For thousands of years innumerable groups of men, women and children, often peaceful, often in the form of an invading army or as groups of nomadic herders, came to this land to conquer to settle and to populate. The story of their cultural encounter with primarily Hindu-Brahmanical and Buddhist-Jain India is dealt here in some detail.

The present study may help discerning scholars to understand an aspect of ancient Indian history, which is primarily reconstructed here from the references as found in the indigenous literary evidences, corroborated by subsequent archaeological findings and interpretations.

The author, Dr. Manjari Ukil (1936-2004), studied Indology at Visva-Bharati University from the mid-1950s till 1964. As her allied subjects she studied three ancient Indian languages, viz. Sanskrit, Pali and Ardhamagadhi. This, indeed, qualified her to conduct an inquiry into an area of Indian cultural past where the appropriate languages with their grammar and etymology, along with epigraphy and numismatics, are probably the only available tools to decipher the mystery.

Manjari was born into the Dey family of Santiniketan and married into the Ukil family of New Delhi, both families of modern Indian painter artists, who were responsible in more ways than one for the enrichment and expansion of India's aesthetic ideals within and beyond the borders of modern political India. We believe this provided the author with some insights into the subject of our common cultural history, which she tried to share as exhaustively as was possible. Whether she was successful in her attempt or not, is for the readers to judge.

In the absence of the author amongst us, we take the opportunity to express deep gratitude to Sh. Pradeep Mittal and Ms. Gita Dua for making this publication possible. Without them the work would never have seen the light of day. Our deep gratitude is also extended to Sm. Rimli Borooah for her editorial suggestions.

Mukul Dey Archives
'Chitralekha' House
P.O. Santiniketan
West Bengal, India
25 July 2006

Satyasri Ukil
Shivashri Ukil

Contents

One

Introduction

Since time immemorial, India had been having intimate contacts with the world surrounding her. A discussion of the main routes of communication from India to abroad in ancient days is of prime importance for a comprehensive idea about the whole. The term '*Mleccha*' often occurs in Indian literature to connote a 'foreign' intruder and therefore a discussion to define the exact significance of the term seems also necessary.

From the dawn of history, foreign tribes, some as peaceful immigrants and others as valiant invaders have come through the north-western mountain passes of Indian peninsula. Many of them were able to reach the very heart of the land while others settled in groups in the bordering regions and worked as intermediaries in between different cultures, that approached India in successive waves. During a foreign domination these tribes took active part in enriching the Indian civilization, in contrast to their status under the Brahmanical rule, when they were despised more so because of their lineage, which according to the Vedic Aryans was considered as 'non-Aryan' in origin, and their peculiar social customs, which went against the Vedic faith. Yet, their cultural contributions are proved to be of lasting value and have come down to us as our national heritage. Some of these ideas and customs are common enough while others remained obscure, the history of their true origin has disappeared into the darkness of oblivion.

Section I

The Political Outline and the Period Defined

From the advent of the Indo-Aryans to their settling down in this country, nearly a millennium passed. Inter-changes of ideas between the Aryan new-comers and the native inhabitants of this land led to a cultural synthesis and crystallized in the form of Brāhmaṇa-dominated society based on the "*Caturvarṇāśrama-dharma*" plan. The period of the present study begins from about c.600 B.C., a date important from many points of view. In this period the thickly populated Janapadas were giving way to the four principal states, which in their turn were dominated by the supremacy of Magadha. The ancient and the more revered laws were being codified. On the other hand the *Kṣhatriyas* were feeling uncomfortable under the all-powerful *Brāhmaṇas*, while some questioned the authority of the Vedas, and the bloody paraphernalia of a Vedic sacrifice. Consequently groups of mendicants known as the *Ājīvīkas* and the *Śramaṇas* branched off from the Vedic religious system and India saw great Masters like Vardhamāna, the Mahavīra and Gautama, the Buddha. The economic activities attracted greater attention of the people; trade and commerce with the western world became brisk. In one word, an urban culture was taking shape in place of the rural society and was aspiring for an imperial suzerainty that was yet to come.

It was in this period (c. 550 B.C.) that Cyrus ascended the throne of Persia, whence started a chain of events important for the political as well as cultural history of India. His contemporary Indian king was Bimbisāra of the *Haryaṅka* dynasty and Puṣkarasārin was ruling in the land of *Gāndhāra*.[1] It is certain the "Cyrus led an expedition against India" and Indian tribes like the *Aṣṭakas* and the *Aśvakas* had to accept the Persian domination.[2] Contacts became more intimate when Darius the Great, sent a Greek sea-captain Scylax of Caryanda to explore the river Sind about c. 513 B.C. This expedition was preliminary to a conquest after which the 'Hindus' (i.e., Hidus) were included within the list of the tribute-paying subjects of Darius. Some more tribes belonging to the bordering regions of India viz., the Gandharians, Sattagydians, and Arians are mentioned, obviously after being reduced by Darius' force.[3] Xerexes maintained his hold on the Indian provinces and Indian soldiers recruited by him stand out in the army that marched against Hellas.[4] The South Tomb inscription of Artaxerexes II mention the Hi(n)dus side by side with the Sattagydians, Gandharians and other Persian subjects.[5] Ktesias, moreover, informs us that Artaxerexes II (c. 405-358 B.C.) received costly presents from India.[6] But for most parts his accounts are 'traveller's tales' and little reliance can be put to them. But there is no doubt, that contact between India and Persia was intimate so he was able to collect his information about India from the Persian court. Even as late as Darius III Codomannus, the 'three distinct group of Indians figured in the army which mustered under the banner of the Persian monarch', with whom Alexander had his encounter. The close contact of India with Achaemenid Iran for a little more than two centuries is of profound importance for Indian culture, as we shall see in the following chapters.

With the final defeat of Darius III in 330 B.C. and progress of the invasion of Alexander in 327-26 B.C., the frontier of India was opened afresh to western influences, this time mainly Hellenistic. Stray references in literature show that peaceful immigrants and captives have infiltrated through the Achaemenid empire and had founded settlements on Indian borderland from time previous to the Macedonian conquest.[7] Alexander's invasion, though a short-lived enterprise, had left its two important results: – the consolidation of the great Maurya empire and the rise of the Indo-Greeks in Bactria, the Kabul valley and north-western India.

The three great rulers of the Maurya dynasty: Chandragupta, Bindusāra and Aśoka had maintained a foreign policy which sustained the cultural atmosphere and the interchange of ideas between India and the west. Thus the Greek ambassador Megasthenes had come and resided in the court of Chandragupta in Pāṭaliputra. Thanks to his observations about Indian life preserved in the quotations of the later writers, without the light of which Indian works, viz., the *Arthaśāstra* of Kauṭilya would have remained in the darkness of negligence. Bindusāra followed the friendly policy and received ambassadors from the kings of Syria and Egypt.[8] The episode of the "private friendly correspondence" between Bindusāra and Antiochos (I, Soter) is well-known and arouse curiosity in the minds of the historians.

The diplomatic relation between the Mauryan Empire and the western powers was utilized and undertaken by Aśoka in a larger scale. His "missions" to the foreign powers viz., Antiochus II Theos, king of Syria and Western Asia (B.C. 261-246); Ptolemy II Philadelphos, king of Egypt (B.C. 285-247); Magas, king of Cyrene, North Africa (c. 258 B.C.); Antigonas Gonatas, king of Macedonia (B.C. 277-239) and Alexander, king of Epirus (B.C. 272-c. 255) or Alexander the ruler of Corinth (B.C. 252-c. 244) have been immortalized by the famous Rock Edict XIII.[9]

Beginning with the death of Aśoka (c. 233-23 B.C.) to the end of Bṛihadratha (c. 187 B.C.) the Maurya power gradually diminished. This synchronizes with the period of the rise of the Bactrian Greeks after they threw off the yoke of their Seleucidan masters (c. 250 B.C.). In or about c. 187 B.C India was threatened by an attack of the 'Yavanas' (i.e., the Bactrian Greeks in this case) from the north-west, and taking advantage of this political crisis Puṣyamitra Śuṅga, a powerful minister of the Maurya king Bṛihadratha usurped the throne. Demetrius was the leader of the invasion who opened the way towards India afresh for the Bactrian Greeks.[10]

From the reign of Puṣyamitra Śuṅga (c. 187 B.C.) who was 'heading the reaction promoted by the *Brāhmaṇas'* we find dual forces working simultaneously in shaping the cultural tendencies of north India. The Bactrian Greeks and following them the Indo-Greeks of north-western frontiers and the Punjab and Sind directly or indirectly introduced some Hellenistic ideas in this land, while the Śuṅgas and the Kāṇvas upheld the orthodox Brahmanical faith in Eastern and Central India. At least two foreign names, one of Heliodorus, the ambassador of

Antialkidas to Bhāgabhadra and the other of Menander, the 'faithful' king have been immortalized for their religious fervor and loom bright in the pages of socio-religious history of India.

About c. 145 B.C. the Bactrian kingdom fell before the invading Śakas from Central Asia. The year c. 129-127 B.C. is important from the fact that during these years the Śakas won a victory over the Parthian monarch Phraates II (138-128 B.C.). But with the reign of Mithridates II, the Great (123-88 B.C.) events took a different course. The Śakas under the strong hand of Mithridates had to quit their further procedure towards Iran and turned eastwards to India. By the way of Ariana (southern Afghanistan) they came to Kandahar, crossed the Bolan and the Mulla passes and descended on the plains of lower Indus Valley sometime before c. 32 B.C. This region was called "Indo-Scythia" by the classical writers because of the tribe's connection with the place.[11] It is generally believed that Maues, the first Scythian king in India came to power in between c. 32-20 B.C.

The Śakas were able to establish several satrapies in different parts of India governed by the House of Maues in Taxila, another at Mathura under the supremacy of *Mahā-kṣatrapa* Rājula. The third satrapy in western India, which comprised the Surāṣ ṭra, Anarta and Avantī regions (modern Kutch, Kathiawar, Surat and Malva) was governed successively by two houses, first by that of Bhūmaka and the second belonging to Caṣṭana. This ruling *Kṣatrapas* of the south-west rivaled the supremacy of the Andhra-Śātavāhanas of the Deccan.

The Taxilan House of Maues was intimately connected with the line of a group of Parthian kings, the most important of which was Gondopharnes (c. 45 A.D.). The chronological history of this period is a hopelessly confused one, and the assumptions are liable to changes with the discoveries of new numismatic and paleographic evidences in future. But as far as cultural history is concerned, it can be said with certainty, that they were considered more or less one and same by the ancient Indian accounts.

By c. 64 A.D. another foreign tribe viz., the Kushana branch of the Yuehchi race established themselves in the Kabul Valley and in 78 A.D. the Great Kushana Kanishka launched upon his dazzling career. Nearly a century starting from c. 44-45 A.D. to 150 A.D. is very important, as it witnessed the rule of illustrious foreign sovereigns like Phraotes, Gondopharnes, Kanishka and Rudradāman, who were men of versatile genius and of liberal outlook.[12] It must have had lasting and profound impressions upon the minds of contemporary literati and intelligentsia.

Nomadic tribes from the west, taking advantage of these foreign dominations came in and settled within the land. It is common in history, that a greater immigration of hordes is followed by smaller ones. Several other foreign dynasties, like the one of Iśvaradatta, the Ābhīra of western India (his coins have been found in Kathiawar, c. 236-239 A.D.)[13] the Śaka Muruṇḍas of the east (Ayodhyā and Pāṭaliputra),[14] and the later Kushanas and Schythians i.e., Śākas (Balkh, Afghanistan and parts of the Punjab)[15] as well as the Sassanids[16] held the ruling authority for some time. In course of time these tribes lost their separate entity and became naturalized Indians.

Thus, from sixth century B.C. onwards one finds India open to western influences. The surge of assimilating the foreign elements rose high under the Śaka-Kushanas, it brought forth its finest products under the Imperial Guptas after 320 A.D.

The cultural development of a land is a continous panorama and cannot be visualized within the scope of age-limited panels. Yet, we have to concentrate in this book that very period when the western influences were imparted on various branches of culture. Bearing this in mind, we close our discussion on the eve of the rise of the Guptas.

References

1. H.C. Raychaudhuri, PHAI, pp. 227-228.
2. Arrian, iii, Indica I, CAI, p. 214, mentions them as 'Astakenoi' and 'Assakenoi'.
3. Bisutum inscription mentions 'Gandhara' with Drangiana, Aria, Sattagydia, Arachosia etc., S. Sen, OPI, p. 6; Persepolis inscription

includes "hi(n)dus" i.e., Sindhuh, Ibid., pp. 93-94; Nax-i-Rustam inscription mentions "hi(n)dus" Ibid., pp. 97-98; Susa inscription mentions "...teak from Gandhara" and "ivory... from India." Ibid., p. 122; Persepolis inscription of Xerexes includes Gandhara, India, etc., Ibid., p. 151, as the land of tribute-paying subjects.

4. Herodotus, vii, 64-65.

5. The South Tomb inscription of Persepolis belonging to Artaxerexes II, points out the nationality of all the subjects of the empire including the Sattagydians, Gandharians and Hindus, S. Sen, OPI, pp. 172-173.

6. Raychaudhuri, PHAI, p. 243.

7. Herodotus, iii, 102, "There are other Indians bordering on the city of Caspatyrus and the country of Pactyice, settled northward of other Indias, *whose mode of life resembled that of the Bactrians*. They are the most war-like Indians and these are they who are sent to procure gold, for near this part there is a desert by reason of sand"(emphasis added). Ibid., iv, 204, vi, I; Arrian v, the tradition of the Mysaeans, Sélincourt, pp. 163-165; Majjhima Nikāya, II, 149; B.C. Law, TAI, pp. 154-56; A.K. Narain, The Indo-Greeks, Introduction, pp. 1-11.

8. Megasthenes, "Those of the second attend the entertainment of the foreigners", McCrindle, p. 87. These officers looked after the comforts and kept watch over the foreigner in Maurya Empire, Raychaudhuri, PHAI, pp. 298-300.

9. Rock Edict II, R. Basak, AI, pp. 7-8; Rock Edict XIII, Ibid., pp. 71-72.

10. Chattopadhyaya, EHNI, p. 6f.

11. The Periplus, 38-41, CAI, pp. 300-301; Ptolemy, vii, i. 55, CAI, pp. 372-373.

12. Apollonius states, "The king Phraotes, in answer said that he was moderate because his wants were few, and that he was wealthy, he employed his wealth in doing good things...and in subsidizing the barbarians.....he drank but little wine as much as he poured out in libation to the sun." CAI, p. 389.

    Though probably legendary in character, the Christian apocryphal Acts of Judas Thomas the Apostle tell that Gondopharnes was eager to receive a skilful foreign i.e., western carpenter for building a palace. To procure one he sent an Indian called Habban. This shows his interest in artistic endeavour. Moreover, his court must have had been renowned for its religious patronage and liberal outlook, so that his name was intentionally connected with the Christian church.

The learned assembly of scholars, theosophists, philosophers and literateur who adorned the court of Kanishka is too well-known to be recounted here.

The Junagadh inscriptions of Rudradāman, Ep. Ind., VIII, p. 44, bespeaks of his versatile genius in arts, literature and administration, his comely body and stately mien.

13. *Matsyapurāṇa*, 273. 18 and 24 mentions ten *Ābḥīra* kings in the dynastic list; The Nasik inscription of Iśvarasena, Ep. Ind. VIII, pp. 88-89. The Gundā inscription of the year 108 = 181 A.D., Ep. Ind. XV, p. 233; Raychaudhuri, PHAI, p. 498, n. 2, pp. 509-510; Chattopadhyaya, EHNI, p. 126 – the Iśvarasena of the Nasik inscription was probably connected with Iśvaradatta of the coins.

14. *Matsyapurāṇa* Ibid., 22; Ptolemy, "Morounda", CAI, p. 377; Pliny, "Molindae", Ibid., p. 342; Chinese accounts quoted in EHNI, p. 118; Raychaudhuri, pp. 401, 430, 546.

15. They are known chiefly from their coins and the Allahabad Pillar inscription of Samudra Gupta, Corp. Ins. Ind. III, I; Ep. Ind. XXII, p. 35; The Vakataka Gupta Age, pp. 12-19f.

16. The evidence is supplied by the Paikuli inscription and Tabari, discussed by Frye, The Heritage of Persia, p. 211; Chattopadhyaya, EHNI, pp. 132-134.

Section II

The Ancient Overland Routes

The Achaemenid kings controlled their realm with the help of a network of roads. India's political relation with the Achaemenid Empire have been discussed in the previous section. Herodotus tells, "A great part of Asia was explored under the direction of Darius. He being desirous to know in what part the Indus, which is the second river that produces crocodiles, discharges itself into the sea; sent in ships both others on whom he could rely to make a true report, and also Scylax of Caryanda. They accordingly, setting out from the city of Caspatyrus, and the country of Pactyice, sailed down the river towards the east and sunrise, to the sea: then sailing on the sea westward, they arrived in the thirtieth month at the place where the king of Egypt dispatched the Phoenicians, whom I before mentioned to sail round Lybia. After these persons had sailed round, Darius subdued the Indians, and frequented this sea. Thus the other parts of Asia, except towards the rising sun are found to exhibit things similar to Asia."[1] The city of Caspatyrus was probably situated in ancient *Gāndhāra*[2] in the upper Indus and the city of Pactyice "is apparently the ancient name of the modern Pathan country on the north-west border land of the sub-continent of India."[3] Ancient routes must have passed through these places and we shall see how Iranian and Greek elements were found in these bordering regions.[4] These frontiers i.e., *pratyantadeśas* were considered as much "foreign" or semi-barbarous by the Indians as they were reckoned "Indian" from the western stand point of view.

From the numerous references the *Jātakas* and the epic[5] we come to know that the *Kāmboja* horses were highly praised for their beauty, strength and speed. The merchants of Sind carried on horse-trade following the *Uttarāpatha* route. Scholars differ as regards the situation of the Kāmboja country,[6] but it can be stated with some certainty that routes must have connected this land with Ferghanah, which produces "the great

Parthian chargers who were said to have descended from the 'heavenly' horse".[7] Trade in horses had been going on from very ancient times and the traders must have come in association with people possessing debased type of culture. So that might have been the reason for Baudhāyana to exhort the abstinence from horse trade.[8]

By the time of Alexander knowledge about India became dim, his campaign with bands of engineers, guides, mercenaries and overseers[9] and the great task undertaken by him to found new ways, equipped with walls, new cities and settlements undoubtedly gave a fresh impetus to the older routes of contact. The old and new routes had reciprocal effects on each other, the Achaenenid roads made it possible for Alexander to penetrate through the heart of the Persian Empire and reach the banks of the Indus while the ancient tracks and harbours were once more repaired and provided with halting stations during his campaign.[10]

Alexander followed the route used by Xerexes through Hellespontine, Phrygia, Cappadocia and Cilicia to Asia Minor. After returning from his visit to Ammon in 331 B.C. he proceeded to Iran and had his encounter with the Persian monarch in Gaugemela and Arbela. He then went down south to Babylon, Susa and Persepolis, from there following the ancient road he proceeded north to Ecbatana, Hecatompylos, Hyrcania and traversed the way to Aria (Alexandria Areion-Herat) and came down southwards to Drangiana. Taking the course of the Helmund river he came to Kandahar, crossed Ghazni and Kabul and through the Khawak Pass (or the Panjshir Pass according to Holdich) entered the land of Bactria. He passed through Drapsaka (Kunduz), Aornos (Tashkurgan), Bactra-Zariaspa or Andareb[11] and entered the land of Sogdiana in the north. He went up to the rivers Polytimetus (Zarafshan) and Jaxartes (Syr Daria) and founded Alexandreschate (Chodjend). By coming down south by the way of Hissar and Faisabad he took the former route and came through the Kaoshan Pass to Paropamisadae. There he founded Alexandria, near Kāpiśa.[12] He traversed the valley watered by the Cophen (Kabul), Choaspes (Kunar), Gouraios (Panjkora), Suastos

(Swat) and entered the Gāndhāra country via Puṣkalāvatī in the Swat Valley. After his decisive winning over the rock of Aornos and victory over Porus he proceeded and founded Niceaea on the east and Bucephala on the west of the Hydaspes (Jhelum), gained Śākala on the stream of the Awak, crossed the river Hydraotes (Ravi) and Hyphasis (Beas) but due to the resentment in the army went back to Bucephala, where from he took the southerly course of the Hydaspes to the Indus. On the spot where the Indus bifurcated he founded Pattala (probably modern Bahmanabad).[13] Craterus was sent by the way of Kandahar and Seistan to Persia. The same route was traversed by the Śakas during their occupation of Seistan and the lower Indus Valley (i.e., Sind) in first century B.C. With a zeal to open an easier sea-route he sent Nearchus on a costal voyage from the mouth of the Indus to Antioch Charax by the Arabian Sea, gulf of Hormuz and Persian Sea. He himself took the difficult land-route through the desert tracts of Gedrosia to Persepolis via Alexandria (Gulashkird). Alexander died shortly after this on 13 June 323 B.C., but his dreams came true when in the years that followed, – "in Seleuceia, like a nerve center met all the great routes across Asia south of the Caspian and of the Steppes; the most important, which traversed the whole of breadth of Asia from the Ganges to the Aegian and which is well-known from Greek and in parts from Chinese and Indian sources."

These routes described by Herodotus, Arrian and others and the northern and southern routes from Central Asia, which joined at Balkh were in constant use during the period of the Bactrian Greeks and especially parts of Central Asia, Afghanistan and Northern India. Fa-Hsien who visited India just after our period of study (he started in A.D. 399 and returned to China in A.D. 414) took the route which "lay through the hills via Karghalik and Tash-kurghan (Aornos) and then along difficult valleys and mountain passes to Kashmir and the neighbouring countries".[14] He visited Nagara-hāra (Jalalabad or Greek Dionysopolis), Uḍḍiyāna and Suvastu (Swat-Valley), Gāndhāra and Taxila, the innermost cultural outpost of ancient India.

Many semi-foreign tribes viz. Sugdas, Cūlikas, Daradas, Pāradas, Tanganas etc., inhabited the fringes of the frontier of India and did not quite come within the pale of Indian culture, still they have found occasional mention in the great epic and other works. The land routes played a much more important rôle in the dissemination of western culture in India, but our study would not be complete without a reference to the sea-routes by the way of which many exotic ideas reached our land.

Unfortunately, we have no itinerary of the western route to India from Persia, except the ghastly description of Gedrosia left by Alexander's historians. Yet, references to the droughtful deserts, dreary mountain-blockades and difficult tracks of the west in the Rāmāyaṇa[15] prove that these trails were not absolutely untrodden by the ancient Indian adventurers.

A dismal and awe-arousing description of the western desert given in the *Vāyupurāṇa* states this:

"Antarāle girau tasmin Subaksaḥ śikhi-śailayoḥ,

Samantād yojana-śatamekabhūmaṇ śilātalam. 37

Nitya-taptaṃ mahāghoraṃ duḥsparśaṃ romaharṣaṇam,

*Agamyāṃ sarvasattvānāmīśvarāṇāṃ sudāruṇaṃ"*38 etc.

(Vayu, 37)

This shows that the frightful deserts were well-known to the Indian *Purāṇa-kāras*.

References

1. Herodotus, iv, 44.
2. Raychaudhuri, PHAI, p. 241; CHI, p. 336; Motichandra, Sārthavāha, p. 46, thinks it identical with Multan.
3. Raychaudhuri, op. cit., p. 214; CHI, pp. 82, 339.
4. Herodotus, vi, I. "...that when conquered in battle, they shall be enslaved; that we will make eunuchs of their sons, and transport their virgins to Bactra, and then give their country to others"..

   Ibid., iv, 204 "The farthest point of Africa to which this Persian army penetrated was the country of Euesperides. The Barcaeans, whom they have enslaved, they transported from Egypt to the king; and king Darius gave them a village in the district of Bactria, to dwell in. They gave them the name of Barce to this village, which was still inhabited in my time, in the Bactrian territory."

The story of the Branchidae told in Strabo xi, ii, 4; xiv, 1.5 and in other classical accounts show that they were a de-hellenized race who still remembered their history uptill the time of Alexander's conquest in Sogdiana; vide Plutarch, Moralia, 557 B; Curtius, vii, 5, 28-35.

H.G. Rawlinson, Bactria, p. 32, "Bactria seems to have been used as a sort of "Siberia" under the Persian kings".. ; Pliny, vi, 23; Strabo xv, II, 9, xv, I, 11; CAGI, pp. 17-18.

5. *Kukkura Jātaka* (22); *Bhojājānīya Jātaka* (23); *Bālodaka Jātaka* (183); *Kuṇḍaka-Kucchi-Sindhava-Jātaka* (254), etc. Mbh. 2.47.8, 2.47.16-18, (B.O.R.I.); 2.49.7, 2.48.16-18 (Haridas); 7.21.1-65 (Haridas); 7.22.1-60 (B.O.R.I.) describes horses in general; 7.22, refer to '*Kāmboja*' and 7.22.17-18 refer to '*Saindhava*' and '*Bāhlījāta*' horses.

6. Raychaudhuri, PHAI, p. 148 states "The Mbh. Connects the Kāmbojas with a place called Rājapura. – 'Karṇa Rājapuraṃ gatvā Kāmboja nirjitāstvayā'. The association of the Kāmbojas with Gāndhāras enables us to identify this Rājapura with the territory of that name mentioned by Yuan Chwang which lay to the south or south-east of Punch. The western boundaries of Kāmboja must have reached Kafiristan. Elphinstone found in that district tribes like the 'Caumojee', 'Camoze', and 'Camoje' whose name reminds us of the Kāmbojas."

   According to Tarn, GBI, p. 138, "Kāpiśa was the outlet for Kafiristan, the land of the Kāmbojas, who were possibly a valuable support to the Greeks – indeed it has been thought probable that Kāpiśa and Kāmboja are the same word; and the dual city was nearer to the Bactra than any other important city and commanded the three routes." vide p. 461 also.

7. Hiuen-Tsang mentions the Shen (excellent) horses of Central Asia and northern Afghanistan, vide Beal, i, pp. 20, 32, 54, 61; Tarn, pp. 308-309; Mbh. 2.47.4 (B.O.R.I.) mentions the "*Śukanāsikan*" or the "Parrot-nosed" horses, cf. bas – reliefs of horses from Pritchard, ANEP, Fig., 27, 28 f.

8. I, 1.2.4, Baudhyāna condemns this practice with other five northern customs.

9. Tarn, Alexander the Great, pp. 85-86.

10. Arrian, iv, 4.24; v. 20; vi, 17 etc.; Tarn, Ibid., pp. 133, 138, 145; For a fuller reference, vide Cary and Warmington, Ancient Explorers, p. 144, 145.

11. Holdich, Gates of India, p. 90, "Zariaspa is identified with Balkh by some authorities, but the name is probably a variant on Adrapsa which almost certainly was Andareb."

12. CAIG, p. 26, Opiane-Alexandria is the Opian near Charikar; pp. 28-30.

13. Ibid., pp. 320-327; CHI, p. 339; But Cary and Warmington prefers to identify Pattala with Hyderabad, Minnagara with Bahamanabad and 'Barbaricon' with Bahardipur, vide pp. 78 and 147.

14. P.C. Bagchi, India and China, p. 64.

15. Kiṣkindhyākāṇḍa, 43.23; –

    "Giri-jālāvṛitāṃ durgāṃ mārgitvā paścimāṃ diśam
    Acchidreṇa vicetabyā deśāḥ sa-giri-kandarāḥ.23"

Section III

The Sea-routes

In acting as cultural intermediary i4n between India and the Western lands the land routes played a much more important role, yet the discussion will not be complete without a reference to the sea-routes along which the western ships steered their courses to the shores of India. The Jātaka stories[1] and similar tales in the *Mahāvastu*[2] describe and refer to the sea-faring merchants and adventurous voyages undertaken by them. Taking other classical[3] accounts in consideration these voyages seem to have been coastal, confined along the western sea-board of India and the dreary coast of Makran,[4] starting from the Pattala on the mouth of the Indus and carried up to the opening of the Euphrates. The first recorded voyage, of this period, that of Scylax of Caryanda was carried on the same line.[5] He was followed by Nearchus[6] two centuries later. The coastal voyage was a perilous job on account of the absence of good harbours, drinking water, and the unfriendly disposition of the people who inhabited the Makran Coast. The country beyond the western Indus inhabited by the Arabitai,[7] the Oreitai[8] and the crude Ichthyophagi[9] or the Fish-eaters who appear from their description left by Nearchus to have belonged to the standard of Late Stone-Age. A group of them, who lived near the "winter torrent" Tomerous (Hingol) are described thus, 'The natives lived near the marshy grounds near the shore in cabins close and suffocating... They carried thick spears hardened at the point by fire... Those they captured had shaggy hair, not only on their head, but all-over their body, their nails resembled the claws of wild beasts, and were used it would seem, instead of iron for dividing fish, and splitting the softer kinds of wood. Things of hard consistency they cut with sharp stones, for iron they had none. As clothing they wore skins of wild beasts, and occasionally also the thick skins of the large sorts of fish.'[10]

Though written history is lacking from the time of Nearchus to the days of Pliny and the Periplus, it would not be improbable to assume that trade was carried on in between India and these regions and the inhabitants became acquainted with the usage of Indian commodities of common necessity. The statement in the Periplus makes it clear that the commodities of Indian manufacture from the country of Ariake were to be found in the kingdom of Zoscales.[11] It also states that the East African ports, where ships from Egypt that came in July were 'regularly supplied with the product of far beyond them Ariake and Barygaza'. Some of the trade centers in Arab like Aeudaemon[12] and Dioscordia[13] were regularly visited and were populated by Indian merchants, earlier to the discovery of Hippalus, who undertook coastal voyages, which were in all probability "used to be performed in small vessels which kept close to the shore and followed its windings."[14]

This trade received a new impetus and flourished greatly after the discovery of the monsoon by Hippalus in first century A.D.[15] Pliny clearly mentions four stages of this voyage.[16] In the first stage he mentions the coastal undertaken by Nearchus. The second stage is marked by the introduction of Hippalus, by the aid of which a direct voyage could be possible from Syagrus in Arabia to Pattala. In the third stage a shorter route was followed from Syagrus to Sigerus.[17] Pliny writes—"For a long time this route was followed until one still shorter was discovered by a merchant, and India was brought nearer to us through the love of gain,"—this marked the fourth stage.

Once the shorter route was discovered following the trend of the south-west monsoon, settlements of foreign traders must have grown up along the coasts of the Western Ghats:—Syrastrene, Sopara, Calliena, Mandagora, Palaepatmae, Melizigara, Byzantium, Togarum, Tyranoboas, Sesecreinae, Aegidioi, Chersonesus, Leuke Islands, Naura, Tyndis and Muziris, where 'a Roman temple amongst the palms would accord with the heterogenous tradition of the scene'.[18]

The great south Indian epic 'Silappadikāram' and other works corroborate the classical evidences by its numerous references to the *Yavanas*, their ships, their dexterity in shipbuilding[19] and carpentry[20] their abodes in the city of Puhar[21] and their love of pepper.[22] Interesting stories regarding the method of pepper-collecting are found in the classical accounts.[23]

These literary evidences are further corroborated by the finding of Roman coins in hordes at various places of south India, and in the ancient port of Poduke of Periplus i.e., the 'New Town' (modern Arikamedu) the coins are accompanied by ceramics of Roman manufacture.[24]

Graeco-Roman merchants became well-acquainted with the South-Indians as might be expected and vice-versa, yet the impact of Roman contact in south remained confined within the limit of purely commercial relationship, and did not reach beyond the superficial surface.[25]

The knowledge gathered from the Periplus becomes more and more vague as it gradually describes the north-east after crossing the Cape of Comari. It seems that foreign contacts were more intimate with the parts of the Western Ghats and with those lying far south than with the far-reaching ones of north-easterly direction. Yet, the famous metropolis of Tāmralipta was casually visited by the Roman ships, as art objects of Roman craftsmanship have been found here.[26] *Yavana* merchants visiting Tāmralipta are referred to in the classical Sanskrit literature of a later date.[27] The Bengali edition of the epic mentions "*Romāṇaḥ*" and "*Tāmraliptakāḥ*" in close affinity. This evidently shows that eastern India knew the Graeco-Roman sailors who frequented her eastern ports.

References

1. *Cullaka-Seṭṭhi Jātaka* (4); *Balahassa Jātaka* (196); *Bāveru Jātaka* (339); *Suppāraka Jātaka* (463); *Samudda-Vāṇija Jātaka* (466); etc.
2. Mahavastu, I, p. 200, ThāpakarṇI sails in ship; II, p. 87, A Brāhmaṇa went over-sea to perform a sacrifice for the merchant of the town beyond the ocean. Is the resident town called "Vāravāli" a corruption for "Dvārāvatī"? III, p. 71 ff. The five-hundred merchants and their Voyage.
3. Pliny, vi, 26.

4. Holdich, Ibid., pp. 135-168; Vide map facing p. 135.
5. Vide supra, p. 9.
6. Nearchus, Indica, CAI, pp. 313-336.
7. Nearchus, xxi, CAI, p. 315, "Then following the winding of the coast they ran a course of 120 stadia, and reached Krokola, a sandy island where they anchored and remained all next day. The country was inhabited by an Indian race called the Arabis,.. it is stated that they derive their name from the river Arbis, which flows through their country to the sea, and parts them from the Oreitai".
8. Ibid., xxiii and xxv, CAI, pp. 317, 319, "On the sixth day they weighed again, and after a course of 300 stadia reached a place called Malana, the last on the coast of Oreitai. In the interior these people dress like the Indians, and use similar weapons, but differ from them in their language and in their customs".
9. Ibid., xxiv, CAI, p. 318.
10. Cf., Strabo, xv. II. 2. 3, CAI, pp. 93-94; the crude Ichthyophagi somehow reminds us of the story of the town 'Meruvraja' related in ch. 169 of the *Śāntiparvan* of the great epic (Bengali version). It tells how a *Brāhmaṇa* became contaminated out-caste in association with the "*mlecchas*" of the north. These "*mlecchas*" are probably identical with the Ichthyophagi of the classical writers. A band of sea-going merchants and titanic bird called "*Bhāruṇḍa*" (cf., Ram. Kish. 43. 4) are also mentioned in Santip. 169.

    It seems that this sea was the bay of Makran bordering on the Malana coast. The "*Bhāruṇḍa*" (Mbh.) or the "*Siṃhika*" birds (Ram.) were adopted from the "Simurgh" of Itanian mythology, the precusor of the famous "Roc" of the Arabian Nights.
11. Periplus, 5, "Below Aduli about 800 stadia.. the king of all country is Zoscales,".
12. Ibid., 26, "In the bygone days when the merchants of India did not proceed to Egypt, and those from Egypt did not venture to cross over the marts further East, but both came only as far as this city, it formed the common center of their commerce".
13. Ibid., 30, "It consists of an intermixture of foreigners. Arabs, Indians and even Greeks who resort here for the purpose of commerce".
14. A study of the Indica of Nearchus and the Periplus testify the truth of this observation. Vide Periplus, 57.

15. Cary and Warmington, The Ancient Explorers, p. 75; Wheeler, RBIF, pp. 154-155; CAI, p. 337 assigns Pliny in between c. 23-79 A.D., so "Hippalus lived some very considerable time before the third quarter of the first century A.D. ...".

16. Pliny, vi, 23 (26). CAI, p. 337.

17. Ibid., p. 350, R.C. Majumdar thinks, "Sigerus has been taken to be the same with Melijigera in para 53 of the Periplus". But Wheeler takes it to be some place south of Bombay. Pliny, L.C.S. II. P. 415 identifies it tentatively with Jaigarh.

18. Wheeler, Ibid., p. 148; Mbh. 6.9.56 (Haridas) mentions Romans:

    "Vānāyavo Daśa-pārśva-Romāṇaḥ Kuśabindavaḥ

    Kacchā Gopāla-Kacchāśca Jāṅgalāḥ Kuru-varṇakāh."

    The same is in Mbh. 6.10.54-55 (B.O.R.I.), with slight variation of '*Lāṅgala*' and '*Paravallka*' for "*Jāṅgala Kuruvarṇaka.*"

19. *Śilappadikāram*, trans., Dikshitar, pp. 201, 323, 335. Their ships are referred to thus, "agitating the white foam of the Periyāru, the beautifully built ships of the Yavanas came with gold and returned with pepper, and Muziris resounded with the noise," P.T.S. Iyengar, The Tamil History of the Tamils from the earliest times to 600 A.D., p. 312, quoted from Wheeler, Arikamedu, Ancient India, No. 2, 1946, p. 21.

20. *Manimekhalai*, trans., K. Aiyangar, p. 159.."carpententers of Yavana." Wheeler, Ibid., p. 21.

21. *Śilappadikāram*, p. 110, "The sun shone over the open terraces, over the ware-houses near the harbours and over the turrets with air-holes looking like the eyes of deer. On different places of Puhar the onlooker's attention was arrested by the sight of the abodes of Yavanas whose prosperity was never on the wane. On the harbour were to be seen sailors from distant lands but for all appearance they lived as one community."

22. Iyengar, op. cit., Pliny, xiii, 14, Wheeler, RBIF, pp. 148-149.

23. Appollonius, CAI, p. 395.

24. Wheeler and others, Arikamedu, Ancient India, No. 2, 1946, pp. 17-125.

25. Wheeler, RBIF, p. 182, "..had no appreciabie or durable effect upon the cultures of the peninsula. It left a superficial imprint here and there sometime in remarkably remote places, but nowhere south of the Vindhyas was that imprint more than a graffito upon an essentially self-sufficient native fabric."

26. P.C. Dasgupta, Indian Folk-lore, Jan.-March, 1958, pp. 17-34.

27. Daṇḍin, *Daśakumara Caritam*, VI, p. 215, "*Dāmalipta*", cf. Mbh. 6.9.56-57 (Haridas), 6.10.54-55 (B.O.R.I.) which mention '*Romāṇaḥ*' and '*Tāmraliptakāḥ*' in close proximity, op. cit., 2.30.70, 2.28.49. (B.O.R.I.) mention "*Roman ca Yavanāṇ āṃ puraṃ tathā.*" These foreign sailors were mostly Greeks (i.e. *Yavanas*), but they are called "*Romāṇah*" because they came from the Roman West, vide Cary and Warmington, Ibid., p. 159. However to the Indians it did not make any difference.

Two

Section I

The Foreigners in Ancient India

A few words seem necessary about the sources of information discussed in this work. This study is mainly based on the data supplied by the contemporary Indian literature: Hindu, Bauddha and Jaina. We will presently see how these different authorities feel about the foreigners and consequently the research has been carried on from the Indian stand point of view.

To this period belong the later Vedic literature compiled in the *Brāhmaṇas*, the *Āraṇyakas* and the *Upaniṣads*. The *Dharma* and the *Gṛihya-sūtras* enlarge the bulk of the information.[1] The three grammatical works, viz. the *Nirukta* of Yaska and the *Aṣṭādhyāyī* of Pāṇini followed by the *Mahābhāṣya* of Patañjali supply us with useful data. [2]

The twin epics: The *Mahābhārata* and the *Rāmāyaṇa* together with the *Dharmaśāstra* of Manu and *Arthaśāstra* of Kauṭilya[3] are indispensable source books of historical information. The facts gleaned from the repository of the four above mentioned monumental works are corroborated by numerous evidences supplied by portions of the earlier *Purāṇas*,[4] viz.,—the *Mārkaṇḍeya, Kūrma, Vāyu, Matsya* and *Viṣṇu*. To the end of our period of study belong the *Khila Harivaṃśa*, full of interesting episode.

The two most interesting treatise on dramatics and music, viz., Bharata's *Nāṭyaśāstra* belonging to second-third centuries A.D., and the later one by Mataṅgamuni called "*Bṛhaddeśī*" of sixth century A.D. are often cited and prove to be of great value because both have recorded the cultural contribution of the foreign tribes.

Among the Buddhistic works, the Pali texts from the *Tipiṭaka* like the *Mahāvagga*, the *Bṛahmajālasutta*, the *Jātakmālā*,[5] as well as the *Māhavastu, Avadānaśataka* and the *Divyāvadāna* appear to be the chief sources of knowledge regarding the names of the foreign tribes, their location and other particulars.

The Jaina canonical works such as the *Nāyādhammakahāo* and others occasionally refer to the foreigners.

These earlier sources are corroborated by numerous contemporary epigraphical data and later literary works, among which the *Bṛihatsaṃhitā* of Varāhamihira, the *Mānasāra*, the *Nāṭakas* and *Kāvyas* by Bhāsa, Kālidasa, Śūdraka and Bāṇabhaṭṭa, and the *Bhaviṣya*, the *Padma* and the *Bhāgavata* purāṇas are important.[6] Later Buddhist and Jaina works the *Lalitavistara* and the *Vāsudevahiṇḍi*[7] are cited wherever the traditions of the foreigners have been found intact.

The question naturally arises, who are these "foreigners", by what name they were addressed in general? The term '*Mleccha*' connotes many different shades of meaning, viz., those who are non-believers in Vedic sacrifices and worship, those who do not abide by the sobrieties of the society i.e., "*Śiṣṭācāra*", those who do not pay homage to the gods and goddesses of Brahmanical pantheon, yet occasionally poured into this land of religion (*Dharmabhūmi*) in disturbing packs and settled in the frontier regions, roamed about in the desolate tracts of deserts, mountains, forest-sea-shores, and spoke in an unintelligible tongue; they are the "*Mleccha*" or "foreigner's".[8] *Śatapatha Brāhmaṇa* takes the term in this meaning and states, "Such was the unintelligible speech which they then uttered [i.e., He 'la vah! He' lavah!]–and he who speaks thus is a Mlekha (barbarian). Hence no Brāhmaṇ speak barbarous language, since such is the speech of the Asuras", So it seems that the earliest connotation of the term involved the idea of a difference of speech, and meant all the people who spoke in non-Aryan dialect, be him a native pre-Aryan or a foreign intruder. The *Dasyu* i.e., the outcaste too had a synonymous connotation, due to their association with the *Mlecchas*.

Though they are vehemently disdained, the usefulness of the people and their language are not overlooked by the ancient Brahmanical authorities. They occupied quite an important place in the political and administrative system of those days.

Baudhāyana (I. 1, 2, 13) mentions the "*Saṃkīrṇayonayaḥ*" i.e., the land of the mixed origin around the *Madhyadeśa*.[9] The Mahābhārata defines the boundaries of *Bhāratavarṣa* and states that *Mlecchajātis* dwell all around it. It also describes the Indian river-system, the water of which was used by the Aryan and the *Mleccha* people.[10] The *Matsya-purāṇa*, Chap. 113, describes the "*Padmarūpi Prithivī*" or the Lotus-shaped earth, and states that there are *Mlecchadesas* beyond the *Keśaraparvatas*; *Jambudvīpa* is situated within the core of the lotus, which is the holy seat of *Dharma*. But unlike the *Matsya-purāṇa* the *Bṛhatsaṃhita*[11] and the *Mārkaṇḍeya-purāṇa*[12] place many *Mleccha* tribes side by side with the well-known Aryan tribes in all directions and parts of the continent. This obviously point to the fact, that once the *Mlecchas* were living all around outside the 'Aryandom' amidst the *Keśaraparvatas*; but later on there was continuous movement and the multitude of people infiltrated into the settled system and thereafter lived together with the Aryan tribes.

Now we shall proceed to see how the *Mlecchas* were looked upon by the political thinkers.

The *Arthaśāstra* states[13] those regions that were inhabited by many caste-less, thieves, *Mlecchas*, and forest people is called "*Nityāmitra*". In other place[14] Kauṭilya states that a king should reinforce his army by recruiting men from *Mlecchajāti*. This immediately reminds us of the observation of Arrian, iv., 17, that, "... these scythians are always ready at a word to take part in any fighting which may be going on; their extreme poverty might be reason enough, but in addition to that, they have no towns, no settled homes, and consequently no cause to fear the loss of what is dearest to them." It is quite possible that Kauṭilya here refers to these "Scythians" by his expression "*Mleccha*". They were evidently outcaste-banditi of whom the epic states that the "*Dasyus*" should not be destroyed all at once by a king. A separate chapter deals with the treatment of the "*Dasyus*" by an wise ruler[15] and states: –

"*Dasyunāṃ sulabhā-senā raudrakarmasu Bhārata*!"

Many a "Mleccha" soldier joined the side of the Kauravas in the war of Kurukṣhetra[16] and are rendered in a most picturesque description. Kauṭilya further states[17] that sometimes the *Gūḍhapuraṣas* (spies) of the state took the disguise of the *Mlecchas*. The *Mukhyapuruṣas* (Officers-in-charge) of the *Mlecchajātis* (i.e., foreign tribes or non-Aryan tribes) should have transferable services at different places, and should not be given charge for long in one place.[18] The *Mleccha* men and women were appointed to induce poison on opponent kings, in the disguise of hunchback, dwarf, Kirāta, deaf, dumb, idiots and blinds.[19]

The well-known episode of the '*Jatugrihadāha*' (i.e., burning of the House of Lac) in the epic,[20] tells how wise Vidura conveyed to Yudhiṣṭhira the means of escaping in a foreign tongue. It was intelligible only to both of them. They two were called "*Prājñā*" because they were well-versed in that 'foreign' language.[21]

The *Matsya-purāṇa* informs us that the *Mlecchas* were born of Dakṣa: "*Janayāmāsa Dharmātmā Mlecchān sarvāna-nekasaḥ*, 4.54". The non-Aryan Mlecchas of dark complexion were thought to be the off-springs of Vena: –

"*Mamanthur-Brāhmaṇa-stasya balāddehamakalmaṣa*

Tat-kāyān-mathya-mānāt tu nipetur-Mlecchajātayaḥ"

The people who are to be avoided during the *Śrāddha* ceremony enlist: "*Mleccha-deśa-nivāsinaḥ*"[22] together with the Barbaras, Drāva, Bīta, Drāviḍa, Koṅkoṇa etc.

King Turbasu was cursed by Yayāti to rule over the *Mlecchas*: –

"*Saṃkīrṇāścāra-dharmeṣu pratiloma careṣu ca*

Piśitāśisu lokeṣu nūnaṃ rājā bhaviṣhyasi

Gurudārā-prasakteṣu tiryag-yoni-rateṣu ca

Paśudharmiṣu Mleccheṣu pāpesu prabhaviṣyasi"[23]

The above *Saṃkīrṇa Ācāras* (i.e., base behaviours) are opposite to the *Śiṣṭācāras* (i.e., gentle behaviours) of the sober society. These are: –

"*Śiṣṭair-ācaryate yasmāt punaścaiba Manu-kṣaye*

Purvaih purvair-matatvācca śīṣṭācāraḥ sa śāsvataḥ.

Dānaṃ satyaṃ tapo'lobho vidyejyā pūjanaṃ damaḥ

Aṣṭau tāni caritrāṃī Śiṣṭacārasya lakṣaṇam".[24]

The *Mlecchas* were notorious for their cruelty. Thus Agni has been vilified by the women of Tripura for being more ruthless than even the *Mlecchas* – "*Dayāṃ kurvanti Mlecchapi dahantīṃ vīkṣya yoṣitam Mlecchaṇāṃ-api kaṣṭo'si durnivāro-hyacetanaḥ*". Numerous literary expressions like this can be cited.

Antyaja (i.e., frontager) is akin to the *Mleccha*.[26] We shall presently see that the Medas,[27] Varuḍas etc., who were probably foreigners, came and settled in the frontiers of India, and were regarded as *Antyajas*. The term came to denote "low-born" in a later age.

Though they were held in utter humiliation still we find that the Indian society was continuously adopting and absorbing many a social, artistic and religious traditions from these *Mlecchas*. In one word, Indian culture was thoroughly imbued with exotic elements received from the native pre-Aryan as well as foreign "*Mlecchas*", who were found in and coming into this land.

For a clarification of the foregoing we shall enumerate some of the more important *Mleccha* or semi-*Mleccha* tribes of India, who appear repeatedly in the pages of her ancient history, recorded in the *Dharmasūtras, Dharmaśāstras, Arthaśāstra*, Epics and the *Purāṇas*. Even works of Astrology, like the *Bṛihat Saṃhitā* and architectural treatise as the *Mānasāra* refer to the *Mlecchas*[28] and *Asuras*. The *Bṛihatsaṃhitā* mention the *Mlecchas* with the Taskaras, Śūdras, artists, artisans, military-men, marching phalanx and those who earn their livelihood by fire.[29] The astrologer, while predicting the results of the luminary functions, obviously, had the whole nation before his vision and the *Mlecchas* occupied quite an important place in that national population. This patriotic spirit which distinguishes the Gupta epoch was the result of the assimilation in cultural life in the period under discussion, and the absorption of the contributions of the different peoples.

References

1. CHI, vol. I, p. 223, "In general, the age to which the Sutras may be assigned cannot well be earlier than seventh or later than the second century B.C. ...Probably the Gṛhyas represent the earlier Sūtras; the Dharmas as a whole came later perhaps: 300 B.C. would represent the earliest."
2. Yāska's *Nirukta* has been dated in c. 500 B.C. by Keith, CHI, p. 105.

   The *Aṣṭādhyāyī* of Pāṇini, according to Keith was composed "not later than 300 B.C." CHI, Vol. I, p. 101; Agrawala IIP, p. 464 ff., dates Pāṇini from 450 B.C.-400 B.C.; Saletore, IDRW, p. 337-338, n. 1, criticizes his views. There is no doubt, anyhow, that the *Aṣṭādhyāyī* forms one of the most important source-book of information for a study of the period under discussion.

   There is fortunately no such discrepancy regarding the date of Patañjali who lived in the second century B.C. and composed his Mahābhāṣya, during the reign of Puṣyamitra Śuṅga (187 B.C.-157 B.C. vide Chattopadhyaya, EHNI, p. 9). But Raychudhuri, PHAI, pp. 9-10 places Patañjali slightly later, i.e., c. 150 B.C.-100 A.D.
3. Incredibly long period has been taken to cover the period of the two epics: the *Rāmāyaṇa* and the *Mahābhārata*. It is found that the *Rāmāyaṇa* was composed at later date than the *Mahābhārata*, but was given its definite shape earlier than the older ballad story. It would not be radically wrong if one assigns c. 1000 B.C. to 600 B.C. to the *Mahābhārata* and c. 600 B.C. to 200 B.C. to the *Rāmāyaṇa*. Most parts of the epics took definite shape before the Gupta epoch, and from the references to different tribes, it seems that the bulk was added to the text in between c. 600 B.C. to 320 A.D. or little earlier. Vide. The Age of the Nandas and the Mauryas, pp. 308-309.

   According to Keith, HSL, p. 42 "Vālmikī and those who improved on him, probably in the period 400-200 B.C., are clearly the legitimate ancestors of the court epic." Vide also J.R.A.S. 1916,

p. 227, the *Rāmāyaṇa* 500 B.C. – 300 B.C.; the *Mahābhārata*, 400 B.C. – 200 B.C.

The *Arthaśāstra* of Kauṭilya helps us in dating the great Epic and the *Manusmṛiti*, because both of them tally in details of administrative and political procedures of the state, ideals of kingship and the measures to be taken by a king. The main bulk of the *Arthaśāstra* was composed under Chandragupta the Maurya (c. 334 – 300 B.C.) and his successor Bindusāra. But mention of foreign commodities like *Cīnasī* and *Cīnapaṭṭa* show that later additions were done until first century B.C. or first century A.D. The commodities, ports and routes referred to in the *Arthaśāstra* reminds invariably of the Periplus, and point to an India which kept close contact with Central Asia and China. It thus proves to be of great importance for the history of the period under discussion. Raychaudhuri, PHAI, p. 9-10, assigns it to 249 B.C. – c. 100 A.D.

4. Hazra, PRHRC, Ch. II, p. 8 ff., Vide also p. 19, Hazra supports the theory of Farquhar that the *Harivaṃśa* is not later than 400 A.D.

5. Winternitz, HIL, Vol. II, p. 15, "Pāli Tipiṭaka, at least the Vinaya and the Suttapiṭaka, docs, on the whole, correspond to the Māgadhī canon of the third century B.C."

6. Hazra, PRJRC, pp. 52-57, pp. 107-127, pp. 167-173.

7. *Lalitavistara*, according to Winternitz was compiled before 850 A.D. but most probably synchronizes with the Gāndhāra School of Sculpture (i.e., from the first century A.D. to six century A.D.), and was known to Aśvaghosa in a rudimentary form.

8. The *Śatapatha Brāhmaṇa* II, p. 32.

   Dr. D.R. Bhandarkar I.A. 1911, p. 180, takes the term to mean this "Yavanas, Śakas, Hūnas etc. from the popular point of view are foreigners, i.e., Mlecchas".

9. Govindasvamin, p. 12

   "*Āvantayorṇga-Magadhāḥ Surāṣṭrā Dakṣiṇāpathāḥ Upāvrit-Sindhu-Sauvīra ete saṃkīrṇa-yonayaḥ*".

10. *Mahābhārata*, 6.10.12.

11. *Bṛihat Saṃhitā*, Chap. 14.

12. *Mārkaṇḍeyapurāṇa*, Chap. 58.

13. *Arthaśāstra*, 7.10.116.

14. Ibid., 7.14.118.
15. *Mahābhārata*, 12. 131.10 (B.O.R.I.)
16. Ibid., 7.19.7-11 (B.O.R.I.); 7.18.6-12 (Haridas).
17. *Arthaśāstra* 12.4.166-67.
18. Ibid., 13.5.176.
19. Ibid., 14.1.177.
20. *Mahābhārata* I. 138, Haridas; 1.132 (B.O.R.I.).
21. Ibid., 1.133. 18-19 (B.O.R.I.); 1.139. 20-21 (Haridas); 1.135.6 (B.O.R.I.); 1.141.6 (Haridas).
22. *Matsyapurāṇa*, 16.16.
23. Ibid., 33. 13-14.
24. Ibid., 145. 37-38.
25. Ibid., 88.47.
26. R.D. Mookerji, The Hindu Conception of the Mother Land, *Indian Culture*, Vol. I, 1934-35, pp. 553-566.
27. Rai Bahadur B.A. Gupte, The Meds of Makran, I.A., Vol. xl, 1911, pp. 147-149.
28. P.K. Acharya, IAMS, p. 166 f.
29. *Bṛhat Saṃhitā*, 5. 29; 5.33.

Section II

The Tribes that Contributed their Shares

In this section a review would be made of the ancient tribes that contributed in the growth and development of Indian culture. Some of them were totally foreign, while others were actually indigenous, but were degraded and repeatedly classified with the barbarians, because of their close connection with the incoming tribes. The term "*Mleccha*" denotes both these groups.

1. **Gandhāris**: The Gandhāris or Gāndhāras were a well-known ancient tribe occupying the eastern and the western banks of the Indus,[1] mainly the area around the modern Peshawar and Rawalpindi districts of Pakistan.[2] Its eastern capital was Takṣ aśilā, with another capital at Puṣkalāvatī[3] on the confluence of the streams of the Kabul and the Swat. As the Gāndhāras occupied the north western frontier territory of India which was held under foreign subjugation from time to time, the life of the people became deeply influenced by foreign traditions and culture.

But these people were quite old and indigenous; they had a long history. Their product of fine wool is referred to in the *Ṛīgvedas*[4] and in the famous Takman hymn in the *Atharva veda*,[5] fever is sent to the Gandhāris and the Mujavants, – "to the Gandhāris, the Mujavants, the Aṅgas, the Magadhas, like one sending a person a treasure, do we commit the fever".

In the *Chhāndogya Upanishad*,[6] in the *Aitareya Brāhmaṇa*,[7] and in the *Śatapatha Brāhmaṇa*[8] the country of Gāndhāra and its king Naganajit are mentioned. Curiously enough in the *Citralakṣmaṇa* a Naganajit is found to be instructed by Viśvakarmā in the art of painting.[9] The *Baudhāyana Śrauta Sūtra*, the *Āpastamba Śrauta Sūtra* and the *Hiraṇyakeśī Śrauta Sūtra*[10] mention the Gāndhāris. They held an equally prominent position in the *Aṣṭādhyāyī* of Pāṇini.

The *Mahābhārata* is full of references about the Gāndhāras. For the present purpose it is worth noting that the people are condemned thus, "the Prasthalas, the Madras, the Gāndhāras, the Āraṭṭas, those called Khaśas, the Vasātis, the Sindhus and the Sauvīras, are almost as blamable in their practices.[11] This evidently shows that the Gāndhāras were not rigorous about the "*śīṣṭācaras*" maintained in the *Madhyadeśa*; this lack of approved sobrieties was due to long foreign contact, and prevalence of Buddhism in Gāndhāra territory.[12] Buddhism disregarded the authority of caste system, which indeed aroused scorn amongst the orthodox Brahmanical society.

Skilful musicians, called Gandharvas from this land, are mentioned in the *Vāyu*.[13] The *Mārkaṇḍeya* places the Gāndhāras in the right-side[14] of the "*Kūrma*" i.e., north of India and the Matsya with the people of the north.[15] Numerous references about the Gāndhāras with Śakas, Kambojas, Yavanas and Sindhu-Sauvīras in the epic and the Purāṇas attest their semi-*Mleccha* status.

Excellent horses from Gāndhāradeśa are mentioned in the *Vāyu*.[16] The *Mahābhārata* has numerous references about the prized horses of Gāndhāra and Kāmboja. It seems that pedigree horses were brought from Kāmboja to India proper via Gāndhāra and Sindhu, consequently these territories rose into renown for fine well-bred horses. The description appears to be most picturesque in the *Sabhaparvan*.[17] The *Jātakas* describe the beauty, speed and the means of ensnaring the horses.[18] The *Śyāma Jātaka* in the *Mahāvastu*[19] states that the horse-dealers spoke in a northern accent, showing that they belonged to Gāndhāra or Kāmboja janapadas.

Wollen blankets (*Kambala*) were manufactured in Gāndhāra, likewise in the neighbouring Kāmboja.[20] Thus we find that the tradition of the fine woolen fabrics was kept intact from the age of the *Ṛig-vedas* to all through the historical period.

The heterogeneous customs and practice of the Gāndhāras, their trade in horse and manufacture of woolen products, unique development of a new school of art, all grew out of intimate contact with the West. Though classified with the *Mlecchas*, the contribution of the Gandharas in music and fine arts are accepted with due regard to them.

2. **Kāmbojas**: The most important tribe after Gāndhāras, who occupied the north-western region of ancient India was the Kāmbojas.

Yāska in his *Nirukta* (c. 500 B.C. or earlier) gives an interesting reference about the Kāmbojas. He states:

"*Śavatir gatikarmā Kambojeṣveva bhāṣyate*
Kambojah Kambalabhojāh. Kamanīyabhojā vā.
Kambalaḥ kamanīyo bhavati."

As the Kāmboja tribe retained the use of the verb root 'śav' and used it to denote 'to go', they appear to be a branch of the Indo-Iranian group of people, who still spoke in a language more akin to the Iranian than the Vedic Sanskrit of the Aryans.[21] Their epithet "*Kambalabhoja*" reminds evidently of the remark of Baudhāyana that the northerners were to be hated for their trade in wool and horse.[22] It attests their connection with wool industry which developed under the patronage of the Achaemenid rulers.[23]

The Janapada of the Kāmbojas is mentioned both by Pāṇini[24] and the Patañjali.[25] It is also mentioned with the list of the sixteen great principalities in the *Aṅguttara Nikāya*.[26] This shows that they were held in importance by the Indian states but kept close connections with other foreign tribes as well. This was possible for the strategic position of their territory which lay to the extreme north-west border of India and was contiguous to the land of Gāndhāra on one side and Ferghana on the other. It commanded the important trade-routes from Iran, Central Asia and Afghanistan.

The Kāmbojas are given an important position in the great epic. The Pāṇḍavas could not win them to their side but it is said that Duryodhana succeeded perhaps because of his kinship with Śakuni, the lord of the neighbouring Gāndhāra country.[27]

The horses of Kāmboja together with those from Sindhu, Āraṭṭa and Pārasya are praised in the epic.[28] Jātakas[29] and in the later literature.[30] Fine carpets, bed-spreads and coverings for horses from the Kāmboja country are often mentioned in the epic.[31]

In the *Droṇaparvan* we find numerous references about the Kāmboja soldiers together with the Śakas, Yavanas, Barbaras, Daradas, and other *Mleccha* phalanx. They are called as "shaven headed" and wearing solid coat of mails.[32] The Yavana soldiers are said to have worn iron and bronze chain mails. Sculptures and reliefs from Gāndhāra supply ample illustration of this type of costume. It is needless to add that these cultures were adopted from contemporary Iran, where Hellenistic, Scythian and Iranian sartorial tradition gave rise to different types of sewn garments and armours.

In the *Karṇaparvan* they are described fighting with the Śakas, Tukhāras and Yavanas, "*Śakastukhārā Yavanāśca sādinaḥ sahaiva Kāmbojavarairjighaṃsavaḥ* (Mbh. 8.65.16.Haridas).

The Kāmbojas had close matrimonial ties with the ruling dynasty of Sindhu-Sauvīradeśa as Kāmboja and Yavana women are described guarding the dead-body of Jayadratha.[33]

They nearly always find a mention with the barbarous people of the north[34] and are said to have been degraded due to an unfavorable attitude of the *Brāhmaṇas* from *Kṣatriya*-caste to Śūdrahood.[35] The same idea is repeated in the *Manusmriti*.[36] The Kauṭilya *Arthaśāstra* refers to the corporation of the warriors of Kāmboja,[37] while the epic states: –

"*Gāndhāraḥ Sindhu-Sauvīra nakhara-prāsa-yodhinaḥ*
*Abhiravaḥ subalinastadbalam sarva-pāragam.*3
Sarva-śastreṣu kuśalāḥ sattvavanto hyuśinarāḥ
*prācya mātaṅga-yuddheṣu-kuśalāḥ śaṭha-yodhinaḥ.*4
Tathā Yavana-Kāmbôjāḥ Mathurāmabhitaśca ye
*Ete niyuddhakuśalā Dākṣiṇātyāsicarminaḥ.*5"

(Mbh. 12., 102, B.O.R.I.)

The *Jayadrathavadhaparvādhyāya* in the *Droṇaparvan* supply with ample references about the valour and prowess of the Kāmbojas who are styled as "*Yuddhadurmadāḥ*".

The *Harivaṃśa* narrates that Sagara, "considering his own promise and the words of his preceptor... violated their religious practices and made them change their dress (15).

Having made the Śakas shave half of their heads he dismissed them. He made the Yavanas and the Kāmbojas shave their entire head (16). Pāradas used to have their hair dishevelled and Palhavas kept beards (17)".[38]

Pāṇini's Gaṇapāṭha mentions along with "*Yavanamuṇḍa*", the "*Kambojamuṇḍa*" and that "he may have seen the 'shaven headed' Yavanas and Kāmbojas, who were probably known as such because, unlike Indians, they wore their hair short".[39] The Kāmbojas are also associated with the Yavanas in the *Majjhima Nikāya*[40] which states, "*Yona Kambojesu dveva vaṇña Ayyo c'eva Dāso ca...*".

The Kāmboja people retained their martial characteristics throughout the period. Baudhāyāna stated that the people of the north lived by military pursuits.[41] We have already seen them fighting in the great epic and in the *Arthaśāstra*. The *Bṛihat Saṃhitā* states (V. 35): –

"*Pāñcāla-Kaliṅga-Śūrasenāḥ Kāmboj-oḍra-Kirāta śastrabvrtāḥ.*

Jīvaṇti ca ye hutāśavṛittyā te pīḍāmupayanti Meṣa saṃsthe."

Here '*Śastravarta*' is defining the Kāmbojas etc. It immediately recalls the "*Vārtāśastrapojivin*" of the *Arthaśāstra*.[42] There are numerous other references of the Kāmbojas with the Yavanas in the *Bṛihat-saṃhitā*.

It is clear from the above discussion that though in all probability the Kāmbojas were an Indo-Aryan tribe,[43] in remote antiquity they became much westernised or went *Mleccha* under the barbaric influence. They were consequently degraded in socio-cultural status from the "mid-land" point of view:

3. **The Madrakas and the Vāhīkas**: For obvious reasons the Madrakas and the Vāhīkas are to be discussed together. Firstly, both of them occupied the same territory; while the term Madrakas always denoted a people, and *Madradeśa* their country, the term Vāhīka denoted the land as well as it's people. Secondly, they are mentioned conjointly in the epic, and possessed a similar social status and culture.

The Madrakas are given quite an important position in the Mahābhārata. Prior to that they find mention in the earlier literature, which show that they were a well-known ancient tribe of north India.[44] The mention of the *Uttara Madras* and *Uttara Kurus* in the *Aitareya Brāhmaṇa* points to the fact that the Indo-Itanian tribe called Madra previously lived beyond the frontiers of India. However, during our period of study, they became 'Indian' as any other Aryan tribes of north India. But we shall presently see, that some Iranian affinities were kept intact in their social institutions till quite late.

In the *Rāmāyaṇa* Sugrīva was sent by Rāma, to Madra country in quest of or Sītā.[45] They held a more prominent position in the *Mahābhārata*. The city of Śākala is stated to be their capital.[46] The Madra king Śalya plays an important role through out the narrative.

In the *Ādiparvan* it is narrated that Bhīṣma went to Madra king Śalya, who was of Bāhlīka lineage[47] asked for the hands of his daughter Mādrī for Pāṇḍu. Śalya having received him mentioned a peculiar custom of taking a fee from the bridegroom's party.[48] Bhīṣma agreed to pay the sum, as it was Śalya's family-custom and brought Mādrī to Hastināpur. This peculiar custom reminds us of Strabo's remark that in Taxila there was a system of exposing marriageable daughters in hope of securing bridegrooms on approved terms.[49] This is reminiscent of the Āsura form of marriage in which the guardian of the bride was enticed by much wealth. The form of marriage was despised in Brahmanical society.[50] In all probability this rule was peculiar to the Madra people alone, who probably adopted it through the Iranian i.e., "Asura" affinity. It may not be out of place to mention that the Indus Valley and the Punjab region was frequented by various tribes from Iran and Afghanistan from hoary antiquity. They brought with them many a outlandish trait, but the history is lost. One such tribe was the Ṭakkas.[51] Whether the Madrakas and the Vāhīkas were affected by close contacts with these tribes, or brought the 'Āsura' custom from the ancient day of 'Indo-Iranian' kinship is difficult to say. But the later possibility seems more plausible in the light of the studies of Przyluski.

In the *Karṇaparvan* Karṇa directly accuses Śalya for the irreligious customs and vulgar practices of the Vāhīkas among whose land reigned Śalya. The *Vāhīkadeśa* i.e., Punjab has been called the dirt of the earth, and the Madra women as the blackspot of the female race.[52] Karṇa relates to Śalya how one Brahmaṇa narrators "said these words blaming the Vāhīka people and the Madrakas." It is clearly mentioned that a clan of Vāhīka people, called the Jarttikas are very much censurable in their practices; a river called Āpagā and the capital town called Śākala are also mentioned in this connection.[53] It is clear from these references that the neighbourhood of Śākala was infested by the barbarous Jarttikas who added to the infamy of the Madrakas. The land of the Vāhīkas is said to be away from the Himāvat, the Gaṅgā, the Sarasvatī and the Yumunā, Kurukṣ etra and lay in between the Sindhu with its five tributaries. In another place it is stated that,

"*Pañca nadyo Vahantyetā yatra pīluvanānyapi*
Śatradruśca Vipāśa ca tṛiyerāvatī tathā.
*Candrabhāgā Vitastā ca Sindhuṣaṣṭha bahirgatāḥ.*35
Āraṭṭā nāma te deśā naṣṭadhrmānna tān vrajet.
Vrātyānām Dāsamīyānām Videhanamayajyanām."36
(8.30. B.O.R.I.)

The Vahīka[54] country which is more or less contiguous with the tract watered by the five rivers and probably stretched a little beyond the Sindhus, had the Madrakas as their ruling house. Przyluski however, thinks that the Bāhīka or Vāhīkas are same as Vāhīkas who came from Bactria, and called this region after their name.[55]

According to Rapson the Madrakas occupied the tract of land in between the Chenub and the Ravi,[56] and according to Cunningham between the Jhelum and the Ravi.[57] The *Malinda-pañha* gives vivid the picturesque description of the Madra capital Śākala. The ruling family of the Madrakas or the Madras are mentioned in the *Jātakas* and in the *Mahāvastu*.[58] Though the ruling families of mid-India sought the hands of the Madraka princesses in marriage nonetheless they are censured all through for their intemperance (Karnap, 27, pp. 74-84). Śalya has been vilified by Karṇa because a sixth part of the demerit of Vāhīkas belonged to him.[59] The orthodox view was so severe and abhorrent towards the Vāhīkas that the tribe was called the offspring of two goblins called 'Vahi' and 'Hika' who lived in the Vipāśā river, and not the progeny of Prajāpati Brahmā. Kātyayana in his *Vārttika* on Pāṇini derives the word Vāhīka from *Vahi* or *bahi* (i.e. outside) suggesting their outlandish manners and customs, probably origin too.[60] There remains every proof that the Madrakas, who were well-known and ancient tribe and in whose land inhabited *Brāhmaṇas* from the days of Prajāpati:[61]

"*Āraṭṭā nāma te deśā, Vāhīkanāma te janāḥ,*
Brāhmaṇāpasada yatra tulyakālāḥ Prajāpatih. 104
Veda na teṣāṃ vedyañca yajño yajanamevaca,
Vrātyānāṃ dāsamīyānām-annaṃ deva na bhuñjate." 105.

(Haridas, 8.34)

They thus fell into this state of disrepute due to their contagious existence with and the possible subjugation under the foreigners (the Vrātyas and Dāsamīyas). Their land lay adjoining the territory of the Gāndhāras, who were held under the sway of the Acheamenid empire. It is clearly mentioned that Vāhīkas had "*varṇasaṃkaras*" amongst them, and the *Brāhmaṇas* to keep the purity of their blood, married in the same family (i.e. Kula) and thus fell to infamy.[62] The Madrakas and their women are condemned althrough.[63]

4. **Yavanas**: In the Persian inscription the Ionians are called Iauna,[64] from which appeared the sanskritized form "*Yavana*" or the Prākṛit "*Yona*" indiscriminately used to mean the Greeks in general. Several other words were derived from *Yavana* such as: *Yonaka, Jabana, Yauna*, etc.[65] Thus Pāṇini refer to *Yavanānī* i.e., the writing of the Greeks.[66] The Prākṛit term Yona finds mention in the *Majjhima Nikāya*, it places the territory of the *Yonas* side by side with the *Kāmbojas*.[67] According to many, this reference was to the Greeks who were known to the Indians prior to the invasion of Alexander.[68] The Mahāvastu mentions the assemblies of various foreign peoples, incorporating the Yonas too.[69] It enlists the *Yavanī* style of script[70] which is also found later in the *Lalitavistara*.[71] The *Maliñdapañha* mentions the '*Yavanas*' as '*Yonakas*' and applauses their capital 'Śākala'.[72]

The term '*Yona*' is also used in the Rock Edicts of Aśoka as "*Aṁtiyoko Yonarājā*" and "*Yonakamboja*"[73] Yavanarājā Tuṣ āspha held high office under Aśoka.[74] Cordial relation, which remained intact in between the Maurya monarchs Chandragupta, Bindusāra and Aśoka and the Greek princes of Syria, Egypt the Seeucid Iran,[75] enhanced the cultural progress of India immensely.

The Yavanas are mentioned in the *Mahābhārata* as participating with the Kauravas. They are represented as valiant warriors, and enumerated with Śakas, Kambojas, Pāradas, Daradas, Vāhlīkas, Gāndhāras etc., in the *Droṇaparvan*.[76] They are prescribed to follow the Vedic rites, to worship and abide by context, the preceptor, the king and parents with other *Mlecchajātis*.[77] They are respected as having high aptitude for understanding.[78] But from the statement of Gautama, it appears that they were thought to have sprung from *Kṣatriya* father and a *Śūdra* mother.[79] Thus probably predicting their future position as *Vrātya Kṣatriyas*.[80]

Patañjalis' statement about the Yavanas and the Śakas is interesting from the point of view that it shows how these foreign people were admitted into the Aryan society,[81] and were given permission to dine together.

Two different accounts about their origin are concocted in the epic. In one place they are said to have sprung from Vaśiṣ ṭha's cow Nandinī[82] with other Mleccha soldiers viz., Pahlavas, Śabaras, Śakas, Andhras, Paundras, Kirātas, Drāviḍas, Siṃhalas, Pārasīkas etc.,[83] while in other places they are descendants of Turvasu.[84]

In the *Rāmāyaṇa* the Yavanas have been mentioned as follows: –

"*Strīṇāṃ śokāvahaṃ sthānaṃ Dattamindrana-ruṣyatā,*

Purāni Yavananañca vicinvantu vanaukasaḥ. 18

Ālokya Pahlava-vāsaṃ Yac-ca teṣāṃ samīpataḥ,

Tataḥ Pañcanadam kṛitsnaṃ vicetabyam samantataḥ. 19.[85]

The Puras i.e., cities of the Yavanas are said to be "*Strīṇāṃ śokāvahaṃ sthānaṃ*" i.e., the place of grief of the womenfolk, which was incurred upon them by Indra, due to his wrath. Now this evidently points to some allegorical or legendary story behind it, but nothing about the curse of Indra's rage is explained in the following verses as was expected. The following verses narrate the abode of the Pahlavas i.e., *Pahlava-vāsam* and then mentions *Pañcanada*, the Punjab territory.

There are variant readings: –

a) *Strīlokā-panhava-sthānam*,

b) *Strīlokā-Pahlava-sthānam dattamindrāmarundhatīm*.

c) *Strīlokā-bahula sthānaṃ dattam-Indrām-arundhatīm.*[86]

The reading: a) "Panhava" and b) "Pahlava" do not make much difference, because anyway the Pahlavas are mentioned in the next verse. The reading, "*Strīlokā bahula sthānaṃ*" than "*Strīṇāṃ śokāvahaṃ sthānaṃ*", is preferred because the former is corroborated by the *Raghuvaṃśam* of Kālidasa.[87] Raghu on his way to Persia, by the land route came across a place where he met Yavanīs, i.e., Greek beauties; the direction points to lower Sind via which route proceeded towards Makran and Gedrosia.

Before going into the evidence supplied by Kālidasa, we would like to say a few words about the passage from *Rāmāyaṇa*. The *Mahābhārata* mentions "*Yavanastriya*" guarding the body of Sindhu Sauvīrapati Jayadratha.[88] Curiously enough the terms "*Dattamindreṇaruṣyata*" or "*dattam-Indrām-Arundhatīm*" do not bear any clear meaning in its context, but may point to something very different altogether. It is tempting to see a "Dattamindra", more correctly "Dattāmitra" i.e., "Demetrias in Sind" in these lines. The Nasik Inscription makes the existence of the Datāmitiya certain in a northerly (i.e., '*Otorāhaso*') direction from Nasik.[89] It is not at all impossible that as different versions went through endless copying, the true significance of the term was lost sight of and well-known mythological names like Indra and Arundhatī took the place of the name of the Greek township in Sind. In the *Vāyu, Matsya* and *Mārkaṇḍeya* Purāṇas the Greeks are mentioned as "Yavanas", and are placed along with Gāndhāras, Sindhu-Sauvīras, Madrakas etc. The *Viṣṇu purāṇa* mentions a Kāla-Yavana,[90] most probably a legendary character. But it is interesting to find mention of the Yavanas in South in the Mahābhārata.[91] These Yavanas are probably the Graeco-Romans who carried on trade and settled in the southern ports, they are identified with those Yavanas mentioned in the *Śilappadikāram* and the *Maṇimekhalai*.[92] The *Matsya-purāṇa* gives the duration of the Yavana rule,[93] with that of the Śakas, Gardabhilas and Ābhīras. They are mentioned together with the Śakas and the Pahlavas in the Nasik inscription of Gautamī Balaśirī.[94] It is to this political phase, the later Purāṇas refer. The evidences supplied by the *Yugapurāṇa* section of the *Gargī Saṃhitā*[95] and the *Malavikagnimitram*[96] of Kālidasa have been much discussed for the clarification of political problems and is needless to quote them here in detail.[97]

The references to the Yavanas and Pārasīkas in the *Raghuvaṃśam* are more important in the present context. In Canto iv. the poet says,

"*Pārasīkāṃstato jetuṃ pratasthe sthalavartmanā*

Indriyākhyāniva ripustattva-jñānena saṃyamī.60

Yavanīmukha-padmānāṃ sehe madhu-madaṃ na saḥ

Bālātapāṁavābja-nāmakāla-jalado-dayah.61."

If Raghu took the land route by trans-Indus desert of Makran to the Pārasīkas of Far[98] he might have met the Greek ladies in the lower Indus Valley, most probably in the Pattala founded by Alexander or the Barbaricum of the Periplus.[99] An interesting notice has been made by Prof. Tarn that the Greek greeting χαιρεω or χαιρε is still current amongst the women folk of Surāṣṭra.[100] This must have been the result of long association with the Greeks in remote past, and the term has been retained in use by the women from their "mother tongue".

It seems plausible that Kālidasa was well-acquainted with the stories of Semiramis, Cyrus and Alexander the Great; to match the valour of his hero Raghu with these famous figures, the poet led the conquest of the Indian hero through the route followed by the western conquerors from India to the Persis.[101]

The *Bṛihat Saṃhita* has numerous references about the Yavanas.[102] In giving the list of the south-western countries it corroborates the *Rāmāyaṇa.*[103] The *Rāmāyaṇa* mentions the *Phenagiri* where the Indus discharges itself into the sea. Bṛihat Saṃhita also mentions the *Phenagiri* mountain near Yavana-mārga.[104] It is very likely that the place from where Alexander took the western land route came to be known as Yavanamārga; or it might be the region through which lay the route taken by Creteurus via mountainous regions of Kalat and Kandahar. The evidences in the *Rāmāyaṇa* and the later work of *Bṛihat Saṃhitā* show that the incident was remembered long afterwards.

Bāṇabhaṭṭa mentions one Yavaneśvara who was murdered by his Chowrie-bearer.[105] Another Yavana merchant is mentioned, who made an air-craft and kidnapped Chaṇḍipati.[106] He refers to the conquest of Caṇḍakośa i.e., Alexander of the kingdom of the women, *Strīrājya.*[107] These late references show that gradually the Yavanas were becoming figures of legends and folk-lores.

5. **Sindhu Sauvīras**: The Sauvīras or Sauvīrakas as a people are for the first time mentioned by Baudhāyana, together with the dwellers of Ānarta, Aṅga, Magadha, Surāṣṭra, and Dakṣ īṇāpatha as "*Saṃkīrṇa yonaya*" or the people of mixed origin. Their country was impure and the Aryans visiting the country of the Sauvīras were enjoined to purify themselves by performing expiatory penances on their return.[108]

The inhabitants of Sindhu were always mentioned along with the Sauvīras, and the compound name Sindhu-Sauvīra is found in the ancient literature. Their territories lay side by side.[109]

The Sindhu-Sauvīra country edged on the western end of India, and through it ran the main traffic routes leading to the more barbarous and rugged west. Sauvira comprised the famous ports of olden times, Pattala and Barbaricum. The country had to face many a western invasions, led successively by the Greeks, the Śakas and the Pahlavas, which made it open to outlandish contacts. The Greeks, Śakas, Pahlavas and the Kushans, also the Sassanid monarchs held their consecutive sway over this land. These *Mleccha* rulers no doubt introduced their ways and customs, which influenced the life of the Sindu-Sauvīras. From the time of Baudhayana to the traditions of the epic this influence shaded the good name of the country and it was looked down upon from the point of view of the orthodox Brahmanical Indians.[110]

Jayadratha, the king of the Sindhu-Sauvīras is a well known character in the epic, and because of his enmity with the Pāṇḍavas the tribes had joined the Kaurava party. They are mentioned along with the Andhras, Kirātas, Kośalas, and the Gāndhāras in one place, and with the Śivis, Vasātis and the Gāndhāras in the other.[111] Moreover, their country is enlisted with the Kāśmīra, Gāndhāra and Darśaka,[112] thus showing their affinity and position in north-west.

The verses in the *Ādiparvan* which mention the *Yavanādhipa* of the Sauvira country, and have been discussed in detail.[113] Its authenticity has been doubted seriously. But if there is a mention of a township called Dattāmitrī in the works of Patañjali,[114] then at least some truth lies in the interpolation, and the "*Datāmitiyakasa*" in the Nasik inscription[115] seems to support the assumption that there was a town in Sauvīradeśa, in the name of Demetrius. Sauvīra was represented as a port in the *Milindapañha*, because it harboured the populous port and dockyards of Pattala and Barbara.[116] Famous trading station of Roruka (Capital ?) and Bhirukaccha (Bhṛigukaccha) were in this country.[117]

It is clearly mentioned by Arrian[118] that Alexander had left a garrison in Pattala; thus, it was not impossible to find a Greek or semi-Greek population in the Sauvīra country. We find numerous references to Yavana women in this territory. In the *Strīparvan* of the epic it is stated that Kāmboja and Yavana women were guarding the dead body of the Sindu-Sauvīra monarch Jayadratha. It is only natural to conclude that the female body-guards of Yavana and Kāmboja nationality were appointed because of their intimate association with this part of India. Probably the Indian Rājas of Sind felt proud of appointing foreign maids and attendants.

The *Rāmāyaṇa* while describing the western routes running through the desolate mountainous regions towards Kekaya kingdom mention the Sindhu-Sauvīra.[119] This reminds us of the reference in the *Matsya*, which states:–

"*Śibestu Śibayaḥ putraś-catvāra loka-viśrutaḥ,*
Pṛthudarbhaḥ Suvīraśca Kekayo Bhadrakastathā. 19
Teṣāṃ janapadāḥ spītāḥ Kekaya Bhadrakastathā,
Sauvīraścaive Pauraśca Nṛgasya Kekayastathā. 20"

(Matsya 48)

Here also the Kekaya and the Sauvira janapadas are located in close affinity.

The Buddhist literature is not silent about this frontier region.[120] The *Jātakas* mention the "*Saindhavas*" (Sind horses). A portion of the population were occupied with the rearing and trading in well-bred steeds.[121] Moreover, they distilled a special kind of wine called the "*Suvīraka*".[122]

The *Mahāgovinda Suttanta* mentions Sauvīra and its kingdom Roruka.[123] The *Divyāvadāna* mentions Bharukaccha and king Rudrāyana of Roruka in Sauvīradeśa.[124] Cunningham is inclined to identify the Sophir or Ophir of the Bible with Indian Sauvīra,[125] as it abounded in docks, harbours and was a flourishing centre of trade.

Certain portions of the Sauvīra was labeled as Abiria, due to the influx of the Ābhīra people into the lower Indus Valley. The Periplus and Ptolemy mention the ports of Barbaricum and Patalene in the Indo-Scythia (i.e., the Śakasthana of Sind).[126] The southern part of Indo-Scythia was called Abiria. According to Tarn the Sindhu-Sauviras "had entered India shortly before the Persian period and had worked southward." The reason for this assumption is probably that the Sauviras are condemned in the Baudhāyana *Dharmasūtra* shortly before whose time a new tide of incomers reached this land and the pure Vedic Aryan blood became contaminated with an admixture.

Tarn has shown from the evidence of the literature that they marched southwards,[127] but they kept close contact with the western neighbours. In the epic the Sindhu-Sauvīras are condemned for their irreligious practices with the Madrakas, Vasatis, Āraṭṭas, Prasthalas,[128] who inhabited the neighbouring tracts. The extreme climatic conditions of this region together with the possible means of livelihood barred the people from following the higher morality and ideals of life as prescribed in the *Dharmaśāstras*.

In the conquest of Rudradāman this land finds mention with Surāṣṭra, Svabhra, Maru-Kaccha, etc.[129] The prolonged Kushan rule was probably supplanted in some regions by the powerful Sassanids.[130]

6. **Ābhīras**: The Ābhīras were a western tribe who, according to Tarn entered India during the confusion following the death of Alexander.[131] Nothing is known regarding their earlier history but from their nomadic and predatory habits it can be assumed that they were pastoral people, probably of Scythian or some nomadic Iranian stock. Interesting is the curious mention of "*Abirāduś*" in Iran in the Persepolis inscription of Darius the Great.[132] It is not known whether the place was so called because of its association with a people who called themselves '*Abirā*' or "*Ābhīra*".

In Indian literature, they are for the first time mentioned in the *Mahābhāṣya* of Patañjali,[133] who connects them with *Śūdras*, the Soydai or Sodrai of Alexander's historians. This together with the evidence supplied by the great epic gives them position in the lower Indus Valley. Thus the epic states:

"*Sindhukulāśritā ye ca gramaṇeyā mahabalāḥ*
Śūdrābhīragaṇaścaiva ye ca-āśritya Sarasvatīm."

(2.29.8 B.O.R.I.)

"*Tato Vināśnam rājan jagāmadha Halāyudha*
Śudrābhīrānaprati dveṣād yatra naṣṭā Sarasvatī"

(9.35.1. Haridas)

They are enumerated with the people of the western zone:

Vāhlīka Baṭadhanāśca Ābhīra Kālakotoyakaḥ
Aparānta parāntaśca Pāñcāla-ścarma-mandalāḥ

(6.9.47 Haridas)

and also with the vicious and dangerous *Mlecchas* of the north:

"*Kṣatriyopanivesāśca Vaiśyaśūdrakulāni ca.*
Śūdrābhīrātha Daradāḥ Kāśmīrahpaśubhiḥ Saha."

(6.10.65-66 B.O.R.I)

Curiously enough the habitates of *Kṣatriya, Vaiśya* and *Śūdra* families are mentioned in the northern region, but not of the *Brāhmaṇas*. In the *Matsyapurāṇa* (114, 40-43) the Ābhīra people has been located in the north with the *Bāhlikas, Bāṭadhānas, Kālotoyakas, Purandhras* etc. The *Bṛihat Saṃhitā* enumerates them with the south-western peoples (XIV. 18) as well as with the southerners (XIV. 12), while the *Mārkaṇḍeyapurāṇa* places them in Deccan (58, 20-28).

This tends to prove that once the tribe entered the land, they divided themselves into groups and dispersed in all directions. Some of them followed the peaceful pursuits of cowherds, i.e., Gopas, while the others were labelled as bandits and outcastes. In the *Kiṣkindhyā Kāṇḍa* (43, verse 5 and 17) a distinction is made between *Bhadrābhīra* and *Śūrābhīra*. The polite Ābhīras are mentioned along with *Surāṣṭra, Bāhlīka, Sūrpāraka, Prabhāsa* and *Dvārāvatī* all described as "*Sphītaṃ janapaṃ*" i.e., they were living near the cultured habitates of the western tribes, while the *Śūrābhīras* or the brave and more belligerent Ābhīras are said to have occupied the desert and forest regions. Those who occupied the more desolate tracts, maintained themselves by plundering the caravans, and were called *Dasyus* i.e., bandits. They were the highwaymen and burglars of ancient India. A group of them ransacked the seraglio of Arjuna in Punjab while he was coming from *Dvārakā* after the death of Śrīkṛṣṇa.[134] Alexander recruited some Scythian bandits in his army,[135] and a similar idea has been expressed in the *Śāntiparvan* of the epic that the king should not destroy the *Dasyus* altogether, because men of arms could be recruited from them during the time of danger.[136] These people, no doubt, were looked upon as professional arms men and acted as hired soldiers. The more peaceful groups occupied themselves in cattle-rearing. Soon the word *Ābhīra* became a synonym for the word *Gopa*. The Gopas were appointed by the kings to look after their cattle.[137] These Gopas lived in temporary encampments and moved with all their belongings in wagons.[138] This is the peculiar nomadic practice of the Scythians.[139] It is not known whether the *Gopa-rāṣṭra*[140] mentioned in the epic had some connection with the Ābhīras, who gradually came to supremacy under the Śaka rule in the Kathiawar region.

The lower Indus Valley came to be called *Abiria* by the first century A.D.[141] The *Mārkaṇḍeya* section of the *Vanaparvan* and the Purāṇas prophesy the period when the *Mleccha* kings would rule, and enlist the Ābhīras. The Gundā inscription (181 A.D.)[142] of the Ābhīra general Rudrabhūti decipher the period of the Ābhīra supremacy. Ābhīra Mahākṣatrapa Iśvaradatta is known from his coins in the Kathiawar region. Another Iśvarasena is known from the Nasik inscription.[143]

The Ābhīras are mentioned along with the Vairāmas, Pāradas, Kitavas who lived by the sea-side dwellings amidst gardens (*Samudraniṣkuṭa jāta pāresindhu ca mānavāḥ*).[144] The term "*Samudraniṣkuṭa*" has been explained as garden-houses on the sea-shore, yet the reference to *Sāmudraniṣkuṭa*. in Bhīṣ hmaparvan (9, 48-49, Haridas) along with Upāvṛit, Anupāvṛt, Surāṣṭra, Kekaya, Kunda, Aparānta, Māheya and Kakṣa makes it apparent that it was the name of some locality on the western sea-board, probably farther beyond the Indus.[145] They are said to be living on paddy grown by rain-water, or the water of the river. This shows that some of them were settled with agricultural persuits. In another place the fishermen and those living on the hills are mentioned just after the enumeration of the Ābhīras.[146] *Uttarajyotiṣa* country, and *Divyakatampura* is mentioned after that. The irrigated fields in the delta of rivers, the fishermen together with the hill tribes faintly recall the Ichthyophagi of Makran,[147] the lateral hills and valleys in the country of the Oreitai and Arabitai tribe living on the sides of the river Hab.

As *Prāgjyotiṣa* on the eastern side was marked by the *Mleccha* Kirātas, so probably the *Uttarajyotiṣa* was inhabited by *Mleccha* tribes of the north-west. But due the lack of details and any other corroborative evidences the identification of *Uttarajyotiṣa*, *Divyakatampura* and *Samudraniṣkuṭa*[148] territory with parts of Makran cannot be carried on too far. The products brought by the Ābhīra, Vairāma, Kitava and Pārada tribes point to the pastoral life of these people. Thus they brought tribute of gold, goats, sheep, cows, mules and camels. The wollen blankets (*Kambalas*) were the products from their sheep. The fruits and syrups were probably obtained from the orchards or groves near their houses (*niṣkuṭa*).[149] It is quite possible that the Ābhīras entered India through the lateral valleys of Makran and first settled along the Malana Coast of Baluchistan.

A few words may be added here about the observation made by Herodotus, who states[150] "The following are the tribes of the Medas, Busae, Parataceni, Struchates, Arizanti, Budii, and the Magi." B.A. Gupte connects the Medes with the Medas of Indian literature, i.e., Meds of Makran. Are the Varudas or the Varāṭas of the *Yama-saṃhitā* identical with the Parataceni or the second tribe of the list given by Herodotus? It seems highly probable that the *Pāradas*, who are a well-known barbarous tribe of the north, but once have been mentioned with the Kitavas, Ābhīras, Vairāmas of the western sea-board, are some way connected with Varāṭas or Varudas, i.e, Parataceni, of whom there is every possibility and probability of being associated with the Meds, and thus consequently with the western sea-board.[151] Moreover, the *Pāradas* are always mentioned as *Pāratas* by Varāhmihira in his *Bṛihat Saṃhitā*,[152] which is nearer to the Parataceni.

The female-slaves from Bausa seem to be of Busae tribe of the Medes and the Vaiśya mentioned in the *Bṛihat Saṃhitā*;[153] the assumption seems justifiable in the light of the fact that the other foreign maids also arrived from the western countries beyond the Indian boundary. The identification of the Arabas with Arabs of Arabia proper, or with the region watered by the river Arabis in Baluchistan and the Parasa from Persis in Iran make this clear. The Lasiya may be taken as an earlier word denoting the region of Lasbela.[154]

The *Bṛihat Saṃhitā* mentions another tribe called Jriṅga.[155] Could it be possibly identified with Zarang or Drangians of Seistan? The Dhoruṇigiṇi of the Jaina texts is possibly the Prākṛt form of Drangians. The verse[156] from the *Bṛihat Samhitā* mentions the following tribes of Pañcanada: Ramaṭha, Pārata, Tārakṣiti, Jṛinga, Vaiśya, and Kanakaśaka together as "*nirmaryādā mleccha*". It is quite possible that as the Ābhīras are said to be *dasyus* and the Pārtas are called *taskaras*,[157] they snatched away girls from the Iranian tribes of Zarangs (i.e., Dhoruṇigiṇi), Lasbela (Lasiya), Parthians (Pahlava), Pārsis (Pārasa), Arabas (Arabs or those inhabiting the regions of the Arabius)[158] and Bousa (Busae=Vaśya) and a slave-trade flourished along the whole coastal line starting from Arab, Gedrosia and Makran upto the mouth of the Indus (Abiria). This is corroborated by the evidence in the *Mauṣalaparvan* that the *Ābhīradasyus* of Pañcanada snatched away the Yādava beauties.[159] The *Matsyapurāṇa* states that they were treated as "*paṇyastrī*"[160] i.e., females sold for money. This is a strong support to the assumption that a trade in female slaves was carried on by the Ābhīras of India. Moreover, the *Harivaṃśa* explicitly states that, "removing the ocean from its own bed the powerful Yādavas settled those thousands of dancing girls in Dvārāvatī".[161] The Ābhīras influenced the attire of the Yādavas, which was different from the costume of the other ancient Indian tribes.[162] The boats of the Yādavas[163] their fortification of the city of Dvārakā[164] and the description of its siege by Śālva all remind us of some foreign affiliation. Kennedy[165] thinks that the mode of defending Dvaraka is very akin to the description of that of Amida,[166] and in the view that the Ābhīras kept contact with the Sassanian realm,[167] it is quite possible that they had imported the story from Roman West.

The *Āvaśyaka Niryukti*, a Jaina commentary mentions the Ābhīras occupied in cattle-breeding, and how they returned the present of a perfumer by giving him two bull-calves.[168]

The *Bṛihat Saṃhitā* places the Ābhīras in the south (XIV. 12) with the Sipika, Khanikāra, Koṅkaṇa etc. As it also mentions Bharukaccha and Daśapura, Vena etc., which shows that the Ābhīras were also in the Deccan proper.

It is possible that during the Ābhīra ascendancy groups of this tribes pushed further south to Deccan,[169] Hence

Vāyupurāṇa (Chap. 45, 126) enumerates Ābhīra with the Āṭavyas, Śabaras, Pulindas, Vaidarbhas, Daṇḍakas and call them "*Dakṣiṇāpathavāsinaḥ*". Bhandarkar has shown that at present the Ahirs have taken up different pursuits and are found scattered all over India.

A few words may be added lastly about the opinion of Suryavanshi regarding the Ābhīras. He thinks that:

1. The Abhiras were not foreigners[170] but were indigenous nomadic people, staying in forests and valleys.

2. The Gaddi speaking folks of the outskirts of Chamba and Kangra hills are the descendants of the Ābhīras whose migration really took place from this northern region.

His conclusions are mostly based on the evidence of the connection of the Ābhīras with the Madrakas in the Allahabad Pillar inscription[171] corroborated by the epic and the *Bṛihatsaṃhitā*.

He, moreover, draws our attention to the reference in the *Mahābhārata* (2.29.8-9). But it is necessary not to loose sight of another verse from the *Sabhāparvan* which enumerates the Ābhīras, Kitavas,. Vairāmas and the Pāradas together. The edition published from the Bhandarkar Oriental Research Institute omits the term "Ābhīra" and replaces it with "*Vaṅgāśca*" (2.47.10). But it seems that the Bengali version edited by Haridas Siddhantavāgīśa is much more convincing in this regard, because, it is accurate in placing the western tribes viz., Pāradas, Vairāmas, Kitavas and Ābhīras together. The word "*Vaṅga*" here would be indeed out of place. This verse again attests their position in lower Sind contiguous to Makran coast.

In the evidence of the Allahabad Pillar inscription, which mention "*Madrakābhīra*", Suryavanshi takes the word "*Parvatavāsinah*" in *Mahābhārata* (2.29.9) as referring to the Ābhīras in the Chamba and Kangra hills. But from the context it appears, that the mountainous regions of Rajasthan are referred to here. The other reference to the Ābhīras with the Daradas, Kāśmiras and Paśus (6.10.66) corroborates the philosophical evidence and actually point to their habitat in the Chamba and Kangra regions. But the earliest mention of the Ābhīras which appears in the *Mahābhāsya* connected them with the *Śūdras* in the lower Indus Valley. The classical writers too, ascribe this region to them. Curiously enough, Pliny does not mention them while enumerating the tribes of India. They had probably dispersed in different directions by this time, but as both Pliny and the Periplus come from the first century A.D. this silence seems peculiar.

Abiria has been identified by Suryavanshi with modern Thar Parkar and Marwar, the ancient Indian name of which was *Marukāntāra* or *Drumakulya*. The episode in the *Rāmāyaṇa*[172] locates the *Vraṇakūpas* in this region, from where gushed forth water, which quenched the thirst of the bandit Ābhīras. This legend may have one or the other fact behind it.

It is thought that the nomenclature of Rhambacia in Makran had some connection with the legends of Rāma.[173] The *Vraṇakūpas* were probably the volcanic eruptions of the region, the largest of which is nowadays called *Candrakūpa*. It is regularly visited by pilgrims proceeding to Hinglaj. So this would locate the Ābhīras in the coastal desert of south Baluchistan. The other possibility suggested by a passage from Arrian's Anabis which states, "he (Alexander) sent men into the adjacent country, which was waterless, to dig well and to render the land fit for habitation. Certain of the native Barbarians attacked these men, and falling upon them unawares slew some of them;...". These "native Barbarians" were no doubt the "*Ugra-darśana-karmāṇa dasyavaḥ Ābhīrā-prāmukhāḥ pāpāḥ...*" of the *Rāmāyaṇa*. The wells dug by Alexander's men were probably rendered with a mythical origin by the ancient chroniclers and possibly none but the barbarous tribes used the water of these springs sought by a *Mleccha* king. Those wells were made in surrounding regions of Patala, i.e., lower Indus delta, and soon fell into disuse. Quite early popular imagination concocted tales which told that marvelous riches were to be found from these deep sunk fountains. One such story is the *Jarudapāna Jātaka* which relates how a band of merchants found immense valuables by digging one old well in a desert.

However, it must be added, that the problem of the original home of the Ābhīras is not yet settled. Their distinct nomadic type of culture expressed in the following aspects are noteworthy.

a. They like the Śakas, spoke in a non-Aryan tongue as noted by Bharata.[174] Keith thinks that it was an Apabhraṃśa.[175]
b. Their moving from place to place in wagons.
c. They are repeatedly called and cited as *Taskaras* and *Dasyus*.
d. Their sewn costumes described and depicted in ancient literature and art.
e. Their loose morality and liberal outlook towards the women.
f. Their food consisting of beef and wine as found from the *Harivaṃśa*.[176]
g. Their entertainments with music and group dances.

All these peculiarities have been accepted by Suryavanshi, and still his view to hold the Abhiras as indigenous nomads[177] seems futile.

We know from the accounts of Pliny[178] and Strabo[179] that the southern part of Iran was infested by rude tribes called Cyrtii, Mardi and Uxii (i.e., the "brigand Oxii and ...savage tribes of the Mizaei"). These tribes generally persued cattle-rearing and farming but often took to predatory habits due to the barren ruggedness of their habitat. It is noteworthy that the Ābhīras are not mentioned in the Vedic literature. The continuity of their settlement and language at Gadderan in north, which has been taken by Suryavanshi as a decisive proof of their indigenous origin, does not then solve the problem finally. It is quite possible that they migrated from Susiana and Persis to the lower Indus Valley and Gujarat via Carmania and Makran. Suryavanshi himself admits, "Amongst all, the Khandeshi or the Abhirani is biggest and has got a vital importance. Khandeshi or Ahirani has much affinity to village Marathi and more with Gujrati. This impact of Ahirani with Gujarati may indicate that the Ahirs (Ābhīras) of Khandesh originally belonged to Gujarat". This then show their affinity with western India and not to the northern hills. Notwithstanding, if we conjecture, that they had close affinity with the later Gurjaras and migrated from the north, there is nothing to show that they were a native people of India. This only changes the focus from the western to the northern parts of this land.

Had they been purely Indian tribe, there remains no other alternative but to accept that, quite early they became amalgamated with a totally foreign tribe from whom they borrowed their dress and modes of social behaviours. But we know of none, who played such an important role, in influencing the Ābhīras, yet left nothing of their own identity. From the above discussion, one finds, that there remains no serious doubt in accepting the Abhiras as immigrants into Indian sub-continent.

7. **Kekayas**: The Kekaya, though a well-known and ancient tribe,[180] was somewhat distinctive for it's alien traits. They were participants with the Pāṇḍavas in the great battle of Kurukṣ etra.[181] The red uniform and the ruddy hue of their chariot and horses are described beautifully in the *Droṇaparvan*.[182]

In the *Rāmāyaṇa* their country is placed beyond the Vipāśā river,[183] and lay contiguous to the territory of the Gāndhāras. It was thus a frontier state between outer Iran and India proper. It is narrated in the *Uttarakanda* how Yudhājit, the king of Kekaya sent Gargya to Rāma with presents of horses, gems, *Kambalas* etc., and asked him to vanquish the fertile land of the Gandharvas which lay on both the sides of the Indus river.[184] By order of Rāma, Bharata with his two sons Puṣkara and Takṣa went to Gāndhāra and established the cities of Puṣkarāvatī and Takṣaśila.

The Purāṇas ascertain the Kekaya lineage from the Anu tribe,[185] who were Iranians.[186] They are moreover mentioned along with the tribes of the north-western frontier of India.[187]

The Kekayas are probably identical with the Ki-kiang-na of Hiuen-Tsang and Kaikan or Kikans of the Arab writers. Cunningham writes, "I am inclined to identify it with the Valley of Pishin itself, which lies between the Khoja Amran hills on the north, and the lofty mount Takalu on the south...and as this valley inhabited by the tribe of Khakas, it is not improbable that the name of Kikan or Kaikan have been derived from them". The Kāka, Kharaparika and the Sanakānikas mentioned in the Allahabad Pillar Inscription are thought by scholars to belong to Western India,[188] but the names sound particularly connected with the Kaikans or Kikans.

According to Holdich[189] the Zarangai was the Kaiani kingdom of Sakastana (i.e., Seistan) and was identical with Sanskrit Kekaya country. Cunningham identifies Girjhak[190] with the capital Girivraja of the Kekayas.

It is not improbable that probably sometime in the first or second century A.D. taking advantage of the Scythio-Kushan rule, branches of Kekayas, known as Khakas (i.e., Kākas) and Sanakānikas probably entered this land and settled in central and western parts of Punjab along with the Yaudheyas, Mālavas, Madrakas and Ābhīras, where Samudragupta had found them.

8. **The Pārasīkas and the Pahlavas**: Some scholars are of opinion that the term Pruth conjointly with the *Parśu* used in the *Ṛigveda*,[191] refer to Parthians (Pruthu = Parthacas = Pahlavas) and the Persians (Parśu = Pars = Persis = Fars = Pārasīkas) respectively.[192] In later days, however, when contact with Achaemenid Iran became more intimate, the term Pārasīkas and Pahlavas were used undoubtedly to denote the neighbouring Persians and the Parthians. Thus Pāṇini refers to the Persians as *Parśu*, from which *Parśavaḥ* and *Pārśava* were derived.[193]

The Parthians are mentioned in the Indian literature as Pahlavas, Pallavas or Panhavas in connection especially with the Śakas, Kāmbojas, Yavanas and the Pāradas. It is indicative of their "*Mleccha*" category and north-western situation. Their numerous references conjointly with the tribes mentioned above have led scholars like Lohuizen-De Leeuw to think that these pair-names actually denoted more or less the same connotation to the ancient Indian minds.[194]

The *Mahābhārata* mentions the Pārasīkas with the Yavana, Cīna, Kāmboja, etc., the people of the North:–

"*Sakṛid-grahāḥ Kulatthaśca Huṇāḥ Pārasīkaih saha,*
Tathaiva Ramaṇāś-Cīna tathaiva Daśamālikāḥ".
(6.9.66, Haridas)

and,

Tīragrāhās Taratoyā Rājikā Rasyakagaṇāḥ,
Tilakāḥ Pārasīkāśca Madhumantaḥ Prakutsakāḥ."
(6.10.51, B.O.R.I.)

The Pahlavas are mentioned as Panhavas in some recensions: –

"*Khāsīraśc-āntacaraśca Panhava giri-gahvaraḥ*" etc.
(6.9.68, Haridas)

or,

"*Khaśikāśca Tukhārāśca Pallavā Girigahvarāḥ*"
(6.10.66, B.O.R.I.)

Some editions of the epic mention the Pārasīkas with the Pahlavas, Śakas, Yavanas, Barbaras etc., brought out by wrathful Nandinī, the wish-fulfilling cow of Sage Vaśiṣṭha.[195]

The dāsīs (i.e., the slave girls) from the Kārpāsika country bedecked with gold: –

"*Śataṃ dāsī sahasrāṇām Kārpāsika-nivāsinām,*
Śyāma-stanvyo dīrgha-keśyo hem-ābharaṇa-bhūṣitāṇ".[196]
(2.49.6, Haridas; 2.47.7, B.O.R.I.)

enumerated after the list of gift presented by the Kāmbojas, are probably a tribute from the Pars (Kārpāsika-Pārasīka-Pars, being an misrepresentation of the form Pārasīka) as this term i.e., Kārpāsika is of very rare occurrence. This seems more probable because, the reference is followed by the list of gifts from Bharukaccha, Gāndhāra and the sea-shore inhabitants of Vairāma, Kitava, Pārada and Ābhīra, those semi-foreign tribes, connected with trans-Indus region. Or it might be a mistake for Pāraskaradeśa, i.e., Thar Parkar region in Sind.[197] It is well known that Bharukaccha did receive many foreign slave-girls from the west. It has been discussed that the coasts of Makran held the trade of slave from very early times. Handmaids from Arab, Parthia, Persia and Drangiana came to India. The Jaina work *Nāyādhammakahāo* refers to the maid-servants from Barbara (North Africa), Bausa, Pakkaṇa (Parakaṇva=Ferghana in Afghanistan), Damila, Siṃhala etc.[198]

In the *Sabhāparvan* of the epic Nakula was able to subjugate the territories occupied by the *Pahlavas* and the Barbaras: –

"*Pahlavān-Barbarāṃścaiva tān sarvānānayadvaśam*".

(2.29.15, B.O.R.I.)

The *Rāmāyaṇa* probably locates the kingdom of the Pahlavas in the trans-Indus western India i.e., bordering regions in between Sind and Makran when it states: –

"*Strīṇāṃ śokāvahaṃ sthānaṃ dattamindreṇa ruṣyatā,*
Purāṇi Yavanānāñca vicinvantu vanaukasaḥ.
Ālokya Pahlava-vāsaṃ yacca teṣāṃ samīpataḥ,
tataḥ Pañca-nadaṃ kṛitsnaṃ vicetabyaṃ samantataḥ".

(4.43-18-12)

It appears from the version that the abode of the Pahlavas was next to the Yavana city. Some recensions put it as, "*strīloka-bahulāṃsthānaṃ*", "*strīlokā-Pahlava sthānaṃ*" or "*Panhava sthānaṃ*".[199] This immediately recalls the statement of the Periplus, that beyond the region of Patalene the Parthian princes were continuously fighting with each other. It seems that this passage was written when the Parthian dynasties, were actually ruling in Sind and Punjab just after the downfall of the Bactrian Greeks, in later half of first century B.C. and the earlier half of first century A.D.

The mountainous and desert routes referred to in the same epic: –

"*Kaikeyān Sindhu-Sauvīran kāntāra-girayaśca ye,*
Giri-jālā-vṛitāṃ durgaṃ mārgadhvaṃ paścimāṃ diśam".

(4.43.10)

and

"*Tathā Gāndhāradeśaśca Marubhūmiśca sarvasaḥ,*
Viceyam ramaṇiyañca Kaikeyānāṃ niveśanaṃ.
Giri-jālāvṛitāṃ durgāṃ margitvā paścimāṃ diśam,
Acchidreṇa vicetabyā deśāḥ sa-giri-kandarāḥ"

(4.43.22-23)

point directly to the roads which connected Sind and Punjab with Drangiana, Arachosia and Seistan in Afghanistan and Iran via Makran, and upper Baluchistan.

Interestingly enough Hiuen-Tsang mentions a country of women somewhere near the Sonmiani Bay in east Baluchistan. The Classical and later Indian sources probably refer to this country, when they mention "Woman's Haven" and "*Nārīmukha*".[200]

In that oft-quoted and important verse from the Śānti-parvan: –

"*Yavanāḥ Kirātā-Gāndhāraścīnāḥ Śabara-Barbarāḥ,*
Śakas-Tusārāḥ Kahvāśca Pahlavāśc-āndhra Madrakāḥ.
Oḍrāḥ Pulindāḥ Ramaṭhāḥ Kācā Mlecchaśca sarvasaḥ
Brahma-Kṣatra prasūtāśca Vaiśyāḥ Śūdrāścamānavaḥ".
(2.65.13-14, B.O.R.I.)

We find the Pahlavas coupled with the Andhras of the Deccan. This immediately recalls the epithet of Gautamīputra Śrī ŚātakarṇI referred to in the inscription of Gautamī Balaśirī.[201]

In the *Harivaṃśa* the Yavanas, Kāmbojas, Pāradas and Pahlavas are said to have received a defeat in the hands of Sagara. King Kuśa is said to have been brought up by the Pahlavas in the forests.[202] The *Mārkaṇḍeyapurāṇa* places the Pahlavas with the Kāmbojas, Ānartas, Daradas, Sindhu-Sauvīras at the other right-foot of the *Bhārata-rūpī Kūrma*, i.e., India in the shape of Tortoise.[203]

The *Bṛihat Saṃhitā* of Varāhmihira has numerous references to the Pahlavas with the Ābhīras, Śabaras, Mallas, Matsyas, Kurus, Śakas and Pāñcalas (v. 38). The term is given as "*Pallava*" here.

A "*Paruṣakasthalī*" (i.e., the land of the Puruṣakas) has been mentioned in *Vāyupurāṇa* and it[204] describes the vineyards and orchards of Akṣota (Akhroṭ=Walnut), dates and pomegranates of that country. It might refer to some tract in Afghanistan or Persia which abandoned in these fruits. Indeed, these four plants are mostly represented in ancient and mediaeval Persian art. So *Paruṣaka-sthalī* can be taken as Persia proper. It finds mention after the fearful desert that lay to the west of India.[205]

In later times, *Pārasīkadeśa* is mentioned with *Kiṣku, Turaṣka* (Turk) and the kingdom of the Śakas in the *Harṣacarita* of Bāṇa.

9. **The Śakas**: The records of the cultural contribution of this powerful people have been fortunately remained intact and archaeological as well as literary evidence help each other in reconstructing their past history.

The term "Scythian" is a loose one and denote innumerable tribes, inter-connected with each other in certain characteristics, diffused over a vast area in Europe and Asia.[206] This place is too confined to give a comprehensive historical outline of these people. The tribe was called "*Sacae*" by the Persians[207] from which the term "*Śaka*" was derived in Sanskrit. India is mainly connected with the tribe when the Sai or Śakas were driven away from Central Asia by the Yueh-chis and settled in Bactria and Seistan.

Agrawal thinks that the epic mentions the home of the Śakas as *Śākadvīpa* in Central Asia before they pushed more southward in Seistan and then again westward to India proper. He moreover presumes that "Pāṇini also must have known the Śakas not in Seistan but in their original home in Central Asia".[208]

The Śakas are referred to in the sūtras "*Śudrāṇām-aniravasitānām*" and "*Śakandhvādiṣu ca*" in the *Mahābhāṣya* of Patañjali,[209] showing that the Śakas and Yavanas were considered as *Śūdras* who could pertook food of an Aryan's dish "without polluting it",[210] and a special type of well (i.e., *andhu*) was introduced by them.[211] These together with the "*Kanthā*"[212] ending place names, and the nomenclature of Śākala in Punjab[213] have led several scholars to believe that a number of Scythian clans must have had immigrated peacefully into India before the actual Śaka invasion of the middle of the first century B.C.[214] Did the recruiting of Scythian soldiers by Alexander[215] show them the way to India and

Punjab? The evidences from Pāṇini[216] point that the Śakas were to be found in India earlier to Alexander's invasion.

The epic has ample references about the Śakas with the Yavanas, Kāmbojas etc.[217] The *Bhīṣmaparvan* gives a detailed description of *Śākadvīpa* and the four *Varṇas* (i.e., classes) of the Scythian society.[218] The *Purāṇas* mention them with the barbarous tribes of the north.[219] A tribe called Tuṣāra is often coupled with the Śakas. They are the *Yueh-chi* or the *Tochari* people, the Tokharoi of Ptolemy.[220] Rightly has Lohuizen de Leeuw pointed out that to the ancient Indians, the Śakas and Tuṣāras appeared more or less as one and same. According to Law the Periplus means the Tukhāras when it bespeaks of "the warlike nations of the Bactrians".[221]

The chapters of the *Purāṇas* which deal with *Mleccha* rulers enlist the dynasties of Śakas and Tuṣāras with Yavanas, Ābhīras. Garddabhilas etc.[222] This undoubtedly point to the illustrious Śaka families that ruled in Taxila, Mathura and Ujjainī regions,[223] and the Kushan dynasty of Kanishka.

Lastly, it may be added that though these virile race played important role both politically and culturally they could not retain their separate entity like the Ābhīras, but became amalgamated with other Kṣatriya clans soon after the ancient period.

Several other frontier tribes find mention as *Mlecchas*, because of their general likeness in the cultural tradition. In the epic and following it, the *Purāṇas* mention their names as fighting bodies in describing the warfare and enumerating the population of the different parts of India. It is possible that these tribes, who were well-known by their names, yet, rendered in meager details were only to be met with during a warfare, in which they joined some party or the other, but were insignificant in other respects and had little to contribute in the sphere of culture.[224]

They are the Barbaras, the Lampākas, the Ramaṭhas, Taṅgaṇas, Parataṅgaṇas, Śūlikas, Sugdas, Pāradas, Daradas, Khaśas, Vasātis, etc., who occupied the north-western or western parts of India proper and lands beyond that came within greater spheres of Indian culture. These people are said to have inhabited the regions watered by the Cakṣu (Oxus), the Sītā (Tarim) and the Sindhu.[225]

10. **Barbara**: The Barbaras are mentioned in the *Mahābhārata*[226] and in one place they are enlisted alongwith the Yauna, Kāmboja and Gāndhāra tribes, who dwelt in the *Uttarapatha*. At other place they are mentioned with the Tuṣ āras, Pahlavas, Pāradas, Śakas, Urjas and Aurosas etc., through whose land flowed the Cakṣu stream of the Ganges.[227] Most often it is found that the *Purāṇas* do not place or mention the names of these tribes in accordance with their geographical distribution but merely put them in a 'class' belonging to northern or western regions, there is a possibility that due to repeated copying, the names got mixed up and misplaced in the manuscripts. The list remained but the location was lost sight of.

Kauṭiliya *Arthaśāstra* mentions the Barbara country, and the commentary states that the river *Srotasī* flowed across the land; the river is said to produce pearls. A city called *Ālakandaka* stood on the river by the name of which a species of coral was called *Ālakandaka*. It has been identified with Alexander's Haven on the Indus.[228] This *Barbara* or *Barbarika*[229] was the *Barbarei* of Ptolemy and the *Barbaricum emporium* of the Periplus.[230]

The Barbaras were then, a people who inhabited the delta portion of the lower-Indus, and possessed a culture similar to that of the Sindhu-Sauvīras. Most likely they belonged to the traders-class, because many important ports like the Barbaricum, which kept intimate contact with Minnagara, and Pattala were situated within their lands. The highroads from Iran via Makran divulged to their port-towns.

11. **Darada**: The Daradas are known from the Sanskrit as well as the classical Greek sources. The account of Herodotus states, "The Caspians, Pausicae, Pantimathians, and ***Daritae***, contributing together, paid two hundred talents; this was the eleventh division"(emphasis added).[231] In another place[232] he describes the gold digging ants. The *Mahābhārata* mentions

them several times and they were defeated by Vāsubdeva along with other northern tribes such as – Khaśas, Śakas, Yavanas etc.,[233] while the *Jātakas* mention their capital Daddarapura. They are associated with the Ābhīras and Kāśmiras in the *Viṣṇupurāṇa*,[234] and in the *Matsyapurāṇa* they are situated with the Gāndhāra, Śivapura, Urjja, Aurasa, etc.,[235] thus showing that they were in the northern extremities of the upper Indus Valley, i.e., in the Darel Valley, now called Dardistan.

They are called differently as Dardanians,[236] Dardae,[237] and Daradrai[238] by the classical writers. The modern name of their country is Dardistan.[239] They have been important for one factor in the ancient Indian history, i.e., gold came through their country. The classical accounts,[240] as well as the epic refers to the gold[241] of the Darada country. These Darada people, to avoid intruders possibly invented the story of the gold-digging ant.[242] Their script is mentioned as "*Daradalipi*" in the *Lalitavistara*.

12. **Lampāka**: The Lampākas mentioned in the epic,[243] the *Matsyapurāṇa*[244] with the Barbara, Pārada, Taṅgaṇa, Parataṅgaṇa, Ramaṭha, Hāra-Hūṇas etc., were a rude mountainous people.

Cunningham identified their territory with modern Lamghan, east of Kapisena, north-east of Kabul,[245] Lassen also thinks that the abode of the tribe was Lambatae, south of Hindukush in modern Kafiristan.[246]

Alexander had passed through their country by the way of the Kabul river.[247] Ammianus Marcellinus gives a sweeping description of the lands of Ariani, Paropanisadae, Drangiani, Arachosia and Gedrosia and then remarks, "All of them without exception, even at banquets and on festal days appear in girth with swords; an old Greek custom...most of them are extravagantly given to venery, and are hardly contended with a multitude of concubines;..."etc.[248] His description of the customs and nature in general makes the reason apparent, for labeling them as *Mlecchas*, the barbarians of the north.

13. **Parada**: The Paradas were a similar crude people possessing debased culture mentioned in the epic[249] and in the *Purāṇas*[250] in association with the Khaśas, Taṅgaṇas etc.

The *Harivaṃśa* states that King Sagara defeated the Pāradas, Śakas, Yavanas, Pahlavas and disheveled the hair[251] of the Pāradas. The *Manusmṛiti*[252] supports the view of the *Harivaṃśa* and enjoins that they were *Kṣatriyas*, but became degraded due to the extinction of sacred rites among them. It is quite probable that they were the Paratacenae of the Medes,[253] and while one branch of them came and settled in the region of the Śailodā river somewhere in the high Oxus[254] and were called Pāradas, the others settled along Arachosia or Gedrosia, and kept close contact with the Ābhīras.[255] These latter are known as Pāratas.[256]

Their association with the nomadic Ābhīras makes it probable that they were ousted from their homeland for some reason and took to predatory habits and turned brigands. They probably inhabited some barren land, unable to produce crops, and consequently became labelled as "*Dasyus*" or "*Taskaras*". Outer Iran was infested with various tribes like this and caused great trouble to the dominions of Iran and India alike.[257]

The Abhīrā, Vairāma, Kitava and Pārada are said to have occupied the sea-shore towns and lived on agriculture.[258] This obviously proves that some of them at least were settled with agricultural pursuits.

Motichandra suggests that Rambakia or Rhambacia was called so after the name of its inhabitants i.e., the Vairāmas,[259] which seems quite probable. This identification places the tribes of the Ābhīrā, Kitava, Vairāma and Pārada in the country of the Oreitai, whose capital was Rambakia near the Arabius. It is the region where three rivers, the Hingol (Tomeros), the Purali (Arabius) and the Hab reach the ocean, and thus signify the term "*nadīmukhaiḥ*".[260] This is the district, which "in addition to corn, produces wine, rice and dates".

The southern Baluchistan, thus served as a gateway to the more fertile plains of north India towards the east.[261] Ammianus Marcellinus mentions famous townships of Ratira and Gynaeconlimen on the fertile soil washed by the river Arabius with other smaller streams.[262] This Gynaeconlimen at once recalls the "*Strilokabahulaṃ sthānaṃ*" of the *Rāmāyaṇa*[263] and the account of Hiuen-Tsang.[264] It is possible that "*Nārīmukha*" of the *Bṛihat Saṃhitā* and the "*Vanitāmukha*" of the *Mārkaṇḍeyapurāṇa* refer to the same "Women's Haven" mentioned by the classical author.

It is possible that the shrine of the Great Mother Goddess at Hingol probably gave rise to this name, as pilgrims disembarked at this port for getting to her resort in the hills.[266]

The foregoing is a general survey about the foreign and semi-foreign tribes that inhabited the north-western frontier territories of India. In the following chapters it will be discussed how these tribes did contribute their shares in enriching India's cultural wealth. But a question may arise as to what extent the tribes like the Daradas, the Pāradas, the Lampākas, the Barbaras, the Taṅgaṇas, and the Khaśas, the Vasātis etc., did help and took initiative in India's cultural synthesis. It is true that our information regarding these tribes is limited more or less in their mere names and geographical situation occupied by them. For this reason some of them like the Vasātis, Taṅgaṇas, Parataṅgaṇas, Prasthalas etc., have discussed with others and no special attention has been dedicated to them. A discussion about the four more important ones has been carried on from the point of view, that, it would help us to understand the subject with greater clarity and ease. In future, fresh data may come to light regarding these peoples, which will estimate their merit and contribution in the cultural development of India. Many of them have not been identified properly so far; it is expected that gradually the task will become easier as our knowledge reaches to its perfection.

Finally, a comparative list of the tribes living in south-western, western and north-western extremities of India has been supplied from the pages of the *Mārkaṇḍeya Purāṇa* and the *Bṛihat Saṃhitā* to enable us to see, how these two later authorities agree and differ regarding the names and situations of these frontier tribes.

Some probable identifications have been suggested below: –

	The Mārkaṇḍeyapurāṇa (The "Apara-dakṣinapāda" i.e., the other right foot of the Kūrma)	The Bṛihat Saṃhitā (South-West)
1.	Bāhyapāda	
2.	Kāmboja	Kāmboja
3.	Pahlava	Pahlava
4.	Vaḍavāmukha	Vaḍavāmukha
5.	Sindhu-Sauvīra	Sindu-Sauvīra
6.	Ānarta	Ānarta
7.	Drāvaṇa	
8.	Argiya	
9.	Śūdra	Śūdra
10.	Karṇaprādheya	Karṇaprāveya
11.	Barbara	Barbara
12.	Kirāta	Kirāta
13.	Pārada	
14.	Pāraśava	Pāraśava
15.	Phala	
16.	Dhūrtaka	
17.	Hemagirika	Hemagirika
18.	Sindhu	Sindhu
19.	Kālaka	Kālaka
20.	Raivata	Raivata
21.	Saurāṣṭra	Saurāṣṭra
22.	Drāviḍa	Drāviḍa
23.	Mahārṇava	Apart from the above mentioned it enlists: –
		a. Ambaṣṭa
24.	Vanitāmukha	b. Kapila
		c. Nārī-mukha

d. Phena-giri
e. Yavana-mārga
f. Khaṇḍa-Kravyāda
g. Ābhīra
h. Cañcuka
i. Vādara
j. Ārava

	The Mārkaṇḍeyapurāṇa (The "Puccha" i.e., the other right foot of the Kūrma)	**The Bṛihat Saṃhitā (West)**
1.	Maṇimegha	Maṇimant and Meghavān
2.	Kṣurādri	Ksurāpaṇa (the Parni = Aparnak tribe?)[267]
3.	Khañjana	
4.	Astagiri	Astagiri
5.	Aparāntika	Aparāntaka
6.	Haihaya	Haihaya
7.	Śāntika	Śāntika
8.	Vipraśānta	Praśastādri
9.	Koṅkaṇa	Vokkāṇa
10.	Pañcanada	Pañcanada
11.	Vāmana	Ramaṭha
12.	Āvara (this is probably the Ārava of the Bṛihat Saṃhita with the region of the river Arabius).	
13.	Tārakṣura	Tārakṣiti
14.	Aṅgataka	Jringa (Drangians)[268]

15.	Śarkara[269]	Kaṇaka-Śaka (discrepancies remain over the term Kaṇaka. It has been translated as "golden Śakas". It might had some connection with the "Sanakānika" of the Allahabad Pillar inscription or with the Ki-Kiang-na of Hiuen Tsang and the Kikano). Vaiśya (this tribe is probably to be identified with the Busae of Herodotus or Bausa of the Jaina literature)

Apart from the foregoing it mentions: –

16. Śālmala
17. Guruśvara
18. Phalgunaka
19. Venumatyā
20. Phalguluka
21. Ghora
22. Guruha
23. Kalaha
24. Ekekṣaṇa
25. Vājikeśa
26. Dīrghagrīva
27. Sucūlika
28. Aśvakeśa

	The Mārkaṇḍeyapurāṇa (The "Vāmapada" i.e., the left foot of the Kūrma)	The Bṛihat Saṃhitā (North-West)
1.	Māṇḍavya	Māṇḍavya[270]
2.	Caṇḍakhāva	Tuṣāra
3.	Aśmaka	Aśmaka
4.	Lalanā	
5.	Kuśārta	Kulūta
6.	Laḍaha (Dahae?)[271]	Halaḍa
7.	Strīvāhya	Strīrājya
8.	Bālika	Vanakha
9.	Nṛisiṃha	Nṛiṣiṃha
10.	Veṇumatī	Veṇumatī
11.	Balāvastha	
12.	Dharma-vaddha	
13.	Aluka[272]	
14.	Urukarma	

References

1. Gandharis

1. *Rāmāyaṇa*, p. 107. 10-11.
2. Agrawala, IKP, p. 28-49; Puri, ITP, p. 74.
3. *Rāmāyaṇa*, 7.108.10-14, describes the flourishing trade and commerce of Takṣaśila and Puṣkalāvatī.
4. I. 126.7.
5. V. 22, 14; Whitney, p. 261.
6. VI. 14.
7. VII. 34, Keith, p. 318.
8. VIII. 1.4.10, S.B.E. Vol. XLIII, p. 21.
9. *Citralakṣana*, pp. 128-29; *Gāndhāra Jātaka* (406); *Kumbhakāra Jātaka* (408).
10. B.C. Law, TAI, p. 11, f.n. 4.
11. P.C. Ray, Karṇaparva, XLIV, 46.

12. The evidences are supplied by the sculptures, the genre scenes in reliefs and account of Fa-hsien and Hieun-Tsang.

13. Chapters 86, 87.

14. *Mārkaṇḍeyapurāṇa*, 58.46.

15. *Matsyapurāṇa*, 114. 41.43.

16. *Vāyupurāṇa*, 99.10, "*Gāndhāra-deśajā-ścāpi turagā vājinām varāḥ*".

17. 2. 47.4 (B.O.R.I.); Ibid., 7.22. 1-60.

18. *Chāmpeyya Jātaka* (506); Cowell, Vol. IV, p. 281 ff; B.C. Law, TAI, p. 4.

19. *Mahāvastu*, Vol. II, p. 169.

20. *Vessantara Jātaka* (547), Cowell, Vol. VI; p. 246. Agrawala, IKP. P. 49, "A special variety of blankets known as Pāṇḍukambala (IV.2.11) was a product of Gāndhāra. Gāndhāra is also known to the Atharvaveda for its wool". The "Pāṇḍukambala-śilā", the seat of Śakra, is referred to often in the Buddhist literature. Was is named thus because of its blanket-like design?

2. Kāmbojas

21. Nirukta, II. 2; B.C. Law TAI, pp. 1-2.

22. Baudhāyana, I. 1.2.4. "The animals that have teeth in the upper and the lower jaws"... certainly imply the horse, donkey, mules etc.

23. Vide infra, Chapter III, Section VII on dress and costume.

24. Pāṇini, IV. 1.175; Agrawala, IKP, p. 37, "To the south of Ferghana lay Kāmboja (IV.1.175) which...may be identified with the region of Badakshan Pamir", and p. 48, "In none of the these three janapadas can Kāmboja be included. It stands as a separate janapada, which Lassen correctly identified with the head-waters of the Oxus comprising the Ghalcha-speaking areas of Pamir".

    But from the point of view of culture the Kāpiśa-Kāmboja territory was more or less the same. Vide Supra. p. 22.

25. Patañjali I, 1.1. Puri, ITP, p. 73.

26. *Aṅguttara Nikāya*, Vol. I, p. 213; Vol. IV, pp. 252-256.

27. 5.160 (Haridas; 7.97.13, "...*Duryadhana-puragamāḥ, Śakāh Kāmboja-Vahlīkā-Yavanāḥ Pāradastathā*".

28. 2. 47.4 (B.O.R.I.); Ibid., 2.47.16-18; Ibid., 7.97.26; 7.21.22-23 (Haridas).

29. *Kukkura Jātaka* (22); *Bālodaka Jātaka* (183); *Saindhava Jātaka* (254).

30. *Harṣacarita*, I.

31. 11. 25.1. (B.O.R.I.), "*Kāmbojāstaraṇocitam*" etc., op. cit., 2.47.3, "*Prāvārājina-mukhyaṃśca Kāmbojaḥ pradadau vasu*,"...op. cit., 7.22.3, "*Darśanīyāstu Kāmbojāḥ Śukapatra-paricchadāḥ*".

32. 7.95.12.13, "*Daṃśutāḥ krūra-karmāṇaḥ Kāmbojāḥ yuddha-durmadāḥ*
śara-bāṇasana-dharā Yavanāśca prahāriṇaḥ. 12
Śakāḥ Kirātā-Daradā-Barbaras-Tāmraliptakāḥ,
Anye ca bahavo Mlecchā-vividhāyudha-Pāṇayaḥ. 13"
Op. cit., 7.95.20-21 (muṇḍān); 7.95.35, 38
Harivaṃśa; 1.14. 16-17,
Ardham Śakānāṃ śiraso muṇḍam-krityā vyasarjayat;
Yavanānāṃ śirah sarvaṃ Kambojānāṃ tathaiva ca. 16
Pārada-mukta-keśāśca Pahlava-śmaśru-dhāriṇaḥ,
Nihsvādhyāya-vaṣaṭkārāḥ Kritāstena mahātmanāḥ. 17"

33. 11.22.9-11 (B.O.R.I.)
"*Tametāḥ paryapasānte rakṣamāṇā mahābhujam*,
Sindhu-Sauvīra-Gāndhāra-Kāmboja-Yavanastriyaḥ. 11"

34. 12.65.14, "*Kāmbojaścaiva sarvasah*" etc., (Haridas).

35. *Mahābhārata*, 13.33 and 35 (Haridas).

36. Manu, X. 43.44.

37. 11.1. 160-61, Shamasastry, p. 407. (Sixth Edition)

38. M.N. Datta, *Harivaṃsa*, 1. 14.

39. Narain, The Indo-Greeks, pp. 1-2; Gaṇapāṭha 178 and 2. 172.

40. *Majjhima Nikāya*, II, p. 149.

41. Baudhāyāna, I.1. 24, "to follow the trade of arms".

42. Shamasastry, p. 407.

43. The Kāmbojas are mentioned in the *Vaṃśa Brāhmaṇa* of the *Sāmaveda*, Vide, Agrawala, IKP, p. 49. Dr. B.C. Law, TAI, p. 1, remarks, "we lay stress on this fact, because it shows that the Kāmbojas in early Vedic times, must have been a vedic Indian and not Iranian as has been supposed by several scholars".

3. The Madrakas and the Vāhīkas

44. *Vaṃśa Brāhmaṇa* of *Sāmaveda*, Vedic Index II, p. 123 *Aitareya Brāhmaṇa*, VII. 3, Keith, p. 331 *Bṛhadāraṇyaka Upaniṣad*, III, 3.1, III.7.1.

45. *Rāmāyaṇa*, 4. 44. 12

    "*Tatra Matsyān Pulindāṃśca Śūrasenānstathaiva ca,*

    *Pracarān Bhadrakāṃścaiva Kurūṃśca saha Madrakaiḥ.*12"

    Other recensions put it as "*Prasthalān Madrakāṃścaiva.*"

46. *Mahābhārata*, 2.29.13, (B.O.R.I.)

    "*Tataḥ Śākalamabhetya Madrānāṃ puṭabhedanam,*

    Mātulāṃ prītipurvena Śalyaṃ cakre vase bali".

    Divyāvadāna, *Asokāvadānam*, p. 282; Ibid., *Śārdulakarṇāvadāna*,, p. 361, mentions the tribes of the north:

    "*Tadā Sauvīrakān Madrān Vāhlīkān Kekayān-api*

    Anaśrayaṃscakravākān Janasthānamapi pīḍyet"

47. Mahābhārata I, Vide, Chapters 94, 95.

48. Ibid., I. 107, 9-16 (Haridas),

    "*Pūrvaih pravartitam kiñcit kule' smin nṛpasattāmaiḥ*" etc.

49. Strabo, XV. 1.62.

50. *Manusaṃhitā*, III. 31, 41; Gautama, VI. 11.

51. O.C. Ganguly thinks that Attok, Ṭakkaśilā as well as Ṭāki in Punjab are reminiscent of the name of the Ṭakka tribe, who were a branch of the Turanian race and were different from the Iranian. Vide, Prajñānānanda, Rāga O Rūpa, pp. 6-8.

    It is possible that the tribe had entered Punjab from the west during the supremacy of the Sassanids sometime in or after 240 A.D. from the neighbouring kingdom of Turan. According to Yazdani, Ajanta, p. 50, the features of the foreigners painted are Turanian. It is exactly in this period (c. fifth to sixth century A.D.) the Ṭakka rāga finds numerous mention in Mataṅga's *Bṛhaddeśī*. But the name of 'Ṭakkaśilā' cannot be called after the tribe, because it is known much earlier.

52. *Mahābhārata*, 8.30.55-56,68 (B.O.R.I.),

    Bhavatyekaḥ kule viprah siṣṭānye kāmacāriṇaḥ,

    *Gāndhāra-Madrakāścaiva Bāhlika'pyacetasaḥ.*55

    Evamanyā śrutaṃ tatra dharma-saṃkara-kāraṇam,

    *Kṛitsnamatitvā prithivīṃ Bāhlīkeṣu viparyayah.*56"

and

"*Kṣatriyasya malaṃ bhaikṣyaṃ Brāhmaṇasyaaṇritaṃ malam,*

*Malaṃ prithivyā Vāhlīkaṃ strīṇāṃ Madrastrīyo malam.*68"

The Bengali edition by Harīdas Siddhāntavāgīśa always put "*Vāhīka*" while the edition of B.O.R.I. give "*Bāhlīka*".

53. *Mahābhārata*, 8.30.10-11

"*Bahiskṛitā Himavatā Gaṅgyācā tiraskṛitāḥ,*

*Sarasvatyā Yamunayā Kurukṣetreṇa cāpiye.*10

Pañcānām Sindhu-ṣaṣṭhāṇāṃ nadīnaṃ ye antarāśritāḥ,

*Tan dharma-bāhyāṇ-aśucin Bāhlīkānparivarjayet.*11"

also: –

"*Śākalaṃ-nāma nagaraṃ Āpagā-nāma nimnagā*

*Jarttikā-nāma Bahlīkāsteṣāṃ vṛittaṃ suninditam.*14."

Cunningham, AGI, pp. 206-219, pp. 212-13, thinks that Śākala was near modern Sangala, and the Awak stream should be identified with ancient Āpagā river. Are the "Āraṭṭas" and the "Jarttikas" to be identified with "Oratae" and "Suarataratae" of Pliny, vi. XXIII?

54. Raychaudhuri, PHAI, p. 24 ff. Discusses the gencalogical list in the epic and shows the connection of "*pururavas Aila*" and "Bālhīka Pratipiya" with "Bāhlī" or Balkh, vide, p. 25, n. 17.

Agrawala, IKP, p. 52, "Pāṇini does not explain the derivation of the name Vāhīka. Kātyāyana, however, derives it from *bahis*, 'outside', with the suffix *ikak* (IV. 1.85.5)".

Notwithstanding, the endeavour to derive the name thus and concoct the story of two piśācas "Vahi" and "Hika" (vide, *Karnaparva*) it seems that the name Vahika for Punjab was actually derived due the settlers from "Bāhlīka" or "Vāhlīka" i.e., Balkh, vide, Agrawala, op. cit., p. 447.

55. Przyluski, An Ancient People of the Punjab: The Andumbaras, pp. 7-8.

56. CHI, pp. 549-550.

57. CAGI, p. 185.

58. *Milindapañha*, pt. I. pp. 1-3.

The *Kalingabodhi Jātaka* (179) mention Śākala as the capital of Madra.

Mahāvastu, II, p. 440.

59. *Mahābhārata*, 8.30.63-64 (B.O.R.I.).

60. Ibid., 8.30.44; in 8.30.65-66, "*Dharmaṃ Pañcanadaṃ dṛistvā dhig-ityāha Pitāmaha*, "etc.

61. Cf., *Bṛihadāraṇyaka Upaniṣad*, vide above, n. 44, it mentions the tradition of Vedic teachings amongst the Madras.

62. *Mahābhārata*, 8.30.55-56 (B.O.R.I.); 8.34.114-115 (Haridas); 8.34.134-135 (Haridas).

63. Ibid., 8.27 71-84 (B.O.R.I.); the Madra women are condemned, op. cit., 8.27.85-89; 8.34.144 (Haridas).

4. Yavanas

64. S. Sen, Old Persian Inscriptions, p. 223, Iauna; CHI, pp. 487 and 540.

65. All the relevant terms have been discussed by Narain, The Indo-Greeks, pp. 165-169, Appendix I; Mbh. 12.200.4, "*Yaunā-Kambojā-Gāndhārāḥ Kirāta-Barbaraiḥ*" (B.O.R.I.).

66. Pāṇini, IV, 1.49.

67. *Majjhima Nikāya*, I, 149.

68. Bhandarkar, Charmichael Lectures, 1921, p. 29.

69. *Mahāvastu*, Vol. I, p. 172.

70. Ibid., Vol. I, p. 107.

71. *Lalitavistara*, p. 125, which describes different types of "*lipis*", i.e., scripts.

72. *Malindapañha*, pp. 1-2.

73. Rock Edicts, II, v.

74. Ep. Ind. VIII, p. 36 ff., the inscription of Rudradāman.

75. Rock Edicts, XIII; vide Raychaudhuri, PHAI, pp. 298 ff., 331 f.

76. Mbh. 7.5.3-6; 7.9.16-18; 7-11; 7.80.41-46; 7.103.41-48; 7.105. 13-14 (Haridas) etc.

77. Mbh. 12.65.13-22 (B.O.R.I.).

78. Ibid., 8.30.80

"*Sarvajñā Yavanā rājañ-sūraścaiva viśeṣataḥ,*

Mlecchāḥ svasuṃjñā-niyatā nānukta itaro janaḥ. 80"

79. *Gautama Dharmaśāstra*, IV, 21, "*Pāraśava-Yavana-karaṇa-śūdrāñchūdrotyeke*" etc. SBE, Vol. II, lvi, p. 198; CHI, Vol. I, p. 215.

80. As found in *Harivaṃśa*, I.14.16-19 and in Mbh. 13. Chapters 33 and 35.

81. *Mahābhāṣya*, II.4.10; Puri, ITP, p. 91.

82. Mbh. I.168.37-40 (Haridas).

    Another myth of origin is also supplied by the epic. Thus I.73.34 (Haridas) states: –

    "*Yadostu Yādavājātas Turvasor-Yavanāḥ smṛitāḥ*

    Druhyoh sūtāstu vai Bhojā Anostu Mleccha-jātayaḥ. 34"

83. Different recensions give slight changes in these names.
84. Mbh. I.73.34.
85. *Rāmāyaṇa*, 4.43.18-19.
86. For different versions, see *Rāmāyaṇa*, *Gauḍīyapāṭha*, Calcutta Sanskrit Series, Vol. IV, p. 3324.
87. *Raghuvaṃśam*, IV. 61.
88. Mbh. II.22.11. (B.O.R.I.).
89. Ep. Ind. Vol. VIII, pp. 90, "*Sidham Otarāhasa Datāmitiyakasa*..." etc.
90. *Viṣṇupuraṇā*, V.23.4-5 ff.
91. Vide. Supra, p. 20, n.27.
92. Vide supra, p. 19, ns.18, 20, 21.
93. Matsya, 273, 19-23.
94. Ep. Ind. Vol. VIII, pp. 60-61, "*Saka-Yavana-Palhava nisūḍanasa*" etc.
95. Keru, *Gārgīsaṃhitā*, p. 37.
96. *Mālavikāgnimitram*, V.
97. Rapson, CHI, Vol. I, pp. 468-69, 491; Raychaudhuri, PHAI, pp. 378-88; Tarn, GBI, pp. 452-456, Appendix IX, 4; Narian, The Indo-Greeks, pp. 174-179, Appendix IV.
98. Upadhyaya, India in Kālidāsa, pp. 55-56.
99. Arrian, vi. XVII, XVIII, XX, CAI, p. 77 ff. Periplus 38.
100. Tarn, GBI, pp. 235, 321.
101. Holdich, Gates of India, p. 147.
102. Bṛi. Saṃ, IV, 22; XVIII. 6, etc.; Vide, op. cit., Vol. II, p. 213.
103. *Rāmāyaṇa*, 4.43.
104. Bṛi. Saṃ, XIV. 18.
105. *Harṣacarita*, VI.
106. The story is probably an ancient version of the one in the Arabian Nights.
107. *Harṣacarita*, VII. Levi, I.H.Q. 1936, Vol. XII. Pp. 121-133.

5. Sindhu-Sauvīras

108. Baudhāyana, I.1.2.13, "The inhabitants of Avantī, of Aṅga, of Magadha, of Sauvīra, of the Dekhan, of Upāvṛit, of Sindhu, the Sauvīras are of mixed origin". Vide supra p. 27, n. 9, for the original. Ibid., I.1.2.14, "*Ārattān Kāraskarān Puṇḍrān Sauvīran Vaṅgān Kaliṅgān prānūnāniti ca gatvā punastomena yajeta ṣarvapriṣṭhāyavā*" Vide Govindasvāmin, p. 12.

109. Agrawala, IKP, pp. 37, 44, 50; p. 44, "To south of Kekaya was situated the Sindhu janapada lying north to south between the rivers Jhelum and Indus. Along the lowermost course of the river Sindhu was situated the ancient Sauvīra janapada (IV.1.148), now known as Sind". Vide Puri, ITP, p. 76; Chaudhuri, ESAI, pp. 122-124.

110. Mbh. 8.30.47 "*Āraṭṭā nāma te deśa Bāhlīka nāṁa te janāḥ, Vasāti-Sindhu-Sauvīra iti prāyo vi-Kutsitāḥ*.47"

111. Mbh. 6.18.13-14; Ibid., 6.9.52-53 (Haridas), "*Kāśmīrā-Sindhu-Sauvīrā*"; Ibid., 7.5.6. Ibid., 7.113.11; 7.114.17 (Haridas).

112. Mbh. 7. 51. 14.

113. Mbh. I. 134. 21-23. (Haridas).

"*Atīva bala-sampannaḥ sadā mānī kuruṃ pṛati,*
Vipula nāmo Sauviraḥ śāntaḥ Pārthena dhīmatā.22
Dattāmitra iti Khyātaṃ saṃgrāme kṛitaniścayam,
Sumitraṃ nāma Sauvīra-marjam' damayaccharaiḥ.23"

For discussion about its authenticity, see Narain, IG, p. 39.

114. Puri, ITP, p. 55.

115. Ep. Ind., Vol. VIII.

116. *Milindapañha*, p. 359; Arrain, vi, XVII-XX on Pattala; Periplus, 38; Shamasastry, p. 90, n.2; Agrawala, IKP, p. 62; on Barbara (IV.3.93).

117. *Divyavadāna, Rudrāyanavadānam*, from the story it appears that Roruka was famous for jewels. Agrawala, IKP, p. 50.

118. Arrian, vi, XVII ff.

119. *Rāmāyaṇa*, 4.43.10,

"*Kalkeyān Sindhu-Sauvīrān Kāntāra-girayaśca ye,*
Giri-jālā-vṛitāṃ durgāṃ māgaddvaṃ paścimāṃ diśam".

120. *Kaṭāhaka Jātaka* (125), mentions *Pratyamtadeśa* (i.e., frontier country) and Kaṭahaka's contemptuous statements about their food, mode of dress and toilet etc.

121. *Kukkura Jātaka* (22); *Bhojājānīeya Jātaka* (23); *Bālodoka Jātaka* (183); *Kuṇḍaka Kucchi Sindhava Jātaka* (254).

122. Mbh.8.27.87-88 (B.O.R.I.), "*Suvīrakaṃ yācyamānā*", "*Putraṃ dadyāṃ pratipadaṃ na tu dadyāṃ Suvīrakaṃ*", etc.

123. *Dighanikāya*, II, pp. 235-36, "*Soviran ca Rorukam*".

124. *Divyāvadāna, Rudrāyanavadānam*, p. 465 ff., Vide, p. 486.

125. Cunningham, pp. 569-71; Carry and Warmington, Ancient Explorers, p. 59 disagrees to identify "Ophir" with "Sovira" i.e., Sauvīra country.

126. Ptolemy, 55, p. 136. Periplus 41.

127. Tarn, GBI, p. 171.

128. Mbh. 8.27.91 (B.O.R.I.).

"*Madrakāḥ Sindhu-Sauvīra dharmaṃ vidyuḥ kathaṃ tviha,*

*Pāpā deśodbhavā Mlecchā dharmānāṃ avicakṣaṇaḥ.*91"

129. Ep. Ind. Vol. VIII, pp. 36-49, Vide, p. 44.

130. Vide supra, p. 6, Section on the Political Outline.

6. Ābhīras

131. Tarn, GBI, pp. 171-72.

132. S. Sen, Persian, Inscription, pp. 122, 126

Ammianus Marcellinus, XXIII, 6.53.62, mentions a Scythian tribe called Abii; Pliny vi. XXXI. Enlists a tribe called Abi while enumerating the tribes of north India.

133. *Mahābhāṣya*, i.II.3.72, "*Śūdrabhīram*", "*Brāhmaṇādugra-kanyāyām-ābhīro nāma jāyate*".

134. Mbh. 16.8.45; Ibid., 8.51 (B.O.R.I.).

135. Vide supra, p. 23, on Arrian, iv. 17.

136. Vide supra, pp. 23-24 for the discussion on *Dasyu*, also p. 28, ns. 14, 15.

137. Mbh. 4.29.5-7 (Haridas), Ibid., 4.32.4-7, etc. Ibid., 4.9.15, the *gavādhyakṣa* saw the welfare of the cows and managed the *gopālas*.

"*Tato gopāḥ pragātāraḥ kuśalā nṛitya vādane,*

*Dhārtarāṣṭram-upatiṣṭhan Kanyāścaiva svalamkritāḥ.*8" (3.203.8, Haridas).

138. *Harivaṃśa*, 2.9; trans., M. N. Datta, *Viṣṇuparva*, p. 271; Patañjali, i.II. 3.72; *Mārkaṇḍeyapurāṇa* 49. 50; *Amarakoṣa*, ii. 633, "*Ghoṣa-Ābhīrapallī syāt*".

139. Herodotus, iv. 46.

140. Mbh. 6.9.44 (Haridas); 6.10.42-66 (B.O.R.I.) give some variants in the nomenclature; Ibid., 6.10.45 mentions the Ābhīras, the Vāhīkas, the Vāṭadhānas and the Kālatoyakas.

141. Periplus, 41; Ptolemy, 55; Vide McCrindle, pp. 136, 140, "Tha Abiria is the Ophir of Scripture is an opinion that has been maintained by scholars of eminence".

142. Ep. Ind. Vol. XVI, p. 233.

143. Ep. Ind. Vol. VIII, pp. 88-89.

144. Mbh. 2.49.9 (Haridas); 2.47.10 (B.O.R.I.) omits "Ābhīra".

145. Ibid., 6.10.45 (B.O.R.I.).

146. Mbh. 2.29.9. (B.O.R.I.).

147. Nearchos, XXIV, CAI, p. 318; Holdich, Gates of India, p. 290; "This remarkable feature of long lateral valleys which, through all ages, has made of Makran, an avenue very much easier to traverse from east to west than it is from north to south".

148. Mbh. 2.29.10 (B.O.R.I.) states the verse as follows: –

"*Kritsnaṃ Pañcanadaṃ caiva tathai-Vāparaparyaṭam, Uttarajyotikaṃ caiva tathā Vṛindāṭakaṃpuram.* 10" its n. 10, gives variant readings viz., "*Vāparapaṭṭanān*" or "*Vāvarapattanāt*" which seems to be the correct reading as these probably allude to "*Āvarapattanaṃ*" i.e., the port-town on the Arabius, or the port of Bābara, (Barbara) i.e., the Barbaricum on the Indus. Vide, 2.31.10. (Haridas).

149. The Sauvīra country in the Lower Indus became famous for its wine (vide supra, p. 53) called "Sauvīraka". Harivaṃśa (vide trans., M. N. Datta, p. 645) mentions various wines such as Maireya, Mādhvika and Āsava. The Yādavas were closely associated with Abhīras and it seems that these tribes owned many distilleries. Vide Mbh. 2.49.8-9 (Haridas); Holdich, op. cit., pp. 213-215; Mbh. 2.49.8-9 (Haridas); Holdich, op. cit., pp. 213-215; Mbh. 2.47.10. of B.O.R.I. edition put "*Vaṅgāśca*" in place of "Ābhīrāḥ", but the Bengali edition seems more correct in this context, as the Vairāma, the Pārada, the Ābhīra and the Kitava are all western tribes. "*Vaṅga*" here would be indeed out of place.

Motichandra thinks that the Vairāmas were the inhabitants of Rambakia or Rhambacia in South Baluchistan, vide Sārthavaha, pp. 11, 73.

150. Book i.101.

151. Rai Bahadur B.A. Gupte, IA, 1911, pp. 147-149.

152. Bri. Sam. X. 5; X. 7 etc.

153. Ibid., XIV. 21.

154. *Nayādhammakahāo*, p. 21.

155. Bri. Sam. XIV, 21,

"*Pañcanada-Ramaṭha-Pārata-Tārakṣiti Jṛiṅga-Vaiśya-Kanakaśakāḥ,*

*Nirmaryādā Mlecchā ye paścimadik-sthitā ye ca.*21"

156. For detailed discussion, see, Chaudhuri, ESAI, pp. 103-104.

157. Vide Bṛi. Saṃ. XVI, 1-5.

158. Nearchos, XVI, CAI, p. 314.

159. Mbh. 16.7.46-63 (Haridas)

Viṣṇup. V. 38.26-28, 50-52, 65 etc.

160. Matsyap. 70, relates the whole episode of the Yādava women and the Ābhīra Dasyus.

161. *Harivaṃśa*, 2.88.8-13; trans. P. 635.

162. Ibid., 2.89.7. "*Taddeśa-bhāṣā-kṛiti-veṣa-yuktāḥ*"; trans., p. 640.

163. Ibid., 2.88.57-70; trans., p. 63.

164. Mbh. 3.15.16; *Harivaṃśa*, trans., p. 682-687.

165. Kennedy, J.R.A.S. 1907, p. 962 ff.

166. Ammianus Marcellinus, XVIII, 9. XIX, 1-8.

167. The evidence of the Paikuli inscription shows that the "Abhiran Sah" had brought tribute to the Sassanian monarch Varhran III.

168. J.C. Jain, p. 94; Āvaśyaka Nir., p. 471; Ava. Cur., p. 28 f.

169. Matsya, 273, while enumerating the *Mleccha* dynasties, twice mention the Ābhīras:–

a. "*Saptaivāndhra bhaviṣyanti daśābhirāstathunṛipāh,*
*Sapta-Garddbhilaścāpi Śakaścāṣṭa daśaiva tu.*18"
and,

b. "*Āndhrāḥ Śrīpārvatiyāśca te dvīpañcāśataṃsamāḥ,*
Saptaṣaṣṭistu varṣāṇi daśābhīrāstathaiva ca.
*Teṣutsanneṣu kālena tataḥ kilkilāḥ nripāḥ.*24.
Bhavisyantīha Yavanā dharmataḥ kamatoṛrthataḥ,
*Tairvimiśvā janapadā Āryā-Mlecchāśca sarvasah.*25"

170. Suryavamsi, The Ābhīras, p. 25 ff.

171. Corp. Ins. Ind. Vol. III, p. 8.

172. *Rāmāyaṇa*, 6.22.29-36 (N.S.P.)

Uttareṇāvakāśo'sti Kaścit puṇyataro mama,

*Drumakulya iti khyāto loke khyāto yathā bhavān.*29

Ugradarśana-karmāṇo bahavastatra dasyavaḥ,

*Ābhīra-pramukhāḥ pāpāḥ pivanti salilaṃ mama.*30".

*** *** ***

"*Tena ten-marukāntāraṃ prithivyāṃ kila viśrutam,*

*Nipātitaḥ śaro yatra vajrāśanisamaprabhaḥ.*33.

Nanāda ca tadā tatra vasudhā śalyapīḍitā,

*Tasmād-vraṇa-mukhatttoyam-utpapāta rasatalāt.*34.

Sa babhūva tadā kūpo vraṇa ityeva viśrutaḥ

*Satataṃ cotthitaṃ toyaṃ Samudrasyeva dṛiśyate.*35"

173. Cunningham, AGI, p. 354.

174. Nāṭyaśāstra, xvii, 50-56,

"*Śakār-Ābhīra-Caṇḍāla Śabara-Dramil-Āndhrajā,*

*Hīnā vanecārānām ca vi-bhāṣā nāṭake smṛita.*50"

*** *** ***

"*Gajāśvājāvikoṣṭrādi-ghoṣa-sthāna-nivāsinām,*

*Ābhīrokti Śābari vā Drāmiḍī vanacāriṣu.*56"

175. Keith, HSL. pp. 32-34, according to him, the "tribe appears to have entered India some time before 150 B.C., when it is mentioned by Patañjali. Its early home was Sindhudeśa, by which is meant not Sindh but the Peshawar district of the Rawalpindi division, where they had as eastern neighbours the Gujaras", and "Both Ābhīras and Gujaras were probably of the Dardic branch of the Indian race; to judge at least from the strong Dardic element in Lahnada, the speech of the Western Panjab".

176. *Harivaṃśa*, 2.88, 89.

177. Suryavamshi, op. cit., Introduction, p. xiv.

178. Pliny, vi. XXXI. Vide L.C.L. Vol. II, p. 439. Are the "Surai" (vi. XXIII) amidst the desert and the "Abi, Suri and silac" (vi. XXIII) up the Indus to be identified with "Śūras" and "Ābhīras"?

179. Strabo, XV.III.1. and XV.III.2, The People of Persis and Susis.

7. Kekayas

180. Vedic Index, Vol. I, p. 22, the Anus, the forefathers of the Kekayas, are mentioned as dwelling on the Paruṣṇī stream; R.C. Chanda, The Indo Aryans, p. 33 the Anus were Semitic people.

Mbh. 1.73.34 (Haridas) states, "*Anostu Mleccha-jātayaḥ*", which means that the Kekayas, the Bhadrakas, Prithudarbhaṣ etc., were of *Mleccha* category.

181. Mb. 7.18.7-11 (B.O.R.I.) the Kekayas are mentioned with the Śūras, the Abhīras, the Daśerakas, the Śakas, the Kāmbojas, the Yavanas, the Madras, the Pārvatīyas, the Vasātis etc., forming the Kaurava phalanx.

182. Ibid., 7.8.53-54 (Haridas), "*Indragopa-saṅkāśā rakta-varmāyudha-dhvajāḥ*".

183. *Rāmāyaṇa*, 2.68.19-22; Ibid., 7.107.2, describes the products of Kekaya country:–

"*Daśa cāśva-sahasrāṇi prīti-dānam-anuttaman,*

Kambalādini ratnāni cīrapaṭṭāṃ-stathottamān.

Bahu cābharaṇaṃ mukhyaṃ Rāmāya prāhinonnṛipaḥ".

184. Ibid., 7.107.10-11.

185. Vayup. 99.12-24; *Harivaṃśa*, I. 31.29-30; Matsyap. 48.10-20, Viṣṇup. IV. 18.

186. Davar, Iran and India, p. 45, *Śarmiṣṭhā*, mother of *Anu*, was the daughter of *Vriṣaparvā*, the Asura king. The Persians or Iranians were designated as Asuras, in ancient India.

187. Matsyap. 114. 42-43, the Kekayas are mentioned with the Ramaṭha, the Kaṇṭakāras, Daśanāmakas, the Prasthalas, the Daserakas; etc.

188. B. C. Law, TAI, pp. 78, 95, 356.

189. Holdich, Gates of India, p. 34; Bri. Sam. XIV. 21, mentions "*Jṛiṅga-Vaiśya-Kanaka-Śaka*". This "Kanaka" might had been a transcript for 'Kikan' i.e., Kaikan of Sakastan.

190. Cunningham, AGI, p. 188.

8. The Pārasīkas and the Pahlavas

191. Ṛigveda, VI. 27.8.,VII. 83.1, VIII.6.46, X.86.23, etc.

192. Davar, Iran and India, pp. 42-45; Monier Williams, p. 711, Pruth=to pant or to neigh.

193. Pāṇini, v.III.117; Agrawala, p. 445 ff.

194. Scythian Age, p. 11, n.1, the same, that the scholar says about the Śakas and Tuṣāras is applicable to the Śaka-Pahlavas.

195. Mbh. I. 165.35-37; Vide n. 36 for "*Pārasīkāṃśca*".

196. Mbh. 2.49.6 (Haridas); 2.47.7. (B.O.R.I.).

197. Patañjali, vi. I. 157; Puri, p. 76.n.1.

198. *Nayādhammakanāo*, p. 21,

"*Vāmaṇi-vadabhi-babbari-bausi-joṇiya-palhavi-isiṇi-dhoruṇigiṇi-lāsiya-lausiya-damili-siṃhali-Ārabi-puliṇdi-pakkaṇi-bahali-muraṃdi-sabari-pārasīhiṃ nānā-desīhiṃ videsaparimaṃdiyāhiṃ*". etc.

Vide infra, Chap III, Section on Position of Women.

199. *Rāmāyaṇa*, Vide, C.S.S. Vol. IV, p. 3324. (Calcutta Sanskrit Series) Periplus, 38, "Before this town lies a small islet, and behind it in the interior is Minnagara, the metropolis of Scythia which is governed, however, by the Parthian princes who are perpetually at strife amongst themselves, expelling each other."

200. Hiuen-Tsag, on Lang-Kie (ka)-Lo, Beal, Vol. II, 276-77; Ammianus Marcellinus, xxiii, 6.73. mentions Gynaecon Limen, a city called 'Women's Haven' in south-eastern Gedrosia, the site exactly pointed out by Hiuen-Tsang for the 'Kingdom of West Women'.

Bṛi. Saṃ. Mentions one Nārīmukha in the south-west with Pahlava, Phenagiri, Yavanamārga etc. Vide Supra, p. 63.

201. Vide supra, p. 71, n. 94.

202. Harivaṃśa, I. 32. 50,

"*Babhūva mṛigayāśilaḥ Kuśikastasycātmajaḥ*
Pahlavaiḥ saha saṃruddho rājā vanacaraistadā".

203. Vide supra, p. 62.

204. Vāyup. 39.63; Ibid., 39.68-69,

"*Drākṣāvanāni ramyāṇi tathā Nāgavanāni ca,*
*Kharjura-vana-khaṇḍāni Nīlāśoka-vanānica.*68
Dāḍimāṇāṃ ca svādunāṃ-Akṣoṭaka vanāni ca,
*Atasī-Tilakānāṃ ca Kadalīnāṃ vanāni ca.*69".

205. Vāyup. 38.37-40.

9. The Śakas

206. Herod. iv.

207. Pliny, vi.XVIII.58-XIX, "To these the Persians have given the general name of Sacae……".

208. Agrawala, IKP, p. 68. The Śakas that came with the Tuṣāras, Kaṅkas (Camacae of Pliny, or Ki-kiang-ni of Hiuen-Tsang?), the hairly folks ('*Romaśaḥ*', are they the Rumnici Scythians of Pliny?), and the "*Śṛiṅgiṇo nara's* (either to be identified with the Jṛiṅgas or

these are the Scythians that used head-gears decorated with ram's horn) brought tribute of wollen and silken clothes, fine leather and very many sharp weapons are Scythians from outside of India, vide Mbh. 2.49.25 (Haridas). Cf. With them the Scythians that were to be found in Madhyadeśa, vide infra, n. 219.

209. *Mahābhāṣya*, II. 4. 10; vi. 1.94.

210. Puri, ITP, pp. 55-56; 91-92.

211. Agrawala, IKP, p. 69, "Kātyāyana mentions Śakandhu, Karkandhu, two types of wells of the Śakas and the Karkas (Karkians), which may be identified with the stepped well (vāpī) and the Persian wheel (arghaṭṭa) respectively.

212. Ibid., pp. 68-69, "How a string of Kanthā-ending place names was found in the Uśīnara country in the heart of the Punjab, is an unexplained problem. It points to an event associated with Śaka history even before Pāṇini, possibly an intrusion which left its relics in place-names long before the Śaka contact with India in the second century B.C".

213. Przyluski, APP: The Audumbaras, p. 8, "It seems that long before the invasion of the Indo-Scythians and the Śakas, even before the expedition of Alexander, some Bactrians, descending from Afghanistan, had already penetrated into India and conquered at least the Punjab". Ibid., Vide n. 19, "If certain tribes – apparently Iranised but never to be affirmed that they were Indo-Europeans – advanced before Alexander to the south of the Hindu Kush, it explains better the diffusion of many ethnic and geographical names and certain phonetic anomalies which appears sporadically in the north of India and in Iran. Śākala which appears to be derived from Śaka (Scythians) is an ancient name of the capital of the Punjab". Ptolemy, McCrindle, p. 261, mentions another city in Hyrcania called "Śaka".

214. Chattopadhyaya, The Achaemenids, p. 21 ff.

215. Arrian's Anabis, vide supra, p. 31, But from the evidence of Pāṇini it is clear that the Scythians had entered the land before Alexander, and his Scythian followers only reinvigorated the earlier groups of settlers.

216. Vide above, n. 211, 212.

217. Mbh. 2.50.16 (Haridas); 2.48.26 (B.O.R.I.), "*Śakas-Tuṣārāḥ*" etc.; 7.6.3-6 (B.O.R.I.), Ibid., 7.10.16-18; 7.9.16-18 (Haridas); 7.96.50 and 7.105.13-14 (Haridas); 8.54.19 (Haridas); 12.165.13 (B.O.R.I.), "*Śakas-Tusārāḥ Kanvāśca Pahlavā...*" etc.

218. Mbh. 6.10.50 (B.O.R.I.), "Śakā Niṣādā (n. 50, Niṣedha) *Niṣadhāstathaivānarta-naitāḥ*" etc.

Ibid., 6.11.27-39 (Haridas) describes *Śākadvīpa*.

Matsyap. 122 chap. Relates the names of the rivers, mountains and peoples of *Śākadvīpa* after the epic.

219. Vāyup. 45.116-118, The Śakas are mentioned along with the Hraḍas (are they the inhabitants of the *Hrādinī* or *Hlādinī* stream of the Ganges?), Kulindas, the Paritas, the Hārapurikas, the Ramaṭhas, the Ruddha-kaṭakas, the Kekayas, the Daśamālikas, the Kāmbojas, the Daradas, the Barbaras, the Priyalaukikas, the Tuṣāras, the Pahlavas, the Prasthalas, the Lampākas etc. Viṣṇup. II. 4. 69-71

"*Maryādā-vyutkramo nāsti teṣu deśeṣu sāptaṣu,*

Mṛigāśca Māgadhāścaiva Mānasā Mandagāstathā.69

Mṛigā Brāhmaṇabhūyiṣṭhā Māgadhāḥ Kṣatriyāstathā,

Vaiśyāstu Mānasāsteṣāṃ Śūdrāsteṣāntu Mandagāḥ.70

Śākadvīpa tutair-Viṣṇu Sūnyarupodharo mune,

Yathoktairijyata samyak-Karmabhir niyatātmabhiḥ".71

Mārkaṇḍeyap. 58.6, curiously enough the Śakas here are placed in the Madhyadeśa with the Vimāṇḍavyas, the Śālvas, the Nipas, the Ujjihānas, the Ghoṣasaṃkhyas, the Khaśas, the Sārasvatas, the Matsyas, the Śūrasenas, the Māthuras etc. This shows that the *Purāṇakāra* had in his mind the inland Śakas of the Mathura region.

220. Vide Ptolemy, McCrindle, pp. 283-297, for Sakai and Scythia; p. 272, overthrew the Bactrian kingdom together with the Tokharoi, Sakarauli etc.

Vide, Chaudhuri, ESAI, p. 106 ff. For the identification of the Tārakṣuras with the Takhāras or Turuṣkas.

221. B. C. Law, TAI, p. 396, Tukharas.

222. Mbh. 3.159.34-35 (Haridas),

"*Bahavo Mleccha-rājānaḥ prithivyāṃ manujādhipa,*

Mriṣānuśāsinaḥ pāpā mriṣāvāda-parāyaṇāh.34

Āndhrāḥ Śakāḥ Pulindāśca Yavanāśca narādhipāḥ,

Kāmbojā Bāhlīkāḥ Śūrāstath-Ābhīra narottama.35"

Matsyap. 50.75-76; 273.18

Vayup. 58.81-84, the *Mlecchas* are destroyed by king Pramati.

Visnup. IV. 14, "Tataḥ ṣoḍaśa Śakā bhubhūjo bhavitāraḥ.

Tataśca aṣṭau Yavanāḥ, caturdaśa Tukhārāḥ, Muṇḍāśca

trayodaśa, ekādaśa Maunāḥ, ete prithivīṃ trayodaśa varṣaśatāmi navanavatyādhikāni bhokṣyanti".

223. Raychaudhuri, PHAI, p. 431 ff.; Chattopadhyaya, EHNI, p. 52 ff; p. 100 ff.

224. The Indian as well as the classical records are silent about the cultural activity of these people. Herod. iii. 102 mention them as "most warlike of the Indians". It has-been cited that the epic, the *Arthaśāstra*, the *Aṣṭādhyāyī*, the *Nāṭyaśāstra* and the *Bṛihat Saṃhitā* corroborate the accounts of Herodotus about the belligerent Northerners. The epic (2.27.17. Haridas, 2.25.17. B.O.R.I.) called the Gandharvas, the Hāṭakas, the Ṛiṣikas, the Lohas, the Paramakāmbojas etc. as "*Kṣatriyair-dasyubhiḥ*", and Pāṇini mentions them as "*Āyudhajīvibhyaśchaḥ parvate*" (iv.3.91). But apart from that the Indians were fully aware of their valuable products of fine clothes: silken, linen or wollen, of the soft leathers, ornaments, weapons and above all steeds of variegated colours (Vide Mbh. 2.27.16.17, Haridas; 2.25.16, 19, B.O.R.I.; 2.26.25-29, Haridas; 2.24.23-27, B.O.R.I.; 2.26.3-7, Haridas; 2.24.3-7, B.O.R.I. and 2.49.22-25, Haridas), which were to be gained from the Śakas, the Tuṣāras, the inhabitants of the Oxus region, the Śriṅgiṇas, the Romaśas, the Ṛiṣikas, thc Hāṭakas, the Gandharvas etc.

S.B. Chaudhuri, ESAI, p. 70-71 thinks that generally the Ṛiṣikas are to be located in the Anūpa country, but from the above references it is clear that the Ṛiṣikas (or Uttara-Ṛiṣikas, according to Chaudhuri, p. 71-n.4) are the Yueh-chis (vide, Agrawala, IKP, p. 62) whose language was Ārśī. They are the Asii of the classical writers (Ibid., p. 68). For the identification of Lohas, vide, Agrawala, p. 40. According to him these tribes inhabited the valleys of Kohistan-Kafiristan.

225. Mbh. 6.6.49 (Haridas) mention the seven streams of the Ganges,

"*Vasvaukasārā Nalinī Pāvanī ca Sarasvatī,*

*Jambunadī ca Sītā ca Gaṅgā Sindhuśca saptamī.*49"

This "*Vasvaukasārā*" might be "*Vakṣu*" or the Oxus, or one of the tributaries.

Ibid., 6.11.31-32, mention the Cakṣu (the Oxus, Vide, Agrawala, IKP, p. 68 and Matsyapurāṇa, A. Study, p. 206 ff.; but according to Chattopadhyaya, The Achaemenids, p. 26 it was Jaxartes) and the Vardhanikā (the Wakhan) streams in *Śākadvīpa*.

Matsyap. 121. 45-46a.,

"*Tuṣārāu Barbarākārān Pahlavān Pāradañchakān*

Etān Janapadaṃś-Cakṣuḥ plāvayitvodadhiṃgatā 46a"

Sītā (Matsyap. 121.42; Vayup. 47.37-51) has been identified with the Yarkand river (Agrawala, Mat. A. Study, pp. 204-5) but it seems that Sītā was the common name for the Yarkand-Tarim stream.

10. The Barbaras

226. Mbh. I. 165.36; 2.29.15; 2.48.n.3 (B.O.R.I.).

227. Ibid., 2.49.19 (Haridas),

"*Cīnān Śakāṃstathā coḍrān Barbarān Vanavāsinaḥ,*

Varṣṇeyān Hārahunaṃśca Kriṣṇān Haimavatāṃstathā.19"

These Hārahūṇas or Hārahūnas are identified with the inhabitants of the Haraguaiti Valley.

Mbh. 6.10.55 (B.O.R.I.); Matsyap. 121, 43-47, it appears that while one branch of them dwelt near the Cakṣu, the other lived near the Indus. They are variously mentioned as "*Barbarān*" (vs. 43), "*Barbarākārān*" (vs. 45) and "*Barbān*" (vs. 47). It is not known whether or how these northern tribe of Barbaras came in and settled in the lowermost region of Indus Delta.

228. CAGI, Notes, 9, pp. 692-95.

229. Ibid., pp. 337-40; Shamasastry, 6th ed. P. 79, ns. 1, 2, "... of the river of Barbara", ... "near the island of the Yavanas".

230. Periplus, 39; Ptolemy, 59, CAI, p. 373, mentions Patala and Barbarei in the island formed by the river.

11. Daradas

231. Herod, iii. 92.

232. Ibid., iii. 102.

233. Mbh. 7.10.16-18; 7.19.7-11 (B.O.R.I.).

234. Mbh. 6.10.66 (B.O.R.I.) states –

"...*Daradāḥ Kāśmīrāḥ Paśubhiḥ saha,*

Khāśikāśca Tukhārāśca Pallavā Girigahvarāḥ. 66"

235. Matsyap. 121.46; Mārkaṇḍeya, 57.38, the Kāmbojas, the Daradas, the Barbaras etc., are called "*bāhyato narāḥ*" i.e., outsiders.

236. Dionysus Periegetes, CAI, p. 423, "Dardanians have their seat by the mighty flood of the Indus".

237. Pliny, 22, CAI, p. 342, "Gold is very abundant among the Dardae".

238. Ptolemy, 42, CAI, p. 370, "Below those (sources) of the Indus are the Daradrai, in whose country the mountains are of surpassing height".

239. CAGI, pp. 95-96.

240. Herod, iii. 102-105.

241. Mbh. 2.50.4 (Haridas).

242. Tarn, GBI, pp. 104-110.

12. The Lampakas

243. Mbh. 7.105.42 (Haridas), they fought with stones and iron spears; Chaudhuri, ESAI, pp. 100-101.

244. Matsyap. 114.43, "*Lampakāstalagānāścaiva*"...

Vayup. 45.119, mentions them with the Ātreyas, the

Bhāradvājas, the Prasthalas, the Kaśerukas, the

Stanapas, the Pīḍikas, the Juhuḍas etc.

Mārkaṇḍeya, 57.40, mention the Lampākas, together with the Śūlakaras, the Cūlikas, the Jaguḍas, etc., all of whom are stated as branches of the Kirāta race.

245. CAGI, pp. 31-32.

246. Ibid., p. 50; Ptolemy, 42, CAI, p. 370, "Below the sources of the Koa are located the Lambatai and their mountain region extends upwards...Komedai".

247. Holidich, GI, Vide Map facing p. 94, vide p. 96.

248. Amn. Marc. XXIII, 6.75-84.

13. The Paradas

249. Mbh. 2.49.8-9; 2.50.3; 2.50.13 (Haridas).

6.84.7 (Haridas); 6.10.64 (B.O.R.I.), "*Pāratakaiḥ*".

250. Vide, TAI, p. 364-65; Mārkaṇḍeya, 57.37, 58.31.

251. *Harivaṃśa*, 1.14.16-17.

252. Manu, X. 43.44.

253. Vide supra, p. 46.

254. Mbh. 2.50.2-3 (Haridas),

"*Meru-Mandarayor-madhye Śailodāmabhito nadīm*," etc.

Matsyap. 121, 22-23, "*Tasya pādāt prabhavati śailodaṃ nāma tat sarah.*22.

Tasmāt prabhavate puṇyā nadī Śailodakā śubhā.

*Sa Cakṣuṣi tayormadhye puṇyā praviṣṭā paścimodadhim.*23"

255. Mbh. 2.47.10 (B.O.R.I.).

256. Mainly in Bṛihat Saṃhitā, X.5, X.7, XIV.21, etc.

257. Holdich, GI, p. 201, "... thieves and brigands".

258. Vide supra, pp. 48-49; the Pāradas and the Ābhīras, are moreover connected in the Paikuli inscription where it is stated that, "the chiefs of Paradan (Paradas), Makuran (Makran), the Ābhīras and the Kṣatrapas of Avantī as vassals under varhran III." This asserts their position in western India touching the southern Beluchistan.

259. Motichandra, Sārthavāha, pp. 11, 73.

260. Vide Holdich, Map facing p. 284. The Kitavas are also mentioned in Mbh. 7.6.6. (B.O.R.I.) with the western tribes such as Śibis, Śūdras, Sauvīras etc.

261. Holdich, GI, p. 167.

262. Am. Marc. XXIII. 6.17.73.

263. Vide supra, pp. 34-38.

264. Hiuen-Tsang, Beal, Vol. II, p. 277.

265. Mārkaṇḍeyap. 58.29.

266. A. Stein, M.A.S.I., 1881, No. 43, pp. 26-27 thinks that the local worship of '*ziarats*' are older then the advent of Islam.

267. Frye, Heritage of Persia, p. 180.

268. Chaudhuri, ESAI, pp. 103 ff.

269. *Śarkara, Śarkarā* or *Śārkara* has been identified with Sukkur in Sind, vide, Agrawala, IKP, pp. 50.

A few lines may be added here regarding the "*Kanaka-Śakas*" which supplement "*Śarkarā*" in the *Bṛihat Saṃhitā*.

Viṣṇup. IV. 18, states, "*Strīrājya Muṣikajanapadān Kanakāhvbayā bhokṣyanti*". This Strīrājya may be well identified with the "Striśvara" or "Women Paramount" of Hiuen-Tsang (Beal, Vol. II, p. 277), and the *Vanitāmukha* (Mārkaṇḍeya, 58.30) or *Nārīmukha* (Bṛi-Sam XIV. 17) all of which denote the same meaning and are located more or less with the western countries. The Kanakas mentioned along with the Śakas (Bṛi. Sam. XIV. 21) are to be identifies with those mentioned by Hiuen-Tsang (Beal, II, p. 282) thus: –"The common report says on the western frontier of this country [Fa-la-na=Varaṇā, sanskritized form of Aornos? Vide, Agrawala, IKP, p. 69] is the kingdom of Ki-kiang-na

(Kikana?). The people live amid the great mountains and valleys in separate clans. They have no chief ruler. They breed an immense quantity of sheep and horses. The shen horses are of a large size, and the countries around breed out few, and therefore they are highly valued".

The Kaṅkas of the epic (vide above, n. 208) after whose name, tributes of speedy-steeds, gold, carpets, bed-spreads, ivory inlaid armours of variegated colours, sharp weapons, and harnessed chariots are mentioned (2.49.26-27, Haridas) appear to be this Ki-kiang-na. (vide supra, p. 51).

Davar, Iran and India, p. 46, writes, "When Bharat with his maternal uncle Yudhājit went to meet his maternal grandfather, the latter favoured him on his return with numerous gifts, which comprised hounds, wollen raiments and the skins of antelopes. From these rather peculiar gifts, it may be inferred that the king of the Kekayas did not belong to India proper but to some province bordering on India". The author does not mention which recension or edition of the Rāmāyaṇa he has used for his informations. Both the Bengal recension and the Nirṇaya Sāgara edition enumerates horses, kambalas, jewels etc.

270. This *Māṇḍavya* may really stand for the Muruṇḍas (vide, Chaudhuri, ESAI, p. 138, n. 1), who lived in the Lampāka, Lamghan (Laghman) reign.

271. They are probably the Dahae Scythians, Vide Pliny, vi, XIX.

272. Chaudhuri, ESAI, Chart III, there remains some vagueness about the name.

Three

Social Life

This chapter reviews the western impacts upon the main aspects of social life. I have pointed out earlier why the discussion on social life has been taken up first. Any change due to the foreign contacts becomes visible first in the society before it can make it's influence evident on other nobler spheres of culture, such as fine arts and religion. The society, it seems, gets agitated at the advent of an alien force, and after the turmoils of the wars are over and conditions come to normalcy, the people start reacting in an affirmative or negative disposition. It is the society, without its knowing discerns, whether some alien elements are to be accepted or rejected.

The social life of a people is manifested in various spheres. In other words, human society consists of modes and behaviours which determine the scope of its activity. India's social life is mainly expressed in it's custom and beliefs which are intermingled with philosophical thinking and religion. The ancient Indians could not think of a life without "*Dharma*", which was inherently connected with human life and was the ultimate goal to be reached. So the epic states:

"*Lokayātrāmihaike tu dharmaṃ prāhurmanișiṇaḥ*"

(12.138.19. Haridas).

Again, there was no bar for a house-holder or an ordinary member of the society to follow the path of righteousness:

"*Yastu dharmaṃ yathāśakti grihastho hyanuvartate,*

Sa pretya labhate lokānakṣayāniti śuśruma".

(12.141.10. Haridas).

It is therefore, not easy to separate religion from the life of the common people. Society as a whole in India has been based broadly on religion and her social life cannot be imagined bereft of religious duties. In a way it would have been proper to give a heading like a study of the "Socio-religious life" to this chapter. But some problems, as for example, of iconography are intimately connected with our idolatrous sectarian cults, and a review of the history of the sculptural art would have been absolutely necessary before discussing the problems of western influence on religion. So this distinction between social life and religion has been made. On the other hand, certain problems fall within the scope of the study of social life, which apparently have little or no connection with religion. Hence, I have given the heading "Social Life" to this chapter.

The first section of this deals with the system of caste distinctions. In order to have a better and fuller appreciation of the ancient Indian society, a clear idea about the caste-system prevalent then is necessary, which would serve as the background for a complete picture of social life.

The following section is devoted to the study of the rules of marriages which were in practice in those ages. Though we do not find any form of wedding-ceremony that was newly introduced by the foreigners, it is only natural to conjecture that the foreigners were admitted into the fold of the Indian society through the observation of any one of those eight known orders of marriages, that legalised the matrimonial contract. It is probably to give a socio-religious sanction to the progenies of mixed-marriages that the Gandharva, Āsura, Rākṣasa orders together with the most despised Paiśāca were recognized and freely permitted to the three lower classes, viz., the Kṣatriyas, the Vaiśyas and the Śūdras, The contemporary Hindu society also thought out a plan so as to admit the descendants labelling them as "*Saṃkarajāti*".

An attempt has been made in the following section to determine the results of this contact on the position of women in India. I have discussed this in a detailed manner as some new interpretation and fresh information have been added to the bulk of the serious studies that have been made on this subject previously.

The fourth section illustrates some peculiar examples of the disposal of the dead, that might have come from far-off western lands beyond India. The Hindu society remained faithful to its age-old tradition of cremation but some novel ideas of preserving the corpse have been sporadically mentioned in contemporary literature.

The fifth section has been devoted to the study of the western influence upon the culinary art of ancient Indian people. Observations have been made about those imported food-stuffs and drinks enjoyed by the ancient Indians. These, no doubt show how India had kept close contacts with the lands that supplied her with these favourite delicacies. This change in taste points to the mutual give-and-take and adaptability of this period.

The section following this presents a study of social enjoyments and pastimes that were probably introduced from the western lands or by the immigrants to India.

A thorough study of the western contribution in the realm of costume art of India has been presented in the next section. This study is quite exhaustive because fortunately the available materials provide a scope for a wide range of research work.

A short section is added to show how western ideas crept into the coiffure art of the ancient Indians. It relates the diverse variations of styles thus produced by the fashionable men and women of the well-to-do classes in this period.

The last section deals with the western designs introduced into the jeweller's craft of India. These last two sections actually supplement the foregoing section on dress and complete the discussion on costume as a whole. But as the study on dress and foreign materials is a lengthy one, these have been separated into two other shorter additional sections. These three studies together are very important from the cultural point of view, because they show the superior refined taste of the then Indians and their decent mode of blending heterogeneous elements into a harmonizing ensemble. These are the happy results of the racial synthesis discussed in the sections of Caste-system, marriage, and the high social status enjoyed by the women.

Indeed, a leading part was taken by the women of India in endowing our rich heritage with the gorgeous variegated panorama of traditional costumes.

Thus the four earlier sections, viz., caste-system, marriage, position of women and the disposal of the dead can be called the psychological reaction of the society, while the culinary habits, the festivities, dress and costume, coiffure-making and the jewellery art can be styled as the materialistic or the visual exposition of that mental adjustment. So much by way of introduction.

Section I

Caste System

By the beginning of this period, i.e., c. 600 B.C. a thorough cultural and spiritual influence on India by the Indo-Aryan was complete. They had long been able to reach the farthest corners of this vast land and inspite of the different racial and social elements, the general plan of the "*Caturvaṇāśramadharma*", i.e. Four Orders and Four Stages of Life was universally applied and introduced to all those diffused group of peoples (janapadas). One need not go into the details of the historical evolution of the caste system propounded by the Vedic Aryans; it would be suffice to take note, that by this period this system, which served as the pivot of Indian social plan, was rendered with a high religious sanctity and divine origin. Thus Krisṇa elucidates the old and revered predication of the Ṛigvedas[1] and say:

"*Cāturvarṇyaṃ mayā sṛiṣṭam guṇa-karma-vibhāgaśaḥ*".

To judge, whether some influences from the west had brought any change in the social life of the contemporary India, we have to find out how far it had influenced the caste-system. In discussing the subject I would prefer to follow two broad distinctions (i) based on the literary evidences, (ii) based on the epigraphic sources.

In the period under study, the set rules of the society were disturbed by the incoming hordes mentioned above. Reviewing all the available data, it becomes obvious that side by side two opposite forces were active in the society. The one more lenient with accommodating tendency admitted the foreigners in it's fold while the orthodox class tried to keep them out of their own society and did not allow to provide equal status. Yet, the latter tendency is, in a way, a negative indication, as it points out that actually cultural and racial synthesis were taking place. The prohibition towards "*Varṇasaṃkaradośa*" in the sacred laws prescribed in the *Dharma-sūtras*, *Dharma-śāstras* and in the epic[2] implied that there were *varṇasaṃkaras* or progenies of mixed-marriages, that took place in between different castes, were to be found in the contemporary society. It is curious to note, that some book contains prescriptions by two opposite view-holders; the orthodox and the more liberal authorities. The *Dharmasūtras*, the *Māhābhārata*, the *Mānavadharmaśāstra* as well as the *Purāṇas* enlist the name of the offsprings of the mixed marriages by the *Anulona* (regular) *Pratiloma* (reverse) Orders and refer to the *saṃkarajātis*.[3]

Several ethnographic names, such as Māgadha, Sairindhra, Niṣāda, Pukkaśa, Ambaṣṭha, Ugra, Meda, Śabara etc., show that, those indigenous aboriginal tribes that came closer to the Brahmanical society and were to be accepted within it's fold, were thus rendered to a lower status, labelled as *varṇasaṃkara*.

Again we find, that some professional bodies, like the *Carmakāra*, the *Maireyaka*, the *Māṃsa*, etc., were incorporated within the *varṇasaṃkarajātis*.[4]

It is interesting to note that while the pre-Aryan tribes of India proper were all taken into estimation within the Anuloma-Pratiloma progeny group, the tribes that inhabited the bordering regions of north, north-west and west were titled as *Mlecchas*, and were kept off from the society. The name *Mleccha* was also applied to the wandering groups of nomads having no special designation and settled home or fixed profession. They could have been thieves, brigands or fowlers. The Jātaka story[5] refers to the "*Milācā*" nomads, who were these *Mlecchas*. Another Jātaka story describes the loathsome habits and crude culture of the front-agers.[6]

Gradually the four so-called pure castes got mixed up with the *Mlecchas* of the frontiers, and this was indicated when the people of Avantī, Aṅga, Magadha, Surāṣṭra, Dakṣiṇāpatha, Upāvṛit and Sindhu-Sauvīra,—all situated in western, eastern and southern fringes of the Madhyadeśa were called as "*Saṃkīrṇa Yonayaḥ*" by Baudhāyana. The name "*Antevasāyi*" probably meant an "inhabitant of the Anta" i.e., frontier, and thus corroborates the other evidences shown above.

But the more important racial and tribal groups, like the Yavanas, the Kirātas, the Gāndhāras, the Cīnas, the Śabaras, the Barbaras, the Śakas, the Tuṣāras, the Kaṅkas, the Pahlavas, the Andhras, the Madrakas, the Puṇḍra, the Pulindas, the

Ramaṭhas and the Kāmbojas—though titled as '*dasyus*' were ordained to follow the rites prescribed in the Vedas,[7] to serve one's parents to conduct the worship of the Manes, show respect to the king, the preceptor, and to abide by the Vedic rules and perform *yajñas*.[8] It is of utmost importance to note that though these people were *Dasyus*, they were permitted to perform the sacred rites of bestowing tanks, furniture, public hydrants etc., for the sake of *Brāhmaṇas*, and welfare in general. This religious sanction to perform different *yajñas* consisting of *dānas* is evident enough to prove how these foreigners or semi-foreigners and pre-Aryans were given the adequate chance to embrace the Brahmanical mode of life and thus occupying a position of respect in the Aryan society.

The Lohas, the Ṛiṣikas, the Kāmbojas, the Gandharvas and the Hāṭakas are called "*Kṣatriyoirdasyu-bhiḥ*" in the epic.[9] Moreover, in the epic[10] and in *Harivaṃśa*[11] we hear an echo of the *Manusmṛiti*[12] where they state that the Kāmbojas, the Śakas, the Yavanas, the Pāradas, the Panhavas, the Kirāta, the Daradas, the Khaśas etc., were all *Kṣatriyas*, but fell to Sūdrahood owing to the negligence of *Dharma* and the absence of Brāhmaṇas amongst them. Here again, the predominance of the *Brāhamaṇas* were extolled once again, for had they respected the *Brāhmaṇas*, and performed the religious duties with the help of the *Brāhmaṇas*, they would not have fallen to this state of disrepute. Moreover, this was probably an indication towards the fact that if these tribes again accepted the authority of the *Brāhmaṇas*, they could have regained their lost position and respectable social status as *Kṣatriyas*.

The above discussion shows that they were distinguished from the Ābhīras, the Kitavas, the Vairāmas, the Taṅngaṇas, the Lampākas etc. who are not mentioned. But it might have been so that, by enumerating some names Manu really meant all these tribes. It has been shown that the Kekayas, the Madrakas, the Kāmbojas, the Gāndhāras and the Sindu-Sauvīras were really Aryan tribes belonging to the *Kṣatriya* caste, but were gradually degraded due to their association with the front-agers. The Vāhīkas, the Āraṭṭas and the Jarttikas were thought to be the lowliest of all. They nearly fell to the category of the untouchables.

Now, why was this difference of attitude made towards the foreigners themselves? Why some of them were prescribed to follow the Vedic rites and the sober duties of a social man while others were branded as the "trash" of human race? This difference was obviously done, because of their disposition towards the Indian society, their barbaric behaviour and customs. While some of them were eager to know and accept the country conquered with its religion,[13] philosophy, it's sacred customs and rites, it's arts, literature,[14] and science, the others kept busy with their frivolous life occupied by revel and mirth, full of distasteful manners and uncouth gluttony.[15] This is clear in the epic. While enumerating the intellectual aptitude of the various peoples, it states that, the Yavanas grasp one half of a certain maxim but the Vāhīkas do not understand at all.[16] The criterion of acceptance and permittance into the Hindu society thus depended on both the parties, the western incomers and the population guided by Brahmanical authorities. It was dependent on the reciprocal attitudes, on how much the foreigners were eager to accept the Indian mode of life, as well as how much they were bestowed with the socio-religious privileges.

The Buddhist society knew no caste, so it was easier for them to render a happy well-cone to the foreigners who were eager to know the law of piety. But quite surprisingly, we find that the Hindu canonical authorities of this period were quite different from their orthodox mediaeval descendants and provide a shelter to this martially vigorous, but spiritually poor people. It seems that if these tribes were ready to change their savage habits, showed respect towards the Vedas, the *Brāhmaṇas* and the sectarian divinities and abide by the rules of *Smārtadharma*, in one word, if they took to the *Siṣṭācāras* the authorities sustained no ill-will against them.

It would not be out of place to recapitulate the definition of *Sistacara*. The *Matsyapurāṇa*,[17] states that the *Śrautadharma* (Vivāha, Agnihotra and Yajña) and *Smārtadharma* (Varṇāśramadharṃa, Yama and Niyama) together mean *Śiṣṭācra*:

"*Tasmāt Smārtaḥ smrito dharmo varṇāśramavibhāgasaḥ,*
Evam vai vividha dharmaḥ Siṣṭācāra sa ucyate."

(145.33)

and then explains these characteristics of *Śiṣṭācāra*, viz., (i) *Dāna*=gift, (ii) *Satya*=truthfulness, (iii) *Tapa*=austerieties, (iv) *Alboha*=uncovetousness, (v) *Vidyā*=knowledge, (vi) *Ijyā*=sacrifice, (vii) *Pūjā*=worship, and (viii) *Dama*=Self-control. Amongst these only *Ijyā* was prohibited to the Śūdras, but one could perform if it was ordained by the *Brāhmaṇas*.[18]

We shall, however, see that the low-born as well as *Mlecchas* did carry on *Dāna* and *Pākayajñas* in this period.

Of course, the way was not smooth always. The epic and the *Purāṇas* enlist the catastrophies that would ravage the society in the *Kali* age, when the *Brāhmaṇas* would act like the *Śūdras* and the foreign tribes would rule the earth.[19] This clearly marks the apprehension of the orthodox hierarchy at the advent of the foreign rule, and Buddhist upheavals that permeated a darkness over the Hindu society.

The so-called *Kali* age of the *Purāṇas*, when the sanctity of the *varṇāśramadharma* and the superiority of the *Brāhmaṇas*, would be demolished, seems to have had commenced from the very outset of our period. The *Ājīvika, Bauddha* and the *Jaina* sects did not believe in the caste-system and the founders of these schools of philosophy, i.e., Maṅkhaliputta Gosāla, Gautama Buddha and Vardhamāna were all born in *Kṣatriya* families. Their preaching disregarded the authenticity of the Vedas and the ritualistic aspects of Brahmanical worship.

The most important ruler of the period following was Mahāpadma Nanda. The *Matsyapurāṇa* states,

"*Mahānandisutaścāpi Śūdrāyāṃ Sarva Kalikāṃsajaḥ,*
Utpatsyate Mahāpadmaḥ Sarva Kṣatrāntaka nṛpaḥ. 17
Tataḥ prabhiti rājāna bhaviṣya Śūdrayonayaḥ,
Ekarāṭ sa Mahāpadmo ekacchatro bhaviṣyati. 18
Aṣṭaśīti tu varṣāṇi pritivyāñca bhaviṣyati,
Sarvakṣatramathotsadya bhavinarthena coditaḥ. 19"

(272.17-19)

Long before Dr. Bhandarkar has pointed out the importance of this statement that hereafter the *Kṣatriyas* became born of *Śūdra* mothers.[20] The contamination of *Śūdra* and *Kṣatriya* castes gave rise to the *Ugras*.[21] This social havoc made the scene ready for the foreign intruders from the west. While the Bṛahmanical society was already passing through a mental shock and dismay they poured in like swarms of locusts and filled the country. Indian society knew not how to avoid them or to get rid of them, as they were far to numerous, and virile to be treated like that. It is unfortunate that our forefathers have not left any vivid description of the foreign invasions, but the pages on "*Yugadharma*" in the *Purāṇas* compensates for it. It thus describes the utter devastation that made the life of women and children unsafe, the property of people were plundered, the royal authority shuffled from hand to hand. A good government disappeared like a mirage, and a vast section of the population became wandering mendicants, who took to this view or that. It is easily imaginable that in this state of events, serious studies on the Vedas could not be followed. Thus the *Brāhmaṇas* became paid staffs of the ruling offices. However, after a while, the panic subsided and the foreigners were found to have settled with their Indian families. Now, these new-comers were to be incorpora'ed and provided with specific profession and status.

More than once, the epic expresses, that one, who provides a good government and security for his people fulfills the obligations of the true *Kṣatriya* and a dutiful king. The main duty of a *Kṣatriya* was to drive off the oppressors of mankind, i.e., the *Dasyus*.[22] But these *Dasyus* are never to be destroyed cruelly.[23] The story of *Dasyu Kāyavya* expresses the respectful attitude of the ancient authorities towards righteous *Dasyus*.[24] It seems from these references, that the *Dasyus* were those tribes, living within or outside Indian frontier but who often caused great disturbances in the settled communities. The social authorities thought out ways of compromising in between the government and these *Dasyus*. Another story relates how Brāhmaṇa Gautama had fallen by staying amongst the northern *Dasyus* who were fowlers.[25] A comparison in between *Dasyu Kāyavya* of the Pāripatra Ranges, and Brāhmaṇa Gautama of the northern town of *Meruvraja* show the reciprocal effects of *Brāhmaṇa* society on Dasyus, and the association of *Dasyus* with a *Brāhmana*

I would briefly recount here the lineage of the ruling dynasties of ancient India, which would show that the boast of a pure "Aryan blood" is as futile as a day dream.

The accounts of the lineage of Chandragupta Maurya, is variously given, but all the sources unanimously accept a most ordinary or so-called low-origin for the scion. Dr. Raychaudhuri has laid more stress on the tradition of the *Mahāparinibbāna sutta*,[26] being the earliest of all, in which the *Moriya* clan is described as belonging to *Kṣatriya* class. But the fact, that, Chandragupta grew up among a group of peacock-tamers in the Vindhya forests, corroborated by the Jaina tradition recorded in the *Pariśiṣṭaparvan* which states that Chandragupta was connected with the family of the chief of *Mayūrapoṣakas*, indicate his low-origin. The *Divyāvadāna* says that Bindusāra, son of Chandragupta was a *Mūrdhābhiṣ ikta*, a term which according to the authorities was differently designated either as *Anulomaja* or *Pratilomaja*[27] in between *Brāhmaṇa* and *Kṣatriya* castes. The Hindu traditions recorded in the *Viṣṇupurāna* and the *Mūdrārākṣasa* say that Chandragupta was the son of a Nanda king born to a *Śūdra* wife called Mūra. It is needless to repeat here, how this half-*Śūdra* Maurya rose into power with the help of a *Brāhmaṇa* and how magnificently his dynasty outshone the long vista of Indian history.

The family that usurped the throne next to the Mauryas, were *Brāhmaṇas*, called the Śuṅgas. Following them came the Kāṇvas, who were called "*dvija*" and "*dhārmika*". If the Śuṅgas, and the "*dvija*" Kāṇvas, were really *Brāhmaṇas*, then they had violated the orthodox rule by accepting the monarchical post, which was to be kept reserved for the *Kṣatriyas* only. After them the trans-Vindhyan tribe of the Śātavāhanas, (also called *Andhras* or *Andhrabhṛityas*) came into prominence, and ruled in the Deccan and western India. On the evidence of the Nasik Praśasti of Gautamīputra Śrī Śātakarṇi and the *Dvātriṃśat Puttalikā*,[28] Raychaudhuri thinks that they were "*Brāhmaṇas* with little admixture of *Nāga* blood". In spite of the distinction in between the melodies "*Āndhrī*" and "*Śātavāhinī*" made in the *Bṛhaddeśī*,[29] the numerous references about the Śātavāhanas as Andhras in the

Purāṇas leave little doubt that the Śātavāhanas were a branch of the Andhras. The *Matsyapūrāṇa* states,[30]

"*Śiśuko'ndhraḥ sajātīyaḥ prapsyatīmāṃ vasudharām*".

It has been seen, that the Andhras are always placed with the foreign and non-Aryan tribes. Their low origin have been described by the *Manusmṛti*.[31] Notwithstanding, the fact that they boasted to belong to *Brāhmaṇa* lineage, the latter was not of a high status. This is apparent from the *Dvātrimśat Puttalikā*. It states that the *Vetāla* found the mother of Śālivāhana (i.e., Śātavāhana) in a *Kumbhakāra-gṛha*, potter's hut, at Pratiṣṭhānagara (Paithan). The progenitor of this Śālivāhana was *Śeṣanāga*. This mythical origin was concocted, no doubt, to render a glorious and mystic colouring to facts, that were not very favourable to the fame of the Andhra-Śātavāhanas. In fact, the *Matsyapurāṇa* states:

"*Saṃkaraṃ durbalātmanāḥ pratipatsyanti mohitāḥ,*
Brāhmaṇāḥ Śudrayonisthāḥ Śūdra vai mantrayonayaḥ".

(273.46)

By comparing the epithets of Gautamīputra Śātakarṇi[32] with the statements of the *Vāyu-purāṇa*:

"*Nādhīyante tathā vedā na yajante dvijatayah,*
Utsīdanti tathā caiva Vaiśyaih sārdhantu Kṣatrutāḥ.38
Śūdrāṇāmantrayonistu sambandho Brahmanaih saha,
Bhavantīha Kalau tasmin Śayanāsanabhojanaiḥ.39"

One is tempted to connect these degraded *Brāhmaṇas* with the progenitors of the Andhra-Śātavāhana dynasty. Moreover, it is mentioned that the *Śūdra* kings of *Kali* age would perform *Aśvamedha* sacrifice, Satakarṇi have been praised for acquiring merit by the performance of *Aśvamedha* sacrifice.[33]

The act by which the Mauryas snatched the throne from the Nandas, the Śuṅgas from the Mauryas, the Kāṇvas from the Śuṅgas can be called traditional usurpation of utter disloyalty shown by the subordinates to their masters. This violation of laws of caste, duty and loyalty by the ruling powers threw a shade of distrust and infamy on India's social life which was further darkened by the vicissitudes presented by the alien hordes.

Before we pass on to the epigraphic records, I would like to mention about the interesting episode of Pramati related in the *Purāṇas*. The *Matsyapurāṇa*[34] states that a scion called Pramati was born in *Bhṛigu-kula*. He was of *Candramasa* gotra. He roamed all over the earth for thirty years and collected arms and four-fold army consisting of infantry, cavalry, elephants and charioteers. He then, with hundred thousand *Brāhamaṇas* destroyed the *Mlecchas*, the *Śūdra* kings, the heretics (*Pāṣaṇḍas*) and sacrilegious persons (*adhārmikas*). He faced the northerners, the mid-landers, the westerners, the easterners, the inhabitants of the Vindhyas, the Aparāntas, the Deccanese, the Drāviḍas, the Siṃhalas, the Gāndhāras, the Pāradas, the Panhavas, the Yavanas, the Śakas, the Tukhāras, the Barbaras, the Śvetas, the Hālikas, the Daradas, the Khaśas, the Lampākas, the Andhras and the Corajātis. He is manifested in the *Kali* age as Candramasa, and an incarnation of Viṣṇu. Having reached the age of thirty-two he set out, and after having wandered for twenty years and destroying the above mentioned armies, died at the confluence of *Gaṅgā* and *Yamunā*.[35]

A question naturally disturbs the mind, that who was this Pramati-Candramasa, was he a mythical personage or a historical figure like Puṣyamitra Śuṅga, or Gautamīputra Śrī Śātakarṇi, both of whom are known to have had fought with the Yavanas, and Śaka-Yavana-Pahlava respectively? Or can this be possibly a deification of Samudra Gupta?

Now I turn to the epigraphic sources that throw new light on the problem. Though the unique piece of evidence supplied by the Garuda Dvaja inscription of Heliodorus from Besnagar[36] has no direct bearing on the subject of caste system, should be reviewed here. It proves beyond all doubt that Vaisnavism was more liberal than generally thought to be, so as to accept a Yavana, who was a fervent worshipper or a *Bhāgavata*. It also proves how a Greek was well-versed in the main precepts of Bhagavatism. It is not difficult to assume that it was this noble disposition of the Greeks, that made them the most esteemed amongst the foreigners and secured the applause of the great Epic.[37]

We shall see how after a century the Yavanas again came into the picture:

There are three inscriptions from Junnar, which mention the gift of two cisterns from Irila, the Yavana from Gartas, another records the gift of the dinning hall from the Samgna of Yavana Ciṭa, from Gartas and the other records the gift of the door of an interior apartment from Camda. The Yavanas are titled in Hindu names of Candra and Citra, like the Śakas only with the exception of Irila, which seems a foreign nomenclature.[38]

The provonance of the above mentioned inscriptions points to the fact that most probably these pious Greeks were wealthy merchants who came on business tours to the metropolis of Ujjainī or Bhṛigukaccha and visited the sacred shrines after a fruitful enterprise. On returning homewards with a thankful heart, they endowed the monastery with pious munificence. Though they made gifts particularly to the Buddhist establishments, culturally they were all really Indian, and it seems they were reverent towards the Indian religion in general. The coins of the Indo-Greeks and specially that of the Indo-Scythians with the galaxy of Hindu divinities on them together with the representation of the Buddha show the same attitude of veneration.

Alike inscriptions hail from Nasik and Karle caves near Pune, where Indrāgnidatta of the northern town of Dattāmitrī, gave the dwelling at Nasik caves "in order to honour all the Buddhas".[39] The name Indrāgnidatta is distinctly Hindu and comprised of the names of two Hindu divinities Indra and Agni. His father was called Dharmadeva and son Dharmarakṣita.

In Karle[40] Yavana Sihadhaya i.e., Siṃha Dhairya, and Dharma made gifts of caves. Dhamma hails from Dhenukākaṭa. The presumptions of Tarn that these Yavanas were the residents of some Greek "polis", were just dutiful citizens and that they had nothing to do with Hindu or Buddhist faith,[41] cannot be maintained owing to the fact, that if this was the case, numerous similar endowments would not have come to light. The number of these records show that these were just not business tactics, but were really outcome of the faith of the much Indianized Greeks. The business could have been conducted smoothly even without this sort of religious pretence. Indeed, in the south and at the flourishing ports of the eastern seaboard where the Romans carried on thriving business with the Indians, no such religious endowments have been recorded and trade seems to have flourished independent of any religious pretext whatsoever.[42] Moreover the nomenclature of these Greeks points clearly that they were much Indianized. If they had, by then retained their separate entity, as Tarn thinks, and remained culturally pure Greek, they would not have had adopted names like Indragnidatta, Siṃhadhairya, Dharma, Chitra and Chandra. If they wanted to retain their separate entity, and had not adopted the Indian religion, if they did not commit to mixed marriages, we would have still found them, as separate social groups like the 'Parsis' of western India, or the Anglo-Indians who are mixed in blood but retain their separate social entity by the common tie of Christianity.

In the Scythian epoch we find Śaka Uṣabhadāta, the husband of Dakṣamitrā, and the son-in-law of Śaka Satrap Nahapāna making endowments of villages and kind to the *Brāhamaṇas* and performing the righteous deed of giving "eight wives to Brāhmaṇas at the religious Tīrtha of Prabhāsa", a place of great sanctity to the Hindu. He moreover caused benevolent endowments at Bharukaccha, Daśapura, Govardhana and Sūrpāraga. This is the epigraphic corroboration of the liberal views expressed in the *Śāntiparvan*. The *Brāhmaṇas* allowed a foreigner of Śaka lineage to conduct sacrifice at Prabhāsa and accepted gifts from his hands. Moreover, Uṣabhadāta acquired the merit of causing eight *Brāhmaṇa* marriages.[43] This is enough to show how far the Śakas were admitted and given a socio-religious status in the Indian society of first century A.D. They could not have done these if the *Brāhmaṇas* did not accept gifts from them or permitted the rest houses, gardens and tanks to be executed.

It has been proved by the record of Śateraka, the minister of queen of Vāśisṭhiputra Śrī Sātakarṇi, who was most probably the daughter of Mahākṣatrapa Ru(dra)[44] that the Sātavāhanas contracted marriage alliances with the house of Rudradāman, the Śaka Satraps of Deccan. The inscription from Nasik of Gautami Balaśrī states the epithet of Gautamīputra Śrī Śātakarṇi as 'Vinivatita-chātuvana-sankarasa' etc. i.e.,' "he prevented the contamination of the four castes",[45] we find that intercaste marriages were actually taking place in the royal houses.

The Śakas adopted Hindu names in general. There are two other inscriptions which record the gifts from devotees of Śaka lineage. Śaka Dāmachika Vudhika, or Vṛiddhika, son of Śaka Viṣ ṇudattā and a resident of Daśapura (Mandasor), is recorded to have endowed cave a two cisterns for the sake of the monks.[46] The other is by a female lay-devotee i.e., Upāsikā Viṣṇudattā, daughter of Śaka, thus titled as "Sakānikayā" Agnivarman and the wife of Gaṇapaka Rebhila.[47] While her as well as her father's names are distinctly Hindu, her husband's name is non-Indian, but her son's name is again a Hindu one, i.e., Viśvavarman. It is quite probable that while the house of Śaka Agnivarman was much Indianized, as found from the names, the house of the Gaṇapakas was not so. But after the marriage with Hinduized Viṣṇudattā the Gaṇapakas became Indianized and their sons were given Hindu names, and the suffix Varmaṇ distinctly showing their *Kṣatriya* status were added after the style of his maternal grand-father. Yet, the appellation "*Śakānī*" and '*Gaṇapaka*' were added to the names of Viṣṇudattā, Rebhila and their son Viśavarman showing their foreign extraction. Rebhila was a Śaka name, which was also found in Ābhīra communities.

The *anuloma* and *pratiloma* system of marrriage [48] was invented for the necessity to accommodate the various foreign tribes within the fold of Brahmanical society. In those regions where the foreign hordes poured in numbers the socio-religious outlook of the society had to undergo a change and was consequently widened. For this reason we find more instance from western India, which have just now been discussed.

Another foreign tribe, the Ābhīras who possibly entered India from southern Iran via Makran, and settled in the lower Indus valley as well as on the banks of the *Sarasvatī*, also dispersed towards the south and branches of them became powerful and well-established in Deccan. The scions of these Ābhīra families, as we know from the inscriptions, adopted Hindu names like the contemporary Greeks and Śakas. Māḍharīputra Iśvarasena is called the son of Śivadatta,[49] both the Hindu names with the appellation of Iśvara and Śiva, point to their venerable disposition towards the Śaiva faith. The Gundā Inscription of Śaka era 102-180 A.D. records the grant of a well and embankment caused to be made by Ābhīra Senāpati Rudrabhūti,[50] son of Bāpaka. Here also the term '*Rudra*' is interesting. It would be found that the Ābhīras contributed certain elements in the growth of the Vāsudeva Kṛṣṇa cult, but here in the names of these rules we find the predominance of Śaiva faith.

The fervent devotees of Hinduism did not remain inert in the activity of arousing faith within the hearts of foreigners. The *purāṇakāras* evidently took a leading role.[51] The *Purāṇas* were then the medium through which messages were to be conveyed to the people in general. Thus the curious piece of evidence supplied in the *Matsyap*. states that once there was an Ābhīra-kanyā who just out of curiously practiced the Bhīma Dvādaśī Vrata to propitiate Śiva, and as the result of her pious observance she was delivered of the mortal bondage and was reborn as the celestial dancer *Urvaśī* at heaven (*Nākapṛṣṭha*).[52] This reference points to three things. Firstly, the foreign tribes like the Ābhīras were permitted to observe *Vratas* which generally incorporated a gift to pious *Brāhamaṇa* at the end of the observance. This evidently points to the fact that the *Brāhmaṇas* had no impediments in receiving gifts from the Ābhīras etc. This has been substantiated by the record of Śaka Usabhadāta already. Moreover this shows that women of foreign extraction were well-acquainted with the particulars of the Hindu rituals. Secondly, this is chiefly prescribed in the *Purāṇa* to arouse faith and curiosity of the foreigners towards the Brahmanical beliefs. Thirdly, it shows that Ābhīras believed in re-birth and the divine results of pious acts, as the said Ābhīra maiden only as the result of her meritorious deed attained the high bliss of becoming the celestial nymph of *Nākapṛṣṭha*, i.e,, a sort of tutelary deity of that sacred spot. While these Purāṇic verses were recited amidst the congregation of different people, it is not improbable that it aroused a keen desire within the hearts of the numerous foreign people to perform similar religious acts and attain such high status.

The Indian *Purāṇakāras* were accustomed to contemplate the other lands on the same basic plan like that of India. The *Dvīpas* of this earth and its *Varṣas* are divided and classified in system of a rather monotonous uniformity,[53] and more than once we find the society of these *Dvīpas* being divided into four groups, corresponding to the *Brāhmana, Kṣatriya, Vaiśya* and *Śūdra*. The *Viṣṇupurāṇa* states:

Daminaḥ Śuṣmiṇaḥ Snehā Mandehāśca Mahāmune
Brāhmaṇāḥ Kṣatriyāḥ Vaiśyāḥ Śūdrāścānu kramoditāḥ.
(II, 4, Verse 39).

In the *Kuśadvīpa* the *Daminas* were the *Brāhmaṇas*, the *Śuṣmiṇas* were the *Kṣatriya*, the *Snehas* were the *Vaiśyas* and the *Mandehas* were the *Śūdras*. Without any other corroborative historical records from any other sources it is not possible to identify these social groups, but this much is clear that the *Purāṇakāras* tried to lend a similar social system to the parts of the globe which was half-known to them. The *Mandehas* classified as *Śūdras* seem to be identical with the *Mandagas* of *Śākadvīpa*, who are mentioned last of all. If the *Daminas* can be identified or connected with the Dāman title of the western Kṣatrapa House, then the relatively high position of the latter can be well-explained.[54]

We are in a better position with regard to the classification of the people of *Śākadvīpa*. Thus the same *Purāṇa* (Verses 70-71) states:

Mṛgā Brāhmaṇabhūyiṣṭhā Māgadhāḥ Kṣatriyāstathā,
Vaiśyāstu Manasāsteṣāṃ Śūdrāsteṣāntu Mandagāḥ. 70

Some account is given in the *Bhīṣmaparvan* of the Epic (Chap. XI. 35-37). This *Mṛga* (Maṅga) or more correctly *Maga Brāhmaṇas* from *Śākadvipa* were the Magis of Persia. They, according to Bhandarkar were ushered into India during the reign of the Great Kushan monarch Kanishka;[55] whose coins attest the prevalence of the *Mithra* or *Mihira* cult.[56] By the sixth century A.D. the sun worship attained a high popularity and the sun temple of Multan was very famous for its riches, munificence, pomp and splendour, as attested by Hiuen-Tsang.[57] The later work *Bhaviṣya-purāṇa* attests that the preceptors of the Sun-temple of Multan were really *Maga Brahmanas* from *Śākadvipa*, who were brought by Śāmba thus proving a long antiquity of the tradition.[58]

References

1. Ṛigvedas, X. 90.12, the idea has been repeated in Manu, I.31. Vaśiṣ ṭha, IV. M.N. Datta, p. 763, etc.
2. Mbh. 12.285.8-9 (B.O.R.I.); 289.8-9 (Haridas).

   Side by side there are interesting statements which show that violation of these established orders was not unknown. Vide. Mbh. 13.20.I-3 ff. 38 (Haridas). Gautama, IV describes the eight forms of marriage and mixed castes; Vaśiṣṭha, XVI; Viṣṇu, XVI; Manu X. 61,

   "*Yatra tvete paridvaṃsā yāyante varṇadūṣakāḥ,*

   Rāṣṭrikaiḥ saha tadrāṣṭraṃ Kṣiprameva vinaṣyati".
3. Mbh. 13. Chap. 40, (Haridas); 13 Chap 48 (B.R.M.) Matsyap. 144; 165,

   "*Āśramāṇāṃ vipariyāsaḥ kalau samparivartate*

   Varṇānāñcaiva sandeho yugānte ravinandana (18)" 273, etc.
4. Mbh 13. 40. 20-22 (Haridas).
5. *Mahaukkusa Jātaka* (486) refers to the "*Milācā*" nomads.
6. *Kaṭāhaka Jātaka* (125) refer to the degraded manners of the frontagers, i.e., *Pratyantadeśas*.

   See R.K. Mookerjee, Ind. Cult. Vol. I, 1934-35, pp. 557-559.
7. Mbh. 12.65.13-16 (B.O.R.I.).
8. Ibid., 12.65.17-21 (B.O.R.I.).
9. Vide supra, p. 81, n. 224.
10. Mbh. 13.23.22 (Haridas).
11. *Harivaṃśa*, vide supra, p. 33, p. 67, n. 32.
12. Manu, X. 43-44.
13. The story of King Menander in the *Milindapañha* is a bright instance of the eagerness of the foreign king to know better the Indian (i.e., Buddhist) philosophy.
14. Ep. Ind. Vol. VIII, p. 44, Rudradāman is said to have "obtained profuse fame by studying the remembering, by the knowledge and practice of grammar, music, logic and other great lores".
15. Mbh. 8. Chaps. 27-30 (B.O.R.I.) have ample references to this.

16. 8.34. 142-43 (Haridas).

17. *Matsyap*. 145, according to Hazra the chaps. 144-145 are most probably to be placed in c. 550-650 A.D. But the idea is quite old and established. *Atri Saṃhitā*, verses 34-41, defines *Anasūyā*, *Maṅgala*, *Anāyāsa*, *Aspṛihā*, *Dama*, *Dāna* and *Dayā*, these are the qualities of a twice-born and to be performed by a householder.

18. Mbh. 12, chap. 60 (B.R.M.).

19. *Matsyap*. Chaps 144, 165, *Vāyup*. 50, *Viṣṇup*. VI. I. 44-74; *Brahmāṇḍap*., II, 31; *Kūrmap*., I. 29; *Bhāgavatap*. XII.2; etc.

    Hazra, p. 207, "...it becomes evident that the Puranic chapters on the Kali age are the records of the state of society during the period with which we are concerned here (i.e., the Hindu society before 200 A.D.). The numerous verses common to these chapters show that these are derived from a common source which must be very old. This source is probably to be traced in a tradition for the origin of which the turmoil in society caused by the forces enumerated above should be held responsible".

20. I.A. 1911, p. 8 ff.

21. Manu. X., 13.

    Mbh. 13.40.7, *Kṣatriya* father and *Śūdra* mother give rise to an *Ugra*.

    Gautama, IV, M.N. Dutt, p. 664.

22. Mbh. 12.60 (B.R.M.).

23. Ibid., 12.133 (B.R.M.).

24. Ibid., 12. 135 (B.R.M.).

25. Ibid., 12. Chaps., 168-172 (B.R.M.).

26. S.B.E. XI, pp. 134-135.

27. Gautama, IV. 19; Yājñavalkya, V.I. mention the *Mūrdhābhiṣiktas* as born from a *Brāhmaṇa* and a *Kṣatriyā*. But how can it be that Chandragupta's (who is born of *Kṣatriya* father and *Śūdrā* mother) son be a *Mūrdhābhiśikta*?

    If we are to reconcile the Puraṇic and the Buddhist tradition preserved in the *Divyāvadāna* (vide Raychaudhuri, PHAI, p. 267) we have to accept that the term M. denoted both *Anulomaja* as well as *Pratilomaja* issues as "anointed Kṣatriyas" (Monier Williams, p. 826). Probably the socio-political situation of that time necessitated a term like that.

28. *Dvātṛṃśat-Puttalikā*, "*...asyāṃ Śeṣanāgendrasaṅgamakarot. Tasmādasyāṃ jātaḥ putroyam Śālivāhanaḥ*".

29. Bṛhaddeśī, Āṅdhrī, pp. 53 (Aṃghṛī), 55, 137, 107, 124; *Śātavāhinī*, p. 118; *Śāravāhanikā*, p. 106.

30. *Matsyap*. 273.2.

31. Manu, X. 8-11.

32. Ep. Ind., Vol. VIII, pp. 60-61

    "who crushed down the pride and conceit of the Kshatriyas;...who stopped the contamination of the four varnas, the unique Brāhmaṇa; in prowess equal to Rāma, Keśava, Arjuna and Bhīmasena; liberal on festive days in unceasing festivities and assemblies,"...etc.

33. Bhandarkar, William Meyer Lectures, 1938-39, p. 60.

    Hazra, PRHC, p. 206, n. 59. The Bengali version of the Vāyu however states, "*Yajanti nāśvamedhena rājānah Śūdrayonayaḥ*". (58.67).

    Cf. Manu. X. 67, certainly the sons begotten by Aryans on non-Aryan women become possessed of the privileges (of instituting Pāka-Yajnas, etc., i.e., they become Aryas), while sons begotten by non-Aryans on Aryan women become non-Aryans. This is the decision (67) "From the evidence of inscriptions we know that the Andhra kings performed many sacrifices including Aśvamedha and the Gavāmayana".

34. *Matsyap*. 144, 50-62.

35. Ibid., "*Saṃsthita sahasāyātu senā pramatinā saha,*

    Gaṅga-Yamunayormadhye siddhiṃ prāpta samādhinā"62.

36. For Garuḍa Dhvaja Inscription, vide Puri, ITP, p. 185; Raychaudhuri, EHVS, pp. 99-100.

37. Vide supra, p. 70, n. 78.

38. O. Stein, Ind. Cult, Vol. I, 1934-1936, p. 349.

39. Ep. Ind. Vol. VIII, p. 90.

40. Ep. Ind. Vol. VII, pp. 53-56 ff. See Stein.

    Ind. Cult. Vol. I, p. 347. "Sihadhayas" i.e., "Siṃhadharas".

    Whether this has to be understood as a family or some corporation it is not possible to decide.

41. Tarn, GBI, p. 256 ff.

42. Of course, it cannot be denied that the Buddhist faith gave these Yavanas a better welcome, than the Brahmanical society. In far South where the orthodox Hindu ideals were zealously guarded, the relationship with the westerners remained confined mainly in commercial terms. It is mostly due to the prevalence of Buddhism

in the western coast of India, that the region and its people have been absorbed in the vast population of India.

43. Ep. Ind. Vol. VIII, p. 78.

44. Raychaudhuri, PHAI, pp. 502, 622.

45. Ep. Ind. Vol. VIII, p. 60-61.

46. Ibid., Vol. VIII, p. 95, "*Dāmachika*" may indicate some connection with the "*Dāman*" family. He is styled as "*Lekhakasa*" i.e., clerk.

47. Ibid., Vol. VIII, p. 88.

48. Vide above, n. no.s 2 and 3.

49. Ep. Ind. Vol. VIII, p. 88.

50. Ep. Ind., Vol. XVI, p. 233-235.

51. Hazra, p. 193, "Besides the staunch followers of these religions, there was another class of people who were rather of a mixed type. On the one hand they had high regard for the sectarian gods and looked upon their worship as the means of attaining salvation; on the other they had valued much the practice of the rules of Varṇā-śramadharama, and regarded the Vedas as the highest authority. We shall see in in-after that the Puraṇic dharma originated with this last mentioned class of people". – We are however, concerned with the first group.

52. *Matsyap*. 69.59.

53. Mbh. 6. Chaps. 11, 12, 13 (B.O.R.I.).

    The epic mentions *Maṅga, Maśaka, Mānasa* and *Mandaga* as *Brāhmaṇa, Rājanya, Vaiśya* and *Śūdra*.

    Matsyap. Chaps. 121-122, "*Tatra puṇya janapadaścāturvarṇya samanvitā*" etc. (12.2.28);

    Vayup. Chap. 33 ff., The *Kuśadvīpa* may correspond to the Hindu Kush region. It is interesting to note that the Gadhā (Jasdan) inscription, Ep. Ind. XVI, p. 236 ff. of the time of Mahaksatrapa Rudrasena (A.D. 205) mentions Pratāsaka of *Mānasa* gotra.

54. Vide infra, p. 115.

    It seems that the Daminas were identical with the *Kāradamakas* i.e., Damans of western India.

55. I.A. 1911, p. 17 ff.

56. Vide infra, chapter Five, Section on the cult of Surya.

57. Beal, II, p. 274; Watters, II, p. 254.

    Alberuni's India, p. 116 (Chap. XI, p. 56).

58. Vide infra, Chapter Five, sec. on Sun Cult.

Section II

The Forms of Marriage

For the sake of better understanding and convenience the subject would be under following divisions, (i) the well-known forms of marriage in Indian society, (ii) some peculiarities of Greek, Iranian and Scythian marital rules, (iii) references to hybrid marraiges in Indian literature, (iv) historic evidences of inter-racial (tribal) marriages in ancient India, and (v) the social status bestowed on the offsprings of the mixed marriages.

(i) It has been stated at the opening of this chapter, that evidences of newly adopted exotic modes of marriage ceremonies are absent. All the literary source, viz., the *Dharmasūtras*, the *Dharmaśāstras*, the two epics and the *Purāṇas* either refer to or describe marriage ceremonies that fall within any one, or a medley of different forms, known as the, *Brāhma, Daiva, Prājāpatya, Ārṣa, Gandharva, Āsura, Rākṣasa* and *Paiśāca*. Amongst these, the earlier four were normally prescribed for the *Brāhmaṇas*, though discrepancies remained regarding the respective superiority *Ārṣa* and *Āsura*, one from the former group, and the other from the latter.[1] The epic disliked the *Ārṣa* system because it involved the acceptance of a *Śulka* comprised of "*Gomithuna*" (a pair of oxen and cow) as a bride-price on the part of her guardian, and thus demoralized their conduct. But according to some the "*Gomithunam*" was not "*śulkam*". The *śulka* or bride-price should only consist of money, irrespective of its large or small amount.[2] It was thought that it made little difference in between demanding or accepting money and selling one's son or daughter:

"*Na hi śulkaparāḥ santaḥ kanyāṃ dadati karhicit*"

(13.37.31, Haridas)

"*Yo manuṣyāḥ svakaṃ putraṃ vikrīya dhanamicchati,*
Kanyāṃ vā jivītārthāya yaḥ śulkena prayacchati," etc.

(13.37.74)

It even describes the horrors of *Kālasūtra Naraka* to be

suffered by those who give prime importance to the monetary question in causing a matrimonial relation and thus tainting the religious act. It enjoins that:

"*A nyo'pyatha na vikreyo manuṣyaḥ kiṃ punaḥ prajāḥ*", etc.

(13.37.79, Haridas)

This shows the humanitarian sympathy and deterrent attitude towards the buying and selling of males and females who have fallen in to a sad plight.[3]

However, four earlier forms of marriage are prescribed for the three *dvijātis*, with the 'Daiva' form especially for the *Brāhmaṃas*. The Brāhma and the Prājāpatya which were conducted chiefly by the guardians of the couple and presentation were given voluntarily i.e., "*Yo dadyadanukūlataḥ*", acquired the general appreciation of the gentle society.

We find something more interesting in the next four systems of marriage, viz., *Gāndharva*, *Āsura* or *Mānuṣa*[4] *Rākṣasa* or *Kṣātra*[5] and *Paiśāca*. These four forms together represented the less orthodox view of the Aryan society, but there was the criterion of approbation and censure. The Gāndharva and the Rākṣasa forms were approved for *Kṣatriyas* while the Āsura form was not culpable for the *Vaiśyas* and the *Śūdras*.[6] But the Paiśāca, though recognized was shunned by all.

In the Gāndharva system, the only necessary item seems to be the mutual consent of the partners, who by knowing each others affection (*snehānugatatvāt*)[7] came to be united in the tie of Gāndharva marriage. It has been stated earlier that the Gāndharvas were a pre-Aryan tribe inhabiting the high Indus region.[8] Their natural euphonic tendencies imparted a general feeling of romantic imagination to their personality. Both the sexes possessed beautiful physique, gifted demeanor kept them off from the populated areas and they gave a strong opposition to people other than themselves.[9] Despite of any direct mention in the literature, it is quite probable and possible that this tribe recognized the mutual consent of the partners as the final wedlock. Quite early, this simple method was accepted by the Aryans who day by day inclined towards securing non-Aryan women, as wives, and there was no other way but to provide them with a social sanction. The *Kṣatriya* errants who took the task of Aryan expansion in the unknown wild woods and rugged mountains came in a closer contact with tribes, some eerie with shyness, the others offering a fiendish reception! Unlike the sedate *Brāhmaṇas* or the industrious *Vaiśyas* settled in the hamlets the *Kṣatriyas* were the pioneers of woodland adventure. So the *Gāndharva* and the *Rākṣasa* modes of marriage which were known and introduced first by the *Kṣatriyas* came to be called "*Kṣātra*" after them. Sooner or later, the actual history was forgotten, only the name of the Gandharvas (which by then popularly came to denote a class celestial beings) remained to indicate the origin.

The *Svayamvara* system, in which the bride chose her cherished hero victorious in the tournament, was designated for the *Kṣatriyas* only. This was a variation of the *Gāndharva* form as the bride's choice had been given the prime importance. It is explicitly mentioned and approved in the epic that the mixture of *Brāhma, Ksātra* and *Gāndharva* can be conducted:

"*Prithagvā yadi vā miśrā kartavyā nātra Saṃsayaḥ*"
(13.37.10, Haridas).

The *Āsura* form was akin to the *Ārṣa* method in respect to the monetary matter involved. In this form the bride's party was propitiated by a gift of bride-price. This form was particularly prevalent in north-western India amongst certain neighbouring tribes such as the Kekayas[10] and the Madras[11] and some cities like Taxila.[12] Strabo writes that girls were exposed in public places by their kinsman who would part with her on receipt of agreeable amount of money. It seems that a custom like that of ancient Babylonia is referred to here. But there remains some difference in between the Babylonian bride-price and the earnings of a hierodoulos.[13] As Strabo explicitly mentions the relatives of the girls, this system, seems to be, a mixture of Assyro-Baylonian marriage contracted by the payment of bride-price,[14] with the tinge of the Hierodoulii custom, which has caused the exposition of the girls in public places like the temple hierodoulos. There is no evidence that Mādrī, Kaikeyi or any other bride were exposed in this manner before the suitor's party previous to the wedding ceremony. It is possible, that Strabo made some confusion between the two forms – interlinked in Babylonia,[15] but not in ancient India. He probably refers only to the "*Āsura*" system, which was more of a "social contract" type than "religious" and was adopted in India by some class from the Iranians (Āsuras), but could not secure the general appreciation of the society. The fact, that it was the "*Kulaprathā*", i.e., family tradition of the Madras, indicate beyond all doubt, that it was introduced from beyond the mountains in hoary antiquity, in the bygone days of the *Uttara Madras*. It is supported by the fact that the Kekayas, whose foreign affinities have been discussed,[16] also retained a similar tradition. In the historic times it was prevalent in Taxila.

The *Rākṣasa* form which was quite popular amongst the ruling classes[17] was adopted from the pre-Aryan tribes whom the Aryan designated as *Rākṣasas*.[18] They were akin to the *Paiśācas*.[19] The depredation of the bride from her kinsmen later on symbolized the valour and prowess of the royal suitor. Some tribal customs prescribe mock fight in between the bride's party and the bridegroom, which are reported to be still conducted at the present-day marriage ceremonies in South India. The marriage of Śrī Kṛṣṇa with Rukmiṇī was completed in a mixed mode of *Rākṣasa* and *Gandharva*. Arjuna first eloped Subhadrā and then defeating the *Yādavas* in the skirmish married the latter in *Prājāpatya* ceremony.

The last but not the least important was the *Paiśāca* form of marriage. As the name suggests – this system was adopted from a tribe, the *Piśācas* or cannibals of Afghanistan and Baluchistan who spoke in a different tongue.[20] Due to an utter contempt towards their cannibalistic manners and uncouth habits the term "*Piśāca*" soon came to denote a goblin or devil. It is interesting to note that while the term "*Gandharva*" denoted those romantic demi-gods inhabiting the nooks of northern mountains and waterfalls, the term "*Piśāca*" connoted something frightful and hideous. This indicate the Aryan attitude and the inter-racial connection of the Aryans with the pre-Aryans or the non-Aryans. The system of the Paiśāca marriage, like the Piśāca people themselves received a bitter detestation in the Sanskrit texts on *Dharma*. However, one point should be considered seriously. Why this ignoble mode was recognized as one of the eight forms inspite of injunctions like:

"*Paiśācaścāsuraścaiva na kartavyau kathañcana*"

(13.37.9, Haridas)

The reason simply appears to be this, that a large number of female members of the society were depredated by the savage tribes during the socio-political translations witnessing the incursions from the west. What would happen to these women and their children if the society would have refused to give them a social admittance? By recognizing the *Paiśāca* form the authorities at least made a providence for the profligates as well as the women who were really to lead a conjugal life, and thus saved the society from farther depravations.

Now, a few words to discuss the peculiarities of foreign modes of marriages:

(ii)The Greeks had things common with the Indo-Aryans. Thus marriage was looked upon a religious act and the procuration of off-spring was the main object of married life. The wife was looked upon as the ideal housekeeper. The close similarity in the discourses of Socrates and Ischomachos reported by Xenophon, the ideals expressed in our epics and the code of Vātsyāyana clearly show the similarity of the Greek and the Indian ideals.[21] Though monogamy was the general rule, exceptions were not unknown altogether. Both bride-price and dowry were known, but in the historic times the dowry became more popular. Thus we see that the Greeks and the Indo-Aryans retained many common aspects of their Indo-European kinship. The only difference was that dissolution of the marriage was easily done in the Hellenic society, while it was not so amongst the Aryans of India. Marriage was considered as a life-long tie, and though terms and conditions were prescribed for a separation where necessity arose, the divorce was not so common as in the Dravidian society.

In the Babylonian and the Assyrian society the marriage was more of a nature of "contract". It was looked upon as a legal act and on the breach of contract, the divorce was easily obtained. Bride price was paid to the girl's father, and each and every procedure were recorded in documentary deeds. This attitude was no doubt the source of the "contract" type marriage known as the "Āsura" that we have discussed earlier.

The most peculiar Iranian custom which distinguished it from the other Aryan forms was that of "*Xvaetvadatha*". This met with a general abhorrence in the Hindu society, who shunned from the very idea of causing marriages in the same "*gotra*" and "*pravara*". The Brahmanical society did not even permit marriages in between pupils under a same teacher as this was regarded as a close kinship like that of a brother and sister.[22] But there were exceptions to this rule.[23]

The Scythians, like the Aryans followed the patrilineal system and encouraged polygamy. According to some, a Scythian had a free access to all the wives of his fellow-tribesmen. But according to Herodotus this was only practiced amongst the Massagetae and the Agathyrsi. About the system of polyandry McGovern observes, "The polyandry of the Tibetans and some of the other later peoples of Central Asia (e.g. the Epthalites) never seems to have affected the Scytho-Sarmatian culture, though we are told that some of the Sarmatian tribes inhabiting the northern Turkistan were extremely lax in their code governing sexual relations".

We do not know whether the Śakas of India adhered to this primitive custom of their original land. The absence of any reference to this uncouth manner seems to point to the negative.
(iii) In spite of the ardent attempt of the Brahmanical Indians to keep the purity of Aryan blood, we are not in want of evidence with regard to the hybrid marriages. The most early forms of these marriages were performed in between separate tribes, that were different both culturally and nationally. The term inter-racial is not a suitable one because many of the tribes were Indo-European stock of the "Aryan-speaking" people, who in the centuries that followed, became distinguished entities possessing particular cultural and political limitations. The title, "extra-Indian" I think elucidates the idea and serves the purpose better. The Indians who in the verses of the epics

remembered these marital connections of their forefathers, were becoming conscious both of their 'Aryan' lineage as well as of the precinct of their home land, which excluded the regions connected with their ancestral activities.

Matrimonial relations with outsiders are commonplace in the age described by the twin epics. Thus, Ila, one of the predecessors of the Kuru clan, had migrated from Bactria to India and settled in Pratiṣṭhānapura in Madhyadeśa. He is described as –

"*Karddamyasya prajāpateḥ,*

Suto Bāhlīśvaraḥ Śrīmānilo nāma sudhārmirkaḥ"

(Ram.7.94.3)

This *Karddama* clan inhabited the regions of the *Kārddamaka* river (modern Zarafshan stream) in Bāhlī (Balkh).[24] The patrinymic "*Karddamaka*" probably later on gave rise to the class-name "Daminah",–of the "*Daminaḥ Śuṣmiṇah snehā Mandehā*" etc. of *Kuśadvipa*, i.e., the Hindukush regions.[25] (Viṣṇup. 2.4.39) and the "*Dāman*" title of the western *Kṣatrapas*, who has brought some tradition of the *Kārddamaka* region with them.[26]

The next two chapters in the Rāmāyaṇa describe the fate of Karddama Ila in the land of "All-Women" and the transformation of himself and his troops into a band of Amazons called "*Kimpuruṣās*". This is reminiscent of the Sarmatian Amazons of Scythia[27] and of the assertion of Pāṇḍu in the epic:

"*Uttareṣu ca rambhoru Kuruṣvadyāpi pūjyate,*

Strīnamanugrahakaraḥ sa hi dharmaḥ sanātanaḥ."

This "Sanātanaḥ dharmaḥ" i.e., the old tradition was the Scythian system of promiscuous sexual relationship extant in Central Asia.[28] These sporadic references in the epics, no doubt, show, that the ancients had intimate knowledge about the different customs prevalent beyond the Indian frontiers but did not discuss them in detail or supported them as they were too busy in building a more cultured and complex society based on higher aspirations and stricter morals of life.

But how did they come to know all about it? It seems from the references of the epic that a lot of tribal movement was still current at that time, but gradually the ways were closed. Legendary as well as historic references show that the northerners did not encourage free communications and infringements into their territory. Mythological stories tell that the door to *Uttarakuru* was closed by the servered head of Mahiṣ āsura:

"*Patatā śirasā tena dvāraṃ ṣoḍaśayojanam,*
Parvatābhena pihitaṃ tadagamayaṃ tatoṛbhavat.
Uttaraḥ Kuravastena gacchantyada yathāsukham"

(3.194.67)[29]

This clearly implies that the way was open to all in the antiquity, but was closed later on. It was re-opened again when the epic was edited finally, i.e., during the period of our study. In more than on place the epic refer to the fact that the Indians were not allowed inside the land of *Uttarakuru* which lay beyond the steep and cold northern ranges. The guarding tribes of these regions made the adventurers return satiated with gifts of deer skins, various kinds of weapons and ornaments, pedigree steeds, gold, woolen fabrics etc.[30]

The problem of the ancestry of the five Pāṇḍava brothers, the Tibeto-Mongoloid features of Bhīma, his drinking of Duhśāsana's blood and the polyandry observed by Draupadī are unique by itself. As these problems need a detailed and exclusive study of the foreign influences on epic India, these fall beyond the scope of this work and are consequently not dealt in here. But as far as the system of marriage is concerned, this much can safely be deduced from the evidences collected, that extra-Indian marriages were not unknown to the Indians. The marriage of Yayāti with Asura-princes Śarmiṣṭhā, the daughter of Vriṣaparvā add one more instance to this. Another corroborative evidence is gleaned from the pages of the *Matsyapurāṇa*. Vikukṣi of the Ikṣvāku race, had fifteen sons, who were born in the north of Mount Meru[31] (Mat. 12.16.16-28). He had fourteen more sons who were born in the south of Meru. What does this signify? It implies that a migration of the family took place, and those who migrated to the south of the Meru became "Indians" by matrimonial relations.

(iv) Let us now search for actual historical evidence. To fulfill his dream of "one community" in the "inhabited world" Alexander undertook the unique role of the leader of a grand cultural conquest. His two decisive steps towards this Hellenic expansion were the cosmopolitan cities and the inter caste marriages.[32] The Graeco-Persian marriages conducted by him symbolized the staring of the future cultural infusion that followed his demise. We are not definite whether this zeal for "common unity" and equality with other ideals, had inspired Chandragupta to enter into a marital alliance in the family of Seleucus.[33] The Graeco-oriental marriages remained the mode of the day in Seleucidan Iran. A similar social environment was nurtured in Egypt under the Ptolemies. It was no wonder, that the newly founded colonies of Alexandria of the Arians (Heart), Alexandropolis (Kandahar),[34] Alexandria (Ghazni), Alexandria of the Caucasus (Kāpiśa), Bactra, Alexandreschate (Chodjend) and the settlements at Nicaea, Bucephala and Pattala (Demetrias Patala)[35] all thrived with mixed population of Eurasian blood. What otherwise had befallen to the Greek garrisons left at Patala and the weary soldiers swooning on the way to Gedrosia, than to "go native" day by day? It would have had been different if Alexander really survived "to send out further-settlers and above all European women to prevent the risk of the towns becoming purely Asiatic".

The previously mentioned nomenclature of the Yavana downers[36] show that they were these native Greeks, and had adopted the names from their mother-tongue i.e., provincial variants of Prākṛit.

We know definitely that the Andhra-Śātavāhana dynasty had entered into a matrimonial alliance with the royal *Kṣatrapas*. Vāśiṣthputra Śrī Śātakarṇi is reported to have had accepted the hands of the daughter of *Mahāksatrapa* Ru(dra). The former had encounters with his father-in-law, Rudradāman I, who "did not destroy" him on account of the nearness of their connection".[37] Curiously enough the daughter of Mahākṣatrapa Rudra claimed her descent from the *Kārddamaka* family,[38] mentioned above. Śaka Uṣabhadāta as well as his wife Dakhamitā (i.e., Dakṣamitrā) both had adopted Indian names and from their devout religious activities it seems probable that they were united in a Indian marriage,[39] ceremonial.

(v) The mention of the Yavanas, Rāmakas, Khaśas, Śaikhas, Ābhīras, Medas etc., show that the above mentioned foreign tribes were coming within the caste-system through the hybrid extra-Indian marriages.

The Yavanas together with the Śakas have been placed outside the society of *Āryāvarta* by Patañjali and are classified with the *Śūdras*. It has been pointed out that they were called degraded *Kṣatriyas*.[40] It is not known definitely whether they were degraded as *Śūdras* for their foreign blood or for their martial associations with other so-called low-classes of India, many of whom followed Buddhism. Gautama however, took them into consideration (which prove that some of them were assimilated in the Hindu society and stated:[41]

"...sons begotten on a Śūdra woman, by a Brāhmaṇa, Kṣ atriya, Vaiśya or a Śūdra are respectively designated as Pāraśavar, Yavanas, Karaṇa and Śūdra". No definite allusion is either supplied with regard to the identification of these *Pāraśavas*[42] with the *Pārśavas* (i.e., Persians) of Pāṇini.[43] This possibility would have thrown a fresh light on the interesting socio-cultural effects of the Achaemenian Persia on India.

Vaśiṣṭha's statement, "That of a Vaiśya, by a Brāhmaṇa woman becomes a Rāmaka",[44] arouses another confusion. This mixed-caste of *Rāmaka* was either a wrong transcription for "*Romaka*" (i.e., Roman) or actually denoted the *Vairāmakas* of Rambakia.[45] It seems a hopelessly puzzling nomenclature denoting both i.e., the *Rāmakas* as well as the *Romakas* because the town of Rambakia had a heterogenous population. Moreover, the place was visited by the Graeco-Roman traders.[46]

It is evident from the *Manusmahitā* (x. 21) that the *Brāhmaṇas* committed mixed marriages and were lax in performing the sacred initiation in the northern and western countries. The progenies of these *Brāhmaṇas* were called the *Bhūrjakaṇṭakas*, the *Āvantyas*, the *Vāṭadhānas*, the *Puṣpadhas* and the *Śaikhas*.

The *Khaśas*, a famous a tribe of the north[47] are said to have been born from parents belonging to the *Vrātya Kṣatriya* class.[48] Thus both the *Khaśas* and the *Śaikhas* (a branch of the Sacae tribe?) are taken into the estimation of the Indian society.

The Ābhīras are said to be the off-springs of a Ambaṣṭha mother (daughter of Brāhmaṇa and Vaiśya) and a Brāhmaṇa father (Manu, x. 15)[49] and the Medas with others[50] were untouchable outcastes. These latter group have "*Saṃkaraja*" ancestry on both the sides.

The list of mixed-castes may be lengthened considerably but only a few instances have been chosen to show the western impacts upon the marital rules of this period, and it's effects on the caste-system.

It is proved beyond doubt, that mixed hordes of Indo-Greeks, Scythio-Parthianas, Kushans and others caused a terrible havoc in the society, in which the Aryans and *Mlecchas* mingled freely:

"*Taiśca vimiśrā janapadāstacchīlavartiṇo rājāśrayaśuṣmiṇo Mlecchāścāryāśca viparyayeṇa vartamānāḥ prajāḥ kṣ aspayiṣyanti*"

(IV.24.19 Viṣṇup.)

and

"*Abhirucireva dāmpatyasambandhahetu*" or
"*Strītvamevopa-bhogahetuḥ*"

(Viṣṇup. IV.24.21-22).

The above quotations show that the stricter regulations for marriage were considerably slackened by the foreign dynasties and their "*sīlavartiṇo rājāśrayaśuṣmiṇaḥ*" wealthy ("*tatāścartha evābhijanahetu...ratnatāmrabhāgitaiva prithivī-hetu*") nobility. In this period mere acceptance or agreement was looked upon as an act of marriage;

"*Svīkarṇaṃ vivāhahetu*", and any person having a decorous look was thought to be competent bridegroom (*satpātra*). These sarcastic remarks indeed, throw a flash on the extremely ostentatious and superficial aspect of the contemporary aristocratic society.

References

1. Sukhamaya Śāstrī, Mahābhārater Samāj, p. 7.
Mbh. 13. Chap. 37 ff. (Haridas); 13.44-46 (B.R.M.); Manu, I, 21-25 ff.
2. Mbh. 13.37.76 (Haridas); Mbh. Samāj, p. 15
3. *Vivāha* was one of the *Saṃskāras*, and was considered as religious duty of the householder. Vide S.C. Banerjee Dharmasūtras, p. 73 ff.
4. Ibid., p. 78, "In the menuṣa form, a man after bargaining with the guardian of a girl, married her purchased with money".
5. Ibid., "the Kṣātra is that in which a man forcibly carried away a girl. "But in the Mbh. 13.37.5-6 (Haridas) the Gāndharva has been assimilated with a Kṣātra thus,..."*Kanyābhipreta eva ya, Abhipreta ca ya yasyā tasmai deya...*" etc.
6. Mbh. Samāj, p. 8, n. 31.
7. S.C. Banerjee, Dharmasūtras, p. 80, "B. is liberal enough in holding that the Gandharva form is free from fault in the cases of all the castes as it is based on mutual affection (snahānugatatvāt)".
8. Vide supra, p. 29 ff. Vide infra. Chapter IV. Section on Music.
9. Mbh. 3.49.39-43 (Haridas).
Mbh. 3.203.18-207.16. (Haridas).
Viswanatha, RSHC, pp. 81-82.
Ram. 7.107.10-11.ffs. 7.108.
Saletore, IDW, p. 353, n. 162, Śailuṣa have been corrected by Dr. Chhabra with Seleucus Nicator.
10. Viswanatha, p. 133.
11. Vide supra, p. 34.
12. Herod, i. 196.
Vide supra, p. 68, n. 49.
13. For the custom of hierodouloi, see ERE, Vol. V, 58, VI. 671, 678.
14. For the Babylonian bride-price, see ERE, Vol. VIII, p. 468.
15. In Babylonia every girl had to act once as a Hierodoulos in the temple of Mylitta, Vide Herod.1.99; ERE. Vol. VIII, 469.
16. Vide supra, p. 51 ff.
17. Mbh. Samāj, p. 8 gives the illustrations of the marriages of Vicitravīrya, Duryodhana, Arjuna and Kṛṣṇa respectively with Kāśīrājakanyā, Citrāṅgadā, Subhadrā and Rukmiṇī which were done in the *Rākṣasa* system.

18. Viswanatha, pp. 82, VII; on the Rākśasas, pp. 132-133, on the *Rākṣasa* ceremony.

Krishna's preference to *Rākṣasa* form, see Mbh. I. 214.3-5 (Haridas).

Agrawala, IKP, p. 448, "By adding a suffix in a pleonastic sense (svārtha) prescribed by this very sutra (v.3.117) we get the word form Rākshasa. They also appear to have been an actual people, probably of the north-west group, and of the same racial character as the Piśāchas. The Rākshas, Nāgas and the Piśāchas faught also in the Bharata war on both the sides. We find an important tribe named Rakshānis settled in Chagai district of North Beluchistan.

19. Ibid., pp. 447-448, "...literally a people who were consumers of raw flesh" etc.

20. Ibid., 448, "The existence of the Paiśāchi Prākrit is so well attested to by literary references that there can be no reasonable doubt about its speakers being real human beings".

21. M. Caroll, Greek Women, p. 175 ff., on Xenophon; The "Young wife, a tender girl of fifteen, reared under the strictest restraint to the end that she might "see as little, hear as little, and ask as few questions as possible" has no difference with an ideal Hindu wife. Vātsyāyana, Chaps. XXI, on domestic life.

Manu, IX, "They should be employed in storing and spending money, in maintaining the cleanliness of their persons and of the house, and in looking after the beddings, wearing apparels, and household furniture" 11.

Cf. Mbh. 13. 146.35 (B.R.M.),

"*susvabhāvā suvacanā suvrittā sukhadarśanā,*

Ananyacittā sunukhī bhartuḥ sa dharmacāriṇī".

With Xenophon, "my mother told me that both my fortune as well as yours was wholly at your command, and that it must be my chief care to live virtuously and soberly". Mbh. 13.146.48-51 (B.R.M.), 2.50.46. (Haridas), 12 ch. 144 (B.R.M.); ERE, Vol. VIII, p. 444, The main object of marriage was to secure male offspring, vide Mbh., Samāj, p. 25, n. 11; Manu IX, 7-9 p.

22. Mbh. I. 65.14-17. (Haridas).

"*Bhagini dharmato me tvaṃ maivam vocaḥ sumadhyame*" etc.

23. Mbh. I. 77. 17 (Haridas); Mbh. Samāj, p. 11f.

Ibid., 8.34.114 (Haridas) clearly refer to the practice of marrying in a same family (ekakule) and this was probably adopted by some degraded *Brāhmaṇa* class.

24. Vide, supra, p. 104

Raychaudhuri, PHAI, 25, n. 17.

25. It is probably because of their long tradition that the Daminas are revered and has been placed in the Brāhmaṇa category. But *Kārddamaka-Ila* and the Dāmans of Western India are to be grouped in the *Kṣatriya* class and not *Brāhmaṇa*. It is however, interesting to note that the Śātavāhanas who had contracted matrimonial alliances with the Scythian house of "Kārddamaka"s, claim to be *Brāhmaṇas*, and here in *Viṣṇupurāṇa* the Daminas are ranked highest among the four.

26. Chattopadhyaya, The Śakas, p. 5, ..."Konow points out that there is little doubt that it is Iranian, of Avestan, daman, place, creation; dami, creation, creator"..."Thus it seems clear that a branch of Śakas migrated from Iran".

27. Herod, iv. 110-117; Arrian, vii. 13.

ERE, Vol. XI, p. 277, "The special points are a close mutual resemblance, a reddish complexion, a flatness, a slackness and excess of humours, a look as of eunuchs, and in certain cases a sexual indifference that amounts to actual impotence...Men thus afflicted took their place absolutely among the women and were called 'Enarees'. He adds that all this applied only to the most notable and rich among the Scyths".

28. Mc Govern, p. 55.

Vide supra, p. 114.

29. This seems to be an allegorical allusion to the fresh incursions of the northern *Mlecchajātis* that began to pour in again during the Scythio-Parthians and especially under the Kushans who ruled Central Asia together with North India.

30. Vide supra, p. 81, n. 224.

31. Matsyap. 12. 16-28.

32. Tarn, Alexander, pp. 110-111, "At Susa too a great feast was held to celebrate the conquest of the Persian empire, at which Alexander and 80 of his officers married girls of the Iranian aristocracy, he and Hephaestion wedding Darius' daughters Barsine and Drypetis. It was an attempt to promote the fusion of Europe and Asia by intermarriage. Little came of it, for many of the bridegrooms were soon to die, and many other repudiated their Asiatic wives after Alexander's death; Selaucus, who married Spitamenes' daughter Apama, probably an Achaemenid on her mother's side, was an honourable and politic exception. At the

same time 10,000 of the troops married their native concubines".

33. Raychaudhuri, p. 272, n. 2, "Appiamus uses the clear term Kedos (connection by marriage), and Strabo (XV) only an epigamia. The cession of territory in consequence of the marriage contract clearly suggests that the wedding did take place".

34. Tarn, Alexander, p. 65; identifies Alexandria with Ghazni.

    GBI, p. 407 ff., see for the detailed account of the same. Alexandroolis=Kandahar.

35. Tarn, Ibid., p. 142, n. 1.

36. Vide supra, p. 100 f.

37. Raychaudhuri, PHAI, p. 496.

38. Vide supra, p. 115 f.

39. Ep. Ind. Vol. III, p. 82, mention Dhakhamitrā but curiously enough Bhandarkar (in WML, 1940, p. 61) writes, "His wife's name, we find, was Saṃghamitrā. Both Ṛshabhadatta and Saṃghamitrā are indisputably Hindu names".

40. Vide supra, p. 93.

41. Gautama, iv. 21. M.N. Dutt, p. 665.

42. They are called either Pāraśava or Parāśava. This has been hinted here because the general derivation of the name, "[The son of a Brāhmaṇa] by a Śūdrā woman [is] a Parāśava. They say that the condition of a Parāśava is that of one who, albeit living, is a corpse. The designation of a dead body is Śava" etc. Vide Vaśiṣṭ ha, XVI, M. N. Dutt, p. 802. This is repeated in the epic too (13.40.5, Haridas) but it seems rather artificial. However there may remain or may not remain any relation between the two.

43. Agrawala, IKP, p. 445, "Parśu (v. 3.117). The whole tribe was called Parśavaḥ, and a single member Pārśava. The Parśus may be identified with the Persians". Cf. the "Pāraśava" tribe, supra, p. 83, Does this reference throw some light on the problem of the tribe as well as the mixed caste?

44. Vaśiṣṭha, XVI, 1, M.N. Dutt, p. 801.

45. Vide supra, pp. 49, 60-61 and notes.

46. Periplus, 37. Arrian, vi. 20, "...continued his (Alexander) advance as far as the village called Rambacia, the largest settlement in the Oreitan territory" etc.

47. B.C. Law, TAI, p. 400 on Khaśas.

48. Manu, x. 22.

49. Vide supra, p. 73, n. 133.

50. The Medas have been mentioned in Manu X. 36, thus, "of Kārāvara and Niṣāda women by Vaidehakas are respectively born the Andhras, and the Medas, who live outside the villages,"

    X. 49 state that the Medas earn their livelihood by killing the wild beasts with the Andhra, Cuñcus and Madgus.

    Aṅgirasa I.3, and Yamasaṃjitā.55, state that the Medas together with the Varuḍa, Kaivarta and Bhillas are low-castes.

Section III

The Position of Women

Before looking into the position of women in ancient India, it would be justifiable to take into estimation her respective status in the neighbouring Iranian and Central Asiatic societies. From the extant literature it appears that legendary heroines like Eshther and queen Semiramis loomed bright in the popular imagination.[1] We chiefly depend upon the information supplied in the accounts of Herodotus, Strabo and Arrian. In the current section some broad aspects denoting the position of women in ancient India is being highlighted.

(i) **Iranian**: To begin with, we would mention some peculiar customs prevailing in the Iranian society. It was an ancient custom to consecrate women as servants to gods, they were called hierodouloi.[2] The custom was prevalent in all Semitic countries and Egypt. The code of Hammurābi mentions the "Women of Marduk".[3] Women were consecrated to other gods too. Herodotus obviously mention the same custom of Babylon that was carried on in the temple of Mylitta, i.e.,Venus. The first earning of a woman was offered to the goddess of love. These women, of course, were not actual courtesans; Herodotus observes, "after that time however great a sum you give her you will not gain possession of her". Yet it seems that regular temple-courtesans were not unknown in the west Asia till the time of Herodotus, and later. They were also known in Greece specially in Athens and in Corinth.[4]

(ii) **Achaeminians**: The Achaemenid kings inherited many a set ways and customs from their Semitic predecessors.[5] One of it was the "strict seclusion of women". It was for the sake of "guarding better a pure lineage and to exhibit a greater state". Persian Harem was more rigorously guarded more then any other, and the kings had "often invited into it daughters of neighbouring kings". After the conquest the harem of the vanquished was treated as one of the spoils of war; after the demise of a ruler it was inherited by the successor of the deceased king. Aristocratic ladies of the harem got used to the tranquility of an idle life, the only flicker being imparted by the palace conspiracies.[6] But the ordinary middle-class women were given much more freedom, most of their time was spent doing domestic duties. The chastity was guarded, and the prime duty expected from a faithful wife was honour towards her husband.[7]

(iii) **Scythians**: The outlook was completely different amongst the nomadic tribes of Iran, Southern Persia and Central Asia. We hear of the Massagatae queen Tomyris who fought valiantly against Cambyses.[8] Herodotus also related how Ariapithes' wife Istria, educated his son Scyles in Greek language and had brought him up under the influence of Hellenistic culture,[9] that was frowned upon by the Scythians. This evidently point to a high degree of power and authority enjoyed by the women in Scythian society.

The introduction of the Amazons amongst the Scythians gave rise to a new race-lineage, i.e., the Sauramatae.[10] It seems that the Amazons were a tribe by themselves, and had a peculiar state of society. The "Strīrājya" mentioned in the "*Alexander-romance*" by Bāṇabhaṭṭa in *Harṣacarita* point to this country of Amazons.[11] They are also mentioned by Arrian (Book VII, 13) to have been sent by Atropates, the Governor of Media to Alexander. Herodotus deals with their customs in detail, which incurred the system of slaying at least one enemy before marriage, wearing men's costume equipped with weapons, riding and hunting, —all of which directly point to the extremely free and self-dependant status enjoyed by these women.[12]

The Parthian women were of totally different disposition as compared to the earlier Persian women of aristocratic lineage. As the Parthians for a long time retained their nomadic habits, their women-folk essentially remained sturdy, hard-working, courageous and quite un-accustomed to the delicacies of palace-life.[13]

In the Central Asia, the home of the nomadic races, the women enjoyed a larger freedom. The climatic conditions, as well as the pastoral life in a nomadic society do not encourage seclusion of women. They took active role in the life of community and had to rely more or less on themselves. This helped towards the development of a particular strength of character, unknown to the fastidious belles reared up in seraglio atmosphere, which encouraged a constant dependance on the attendance of a rank of servitors. The nomad women often had to take care of themselves, their children and belongings. Herodotus informs us that when Darius led his army against the Scythians, the Scythian women with their children, livestock and wagons retired to farther north.[14] The upright and the self-reliant characteristic of a nomad woman is "evident from the notable fact, that the wife from the nomad stock rules the harem, and often rules the house". Huntington has ably proved that the mental and physical idiosyncreasies of a race are the results of physiographic condition,[15] and there is every reason to believe that social conditions amongst the Central Asiatic nomads were not very much different in centuries around the beginning of the Christian era from the present. On the contrary, we can safely presume that women were bestowed with much more freedom and were treated liberally before the advent of the Islam.

** *** **

India from quite an early date, had systematized rules and regulations regarding duties, social status and position occupied by women. From the Ṛigvedic times onwards some concepts changed,[16] but on the whole rules were so rigidly fixed that successive waves of foreign invasion could not change the basic foundation of it. Still we find some changes in social phenomenon which did take place due to foreign contact.

(iv) **Seclusion of Women in India**: The *Dharmasūtras* became increasingly strict in debarring women from several social privileges which they used to enjoy previously. Purity of blood and the importance of male-offering, as expected in a partriarchal society, were highly valued. So people grew conscious about the careful guarding of wives.[17] this tendency paved the path for the absolute seclusion of women, which more over received a new impetus from the west through the contact with the Iranians. In the Semitic society wife is looked upon as a prized possession to be guarded jealously, more than as the life-long companion of man in his socio-religious and family life (*sahadharmiṇī*).[18] This general deviation from the Hindu ideal, indeed degraded the status of the wife during the post-Achaemenid rule in north-western India. Pāṇini's mention of *Asūryampaśyā*[19] together with Kāśikā's explanation as "*rājadārāḥ*" i.e., king's wives, show that by Pāṇini's time (c. 500 B.C. or a little later) the ladies of the royal house-hold were confined into the harems, where even the sun could not penetrate, i.e., they were kept in strictest privacy and seclusion. S. Shastri[20] and Altekar[21] studying the above mentioned evidences rightly conclude that the custom gained ascendancy in Gandhara region where many western incursions and consequent settlements had taken place,[22] and which for some time experienced the Persian rule.[23] Pāṇini evidently belonged to the north-west,[24] where he found the system of seclusion prevalent among the ladies of the *Kṣatriya* clans.

(v) **The Antaḥpura, (Kumārīpura or Kanyāpura)**: The custom of polygamy amongst the *Kṣatriya* princes and kings increased the body of the royal seraglio; and a portion of the palace, kept reserved for the women-folk, came to be known as "*antaḥpura*" (interior) or "*Kumārīpura*" (the maidens' apartment). Kauṭilya's *Arthaśāstra*,[25] the epic[26] and)ther Sanskrit works give description of the *Kanyāpura*. Kauṭilya informs us that entrance to this secluded portion of the royal household was guarded by the *daṇḍadhara*,[27] a door-keeper with *Daṇḍa* or a batten in his hand. The king himself, the eunuchs and the officer-in-charge called *Antarvaṃśika*[28] as well as the old *Kañcuki*[29] could enter the harem.

Eunuchs[30] were appinted in the Achamenid harem, and the story of the appointment of Bṛhannalā in Virāṭa's *Kumārīpura* and the numerous mentions of *Varṣadhara* (*Varṣa-vara*) in other works show that they were appointed in numbers in Indian harems too, and constituted an important rank in the hierarchy of harem-officers.

Virāṭa carefully examined Bṛhannalā's skill in music and dancing and having questioned him, sent him in his *antaḥpura*.[31] It seems that the institution of a complex harem system with all its component parts and a hierarchy of officers, attendants servants, guards, couriers etc., was borrowed from Achaemenid Iran wherefrom cane the stricter modes of the seclution of women. This is evident from Baudhāyana: "*Idānimahabhirṣyāmi strīṇam, Janaka, no pura*" (i.2.34) "Now O Janaka, I jealously watch my wives, (though I did) not (did it) formerly".[32] This clearly shows that it was not done before but was introduced shortly prior to the time of Baudhāyana. From the detailed account of Kauṭilya it is evident that the Indian *antahpura* of a king was a complete unit by itself like the Greek gynaeconitis.[33]

From the Sanskrit dramas and the *Nāṭyaśāstra*[34] it becomes evident that the *Kañcukīn* held the sole authority over the *antaḥpura*. He evidently took the office of the *Antarvaṃśika*. He is said to have worn clean (*śuddha*) dress like a *Brāhmaṇa*[35] and had a turban tied around his head.[36] In *Śakuntalam* (Act. V) we find him holding a staff as the mark of his rank.[37] The *Kañcukīs* were normally of matured age.[38] *Kañcuki* was evidently called so due to this long clock i e., *kañcuka*,[39] the uniform of his office. Though he was a *Brāhmaṇa* by caste, and of mature age, he obviously had to wear this peculiar garment to mark his office and rank. It is quite possible that the system of appointing an aged man of noble birth in the charge of the harem came from Iran, wherefrom also came the uniform of this long cloak.[40] Scholars have rightly identified the relief figure from Nagarjuni as that of a *Kañcukī*.[41] (See, plate I).

Architectural remains at the Parthian City of Sirkap, Taxila show that the palace was built after the plan of Mesopotamian palaces. The women's apartment (*Kanyāpura*) was secluded and was separated from rest of the palace containing the men's apartments, the court, the audience hall, the attendant's quarter etc. The women's quarters were all complete with its constituent parts[42] and even had its own votive stūpa. The epics, the *Purāṇas*, the *Harṣacarita* and numerous other earlier and later references in Pāli and classical Sanskrit literature show that the *antaḥpura* had its own garden decorated with bowers, arbours pavilions and pools.[43] It is not unlikely that contemporary Indian *antahpuras* were built likewise the palace unearthed at Sirkap.

(vi) **Foreign Maidservants**: Trade in foreign-born females into India continued from the earliest times to the centuries after Christian era.[44] The "fair maidens" and the "singing boys" from afar found place in the harem of the Scythian ruler Nahapāna of Ujjaini.[45] Delos in Greece was an important center of slave export.[46] It seems that the Ābhīras together with the Medas and Pāratas took active role in slave business along the coast of Makran and Sindh.[47] The Jaina works like *Nayadhammakahao*[48] mention well-trained maid-servants from the countries of Babbara (Barbara–North Africa), Bausa (Busiae?), Joṇiya (Yavana–Ionian), Iṣiṇaya (Ṛṣika), Dhouruṇigiṇa (Darangians), Lāsiya (Las Bela region?), Lakusika, Drāviḍa, Sāṃhala, Āraba (Arab or Arabius in Baluchistan), Palinda, Pakkaṇa (Ferghana), Muruṇḍa, Śabara, and Pārasa (Persia).[49] This evidently shows that an Indian 'king's harem was comprised of cosmopolitan population. These female slaves received respective position in the king's harem and served at the court according to their age accomplishments and beauty. Some of them were appointed as paid courtesans who performed the duties of parasol, cup and chowrie-bearers, massures, bathers and wine replenishers of the king. The king was attended by a galaxy of beautiful courtesans in every necessity of his daily life.[50] *Harivaṃśa* describes how hundreds and thousands of courtesans, besides the queens went with the princes on their pleasure-trip to the sea-side.[51] One of the later sources tells that Harṣa was attended by a band of courtesans who were a joy to the eye and were objects to behold.[52] In the aristocratic Indian society the drinking and bath was performed with most luxuriant paraphernalia like the Romans, and it might be due to the large number of maids of foreign extraction, that Indian kings became acquainted with foreign luxuries.[53] The foreign maid-servants who are called as "*videsa-parimaṇdi-yāhiṃ,...sadesa-nebattha gahiya-vesāhiṃ...*" etc. (i.e., dressed in their national costume) were so large in number and influential, that their dresses were adopted as the uniform of the king's female attendants in general. Thus Bāṇini Mālatī, evidently of Indian lineage, was garbed in a western apparel.[54] *Harṣacarita* moreover mentions the "women of the night watch...", signifying that women *pratihāriṇīs* were appointed to keep the harems by night.

(vii) **Yavani Pratihāriṇīs or Amazons**: The foreign *patihārinṇīs* occupy an important role in Sanskrit dramas.[55] Kauṭilya mentions the body of armed women,[56] who surrounded the king after he rose from his sleep. The appointment of foreign Amazons probably came into practice, from the fact, as Rawlinson presumes,[57] that, foreign women would not enter into the palace conspiracy as easily as a native woman, because of the former's difficulty in understanding local language.[58] The Gāndhāra school of sculpture presents numerous figures of these Yavanī *pratihāriṇīs* dressed in Greek costume.[59]

The composers of the *Rāmāyaṇa*[60] and the *Mahābhārata*[61] were acquainted with the beauty and the fair complexion of the women of the north-western lands, the half-mythical lands of *Gandhamādana* and *Ketumāla*. It seems that all was not myth, and actually fair-featured women were brought from these far-off lands in Central Asia for the Indian gyneceums.

Holdich mentions[62] the mediaeval Arab geographer's account of the most beautiful Turk slave girls of perfect complexion and feature, on which he deduces that, "the Tibet of Idrisi was a town on the highroad to China, which followed the Tarim river eastwards to its source in Lake Burhan". The Tarim river was known to the Indians as the Sītā[63] and it has been shown that the adjoining country and its different peoples were well-known to the Indians during this period. Vyātsyāyana describes the different disposition of women belonging to various countries.[64]

He moreover, enjoins more rules and regulations for the *antaḥpurikās*, and Nāgaraka's wife (common house-wives),[65] which point that aristocratic or middle class women, though accomplished and educated[66] received little independence to act according to their own will.

(viii) **The Gopa-narīs**: We are presented with a completely different picture when we turn to the incoming tribes of India. The Epic, the *Harivaṃsa*, and the *Viṣṇupurana* describe the frivolous and carefree life led by this beautiful young maidens of herdsmen i.e., *Gopa* class. They were apt in music and dancing; the *Kṣatriya* princes often went into these herd-settlements to enjoy the company of the mirthful *gopa-kanyas*. Duryodhana went to his herd settlement near Dvaitavana, and after spending a leisure amidst the gaiety he bestowed them with gifts of money, food and drink etc.: –

"*Tatoh Gapāḥ pragātārāḥ kuśalāḥ nṛtyavādana*
Dhārtaraṣṭram-upātiṣṭhan kanyāścaiva svalaṃkṛitāḥ.8.
Sa strīgaṇā vrito rājā prahṛisṭaḥ pradadauvasu
Tebhyo yatharham-annāni pānāni vividhāni ca.9".

(Vana.203, 8-9, Haridas)

The *Harivaṃśa* describes the dalliances and the *Hallīsaka* dance of the *Gopa-kanyās* at the Kamudī (Harvest Moon) of the Autumn nocturnes. The style of the ballet in which a youngman is surrounded by a circle of female dancers or the *Rāsa* dance[67] mentioned in the *Viṣṇupurāṇa* present a typical nomadic style recalling the Garbā dance of Gujars of Kathiwawar or nomads of Rajasthan. The nocturnal folk-dances in which both men and women participate, point to the mirthful, and somewhat lax morality amongst these nomadic women. It is explicitly mentioned that the Gopa-women[68] did not pay heed to the inhibition of their guardians but came out to play with Kṛṣṇa.

The Yādavas were of course closely associated with the Gopas.[69] It seems that during this period the Yādavas who ruled successively in Mathurā and in western India, mingled with the Ābhīras and some of their characteristics were engrafted on the former. The Ābhīras probably to make themselves more at home in this land took over the Kṛṣṇa stories and associated his name with their tribal deity. However, we find that Yādava women were much addicted to drinking,[70] and wine was lavishly consumed by both the sexes during the festive celebrations in Dvārakāpuri.[71]

Different auditoriums wee built in occasion of some performances for the *Bāramukhyās*, (courtesans), *Nāgarayoṣ itās* (Public women) and *Antaḥpurikās* (ladies of the royal harem and household). But Devakī sat with the *Nāgarayoṣitās* so to see the feats of his son. This again shows that rules were not very rigid amongst the Yādavas, so they permitted Devaki to sit within the demi-monde, outside of the curtain or the grill, that meant to hide the seats of the *Antaḥpurikās* from the public view.

"*Antaḥpuraṇāṃ mañcāśca tathānye parikalpitāḥ*

*Anye ca bāramukhyānām-anye ca nāgarayoṣitam.*26

** **** **

Nāgarīyoṣitāṃ madhye Devakī putra-gṛiddhinī

Ante-kale'pi drakṣyāmi putrasya ruciraṃ mukhaṃ".

(Viṣṇup.V. 20.26,28)[72]

The Yādavas, however, did not make much distinction between the courtesans and the wives of Kṛṣṇa.[73] It is conspicuous that while the eight queens entered the funeral pyre after the demise of Kṛṣṇa, the sixteen thousand women who were rescued from the seraglio of Narakāsura and was wedded by him started with Arjuna towards Hastināpur. On the way, in Punjab they were attacked by the Ābhīra *dasyus*. But it is said, that while some of them were ravaged forcibly, the others followed the Ābhiras of their own free will:— "*Kāmācānyā pravravajaḥ*".[74]

The hetaerae like behaviour of these women is attested in a highly interesting episode in the *Matsyapurāṇa*.[75] In explaining the duties of a courtesan, the story of Vāsudeva's sixteen thousand women is related. They were cursed by Kṛṣṇa on account of their lack of devotion towards the latter and infatuation on Śāmba. The curse enjoined that, they were to be spoiled by Dasyus on the sea-side. There Dālbhya muni would come and expose their former identity as the daughters of Hutāśana (70, 22). By performing "*Anaṅgavrata*" they would be exempted from the wretched condition of the "*Paṇyastrī*" and would be elevated to the *Apsaraloka*, or the *Viṣṇuloka*.

Another story relates here the origin of courtesans residing in '*Devakula*' temples, and in King's courts (*Nṛpamandire* 70.28). They were the widowed wives of *Dānavas*, *Asuras*, *Daityaṣ* and *Rākṣasas*. These stories evidently point to the important fact that, the number of foreign[76] or semi-foreign destitute women (probably due to the wars) was so large that the contemporary Brahmanical society had to admit and provide them in the king's courts or as temple-attendants, and though out various stories to render a mythological origin to them. This reference to courtesans in the *Devakula* is probably earlier than that supplied in Kālidasa and in the *Padmapurāṇa*.

The fact that the *dasyus* carried these women to the seaside, and they became "*paṇyastrī*" (sold for money) may actually point to a sea-borne[77] slave-trade carried on by the Ābhīras on these coastal regions of Sind. It might have had been that the courtesans from the western coast of India (Kutch, Kathiawar and Gujārat) of the time of *Matysapurāṇa* claimed their descent directly from the *Yādavanārīs* of the days of yore.

The mention of these *paṇyastrīs* in "Devakulas (Matsya 70, 28) as prescribed by Indra, opens a new line of discussion, which should be made in some detail.

(ix) **The Courtesans**: It has been said that as the Indian society was giving more stress on the guarding of women, it consequently led to a state of social problem similar to that Athens had confronted centuries ago. The Brahmanical zeal to avoid "*Varṇasaṃkaradoṣa*", which can be compared with the enthusiasm of the ancient Greeks to guard the purity of their "citizen-blood", led to the prohibition on women a knowledge of public affairs.[78] The consequent limitation of their culture, "made it impossible for them to be in every sense the companions of their husbands" those the aesthetically refined and high sophisticated citizens or *Nāgarakas*. The vacant place of the wives was occupied by the all-accomplished courtesans.[79] Though India attached high admiration and respect towards accomplished courtesans from very early times, the "class" as a whole reached it apex of popularity from the time of the Śaka satraps[80] to the days of Vātsyāyana (sixth century A.D.) under the Imperial Guptas.[81] The city courtesans of the cosmopolitan metropolis like Takṣaśilā, Ujjainī,[82] Mathura[83] and Pāṭaliputra[84] evidently enjoyed a position and royal privilege comparable to that of the Hetaerae of Athens.

(x) **Temple-Dancers**: It seems that during the Scythio-Kushan supremacy the institution of "*Devadāsīs*" or temple-dancers was introduced in India. Its earlier references in Iran, have been discussed,[85] in India the first evidence seems to have supplied by the Jogimara Cave inscription on Ramagarh hill. If the reading of Prof. Bloch i.e., "*Devadasikyi*" is accepted[86] we find that the custom came into vogue in between the 1st century B.C. to the 1st century A.D. However, the institution was flourishing at the Mahākāla Temple of Ujjaini in the days of Kālidāsa,[87] and it would not be wrong if we take that it was introduced by the Scythians, who brought many Iranian traditions with them . The custom was also prevalent in the Sun-temple of Multan,[88] where the Chinese devotee found "a constant succession of females performing music". Both *Padmapurāṇa* and *Bhavisyapurāṇa* state that it is a pious act to consecrate *Devadāsīs* in temples,[89] and thus prove the popularity of the institution in later times.

(xi) **The Tribal Women of Punjab**: A much more wanton picture is drawn in the pages of the epic about the women of Madra or Vāhīka country (Punjab).[90] It seems that a fresh incursion of barbarious nomad tribe called *Jarttikas*[91] took place and they settled in the land called Āraṭṭa in Punjab. Their womenfolk were shameless, gluttons and of uncouth behaviour. Due to the close association of these with the earlier Madras their women were also condemned vehemently.[92] The Madra women are called shameless and were much addicted to drinking wine obtained from Sauvīra country.[93]

The epic also mentions a worship of a demoness in the city of Śākala.[94] The ritual involved a large consumption of various kinds of flesh and wines; from the references it seems, that it was carried on in company of women. She was obviously, the Greek Demeter or Iranian Aṛdoksho, often portrayed with children, and later on identified with Hāritī of the Buddhist pantheon. She was worshipped by the womenfolk for the procurance and benefaction to the children. Soon the worship was amalgamated with the rituals of the "*Mātṛkās*" of the Hindu pantheon.[95]

Thus we find, that the large number of influx of this type of tribes, indirectly, if not directly, influenced the position of women of upper classes of the Hindu society. The notoreity of their womenfolk in general, compelled the *Śāstrakāras* lay more stress on the seclusion of the sober housewives (i.e., *Kulastrīs*) of Brahmanical society.

(xii) **The System of Satīdāha**: The discussion on the position of women would not be complete without a few words regarding the system of *Satīdāha*. From the available data, scholars[96] have come to the conclusion that the system was prevalent amongst the Indo-Europeans in archaic days. But probably from some time previous to the *Ṛigvedic* period onwards it fell into disuse. The *Dharma* and the *Gṛhyasūtras* which dealt with the minutest detail of the duty of man, remain silent about this system. *Manusmrti* also does not mention any such rule. But from the epic period onwards we find casual references, and the historical evidence supplied by the Greek historians[97] lead us to assume that as early as c. 316 B.C. the custom was practised in Punjab, and was popular amongst the Cathaeans (Kaṭhas). It was attached with meritorious sanctity. Altekar[98] from the Sanskrit references has come to conclude that the custom came into vogue again in c. 400 A.D. or little earlier.

It is not without justification to believe that a foreign inspiration was at work under this fresh impetus on "*Satīdāha*". We know that amongst the Scythians it was current, to "bury one of the concubines, who was specially strangled on this occasion, " with the deceased chief.[99] In China a princess who followed her dead husband by taking poison, was respected as a great soul.[100] It is quite possible that the incursion of the Scythian tradition and together with the fact that the royal seraglio was ravished after a political fall, obliged the wives of the harem to commit self-sacrifices on the funeral-pyres of their diseased husbands. This presumption find strong support from the fact that the "*Satīdāha*" remained much more popular amongst the *Kṣatriya* caste[101] than amongst the women of other castes, whose fortune did not change so tragically, after the vicissitudes of war. The earliest historical evidence was also that of a wife of a *Kṣatriya* general belonging to Hindu society.[102] The account moreover, throws an interesting light on the fact that the ancient *Kṣatriya* wives accompanied their husbands in foreign lands.

From the above discussion, about the various aspects of a woman's life and her activity it becomes clear that the western influences are more profound with marked effects than generally thought to be.

References

1. Herodotus, i. 184; Diodorus, ii. 4-20 on Semiramis whose name denote "doves", cf. the origin, name and childhood of Indian heroine Śakuntalā.
2. Vide supra, p. 120; n. 15; ERE, v, p. 58; p. 671 ff. Delaporte, Mesopotamia, p. 158.
3. ERE, vi, p. 673.
4. Mitchell Carrol, Greek Women, p. 208 ff. for Aphrodite Pandemus and her worshippers, – "In Corinth, hetaerism was invested with all the sanctity of religion".
5. E.B. Pollard, Oriental Women, pp. 187-189.
6. Diodorus, ii. 23, the concubines spent their leisurely hours in "spinning purple garments and working the softest of wool".

   The *Virāṭaparvan* in the epic supplies ample references about the daily life in an ancient Indian harem, and the occupation of the women there in. The device in between queen Sudeṣṇā and her brother Kīcaka, for getting possession of Draupadī show that meanness vitiated the air of *antaḥpuras*.

   Bāṇabhaṭṭa in *Harṣacarita* VI, mentions some famous episodes current in his time. Many relate that the queens, *pratihāriṇīs* or the court-dancers took the leading role in the stratagems.
7. ERE, V, p. 271, The outlook was very similar about the ideal of housewives (*Kulastrīs*) in India too.
8. Herod. i. 205-206; 212-214.
9. Herod. iv. 78.
10. Ibid., iv. 110-117.
11. *Harṣacarita* vii.
12. McGovern, p. 341, the Amazon attendants of Hunnish kings. It seems that from the conquest of Alexander onwards, the system of keeping Amazon body-guards increased in Asia.
13. E.B. Pollard, op. cit., p. 192; the portraiture of women from Palmyra (Ghirshman, Iran, Pls. 92, 93, 94, 95) belonging to the Parthian period depict them not with a motherly grace or feminine

delicacy, but with a feeling of sedate dignity, pride and domination; cf. noticeable absence of female figures in the earlier art of Achaemenian epoch.

14. Mbh. 13.102 (B.R.M.) mentions the women of *Uttarakuru* (Central Asia) governed by their own will i.e., *kāmacāriṇī*. This evidently points to their highly independent status enjoyed in a tribal nomadic society.
15. E.B. Huntington, The Pulse of Asia.
16. The high status of women was limited in the days of Bandhāyana, II. 2.3.46, who states, "they are weaker naturally in their limbs – says the Śmuti," vide Govindsvamin, p. 187; SBE XIV, p. 231. This change naturally tended towards the limitations in socio-religious life. Later on Atri (135) even goes so far as to put the women in the same category with the *Śūdras*, Dutt, p. 302.
17. Ap. II, 13.7; Ba. II. 2.3, 34, 35; as the Iranians and the Indo-Aryans both had patriarchal society and strong belief in after life, the son was looked upon as the sole resort of man. The son was the legitimate conductor of the funerary rites. Among the different types of progenies, the "*aurasa putra*" was considered best and cherished most. Naturally stricter rules for maintaining the chastity of women were evolved out, to guard a better lineage and purity of blood. It is obvious from the words of Baudhāyana that during his time a fresh emphasis was laid upon the rules of constant vigilance on women.
18. Mbh. 4. 3.17; 13.46. 15; 13.149.34 etc.

    Atri states "...women are therefore always holy (139)", Dutt, p. 303. Dakṣa, IV. 2-4, 15-16, etc. Dutt, pp. 445-448.
19. Pāṇini, III, 2.36; Kāśikā, "Āśūryampaśyā rājadārāḥ" Agrawala, IKP, p. 87.
20. S. Shastri, Woman in Sacred Laws, pp. 61, 64, 69.
21. Altekar, PWḢC, pp. 170, 177.
22. Vide supra, Chapter Two, Sect. II, 1-8.
23. Vide supra, pp. 2-3.
24. Agrawala, IKP, pp. 9-11.
25. Shamasastry, pp. 39-41, i.xx
26. Mbh. 4. Chaps 2-10 (B.O.R.I.) relates how Draupadi was appointed as a Sairindhri in Virāṭa's *antaḥpura*, where the sole authority lay in the hands of queen Sudeṣṇā.

27. J.C. Jain, p. 56, n. 43.
 Shamasastry, p. 41.
28. Basak, p. 48.
29. Shamasastry, p. 41, "he shall be received by the Kañchuki (presenter of the king's court); Nāṭyaśāstra, XXI. 126, 133-134, "*Kāṣāyakaneukapaṭāḥ*", 149, "*Veṣṭanābaddha-paṭṭāni pratiśīrṣāni*" etc.
30. Ibid., p. 41, eunuchs (*Varṣavara* or *varṣadhara*) *Nāṭyaśāstra*, XXIV, 67-71.
31. Mbh. 4.10.11 (B.O.R.I.).
32. Bau.II.2.34, 35, Govindsvamin, p. 184; SBE XIV, p. 229.
33. Vide above, n. 25; Basak, pp. 45-47.
34. *Māavikāgnimitram, Śakuntalam, Vikramorvaśī* etc.
35. Nāṭya, XXI, 126.
36. Ibid., 149.
37. Śakuntalam, v, "*Ācāra ityadhikiṛtena mayā grihitā vetrayaṣṭ hiravarodhagṛheṣu rājñaḥ*".
38. *Vikromorvaśī*, III, the words of *Kañcukī*.
39. Vide above, n. 29.
40. According to Shamasastry, p. 41, *Kañcukī* was the "presenter of the king's court". But Basak translates it as the *Varṣavara* (eunuch) wearing the *Kañcuka* and the *Uṣṇīṣa*, see, p. 48. However, this is evident that the wearing of a cloak over the dress, signifying the royal rank came from Achaemenid Iran, where the king's portraiture show him garbed in a loose cloak covering the body. This was most probably introduced into India during Chandragupta Maurya with other Iranian customs.
41. This may be a *Daṇḍadhara*. We are tempted to identify the figure with a Yavana guard mentioned in literature.
42. Cf. The Greek gynaeconitis.
43. *Harṣacarita* V, Cowell, p. 149.
 Matsyapurāṇa, 130. 24-25.
44. Rawlinson, IIW, p. 117.
45. Schoff, Periplus, 49; according to CAI, p. 304, "instruments for music".
46. Tarn, GBI, p. 374.

47. Vide supra, p. 46 ff., p. 133 ff., cf. Viṣṇu, XVI. 12. the Vaidehakas who earned "their livelihood by keeping dancing girls and other public women".

48. Nāyādh, p. 31, J.C. Jain, p. 107.

49. These identifications are suggested by Motichandra, PBV, p. 141, f.n. 6; vide supra Chapter Two, Section II-6.

50. Shamasastry, pp. 40, 136; Ingholt, pls. 38, 39 note the dress of the women surrounding prince Siddhārtha; Nāṭya. XXIV. 53-56.

51. Hari, II, 88.

52. *Harṣacarita*, II.

53. Cf. Mbh. 1.214. 59-60 (Haridas), I. Ghosh, Vol. I, p. 112, f.n. *Yavanapuṣpa, Turuṣka* etc. Bri. Saṃ. 77. 24-30.

54. *Harṣacarita*, I, Cowell, App. I, pp. 261-263; cf. Inghott, Pl. 39b – the four female night-guards under the arches.

55. *Śakuntalam V*; *Mudrārāksaṣa III*; *Raghu XVI*, 57, "*Kirātī*"; Keith, SD, p. 61; Rawlinson, IIW, pp. 47-48; "Megasthenes says that these [Strabo XV. 1.55, Q. Curtius, VIII. 9.] women were bought from their parents and brought up in the palace;..." Upadhyaya, IK, pp. 135-136.

56. Shamasastry, p. 41, "the king shall be received by troops of women armed with bows".

57. Rawlinson, p. 47-48.

58. Still, we find that Bāṇa (Harṣa, VI) mentions one *Yavaneśvara* was killed by his woman-guard at the strategem devised by the opponent party. Vide Cowell, p. 193.

59. Vide Ingholt, GAP, pl. 361, this female figure appears to be a *pratihāriṇī* (woman-guard) with a spear; Pl. 443. Athenas' dress show the typical garb of a *Yavanī*; Pl. 39, the *sāri* is draped in typical Gāndhāra fashion in the figure carrying the lances; *Vivagasuya*, III. P. 23 mention women dressed in men's attire.

60. Ram. 4.43.

61. Mbh. 6.7.29-34; 6.8.15-16 (B.O.R.I.); the Nāṭya, xxi. 102 enjoins that the characters from *Uttarakuru* should be painted in a golden complexion while those from *Bhadrāśvadvīpa* should be white.

62. Holdich, GI, pp. 282-83; Kūrmap. 46.19 mentions the women of Harivaṃśa as "*sadāmaṇḍanatatparāḥ*".

63. Mbh. 6.7.45 (B.O.R.I.).

64. Vātsyāyana, XVI, Women from *Strīrājya*, *Bāhlīka*, *Ābhīra*, etc.

65. Ibid., XXI; Chakladar, pp. 121-23; *antaḥpura*, pp. 125-126.

66. Ibid., pp. 121-123, pp. 126, 127.

67. Viṣṇup. V. 13. 49-56; Hari, II. 20, "*Hallīsaka Kṛḍanam*" M. N. Dutt, p. 317-18 f.n.

68. "*Ghoṣa Ābhīra-pallī syāt*", hence *gopa-narīs* are Ābhīra women; Mārkaṇḍeyap. 49. 50.

69. The Yādavas were notable for their cattle and had migrated from Mathura region to western India. Later when the Ābhīras entered India and took to the pursuit of cattle-rearing, the identification with the former became easier.

70. Mbh. I. 212. 7-9; 1. 215. 24-29 (Haridas), Hari II. 88; II. 89.

71. Ibid., 16.3.

72. Cf. Kalpāsutra, 4. 63; Nāyā, I. p. 8 – "*Javaniyā*" (i.e., *Yavanikā*) vide J. C. Jain, p. 163.

73. *Harivaṃśa*, II. 88, were these accompanying the Yādava princes were concubines?

    Cf. Visnup. V. 31.14-18 which state that Kṛṣṇa wedded the bands of women rescued from the seraglio of Narakāsura.

74. Vide supra, p. 75, n. 159; Viṣṇup. V. 38. 26.

75. Matsyap. 70, the whole chapter provides many references.

76. Basu, Purāṇapraveśa, pp. 70-71 thinks that the *paṇyasrīs* came from the nomadic tribes.

77. Vide supra, pp. 46-47.

    The Ābhīras were powerful all along the desert routes from Lower Sind to Gujarat Kathiawar.

78. Greek Women, p. 109.

79. It is obvious from the fact that Vyātsyayana laid so much stress on the accomplishments and behaviours of the courtesans, vide *Kāmasūtra*, chaps. III, XXIX-XXXIII; *Arthaśāstra*, XXVII, *Nāṭyaśāstra*, XXIV, 44-51.

80. Ep. Ind. II, p. 199; IX, pp. 243-244; Amohini; The Yakṣinī figures of Mathura school indeed, display the charms of these courtesans.

81. Chakladar, p. 138-142.

82. *Meghadūta*, *purvam*, 32, 38, 40 etc.

83. It may be well-assumed that Amohini was one only of the most renowed courtesans of Mathura.

84. The *Arthaśāstra* no doubt show the condition of Pāṭaliputra. Vide J. C. Jain, pp. 163-166, for courtesans in Jaina canon.

85. For detail vide infra, Chapter Four, Section V.

86. A.S.I. 1903-4, p. 123 ff.

87. *Meghadūta, Pūrvam*, 38, "*Veśyāstvatto padanakhasukhān*" imply their fatigue by constant dancing.

88. Vide supra, p. 108, n. 57.

89. Altekar, p. 183.

90. Mbh. 8 Chpas 27, 30, (B.O.R.I.).

91. Ibid., 8.30.14, 8.30, 16-18 (B.O.R.I.).

92. Ibid., 8.27.85-89 (B.O.R.I.).

93. Ibid., 8.32.35-39 (Haridas); 8.32.72-73 (Haridas).

94. Vide supra, p. 185.

95. The *Rākṣasī* is called "*Mahā-ulūkhalamekhalā*" in 8.30.46 (B.O.R.I.) "*Ulūkhalamekhalā*" is the name of a *Mātrikā* of Skanda. The mother-goddesses Demeter, Ardoksho and *Hāritī* (Hindu, *Rākṣasī Jarā*) were all conjointly worshipped as Matṛka guarding children. This Rākṣasī (i.e. Matṛkā with malevolent aspects) mentioned here was evidently worshipped as Hāritī in the Buddhist city of Śākala, the capital of Menander. Her oblations comprised of flesh and wine, which aroused a general repulsion among the orthodox Brahmanical Hindus. Was the name "*Ulūkhala*" derived from "Ardoksho" which sounded peculiar to the Indians? It seems probable because "*Ulūkhala*" does not make any appropriate sense.

96. Altekar, p. 116.

97. CHI, pp. 372-73.

98. Altekar, p. 122; *Dakṣa Saṃhitā* however mentions the custom thus, "A woman, who, after the demise of her husband ascends the funeral pyre, becomes a good conduct and lives gloriously in the celestial regions. (19)" M. N. Dutt, p. 447.

99. McGovern, pp. 56, 108.

100. Altekar, p. 166.

101. Strabo, XV. C. 700, it was specially prevalent among the Cathaeans (*Kaṭhas*) or *Kṣatriyas* (Vide CHI, p. 372).

102. Diodorus, XIX, 34, CAI, pp. 240-241, Keteus was a *Kṣatriya*.

Section IV

Disposal of the Dead and Funerary Rituals

From the *Dharmasūtras* and other works belonging to this period, no evidence has been found which can tentatively show or indicate any foreign mode adopted for the disposal of the dead. The cremation seems to be the age-old and sanctioned mode of disposing the deceased body[1] among the Indo-Aryans. But the Indians were conscious of other types of death ceremonials. Thus the epic relates about the land of *Uttarakuru*:

"*Bharuṇḍā nāma śakunāstīkṣṇatuṇḍā mahābalāḥ,*
te nirharanti hi mṛtāndarīṣu prakṣipanti ca." 11.

(6.8.11. B.O.R.I.)

The reference is, no doubt, about the Zoroastrian or Magian disposal of the dead in the grottos (*darīṣu*).[2] But this is related not about India but *Uttarakuru* and no other Indian sources directly mention that similar custom was prevalent in India. This is however, reminiscent of the customs observed in Taxila[3] and by the Oraeitai in Baluchistan[4] who threw the corpses to the vultures to be devoured. There is no particular mention to show that the Indians belonging to Hindu or Buddhist Orders practiced this. It might have had been confined only to the Zoroastrian Iranians of those regions.[5]

A striking similarity is to be found in "*āmaka susāna*" of the Jātakas infested by vultures,[6] jackals,[7] and robbers,[8] but it does not seem to have any foreign bearings. There is no reason to assume that the desolate haunts of the ghouls[9] have anything to do with the Iranian Ossuary.[10]

The system of burial was known in India and was prescribed in some special cases.[11] In this the body was placed inside a coffin. That the rich and the able provided fine wooden coffins with metal decorations is proved by the scenes of Buddha's life in the Gāndhāra reliefs (see plate No. 2). This placement of Buddha's body in a coffin seems to be a foreign innovation, introduced by the Graeco-Iranian artists, who were accustomed with the idea.[12]

Sporadic mention about the preservation of the corpse for one reason or other, draw our attention. Thus we are told that body of Daśaratha was kept saturated with oil for a few days after his demise. This was not the general rule out but was done in emergency urged by grave circumstances.[13]

Similarly we are told that Ubbarī's body embalmed with oil and ointments, was placed in a coffin by her lamenting husband.[14] But this was too, a case of exception.

The single reference to a corpse placed on a tree cannot be taken to indicate any custom, neither it has been dealt in detail[15] in the course of the narrative.

From the above discussion it seems that except the mention of the custom observed by the Oreitai and the Taxilans the systems of the disposal of the dead remained unhampered by any foreign impacts. The foreign tribes who entered and settled in India must have had followed their own customs but later on probably took to the Indian mode of cremating their dead.[16]

The absence, till now, of any sarcophagus or funerary vaults point to the probability of the above assumption. But that the Scythio-Parthians and following them the Kushans introduced the custom of installing posthumous statues is attested beyond doubt by the Scythio-Kushan royal images found at Mathura. The custom was accepted with a general welcome in all the regions under the Parthian-Kushan cultural sphere.[17] For some time at least, it was probably adapted by the contemporary *Kṣ atriyas*, so that we find, Bhāsa alluding to a similar custom in his *Pratimānāṭaka*.[18] The departed souls were deified and the effigies were placed in a *Pratimāgṛha* which was as sacred as a *Devakula*. The nomadic Scythians believed in after life, and the installation of posthumous images in more durable material like stone evolved out in Parthian Iran and imparted a lasting impression on India.[19]

It has been shown that the foreign tribes are prescribed to worship the manes[20] but there were some outlandish tribes of whom it has been said, "The gods, the *Pitṛs* and the Brāhmaṇas never accept gifts from those that are fallen, or those that are begotten by Śūdras on the girls of other castes, or the Vāhīkas who never perform sacrifices and are exceedingly irreligious".[21] This again show that the throwing of the dead without any funerary rites and the absence of oblations to the manes (pitris) among the Jarttikas and Āraṭṭas (Oreitai) of Vāhīka (Punjab) aroused a general contempt about them. It proves beyond all doubt, that during the later half of our period (i.e., after the retirement of Alexander to c. 320 A.D.) the Oreitai and probably some other allied tribes like the Jarttikas (Suarataratae) did not remain confined to the west of Indus but spread along the Indus Valley from south to north and infested Punjab. About this migration the classical writers as well as the epic point to a period about first century B.C. to first century A.D.[22] This evidently show that previously during the time of Alexander they were confined in Baluchistan but later on gradually spread towards Punjab along the footsteps of the Śakas.

References

1. ERE, vol. IV, pp. 473-475, both burial and cremation was practiced by the Aryans. But while burial was more popular among the Greeks the cremation was prevalent among the Vedic Indians.
2. Ibid., II, p. 16.
3. Strabo, 62; CAI, p. 279.
4. Diodorus Siculus, xvii, 105.
5. ERE, Vol. II, p. 16 suggests that it spread from the Oreitai. According to McGovern this non-Iranian custom was adopted by the Bactrians and Eastern Iranians. But the case might have been vice versa. It is not known whether the bordering tribes (i.e., the Oreitans and Taxilans) adopted the system from Zorastrians, or whether it was prevalent among them from bygone days previous to the spread of Zoroastrianism; vide McGovern, pp. 82-83.
6. *Maṅgala* Jāt (87); *Gijjha* Jāt (399).
7. *Sigāla* Jātaka, (142).
8. *Padakusalamānava* Jātaka (432).
9. *Jayadissa* Jātaka (513).
10. These Ossuaries were especially hewn out of living rocks in Iran; there were niches to place the dead body.

11. Mbh. Samāj, p. 274.
12. Cf. Arrian, vi. 29 "Inside the chamber there was a *golden coffin* containing Cyrus' body, and a *great divan with feet of hammered gold*, spread with covers of some thick, brightly coloured material, with a Babylohian rug on top." etc. (emphasis added)

    This shows the pomp and splendour of lying the body in its eternal rest.
13. *Rāmāyaṇa*. 2.

    This was done because none of the sons of the deceased king was present at Ayodhyā. Cf. Herod. i. 140, iv. 71, "protective envelopment of the body in wax".
14. *Assaka Jātaka* (207).
15. Mbh. 4.5.31-33 (Haridas), "*Kuladharmo Yamasmākam*", etc. show that this peculiar custom was probably observed by a few people.
16. For Greek funeral, vide ERE, Vol. IV, p. 473 ff. for Scythian burial, vide ERE, Vol. XI, pp. 277-781 II, p. 16. Herod. iv. 71.
17. Ghirshman, Iran, for the Iranian funeral customs through the ages, p. 69 ff.

    For Palmyrene and Sassanian sarcophagi, ERE, Vol. IX, p. 595-596.
18. Vide infra, Chapter Four Sect. I.
19. Vide infra, Chap. IV, section on Sculpture.
20. Mbh. 12.65, discussed previously.
21. Mbh. Trans. P. C. Ray, Karṇap, XLIV, 33-34.
22. Diodorus' information in XVII belong to Alexander's epoch; Pliny worked in c. 23-79 A.D.

    This was also the length of period of the compilation of the epic. These tribes from South Baluchistan must have pressed inward to the Indus Valley with the advance of the Śakas.

Section V

Food and Drink

A study of the habits of food and drink indicate the social environment and the physical abilities of a race. But that is not all, – the manners and etiquettes connected with the partaking of food show the cultural level and the higher aspiration of the people.

Thus the epic states that,

"*Āyuḥsattva-balārogya sukhaprītivivardhanāḥ,*

Rasyāḥ snigdhāḥ sthirā hṛdyā āhārāḥ sātvikapriyāḥ". etc.

(6.41.8-10, Haridas).

Here different kinds of food are mentioned which increase Sātvika (spiritual), *Rājasa* (passionate) and *Tāmasa* (gross) qualities in human beings.[1] So it was food that controlled and influenced the different disposition and abilities of man.

Though the sources are meagre, we will try to show that the western contacts brought something new to the cuisine of ancient India, and caused a change in the taste of the people. I would discuss the subject under the following heads: (i) Dinner Etiquettes, (ii) The food-stuffs (a) Vegetables, (b) Meat, (iii) The consumption of alcoholic drinks.

Before going into the list of food-stuffs and drinks it would be better to take a note on the dinner etiquettes maintained by the Indians, and prescribed for the gentle society. The epic[2] and the *Dharmasūtras*[3] prescribe certain food-stuffs, defilation and cleanliness of the vessels and rules for the partaking food which was thought as an pious duty to be performed in the *Gṛhasthāśrama*. It was thus involved with religious significance. The rules were stricter for the *Brāhmaṇas* but the other three classes too, had to observe certain general rules. This point at the high ideal of welfare, dignity and sobriety maintained by the ancient Indians.[4] The members of the household and above all the guests were given the highest place in the bestowal of food-stuffs by a pious householder.

But side by side some distasteful manners have been illustrated which show that the Brahmanical authorities were quite orthodox about keeping their own stricter observations. It seems that the Persians differed a lot regarding the dinner etiquettes.[5] Thus the Brahmanical authorities condemn one who takes his food having a turban on his head, and shoes covering the feet:[6]

"*Yadveṣṭitaśirā bhuṃkte yadbhuṃkete dakṣiṇā mukhāḥ*
Sopānatkaśca yadbhuṃkte sarvam vidyāttadāsuram".

(13.90.19).

There were set rules in the orthodox Hindu society about accompanying one during his dining. The house-holder, after having fed his guests, other members of the house-hold and servants ate himself. But it seems that it was the duty of the lady of the house to dine after having fed all.[7]

But there were the Ārattas and Jarttikas who used to take stale food stuffs, and dine together, maintaining no bar of segregation in between the females and males and other relations:

"*Pumbhirvimiśrā nāryāśca jñātājñātāḥ svayecchayā,*
*Yeṣāṃ gṛheṣvaśiṣṭānāṃ saktumatsyāśināṃ tathā.*26
Pītvā sidhu sagomāṃsaṃ krandanti ca hasanti ca
Gāyanti cāpyavardhāni pravartante ca kāmataḥ".27

(8.32.26-27, Haridas).

It is evident that not only the *Brāhmaṇas*, but the other castes of the gentle societies too, avoided the company of these "*Naṣṭaśauca*"..."*Śīlavarjita*" Jarttikas.

Here we are inevitably reminded about "The Śakas and Yavanas, living in Aryan villages and hamlets outside Āryāvarta" who "were not ostracized; and they enjoyed the privilege of using a plate without polluting it".[8] (Puri, ITP, pp. 91-92). This if it is correct, then we may presume that the purification of the vessels used by them was not necessary. It also follows, that the Greeks or the Yavanas were far better and maintained the decorum of a higher culture than these Jarttikas and Ārattas (Oreitai) of Punjab, Sind and Baluchistan.

It is said about latter that the "Vāhīkas, without any feeling of revulsion, eat off wooden vessels having deep stomachs with pounded barley and other corn. The Vāhīkas drink the milk of sheep, camels and asses and eat curd and other preparation from those different kinds of milk". This obviously show that they did not observe the cleanliness of the vessels and partook Kumys, cheese and curds all from the milks indiscriminately.

The main diet consisted of cereals, vegetables and preparations from milk. The cereals were the staple food but people used to diversify their menu with the addition of sweet-meat, fishe and meat according to their ability. This was mainly done during the *Yajñas*, some other socio-religious functions and popular festivities.

(a) Vegetables: Interestingly enough we see that certain vegetables are interdicted by the *Dharmasūtras* and *Dharmaśāstras*. These are *Karañjā* (ka) (Pongamia Glabra, Verbesina Scandens, Monier-Williams p. 254); *Kisalaya* (a sprout of shoot, Monier-Williams, p. 284); *Kyāku* (fungus, and gout Monier-Williams, p. 318); *Laśuna* (garlic, Monier-Williams, p. 899); Niryāsa (exudation of trees and plants, juice etc., Monier-Williams p. 557 *Parārīka* (leek, Monier-Williams, p. 590); *Viraścana* (the juice flowing from an incision in a tree, Monier-Williams, p. 1043) etc.[9] Discrepancy may remain about the meaning of *Griñjana* (turnip) which may also denote animal flesh.[10] Manu states "*Varjayenmadhu māṃsañca bhaumāni Kavakāni ca, Bhūstriṇaṃ śigrukañcaiva ślmeṣ māntakaphaāni ca*".[11] (vi, 14) *Śigruka* has been explained as a *śāka* from Bāhlīka. This then was avoided because it was imported from a foreign country. Many of these were taken by the Scyṭhians. We know that they used to take grains, wild bulbs, onions and garlics. It may be the reason that as these wild nomads[12] used these edibles, these were avoided by the *Brāhamaṇas*. An interesting verse states that the garlic, turnips, onion and bulbs were created out of the blood-drops of Balī.[13]

(b) Meat: Various kinds of flesh have been mentioned and it seems that though a deterrent attitude developed towards meat and especially beef eating, it was consumed profusely during some oblation to manes and to the gods in sacrifices. Various kinds of meat other than the beef were to be found in the daily menu of the household of the wealthy and the rich.[14] It is interesting to note that meat could have been accepted without unnecessary violation to living beings and eating of "*bṛthāmāṃsa*" (meat that is not sacrificed) caused the degradation.[15] It seems that meat-eating was gradually increasing in this period due to the influence of the savage tribes. The description of the ritual of "*Rākṣasī Ulūkhalamekhalā*" at the city of Śākala shows the different varieties of meat consumed on that occasion.

Gavyasya triptā māṃsasya pitvā Gauḍaṃ mahāsavam,
Gauribhiḥ saha narībhirbṛhatibhiḥ khalaṃkrtāḥ
Patāṇḍugaṇḍusa yutān khādante caiḍakānbahun.31.
Vārāhaṃ Kaukkuṭaṃ māṃṣam gavyaṃ gārdabhamauṣṭrakaṃ
Ceḍaṃ ca ye na khādanti teṣāṃ janma-nirarthakam".32

(8.30.31-32, B.O.R.I.)

The *Yakṣas*, *Piśācas*, *Bhūtas* and the gnomes guarding over the wealth together with their overlords Śiva and Kubera, i.e., the deities of non-Aryan pantheon were to be propitiated with oblations of meat,[16] with other offerings of cereals and grains. The description of the roasted flesh ("*Niṣtaptaśūlāñcchakalānpaśuṃśca"*) and young buffalo fried in ghrita, ("*Susvinnaśūlyān-mahiṣāmśca bālāñcchūlyānsuniṣ ṭapta ghṛtāvasiktān*") enjoyed with different condiments and fruits (v. 61) no doubt point to a foreign culinary art. The beef and buffalo went out of mode by the age of *Harivaṃśa*. But a vivid description of these savory exotic dishes, no doubt, point to a highly west Asian taste of the wealthy aristocracy of western India. A similar description of the lavish consumption of flesh is to be gleaned from the pages of the *Mṛcchakatika* (Act IV) where the cuisine in the fifth court of the courtesan's household is described by Maitreya.

(iii) **The consumption of Alcoholic Drinks**: There is ample reference to show that during this period the wine drinking was one of the most favourite pastime enjoyed by the fashionable men and women. Inspite of the vehement opposition in the *Dharmasūtras* and *Śāstras* the habit, it seems, gained its way into the society.[17] Various kinds of wines called *Gauḍī*, *Paiṣṭī* and *Mādhvī* were manufactured by professional distiller castes.[18]

The interesting episode in *Kumbha Jātaka*[19] tell that how "*Surā*" and "*Vāruṇī*" were discovered, and unbridled drunkenness spread in the society. It also alludes to the fact that strong liquors came from the Himālayan regions. This evidently reminds of the Kairātaka surā consumed by Bhīma before his march.[20] These references show that several well-known liquors were obtained from the tribes inhabiting the northern extremities of India.

From the west came the famous *Kāpiśāyani*. This wine was called after the region of Kapisi[21] from which the name of the colour *Kāpiśa* (brown or wine-red)[22] was derived.

The distilleries of Sauvīra country were famous for producing *Sauvīraka* wine.[23] The intemperate vulgarity of these people have been alluded to in the epic.

Two historical evidences gleaned from classical literature have left permanent marks in the history of the drinking habits of ancient Indians. We know that Bindusāra asked Antiochus I (Soter) king of Syria to send him sweet wine, dried figs and a sophist; and wine and silver and glass vessels were imported at Barbaricum and Barygaza for consumption at the royal courts of the contemporary monarchs.[24]

The innumerable literary evidences from the epics, the *Jātakas* and the *Purāṇas* have been delineated by the famous sculpture depicting Bacchanalia from Mathura[25] panels from Ajanta paintings[26] and other large and small sculpture pieces.

The *Harivaṃśa* refer to the fragrant *Maireya, Mādhvika, Surā, Āsava* drunk from a special cup called "Pālavī".

"*Tathāranālāṃśea bahuprakārānpapuḥ sugandhānapi pālavīṣu,*

Śṛtaṃ payaḥ śarkarayā ca yuktaṃ phalaprakārāṃśca bahuṃśca khādan".65

The epic also describes cups with golden coverings that were used for drinking, The drink party was moreover enriched with various kinds of snacks:

"*Nānāprakārānapi kaṇḍakhādyān*.63

Apānapāścoddhava-bhoja miśrāḥ śākaiśca supaiśea bahuprakāraiḥ

Peyaiśea dadhnā payascā ca virāḥ, svannāni rājan bubhūjuḥ prahriṣṭā".64

It seems that various types of rhytons or cups were also imported along with the foreign wines,[27] and permeated the drinking parties with an air of fashionable exoticism.

Numerous references in the *Jātakas* about the drinking booths and Bacchanalian festivals show the height of the popular addiction towards drinking.[28] Though the gift of Suna was useless, there is a curious reference that Vessantara arranged for the bestowal of Surā among those who were addicted to it.[29] The *Āpānabhūmi* (drink booths with open courtyard to accomodate the revellers), *Sūnas* (slaughter houses) and *Odanikagṛhas* (where cooked rice were sold) were to be found side by side.[30]

References

1. "*Āhāraniyamenāsya pāpnā śāmyati rājasaḥ*" 12.214.18. (Haridas).
2. Mbh. 12. 220 (Haridas); Ibid., 13.193 (B.R.M.) deals with details regarding food and dinner etiquettes.
3. Manu, IV. 75-76, IV. 131, 211, 205-225 in general Śūdra's food could be accepted, IV. 253-54. Viṣṇup. III. 11. 76-79.
4. Mbh. 13. 104 (B.R.M.) the whole chapter deals with various rules to be observed during a daily routine.
5. Herod. i. 133. "The rich then (on birthday) produce an ox, a horse, a camel, and an ass roasted whole in an oven; but the poor produce smaller cattle. They are moderate at their meals, but eat of many after dishes, and those not served up together...The Persians are much addicted to wine." etc. cf. Mbh. 8.30.32.
6. Cf. Matsyap. 130.43, "*Dadhi śaktun payaścaiva kapitthāni ca rātriṣu Bhakṣayanti ca śeranta ucchiṣṭā saṃvritā stathā.*"43

   This shows that those food-stuffs interdicted to be taken at night were consumed by the Asuras before retiring to sleep. It is not known whether this was their regular custom, or was the ominous sign anticipating their final fall.
7. Mbh. 12.193.9 (B.R.M.).

   "*Atitithināñca sarveṣāṃ preṣyāṇāṃ svajanasya ca,*

   Sāmānyaṃ bhojanaṃ bhṛtyaiḥ puruṣasya praśasyate." etc.

   Ibid., 3.217, 21; 3.218.1-19 (Haridas)

   "*Bhojayitvā dvijān sarvān patiṃśaca varavarṇinī,*

   *Viśrānta ca svavam bhuktvā sukhāsīna bhavedvathā.*21"

8. Puri, ITP, pp. 91-93.

9. S.C. Banerjee, Dharmasūtras, p. 158.

10. Mahābhārater Samāj, p. 283, *Griñjana* has been explained as the meat of a beast (*Paśumāṃsa*) that has been killed with poisonous weapon (*Viṣayuktaśastra*). Vide Mbh. 13.91.38-42 (B.R.M.).

11. Manu, (VI, 14), n. "*śigrukaṃ Bāhlīkeṣu prasiddhaṃ śākam*". These are to be rejected while in *Vānaprasthāśrama*.

12. ERE, Vol. IX, p. 277, The Scythians "eschewed the pig". Curiously enough in the *Karṇaparvan* we do not find the mention of pork or pig. They drank but "unlike the Greeks they drank it neat".

13. "*Laśunaṃ Griñjanañcaiva palāṇḍuṃ piṇḍa mūlakam,*
Karambhādyāni cānyāni hīnāmi rasagandhataḥ".

14. Vide S. C. Banerjee, Dharmasūtras, p. 155, 157.

    Mahābharater Samāj, p. 165. *Gomāṃsa* was censured during the age. Vide Mbh. 8. 45.29. But 13.88. (B.R.M.) prescribes the meat of *Meṣa, Śaśa, Chāga, Varāha, Chitra* and *Kriṣṇasāra* deers, *Gavaya, Mahiṣa* and *gavya*. The Gavaya, mahiṣa and gavya meat cause a satisfaction to the manes for ten, eleven and twelve months respectively, which show the supcriority and sanctity of flesh of these beasts.

    Vide Mbh. Samāj, p. 283.

    Ibid., pp. 159-162 on the lavish consumption of meat in the society.

15. Ibid., p. 161; Manu. V. 31-39; *Mahasutasoma Jātaka* (537) tells that meat was preserved even for the *Poṣadha* day. Vide Gautama's story in Mbh. 13.168-172 (B.R.M.).

16. Mbh. 14, Chap. 65.

17. Agrawala, 114, many new words, such as the Maireya etc. were introduced in Sanskrit. "The word is unknown in the Brāhmaṇa and Āraṇyaka literature, which suggests its origin in post-vedic period".

    Manu XI, 94-95.

    "Wine (Surā) is the impure essence (lit. refuge matter) of grains, and sinful is a refuge matter; hence, let no Brāhmaṇas, Kṣhatriyas and Vaiśyas drink wine (sura)". (94).

    Gaudī (treacle wine), *Paiṣhṭī* (wine of pasted rice) and Mādhvī (wine made from the flowers of Mahua tree) are known to be the three species of wine; all of them, like any, must not be drunk by the foremost of the Brāhmaṇas (95).

    Flesh, wine and fermented saps are the food of Yakshas, Rakshas, and Piśāchas; they should not be eaten or drunk by Brāhmaṇas, who partake of the oblation of gods". (96).

18. Vide supra, p. 92; Viṣṇu, XXII, 81-83, "...These ten intoxicating drinks are unclean for a Brāhmaṇa; but by touching them, a Kṣhatriya, or a Vaiśya commits no sin (83).

    Vide supra, p. 46, p. 74, n. 149; cf. Mbh. 2.49.10 (Haridas), "*Phalajaṃ madhu*".

19. Kumbha Jāt. (512) refer to the intemperate behaviour of the women. It relates the ingredients of the wine and labeling the drinks after the names of the discoveress.

20. "*Kairātakaṃ madhu*", vide Mbh. Samāj, p. 164.

21. Pāṇini, iv. 2 . 29: "Kāpiśyāḥ ṣphak".

    Agrawala, I K P , pp. 118-119 "The grape exported from Kāpiśī was knows as Kāpiśāyanī drākshā and it's wine Kāpiśayanani madhu. Kāpiśī is even today the home of the grape. In ancient days an excellent quality of raisin wine was manufactured at Kāpiśi and widely exported." etc.

22. Monier Williams, p. 251. for *Kapiśa* colour (reddish-brown).

23. For distilleries, vide Agrawala, pp. 114-115; Ibid., p. 110, "Eastern India was fond of wines (*surā-pānāḥ prācyaḥ*) Bālhīka of Sauvīra (a kind of sour drink); Gandhāra of *kashāya* wine" (Italics mine).

    Vide supra, p. 42; p. 73 n. 122. But it was lesser than other finer qualities of wines; Mbh. 3.2.32. 37 (Haridas),

    "*Kathaṃhi pītvā Madhvīkaṃ pītva ca Madhumādhavīm,*
    Lobhaṃ Sauvīrake kuryānnārī kāciditi smare".

    This again show that women of aristocratic classes were used in cosuming the superior qualities of wine.

24. Raychaudhuri, PHNI, p. 299

    Saletore, IDR, p. 134, n. 201.

    Periplus, 39, imports at Barbaricum were wine, glass vessels, silver plates etc. 49, imports at Barygaza were costly silver vessels. Vide CAI, pp. 300, 304.

25. For detailed description vide infra, Chap. IV, the Mathura School of Sculpture and Chapter V, the cult of Baladeva.

26. For detailed discussion vide infra, Section on Dress and Costume.

27. Vide infra, Section on Sports and Pastimes.

28. Vide Infra, p. 156.

29. Vessantara Jataka, (547).

30. Vidurapandita Jataka, (545).

Section VI

Sports and Pastimes

The discussion on social life cannot be complete without a study of the sports and pastime enjoyed by the contemporary people.

(i) **Water Sports**: From the picturesque and vivid description of swimming and rowing supplied by the *Harivaṃśa*[1] it appears that these were favourite sports of the people in ancient India. In the detailed account of the different types of pleasure-boats,[2] and some other evidences supplied in the contemporary literature one may see the probable foreign contribution in this aspect of ancient India's social life.

From the numismatic evidences we find[3] that the Andhra-Śātavāhana dynasty possessed different types of boats. The Periplus informs us that pilots from the coast came and helped the foreign ships to steer their courses to the shore.[4] These undoubtedly show the eagerness of the Indo Scythian as well as the Andhra rulers, to patronize sea-borne trade and maritime activity. In the view of this it is not improbable to presume that the wealthier class of people must have enjoyed rowing and sailing. The rich delighted in the luxury of cruising the pleasure boats. The Alexandrian Greeks who frequented the western coasts of India, and the native Indo-Greeks who were left to survive the conquests of Alexander, Demetrius and Menandar most probably had a hand in the building of these boats of diverse designs.[5] The Greeks were by nature a sea-faring nation and excelled in the art of ship building. Thus we hear of the "beautifully built ships of the Yavanas".[6]

(ii) **Enjoyments**: It has been discussed that the *Harivaṃśa* betrays some foreign affiliation where it describes the Yādavas partaking a meal consisted of varieties of wine and meat roasted on iron roads.[7] The mention of 'beef' in a later work like this essentially makes it alien to Indian taste. It certainly bespeaks of a highly sophisticated society with rather lax morals.[8] It is more in accordance to the ostentatious taste of Oriental Rome than to the prescribed social moralities and native decencies known and advocated by the Brahmanical *Dharmaśāstras* and *Purāṇas*. This peculiarity point to an epoch, when contacts with Alexandria were most intensive, and when the Indian society was ruled by monarchs luxurious and cosmopolitan in their outlook.[9] This is just the period and picture described by the Periplus, i.e., the region of the Scythian Kṣatrapas in western India in the later half of the first century A.D.

(iii) **Festivities**: Special festivities known as *Surotsava* (drink festival) reminiscent of Greek Bacchanalia and Roman Saturnalia[10] were known in the days of the *Jātaka*.[11] There is reason to believe[12] that these ancient festivities were revived by the introduction of the Indo-Greeks and Scythio-Kushans, especially in the Mathura region. Bacchanals were very popular in the Hellenistic times and the Hellenized Bactrian Greeks and their successor the Scythio-Kushans soon identified these two festivities.[13]

The available facts indicate that the most celebrated festival of "Holi", which is an amalgamation of more than one ritual, owes its origin to this epoch. It was about this time that Kṛṣṇa was identified with Kāma or Madana,[14] and the ancient *Vasantotsava*[15] or *Madanamahotsava* concentrated around the cult of Kṛṣṇa.[16] The *Surotsava* and the Bacchanalia imparted the aspect of intemperate revelry to it while the other lesser local customs were added to diversify the observation.[17] That a foreign impetus worked under the development of the national festival "Holi" is attested by the fact that it is celebrated with a greater pomp and hilarious mood in north India, than in the southern part of the country. The evidences of Jātaka show that the "*Surotsava*" and the *Kārttikotsava*[18] too, the two precursors of Holi, were popular in north-eastern and north-western India, i.e., in the *Aryavarta*. To this day, the *Vasantotsava* is known as *Kāmadahana* in the South, where the tragic aspect of the festivity is stressed. But in the pages of *Ratnāvalī*[19] and *Bhaviṣyapurāṇa*[20] the more unbridled extravagant aspect of the festival is depicted, which betrays the colouring of Bacchanalia.

References

1. *Harivaṃśa*, M. N. Dutt, CCXXXV, "Some handsome damsels began to row in wooden boats in the shape of herons and serpents (27) etc.
2. Ibid., 27-28; 58-67.
3. R. D. Mookerji, Shipping, pp. 35-36, Pl. facing p. 36.
4. Periplus 44.
5. Mookerji, Pl. facing p. 33, boat decorated with the griffin's forepart from Sanchi.
6. Vide supra, p. 19, n. 19.
7. Vide supra, pp. 149-150.
8. The Yadavas whose mode represent the western Indian cultures are much addicted to hedonistic aspects of life.
9. All the great rulers of the period discussed viz., Chandragupta, Bindusāra, Aśoka, Gondopharnes, Kanishka, Rudradāman were more or less cosmopolitan in their outlook.
10. J. Ghosh, Jāt, Vol. V, p. 6.
11. The drink festival has been described in *Surāpāna Jātaka* (81); *Pāniya Jātaka* (459) – "it is the time honoured drinking festival"; *Mahāsutasoma Jātaka* (537) etc.
12. Vide infra, Chapter Five, Section on the Cult of Baladeva.
13. From the heterogenous style of depicting the Bacchanalian scenes on Mathura art there is every reason to believe that the foreigners took part in this festival.
14. Matsyap., 70, 37-40, *Madana* is identical with *Nārāyaṇa*.
15. *Śakuntalam*, VI.
16. *Pūjāpārvaṇa*, pp. 1-9.
17. N. K. Bose, I.A.C. Vol. II, 1953-54, pp. 375-387.
18. Vide above, n. 11.
19. Kārttikotsava is described in *Puppharatta Jātaka* (147), *Ummadanti Jātaka* (527) etc.
20. *Ratnāvalī* I; Bhavishyap. *Uttaraparva*, 132, 135.

Section VII

Dress and Costume

Foreign influence is much more conspicuous on dress and costumes of the Indian people, than on any other aspect of life. For the sake of clarity the section is divided into two parts and discussed separately: (i) first, the materials for the garments that came from outside, known chiefly from the literary sources, and (ii) secondly, the foreign elements that can be detected on sewn costumes, depicted in art and contemporary coins.

It is necessary to note the geographical zone with which India kept close contact and imported such merchandise. Scholars generally believe that India had trade relations with the Ancient Semitic world. The *Jātaka* stories like one of the *Bāveru Jātaka* relates how merchants of this land went in that far-off region and traded in peacock and other materials. Later on, when the Achaemenid rule in Iran and following it the Seleucid and Maurya governments assured safety in communications, trade with the occident received a new impetus. It thrived well under the Seleucid, the Parthians and Scythio-Kushans in the period that followed.

The region lying beyond the great mountain barrier of India, specially the countries of Bāhlīka and Central Asia also came within the scope of India's economic activities. The fine stuffs of Bāhlīka were much appreciated in India, while Cīna or China supplied her with silk, popularly known in the Sanskrit works as *Cīnapaṭṭa* or *Cīnāṃśuka*.[1]

(a) **Woolen stuffs**: Lying within the natural boundaries of India, countries like Kāmboja, Oḍḍiyāna (Swat Valley) and Gāndhāra developed industries inspired by foreign influences and aid. It may be noted in this connection that all these countries had been under Iranian rule (c. 520 B.C. to 330 B.C.) and Iranian traditions and art must have influenced to a great extent the craftsmen of these regions. The *Jātakas*[2] and the *Arthaśāstra*[3] refer to the *Kambalas* or blankets of these places while the

Sabhāparvan of the epic[4] enumerates numerous silken and woolen goods presented by Kāmboja to Yudhiṣṭhira.[5] Persia excelled in the art of carpet and tapestry-making from the very ancient days.[6] Various types of fine embroidery work were done in Achaemenid Iran, and in fact, "wagons had come over the mountains bringing from the store-houses of the old Persian king...Babylonian and Persian embroideries and many of this now found a home in the palace of Takṣaśilā".[7] It may be noted here further that the "*Vikaṭikā*" decorated with figures of lions and tigers referred to in the *Brahmajāla Sutta*[8] seems to have been manufactured after Persian design as these animals often found a place in the Achaemenid as well as early Sassanid art.[9]

Various types of skins having white, black or variegated wools on them were imported from the frontier region.[10] The different varieties of these products, dealt with a greater detail and care, show that the contemporary Indian nobility highly praised these stuffs. Many of them were imported from inner and outer Himalayas and were used as bed-spreads, sheets and coverings. Some derived their name from the place of manufacture, viz., *Auttara Parvataka* while others after the animal from which it was produced, viz. *Kadali, Rāṇkava* etc. Some were skins (*ajinas*) while others were woven woolen materials (Kambala, *aurṇa*). The material entitled as "*Bāhlīcīnasamudbhūtam*" was woven from the wool of the Ranka goat of the Pamir region.[11] It is also interesting to note that neighbouring Nepala supplied India with two distinct types of *Kambalas*, viz. *Bhiṅgisī*, and *Apasāraka*, which also served the purpose of water-proofs.[12] The *Matsyapurāṇa* (22.86) mentions *Nepala-Kambala*. Wollen materials, then as now were manufactured better in mountainous regions, and were imported from the frontier countries of north-west and high north.[13]

(b) **Silk**: After woolen materials comes the silk. The available evidences show that the silk industry became known to India in remote past, as early as the days of the *Śatapatha Brāhmaṇa* (c. 800 B.C.) and the *Aṣṭādhyāyī* of Pāṇini[15] which mention *Kauśeya*. The Chouli states that from eleventh century B.C. silk industry in China prospered into activity, the district of

Ping Chou (modern Shan-si) was noted for the finest texture.[16] It can be surmised that in India the art first reached the north-eastern frontiers, and the Kośakara country beyond the Lauhitya river, i.e., Assam reared this infant industry.[17] Most probably the native Kirātas of Assam learnt it from the Cīnas,[18] through silent barter carried on "by nods and signs".[19] Consequently the eastern part of India became the reputed silk producing area. Kauṭilya first enumerated the more famous Indian silks of his time and later on mention the *Cīnapaṭṭa*. Thus it is evident, that the art of silk manufacturing became known from China earlier, and the actual Chinese silk which reached this land at a later date through trade.

Numerous references to *Cīnapaṭṭa*, *Cīnāṃśuka* and "*Cīnasamudbhutam kītaja*" stuff in the *Āyāraṅgasutta*, the *Arthaśāstra* and in the epic show that during the early centuries of Christian era Chinese silk became quite well-known in India.[20] We reach a somewhat definite date by the evidence supplied by the Periplus of the first century A.D., which makes us believe that during the Rome-Parthian War, there had been no other alternative for the Roman traders but to get the Chinese silk from the west Indian ports.[21] Also the Greeks in India during the first century B.C. "imported for themselves silk and other articles from China".[22]

(c) **Skins**: Not only the silk, the *Cīnasī* (Chinese leather "the most valuable product which the Seres dye") were imported from Tibet (sometimes called Mahacina) and Turkestan to India via Bāhlīka and was titled Bāhlaveya. These were exported from Barbaricum to the Roman West. The "*Ajinas*" i.e., skins were highly praised in the epic.[23] We need not be surprised to find that exotic names came with the materials, and were incorporated in Indian languages. The Pāli term "*Gonako*" in *Brahmajālasutta*[24] as pointed out by Motichandra was derived from the Iranian sometime during c. 500 B.C.[25] Its Greek equivalent was "Kaunkes" or coats of skin enumerated in the Periplus,[26] The overcoat decorated with fur-trimmings in the Gāndhāra sculptures[27] is probably more akin to the Greek Kaunkes, than Pāli Gonaka which meant some bed-spread of fleecy texture.

(d) **Decorated Materials**: The same work mentions "*Paṭalikā*" or flowered sheet, probably identical with Polymita of the Periplus.[28] It is not altogether impossible that the famous Patola weaving of Gujarat owes its origin to this Polymita from Alexandria.

It may be suggested with some plausibility that both the rich and poor used foreign stuffs for their apparel. The thin clothings "of the finest weave" presented to Scythian king Nahapāna were evidently for the royal usages, while the coarser varieties imported were for the commoners. Schoff, thinks that the "bright coloured girdles" were worn by the Bhils, but it should be noted here that about this time the Bhils or the "phyllitai" of Ptolemy were living at a distance from the kingdom of Nahāpāna. It is not unlikely that these girdles were used by the Śabaras, (Suaries of Ptolemy) who had been living within the territorial jurisdiction of the Scythian king.[29] However, the ancient sculpture and literature amply show that decorated girdles were in general use also in ancient India.[30]

** ** **

(ii) Indians from the earliest times laid stress on unsewn garments. The graceful arrangements of the *Adhovāsa* (i.e., dhoti or sāri) and *Uttarīya* in pleats, kept in position with knots and elaborately decorated *Mekhalās* (gridle, belt) formed the characteristic national dress. All kinds of cut and sewn costumes, cloaks, chitons and trousures were "distinctive and novel in this land" and foreign to the taste the people. But was adapted as its utility was realized. First we would discuss the (a) dresses of men then (b) that of the women.

(a) **Men's costume**: The Indian soldiers, who were recruited by Xerexes from the north-western part of India, faught side by side with the Medes, the Sacae and the Bactrians possibly came to know the usage of scaled armours, and boots.

Here a few words about the shoes and sandals would not be out of place. Shoes were used by both males and females of wealthier classes.[31] The shoes were decorated with gemstones and were probably done with golden-thread or embossed with gold-work.[32] The *Mahāvagga* has quite an exhaustive discussion on different types of shoes and it is possible that some new varieties of shoes were introduced by the foreigners.[33] The leather shoes of Patañjali[34] were probably one of these while the wooden clog ones seems to be indigenous. It is also interesting to note that the *Carmakāras* (cobblers) are mixed in origin[35] and were untouchables. Probably a goodly portion of them were foreigners, i.e., *Mlecchas*, and settled in India with the invaders. From the detailed rule on the wearing of shoes laid down by Aṅgirasa it appears that the habit of wearing shoes and sandals was common enough.[36] Shoes are, however, depicted more often in the Gāndhāra sculpture and Mathura where western influence was profound. The most interesting reference to the highly polished shoes of Vasantasenā's mother[37] in the *Mṛchakaṭika* indicate that it was the result of a thorough Scythian environment of the city. It seems that shoes were more in use in the north-west, Punjab, Gujarat, Kathiawar, Rajasthan and Delhi-Mathura region than in the South and East where foreign impacts were not so predominant.

The epic has numerous references about strong armour decorated with coral and other gems. The epic heroes had uniform of their favourite colours. New varieties and designs were no doubt added by the increasing number of foreigners who migrated to India. The Greeks evidently introduced the himation and the chiton seen in the terracottas from Taxila and the short kilt worn by the soldier on the Sanchi relief.[38]

Another relief from Bharhut shows the sun-god in a north-western short-sleeved coat, *dhoti*, a ribbon around his head and with the typical Greek leggings.[39] The relief on the north-gateway depicts several figures wearing conical cap and close-fitting skull-cap with curious tuft floating behind.[40] Some of the skull-caps are thickly flowered with rosettes reminiscent of Graeco-Persian design. They are wearing short sleeved blouses with 'V' shaped fold on the chest, and a knee-length tight skirt having a flare at the rear. Some are wearing Chlamys knotted at the front in Greek fashion. All of them are depicted wearing laced sandals in Graeco-Roman fashion. It is not definitely known, whether this band of musicians in hybrid costume were foreigners, or natives of the land. Sculptors and craftsmen of Sanchi, and its vicinity, were acquainted with the foreign dresses from the neighbouring township of Vidiśā, where foreign envoys were received.

The kilt and the tightly worn *dhoti* soon gave place to the Scythio-Kushan trouser, which originated in Central Asia necessitated by the constant riding.[41] The uniform consisting of an armour or long coat, trousers, and high boots, brought by the nomadic tribes from Central Asia became very popular in Northern India, and was titled as the "*Udīcyaveśa*". The sun-icons of later ages were delineated in this costume.[42] All the Scytho-kushan rulers both in their coins and in their portrait statues are depicted in this dress, with a little variations probably due to personal taste and likings. Azelises is shown wearing tall helmet or headgear, coat and trousers.[43] Wima Kadphises in his royal statue appears in a coat finely embroidered around the cuff and front-opening and having been strewn rosettes all over.[44] The same type of border embroidery is found on the tunic of Caṣṭana.[45] It was a Scythio-Kushan fashion no doubt, as the foreign-ruler in Ajanta fresco is painted with the same kind of embroidered coat, "for in the early centuries of Christian era Śaka satrapies were established in Surāṣṭra and Malwa, in close vicinity to the Deccan, and artists of Ajanta must have known intimately foreigners of the type represented in the frescoes".[46]

In the squat seated effigy of an unknown Kushan chief, the latter wears a short-sleeved blouse decorated in front with inverted scale ornamentation. The characteristic heavy boot, a plain torque, a pair of bangles and a peculiar squat cap constitute the accessory. Kanishka, in his royal statue and in his coins is found wearing the stiff long coat, belowing trousers and high boot (See Plate No. 3).[47] His successors Vāsudeva and Huvishka appear in their gold coins,[48] as wearing respectively, a coat with front opening, tapering sides, sleeves reaching upto elbow, and tight trousers, the latter appears in jeweled helmet and open front coat. In the coin of later great Kushan[49] the trouser is rather close-fitting than the looser and heavier one of Kanishka. Loose trousers and full sleeved tunic with matching brocade or embroidered borders on edges, centre and around the ankles, popular among the Parthian high class nobles are carved patiently on the Hypogeum of Atenatan in Palmyra. It seems the men of highest rank wore a loose full-sleeved coat over the inner tunic.[50]

These tunic and trouser were adopted by the Indian rulers. Both Chandra Gupta I and his successor Samudra Gupta are seen in their coins in tight breeches and bead decorated coats.[51] Harṣavardhana and his contemporary chiefs used different varieties of tunics and trousers.[52] From the Gupta period onwards the long coat *Kañcuka* or *Vāravāṇa* became the court-dress of the king. Bāṇa saw Harṣa wearing a *Kañcuka*.

Several types of caps were introduced by the foreigners into this land. The high conical head-gear or helmet worn by Vāsudeva in his coins[53] appears with its variants on several heads found from Mathura region. (Pl. 4).[54] The high conical cap of the "Tigra-khaudā" probably gave rise to the *Kirīṭa* of the later sun-icons. It is not altogether improbable that the elegantly bejeweled high crowns of Bodhisattva in Ajanta painting[55] developed out of this foreign head-gear. There is ample proof to show that Indians, before the advent of the foreigners, used *Uṣṇīṣa* or turbans but this high conical head-gears were brought by the foreigners. Bharata in his *Nāṭyaśāstra* lay rules regarding the use of different types of *mukuṭas* (head-gears).

Another common type was the modern kulah-like cap with conical protuberance at the center. It is seen in foreign associations in the figure from Jaulian, Taxila[56] and in the scenes of 'Persian envoy' and 'wine-drinking' in Ajanta.[57]

Besides the close-fitting skull cap, two distinct types have been identified by scholars. The first, described as, "caps or helmets with crenellated front and knobbed top are generally worn by the soldiers of foreign extraction". The second variety "turban with a kula-like on creast or on the left side...Head on 2702 showing a peaked cap sloping backward".

(b) **Female costume**: It is curious enough that whereas the Scythio-Kushan costumes served as the model for male attire, Indian female dress was more susceptiable to Greek fashions.

The earliest archeological evidence during our period can be gleaned from the terracotta figurines of Bhir mound, Taxila, classified by Marshall. They show no trace of foreign influence except probably in one, in which the figurine "wears wide trousers (?) and veil hanging from top of the head down the back to each side". All the other figures are draped in full skirts or *dhoti* and *sāri* and scarf on the head, and show no noticeable foreign influence on their costumes. In both the Greek and Indian modes a voluminous sheet either *sāri* or the himation was draped around the body in different ways and was fastened with the help of knots or broaches. A loose chiton or petti-coat was worn by the Greek ladies with a peplos of considerable length arranged in various ways over-lapping the body. Both the apparels were loose enough, and sometimes the peplos was arranged in such a way as to raise difficulty in distinguishing it from the tunic underneath. Sometimes the peplos came under the right arm and went up the left shoulder covering the breast and the right shoulder. It thus assumed the appearance of the modern style of wearing the *sāri*. A peplos could cover both the lower and the upper part of the body, while the Indian *sāri* formerly covered only the lower part, and the remainder was hung down the front in graceful folds.

Various ways of draping the *sāri* have been delineated by the Gāndhāra artists. In the terracotta statues from Jaulian the wife of the donor is clad "in a long tunic like the Greek chiton, with a shawl (Indian *sāri*, Greek himation) draped loosely over the left arm and shoulder and round the legs in front, leaving the tunic visible over the upper part of the body". Here evidently the Chiton constitutes the main covering, and the "*Sāri*" or "himation" is merely added, to increase grace and modesty to the ensemble.

In another relief the *sāri* is wrapped in more concealing fashion and forms the chief garment, with an ensemble of scarf covering the head which "Perhaps indicate the married state". It is interesting to note that the dresses of the terracotta figurines found from the earlier Bhir Mound show no trace of foreign influence, except in one case where the figuriue wears a wide trouser (?) and veil hanging from top of the head down the back to each side.[58] All the other figures are draped in dhoti or *sāri*, and use a scarf on the head, and shows no noticeable foreign influence on their drapery.

Taking in view all the available data, Dr. Ghurye[59] comes to the conclusion that the modernistic mode of wearing *sāri*, i.e., to cover the lower and the upper part of the body with a single large piece of clothing "is first attested in foreign associations" on the females depicted in Gāndhāra sculptures. Once this mode evolved out of Greek fashion it became the most popular way of draping among the aristocratic ladies of north and north-east of India.[60]

The other most conspicuous way of draping the *sāri* that has been delineated by the artists of this country is the ensemble of *sāri* with an upper shirt or chiton. It seems that in this ensemble the *sāri* was worn in the "*Sakaccha*" style which resembled the *śilwār* and the blouse resembling the *pājāmā* and *kurtā* of the modern Punjabis. Sometimes a portion of the *sāri* was draped over the bosoms but generally the right breast was left uncovered.[61] The "*Sakaccha*" style left the legs free for more active movements and this was thus especially suited to the women guards and female attendants of the aristocratic household. Sometimes actual *śilwār* replaced the *sāri*. Noble ladies of foreign extraction adopted the long gown and the stole of Hellenistic origin.[62]

That the South Indian artists were well-acquainted with the more modernistic way of sāri-wearing is proved by the draped female figure in the bas relief of Nagarjunikonda, 3rd century A.D.[63] The pedestal of a Mathura inscription[64] shows four females standing wearing the *sāri* in a typical modernistic look (i.e., the material was taken upwards from the right waist, covering the breasts over the left shoulder).

Startling from the invasion of Alexander down to the early centuries of Christian era, –Iran, Bactria and Afghanistan, remained the melting pot of different cultures, viz. Iranian, Graeco-Roman, Scythio-Parthian and Kushan and consequently the successive waves of art and styles that reached India were a medley of traditions. This was strongly felt in the sphere of dress and costume too. But it is not difficult to determine among the various costumes, which were purely Greek, and which were brought by the nomads of Central Asia. It is obvious that while the more civilized people like the Greeks and Iranians added more delicacy and finery to their female costumes, the nomadic races attached no special grace to their female garments, both their male and female dresses remained quite coarse and heavy.

The genre-scenes from the Gāṇdhāra school display a large variety of cut and sewn costumes.[65] It is certain, that these coats and full-sleeved blouses were more in use in Gāndhāra, Kāmboja, Oḍḍiyāna and Kashmir where cold was severe. The womenfolk of Punjab are described in the great epic as "*Madrakāḥ kambalāvṛtāḥ*".[66] The Vāhīkan females are called "*sūkṣmakambalavāsinīm*"[67] and "*Kambalājinasaṃvītā*".[68] Their dresses were evidently made of woolen material and were in all probability sewn. A pair of donor couple from Sahri Bahlol furnish us with plastic representation of woolen costumes. The donor "is dressed in a long sleeved undergarment... ...made of some woolen material". His consort "seems very warmly dressed, having besides the shawl, which covers most of the body, an undergarment of similar material visible on the chest and left arm, and a second thick undergarment, which can be seen on both forearms and recalls that of the male donor".[69] Their heavy and bold features point to their foreign nomadic origin.

The Scythio-Kushans introduced the *śilwār* or female trousers. In the Harwan terracotta a dancing girl is depicted wearing *śilwār* and a Kāmiz-like shirt with tapering ends[70] reminiscent of the tunic worm by Vāsudeva in his gold coin. The ensemble of this type of tunic and tight trouser evidently became very popular among the *Narttakīs* in Gupta period. Two sculpture pieces from Deogaḍ (c. 500 A.D.) depict dancing girls wearing this very ensemble.[71] Dancing girls in Ajanta painting and musical groups in Bagh represent slight variations of these dresses. Rightly ḥas Altekar remarked that foreign fashions were first copied by the courtesans and dancing girls before it came to be generally accepted in the aristocratic society.[72]

Another type of costume generally used by the Śaka females, is seen on the figure of incense-bearer found from Fatehpur, Mathura. Same type of heavily embroidered *Kañcuka* or coat with a very light undergarment is worn by a female donor from Sirkap, Taxila, (See Plate No. 5)[73] As "found in stratum II (Pre-Kushan), the figure is dated by Hargreaves in the early first century A.D.", so the dress is all probability purely Scythian. The Śaka wine-bearer in the Bacchanalian scene of Ajanta, is described as, "wearing a round cap of red material (broad cloth or velvet) with a white border, which is either of fur or some woolen material. A white plume springs from the top of the cap. Her upper garment is a long coat, with tight sleeves; it is embroidered at the collar, the shoulders and cuffs. The lower garment is a long white shirt with a frilled border of pale blue colour. The style of the skirt may suggest Greek influence, but it is difficult to affirm this with any authority, for no dates are available regarding the dress of the people of the north-west before the advent of the Greeks".[74]

Especially the attendants and servants of royal household came under the exotic influences. Motichandra draws our attention to the interesting fact that, "the Nāyādhammakahao mentions female foreign slaves wearing their own national costumes (Videsaparimaṃdiyāhiṃ). These slaves serving in the palaces must have exercised certain influence on the costume of the servant class as a whole".[75]

The most eloquently and poetic description rendered by Bāṇabhatta in Harṣacarita (Ucch. I) of Bāṇinī Mālatī attests how far the dress of female couriers of Indian court were evolved out of the Scythian dress. Mālatī wears a diaphenous *kañcuka* of white *Netravāsa* over her undergarment, which is described thus, "Underneath gleaned a petticoat of safflower tint and variegated with spots of different colours, as if she wore a crystal ground enclosing a treasure of jewels". Her long pendant ear-drops of pearls and the blue net over half of her face are clearly western and foreign to typical Indian taste.[76]

Another distinct type of dress is referred to in the epic while describing the bridal costume of Subhadrā. She is called "*raktakauśeyavāsinīm*"[77] and "*gopālikāvapuḥ*". *Harivaṃśa* too, refers to the colourful costumes of the *gopakanyās*; but both the works remain silent about the particulars of the dress. The gap is probably filled up by a sculpture from Deogaḍ depicting the "Turning of the Śakata" in which Yaśodā is wearing a shirt with sides open, showing the heavy flares of the *ghāgarā* tied around her waist. The hair is piled up high on which rests a flowing scarf, while an ornamental band is fastened around the forehead. (See Plate No. 6). The *Bhāgavatapurāṇa* describes this dress vividly.[78] This delineation is reminiscent of modern Jāṭ and Gujarati women of northern and western India, the head-dress being specially akin to that of the womenfolk of Rajasthani peasants and the Banjara nomads.[79]

References

1. Shamasastry, p. 83.
2. Mahāvāṇija Jātaka (221), Mahāummagga Jātaka (546) and Vessantara Jātaka (547) refer to the red *Kambalas* of Gāndhāra which was a highly praised stuff like the cloths from Kāśī and Kauṭumbara.
3. Shamasatry, pp. 81-82.
4. P.C. Ray, Sabhap. Sect. LI, "The king of Kāmboja gave innumerable skins of the best kinds, and blankets made of wool of soft fur of mice, and other animals living in the holes, and of the hair of the cats, and all inlaid with threads of gold". cf. Shammasatry, p. 81, "Sātinā, Nalatūlā and Vātapucchā are the skins of aquatic animals (Audra)", – these evidently remind us of the garments of the beaver skins worn by Anāhita of Bactra and the beaver-hunting scene in the ivory reliefs from Begram.
5. P.C. Ray, op. cit., "...the Vāhikas presented numerous blankets of woolen texture manufactured in China, and numerous skins of the Raṇku deer, and clothes manufactured from jute and other from the threads of the insects".
6. Holdich, GI, p. 52ff.
7. CHI, Vol. I, p. 322.
8. Rhys Davids, p. 12, "embroidered with figures of lions and tigers".
9. Ghirshman, Iran, pls. 275-281 ff.
10. Shamasastry, pp. 81-82, "Blankets made of sheep's wool may be white, purely red or as red as a lotus flower" cf. Mbh. 2.49.22

(Haridas) – "*Kamalābhaṃ*".

11. Motichandra, PBVB, p. 59.
12. Shamasastry, p. 82, Products of Nepal: Apsāraka and Bhiṅgisī.
13. Ibid., p. 81, f.n. 10, *Dvādaśagrāma*, i.e., Twelve Villages on the Himalayas were inhabited by *Mlecchas*.
14. *Śatapatha Brāhmaṇa*, ii. II.1.8; Motichandra, p. 23.
15. *Aṣṭādhyāyī*, IV. 3.42.
16. Sehoff, p. 263.
17. Rām mentions the Kośakara country; Motichandra, p. 51.
18. The Kirātas and Cīnas generally find mention together in the Sanskrit literature.
19. Schoff, p. 267; Ammi Marcellinus, "they interchange no conversation but settle the office of the articles by nods and signs". etc.
20. Mbh. 2.47. 22-23 (B.O.R.I.); 2.49.21-22 (Haridas).
21. Schoff, p. 172.
22. Tarn, GBI, p. 364.
23. Periplus, 39; Schoff, p. 172; Shamasastry, pp. 80-81, see for various types of skins, "Sāmūra, Chīnasī, and Sāmulī are (skins) procured from Bāhlava (Bāhlaveya)". Cf. Mbh. 2. 49.23 (Haridas) "*Mṛducājinam*".
24. Rhys Davids, p. 12 "(3) Goat's hair coverlets with very long fleece (Gonaka)".
25. Delaporte, Mesopotemia, pp. 69, 182, 194, etc., Motichandra, PBVB, p. 32.
26. Schoff, p. 7, 72.
27. J.B. Bhusan, Costumes and Textiles of India, p. 17, fig. 2.
28. Schoff, p. 167, "Polymita" has been translated as "figured lines".
29. McCrindle, p. 159-60, Var. "Bhyllitai".
30. The girdles were made of metals or stiff materials studded and fringed with beaded decorations. See Zimmer, pls. 33 (a,b,c), 34 (a,b), 35 (a,b), all belonging to first century B.C.
31. Vessantara Jātaka (547) refers to shoes used by Mādrī.
32. Mahāummagga Jātaka (546).
33. Mahāvagga, pp. 246-247, f.n. 7, note especially the "*Puṭabaddha*" i.e., the knee-boot called "*Yonaka*" cf. Arr. Faga, ICGW, p. 113.

34. Patañjali, "*Upanaḥ carmāḥ*", Puri, p. 103.

35. Vide supra, p. 92.

36. Aṅgirasa, 62-63; Dutt, p. 275.

37. *Mṛcchakatika*, IV.

38. Marshall, Taxila, II, pp. 448-449, nos. 30, 31, 33, – "wears long coat crossed over chest, with waist band and trousers". Zimmer, pl. 30, from Stupa No. 2, c. 110 B.C.

39. B.M. Barua, Barhut, III, Fig. LXII. 71, "Mihita, the sun-god of Uttarāpatha" is delineated in a combination of a string-tied coat and pleated *dhoti*. A fillet around the forehead and knee-boots (*yonaka*) complete the costume.

40. Zimmer, pl. 10, from the Great Stupa, north gate, early first century A.D.

41. McGovern, p. 2.

42. Vide infra, Chapter Five, Sec. on Sun Cult.

43. PMC, Pl. XIV 356.

44. Zimmer, Pl. 59, cf. Delaporte, pp. 182, 194, the rosettes came to the Babylonian costume from Hittite art. The Indo-Scythians then adopted it from the Achaemian art that evolved out from Babylonian style.

45. Agrawala, Hand book, no. 212.

46. According to Ghirshman this panel was copied from Sassanian repertory in toto; cf. Yazdani, pp. 46, 50, "the general contour of the face proves him to be of Turanian race rather then Persian...He is wearing a long coat (Quba) of pale blue broad-cloth, the collar, arm-bands and cuffs of which are of a lighter colour and probably embroidered".

47. Agrawala, MMC, p. 39; Zimmer, pl. 61; cf. the statue of the Kushan monarch wearing a pair of fuller trousers with decorated ankles and caftan from Surkh Kotal, Ghirshman, p. 5.

48. National Museum, New Delhi, coins nos. 51, 151, 54.24/26.

49. C.I. Brown, pl. IV, Fig. 10.

50. Ghirshman, pls. 90, 91.

51. Altekar, Bayaya Hoard, pls. XXXVIII-XLIII, pp. cli-clvii. cf. the dress of the Iranian donor from Sahr-I-Bahlol, Ingholt, pl. 417, See Plate No. 3 (b) in the Illustration. "The caftan is visibly longer at the sides than at the centre and has a beaded decoration at the neck down the front to the waist, and down the fronts of the

trouser's legs. The beaded line on the left breast no doubt indicates a fastening of the caftan".

52. *Harṣacarita*, II, Cowell, p. 59, "...thin upper garment spangled with worked stars" reminds us of the embroidered rosettes of the Scythio-Parthan caftans. Ibid., p. 202.
53. PMC, pl. XIX 216, "peaked helmet".
54. cf. Agrawala, Handbook, Fig. 13 and no. G32; Motichandra, IISOA, pp. 201, (Fig. 31-32), 203, 210 (Fig. 65-7), 211. Ingholt, pl. 287 note the high crown of the foreign donor.
55. Zimmer, pl. 151, from innumerable other sculpture pieces belonging to Gupta period it seems that the high tiara adopted from Iran became the fashion of the day.
56. Marshall, Taxila III, pl. 471.
57. Yazdani, Pls. XXVIII, XXXIV.
58. Marshall, Taxila, II, p. 443.
59. Ghurye, Indian Costumes, pp. 83, 85 ff.
60. This style has been unanimously adopted all over India at present.
61. Ingholt, Pls. 39A-B, 43, 361, 362, 364.
62. Ibid., Pls. 310, 341, 400, 401.
63. Stella Kramrisch, The Art of India, Pl. 35, Andhra third century A.D.
64. Lohuizen du Leeuw, Pl. 66.
65. All these types have been classified and discussed in detail by Motichandra and Ghurye.
66. Mbh. 8.27.89 (B.O.R.I.).
67. Ibid., 8.30.20.
68. Ibid., 8.30.22.
69. Ingholt, pp. 161, Pls. 415, 416.
70. Kak, AMK, Pl. XXVIII. 12.
71. National Museum, New Delhi.
72. Altekar, PWAI, pp. 288, 295.
73. Ingholt, Pl. 144, p. 167, "She is dressed in a cloak open in the front and recalling those worn by both Parthian and Kushan nobles and known from Hatra, Shotorak, Surkh Kotal and Mathura. Over the cloak at the back two plaits of hair can be seen. Under the cloak she wears a transparent undergarment reaching to the feet, and besides crossing breast-bands, she has a neck-lace, a jewelled girdle and anklets". Curiously enough the cloak remained the

costume of the female couriers till quite late, Vide Illustration Plate No. 5 (b).

74. Yazdani, p. 48.

75. Motichandra, TISOA, 1944, p. 5; PBVB, p. 141.

76. Cf. Cowell, Appendix I, pp. 261-62, with the translation rendered by P.N. Tagore which seems more appropriate for the original "*nīlāṃśuka jālikayeva niruddhārdhavadana*," etc.

77. Mbh. I. 214, 19.

78. *Bhāgavatapurāṇa*, X.IX. 3, "*Kṣaumaṃ-vāsaḥ pṛithukaṭitaṭe vibhrati sūtranaddam*".

79. Bhushan, Costumes & Textiles of Ind., Pls. XXXVII, IX.

Section VIII

The Art of Coiffure

A few lines may be said to show that foreign hair styles were adopted by fashionable Indians of the day. The female figures from Mathura show rich and diverse hair-styles.[1] A curious passage from *Viṣṇupurāṇa*[2] states that the women in the *Kaliyuga* would be proud in displaying their coiffures, and would not care for riches of other kinds. This is a sure proof to the sarcastic view of the orthodox Brahmanical society towards the extravagance of the ladies towards showy coiffure-making with costly decorations. This is moreover corroborated by the variety of names used for the different hair-styles in Bharata's *Nāṭyaśāstra,* in the *Amarakoṣa* and in the works of Kālidāsa.[3]

Prof. Goetz has found at least two distinct 'foreign' types of coiffure,[4] that came to India from Roman Empire. One is the '*Alaka*' in which masses of curled hair are arranged in wig-like fashion, this was specially in vogue amongst the men. The other was the '*Kumbhabandhana*', which was derived from the aristocratic ladies of Roman East, chiefly from Palmyra. In this style the hair was arranged in a flat knot over the head like a cushioned cap that was held in position with a fillet or a diadem. This style was very popular in the north western parts of India as seen from its numerous representation in the Gāndhāra sculptures.[5] The '*Bhramaraka*' style[6] in which a row of short curls resembling the black-bumble-bees were pearched on the forehead was also in vogue among the ladies of the royal society during the Gupta of period. It is needless to add that these influences reached India in the Kushan and later Kushan periods when contact with the Roman west was most prevalent.

The varieties were increased by the advent of the new nomadic races such as the Ābhīras, Śakas, Kushans etc. and the new styles combined with the traditional Indian ones gave rise to innumerable chignons that are attested from the late Kushan and Gupta sculptures, terracottas and Ajanta paintings.[7] The 'held-high'[8] arrangement so common amongst the aristocratic ladies had a singularly western look and was the outcome of foreign modes introduced.

*** *** ***

Lastly we may take note of the festival of hair-washing mentioned by Strabo.[9] Though it had not direct bearing on the art of coiffure, it seems , from the reference of Herodotus[10] to a like custom prevailing in Persia, that it was adopted in India from Achaemenid Iran, The vivid description of the festive occasion no doubt show how this foreign royal ceremony may have been adopted with all its ostentatious pomp and grandeur by the ancient Indians of this period.

References

1. Agrawala, MMC, p. 54, F 6; p. 55, F. 16; p. 60, KT 146, KT 242, 261 etc.; K.M. Munshi, The Saga of Ind. Sculp. Pl. 31 (a).
2. Viṣṇup., V. I. 16-17, 21, "*Strīyaḥ kalau bhaviṣyanti svariṇyā lalita-spṛihā*". etc.
3. Nāṭya, XXI. 67-70, note the "*dviveṇī*" or the double plaits of the Ābhīra maidens, included within the description of the other provincial coiffures. It appears that the "*alaka*" i.e., the "wig-like" style was prevalent in Avantī region and the "*sumunnaddha*" i.e., "held high" fashion was popular in the northern regions. Cf. Strabo, xv. I. 71, ICGW, p. 111.

   Amarakoṣa, ii., 1266-1270; Kālidāsda *Meghadūta*, Pūrva, 33; *Ṛitusaṃhāra*, II 21; IV 5 etc. refer to the treatment of the hair with frankincense, which undoubtedly came into vogue, due to the intimate trade contact with Arab.

   The interesting reference to "long tresses" of women in *Mṛcchakaṭika* (IX) show the hair-style was the centre of beauty.
4. Goetz, East & West, Vol. X, 1959, no. 3, p. 177 ff.; DCA, pp. 266-268.
5. Marshall, Buddhist Art, pl. 30; cf. The cushioned effect Zimmer, Pls. 227, seventh century A.D., the female head at the left, 228, 236 etc; Motichandra, JISOA, 40 Vol. VIII, p. 113, "Pliny has noted...there was a demand for chaplets imported from India, made of nard leaves on fabrics or else of silk of many colours steeped in unguents".
6. Roman Panorama, Pl. III. Fig. (i); cf. The coiffure from Ajanta, Motichandra, op. cit., p. 112, Fig. 23; p. 137 ff. Fig. 82 (*Alaka*

worn by men); 90, 112. Cf. Zimmer, pl. 108 (b), "Angel of the Discus" wears a peculiar combination of "*Bhramaraka*" with three top-knots. The treatment is somewhat reminiscent of Gāndhāra style.

7. Marshall, Buddhist Art, pls. 61, 77 (Fig. 112), 84 (Fig. 110); Zimmer, Pls. 63, 64 (a) note the highly sophisticated arrangement of curls on Buddha's head, 64 (b), 68, 76 etc. Marshall thinks that this top-knot held within the circlet of chaplets or wreaths was the mark of Scythio-Parthian nobility and was adopted by the Indians to stress the high-rank or often divine or super-human rank of the wearer, see Nāṭya, on the coiffure of *Devīs, Vidyādharīs, Nāginīs* etc. "*Dhammilla*" or the "*cūḍā*" marks the aristocracy.
8. Note the hair-do of the females in Gupta sculptures, Zimmer, Pls. 105 (b), 105 (c), 111 (the female figure at the right corner), 114, 118, 233 etc.
9. Strabo, XV. I. 69, ICGW, p. 109-111.
10. Herod. ix. 110.

Section IX

The Art of Jewellery

A short section may be added to see how far western motifs and craftsmanship enhanced the growth of jewellery and ornamental art of India.

The Indians from very ancient times were inclined towards wearing ornaments on nearly every part of their body, and in this field of craftsmanship the goldsmiths and jewellers showed their indigenous genius. The Graeco-Scythian influence added only some novel motifs and characteristic to their repertory.

The Iranians were very fond of the lion motif, and in fact bangles or bracelets and rhytons with lion's head have been found from Iran.[1] The *Sihañgadā* mentioned in the *Mahāvastu*[2] probably refers to this bangle with the lion motif.

Some jewellery, specially ear-pendants have been unearthed at Sirkap[3] which must have been imported or may be the works executed directly by the Greek artists. The ear ornaments and necklaces with cupid or Eros and Psyche riding sea-lions are also of pure Greek taste. They were used by the Bactrian Greeks, but their association with the Bodhisattva figures,[4] show that Indians of noble birth also appreciated and adorned themselves with Greek jewellery. The much ornamented sandal which is seen on the feet of the Bodhisattva[5] and allusion to which are found in many a Buddhistic works,[6] must have been the combined products of a Greeco-Indian taste, and much more suitable and decent-looking to Indian climate than the Central Asian high boots of Scythio-Iranian import.

A peculiar cylindrical ear-hanging is seen on the figure of Hārītī[7] from Skarah Dehri and from Sikri[8] it was indeed, popular amongst the Scythians, but did not find much appreciation with Indian taste.

The other types of long hanging ear-pendants, in the shape of lozenge, a cluster, or a triangular "*jhumkā*" seem to have gained popularity in India;[9] the leaf-like shape (*pānpātā*) or a cluster of trinkcets, cat-bells or foliage forms in ornaments are still found in Pakistan, Punjab, Rajasthan and western India,[10] and at a much later point of time the aristocratic ladies of Mughal court were seen with it. The womenfolk of these regions wear ear-ornaments more elongated and pendant type than in any other parts of India.[11] For example the ear-ornaments of Eastern India, Deccan and South are shorter, have a floral roundel, or of the simple ring (i.e., *Kuṇḍala*) type. It is evident, that the original Indian ear-ornaments were of *Kuṇḍala* or *pāśā* (roundels), while those brought from the nomads of the west were the longer ones embellished with a profusion of bells and trinkets. Tiny bells and trinkets form a characteristic part of the ornaments used by Indian nomadic tribes of Bānjārās, Jats etc. of Rajasthan, and the village-folks of Kashmir and Kāngra[12] and the Ārāvalli.

The necklaces formed by attaching a number of plaques: round, oval, square and rectangular by means of hinges seems to have come the west i.e., Parthian,[13] Iran; and is still current in Pakistan, Punjab, Afghanistan and Rajasthan.[14] Some of it are strung on cords and the shapes are variegated, into triangles, half circles, or hearts. However, the similar designs could be indigenous Indian as well.

The art of enamelling (*minā*) on gold for which Jaipur (Rajasthan) is famous, seems to have its foundation in this Graeco-Scythian epoch,[15] because Taxilan city of Sirkap have yielded the oldest specimens of enamelling art,[16] found on necklaces and bracelets. The setting of stones also owes its origin to the Scythians who were masters of encrusting gold with variegated stones. This craft was no doubt the precursor of the '*Kundan*' jewellery of Rajputana and Delhi. '*Kundan*' work especially present a polychrome effect, while the South is distinguished for setting precious stones of uniform colour like diamonds rubies or beryls, and Bengal and Orissa for finest work in pure gold or silver. The peculiar colourful effect of a planned design is presented by the '*Kundan*' of north-west, and sometimes in the typical Tibetan or Nepalise jewellery, which had every chance to come into contact with the Central Asian tribes. The belt of the headless torso of Caṣṭana from Mathura, made up of alternative round and square plaques present a typical stone replica of polychromed gold waist band.

It seems that while Indians used bangles to adorn their fore arms, the brancelets were used in the west. Bracelets have been found in Iran[17] and similar one in Taxila, Sirkap.[18] Bracelets of two different types are known as "*Khāḍu*" and "*Māntāsa*", while the "*Valaya*" or bangles are more in use in South and Eastern India, the clasped bracelets are popular in the west and north-west.

The particular triangular and diamond shape in jewellery as found in so many north-west Indian ornaments[20] was introduced by the Scythians and Persians among whom geometrical and animal forms[21] were prevalent.

References

1. *Sihāñgadā* is identical with the gold bracelet from Oxus Treasure, Ghirshman, Pl. 41 rhytons with winged lions; cf. Tamara Talbot, p. 145, p. 17.
2. *Mahāvastu*, II, p. 56, n. 1, "*Sihañgadā*" ise. Lion Bracelet.
3. Marshall, Vol. III, Pl. 190, for description see Vol. II, p. 620 ff. cf. Greek Women, p. 173, the ear-rings represented "swan ...a dove on a delicate pedestal, a bunch of grapes...or a sphinx..." etc. For similar ear-rings with crouching griffins see Tamara Talbot, p. 146, Fig. 51.
4. Rowland, Pl. 35.
5. Lohuizen de Leeuw, |Pl. XII. 18.
6. Vide supra, p. 170, ns. 32, 33.
7. Lohuizen de Leeuw, Pl. XII, 19, the torque is better executed than the ear-pendant.
8. Ingholt, Pl. 340, pp. 145-46.
9. Lohuizen de Leewu, Pl. IV. 6; XVI. 25; J.B. Bhushan, Jewellery, p. 62.2; Ingholt, Pl. 443, see the ear-pendant of Roma.
10. Bhushan, op. cit., Pl. LXVIII.1,2; Pl. XXXIX ear-rings; LXXV. cf. Ghirshman, Pl. 112, the ear-ornament with pendants.
11. Ibid., pl. LXX. 2; pl. LXXIV, 1.
12. Ibid., pl. XIX.
13. Ghirshman, Pl. 112, Parthian jewelleries (1st-3rd centuries A.D.). Similar ones are noted on the necklace of the royal lady from Palmyra, see Pl. 92; cf. the jewelleries of Aqmat with those on Gupta female figures; Zimmer, Pl. 233 note the diadem on the head.

14. Bhushan, Pl. XLI, 3; XXIV. 1; XLII, LXXV. See Tamara Talbot, Pl. 18, the precursor of "Champākali" style.
15. Bhushan, p. 53.
16. Marshall, Taxila, Vol. II, p. 606 (427); III, Pl. 191, inlay works, nos. 167, 168, 173. McGovern, pp. 49, 59 on polychromy practiced by the Scythians.
17. Ghirshman, Pl. 80.
18. Marshall, Taxila, III, Pl. 196, for description see II, p. 635.
19. Bhushan, Pl. XXII. 2.
20. Vide the Plates of North-Western jewellery in Bhushan's volume, Pls. XXXV. 7; XXXIX, XLI, LXV etc.
21. McGovern, p. 59; Tamara Tablot, pp. 27, 133; Pl. 14, 144; Ghirshman, Pl. 124 note the triangular ear-pendants of the goddess (2nd-1st centuries B.C.).

Plate No. 1
Danda-dhara in Iranian costume
from a stone pilaster (in relief)
Nagarjunikonda; second century A.D.
Now at: National Museum, New Delhi

Plate No. 2
The Coffin of the Buddha
Gandhara School, Peshawar
From: Ingholt, Pl. 144

Plate No. 3
Gold Coin of Kanishka
Showing the Scythian Royal Dress
Second Century A.D.
Now at: National Museum, New Delhi

Plate No. 3b
Donor in Scythian Costume
note the caftan and the trousers with studded decorations
Gandhara School, Sahr-i-Bahlol
From Ingholt, Pl. 417

Plate No. 4
Head of a Scythian with Conical Cap
"Tigrakhauda"
Scythio-Kushan period, Mathura
Now at: National Museum, New Delhi

Plate No. 5
Female Donor garbed in Scythio-Parthian Court Dress
Sirkap, Taxila, first century A.D.
from: Ingholt, Pl. 441

Plate No. 5b
A Gopini Duti, i.e., messenger
note the short coat worn over the kanculika and ghagara
from: Maukhira, Burdwan, West Bengal
19th century A.D.

Plate No. 6
Bala-Krisna thwarting the Sakata
note the Scythian Costume of Yasoda consisting the high head-gear, chaplet, open-sided shirt and petti-coat
Gupta School, Deogarh, Sixth Century A.D.
Now at: National Museum, New Delhi

Plate No. 7
The City-wall of Kusinagara
note the concave curve of the towers, the battlements, the triangular openings and the western entablature of the doorway
Gandhara School, Peshawar
from: Ingholt, Pl. 152

Plate No. 8
Guards at the Citywall and the Gate
note the oblong and the cross-shaped watch-holes on the towers
Gandhara School, Peshawar
from: Ingholt, Pl. 464

Plate No. 9
Erotes, carrying the Laurel-wreath
note the highly stylized treatment of the leaves and the fillets
Gandhara School
Now at: National Museum, New Delhi

Plate No. 10
The Iranian Tutelary Couple
Farro and Ardoksho, the Kushan substitutes for Buddhist Pancika
Hariti and Brahmanical Kubera and Lakshmi
note the wreath, cornucopia and the leggings. The purse, the horn of plenty and the upturned jars indicate abundance and riches
Gandhara School, Sahr-i-Bahlol
from: Ingholt, Pl. 345

Four

Fine Art

This chapter needs no special introduction because it is obvious that fine arts itself is the most prominent aspect of culture. By this time, we have seen that one has to depend mostly on the evidences of fine arts while reconstructing the history of western influences on Indian culture.

The first section of this chapter deals with the question of foreign influences on contemporary Indian architecture. The second section describes the different schools of sculpture that flourished under the patronage of foreign dynasties or imbibed a great deal of exotic materials. The following section deals with the aspects of the art of painting, that were enriched by a compilation and assimilation of foreign ideas and techniques. A section has been added to indicate exotic impacts upon some miscellaneous branches of minor arts. A discussion of foreign influences on music, dance and drama has been added at the end.

This chapter actually connects the foregoing chapter on "Social Life" with the following chapter on "Religion" and serves as a bridge in between. The foreign impacts are much more conspicuous and the borrowing on part of India is more in the aspect of culture. So this discussion helps the interpretation and understanding of both the other branches that have been dealt with in this book.

It is obvious that art is not an isolated expression but is intimately connected with the political, economic as well as socio-religious atmosphere prevailing in a country, the spiritual and aesthetic emancipations of a particular age. Consequently, strong exotic influences found in the visual expressions of art belonging to this period mark a extant mode in the socio-religious life of India.

In the guiding light of the evidences gleaned from the vast repository of artistic representations, our assumptions on the vague probabilities become more definite possibilities; thus, this chapter by itself possesses an immense value for the understanding of the whole subject undertaken and reviewed in the pages of this proposition.

Section I

Architecture

The extant monumental remains on which some traces of foreign influence are seen may be divided into several groups, according to their age and their architectural design.

Group i. Maurya Age

Court: (a) The remains of the Maurya Court at Kumrahar, Patna (c. 272 B.C.–232 B.C., but probably earlier).

Fortification: (b) The palisade at Bulandibagh, Patna[1] (c. 321 B.C.–232 B.C. but probably during the earlier part).

Columns: (c) The monolithic columns of Aśoka belonging to his 26-27 reignal year (c. 245 B.C.) But some columns might have been pre-existing at his time.

Rock-cut Sanctuaries: (d) The Sudāmā and the Lomaś Ṛiṣi group of caves in Barabar and Nagarjuni Hills, Bihar (c. 250-220 B.C.)[2]

Group ii. Śuṅga Period

Stupas: (a) The *Stupas* and *Toraṇas* of Bharhut and Sanchi. The architectural development marked here is indigenous but some occasional ornamental motifs of western Asiatic origin are found.[3] (Third Century B.C. to First Century A.D.).

Colums: (b) The Besnagar *Garuḍadvaja* of Heliodorus (c. 150 B.C.).[4] Though this was endowed by a Greek resident from Taxila, the column and the shaft show nothing very typically foreign except the Persepolitan shape of the bell and the palmyra branches on its capital.

Caves: (c) The rock-cut sanctuaries at Bhaja (c. 50 B.C.) which is the stylistic development from the tradition of the Lomaś Ṛiṣi cave and forms an intermediary stage in between the earliest at Bihar and the later ones in the Western Ghats. Except for the idea of carving shrines out of living rock, the entire stylistic development was purely Indian.

Group iii. The Graeco-Parthian and Scythian period

Secular Buildings: (a) The city of Sirkap,[5] Taxila (from second century B.C. to the reign of Wima Kadphises shortly before c. 78 A.D.).

Group iv. The Kushan period & Later

Secular Buildings: (a) The city of Sirsukh, Taxila[6] (from c. 78 A.D. to its destruction by the Huns in the middle of sixth century A.D.)

(b) The monasteries of Jaulian and Mohra Moradu (end of first century or beginning of second century A.D. to sixth century A.D.).

(c) The ivory works from Begram[7] show the representations of contemporary architecture (flourishing period c. 78 A.D.-241 A.D.)

Caves: (d) The rock-cut sanctuaries at Bamiyan[8] (early second century A.D-sixth century A.D.).

Shrines: (e) The remains at Harwan and Ushkar, Kashmir[9] (the former shrine probably belong to c. 300 A.D. and the stupa structures below the existing stupa dates from third-fourth century A.D.).

The type of masonry i.e., diaper pebble applied at Harwan show it's intimate connection with the Kushan city of Sirsukh.

The study of foreign elements in Indian architecture is greatly supplemented by the representations of architectural motifs in the contemporary religious and genre scenes depicted in reliefs.

The Achaemenid influence on Indian architecture can be called posthumous, because during the dynasty ruling over parts of Gāndhāra and Sind any such influence was unknown farther east, even if any trend of it had possibly reached this land it remained confined to the courts of the local rulers of Punjab as presumed by Rawlinson.[10] But this is only an assumption because no extensive archaeological remains of sixth-fifth century B.C. from this part of India have come to light so far. The Achaemenid Order, if it may be called so in architecture came into India by the artists from Seleucid Iran from Chandragupta Maurya's reign onwards.[11]

(Group i, a & b): No such archeological finds, is extant at present or have been unearthed so far, except the great pillared Hall at Kumrahar and the palisade at Bulandibagh, Patna, which can be dated to Chandragupta's reign. The massiveness of these constructions still to be found, together with the grandeur of the then Pāṭaliputra, described by Megasthenes[12] and Strabo[13] and other classical writers, and the description of fortress building given by Kauṭilya[14] offer an impressive and picturesque idea about the Mauryan capital which vied with the magnificence of Ecbatana and Susa.

The Indians, of that time were no doubt skilled builders and engineers in wooden architecture as the huge palisade at Bulandibagh proves; but workmanship and the usage of large stones for construction was indeed a memorable contribution of the West, the fruitful result of India's cultural contact with Achaemenid and Seleucid Iran.[15] The Greeks gained mastery over this craft quite early and those Greek or semi-Greek artisans who worked under the powerful heirs of Babylonian and Assyrian sovereigns naturally became well-acquainted with the popular repertory of the set-motifs used by the earlier western Asiatic artists. The stone-carvers of Susa and Persepolis were in fact Ionian and Sardian Greeks,[16] who worked out the designs in a hybrid style combining the Greek and Assyrian forms.[17] This mixed style reached the soil of India through the foreign western artists and thus we find Ionian columns with Assyrian palmette motif and Ionian side-volutes at the Hall of Chandragupta or Aśoka.[18]

It has been unanimously accepted by most of the scholars that the superb quality of hyaline polish which singularly adorn the Mauryan constructions and carvings owes its origin to Achaemenid Iran and marks the cultural indebtedness of India to Seleucid Iran.[19]

It has been long since scholars have devoted their time and energy to find out how this imported foreign art aroused the popular imagination to invent or create tales. This single and unique extant archaeological evidence of a Court with rows of pillars inspired by the foreign impetus is probably referred to an allusion in the respository of the great epic. In the Sabhāparvan Kṛṣṇa orders Maya, the Dānava (i.e., Asura) architect, "Build, thou a mansion, in which we may be hold (a mixture of) celestial, Asura and human designs".[20] Though any detail with regard to the three types designs is not supplied, or to deduce something from this legendary account would be too far-fetched, yet, this much can be surmised that notions about three types of buildings were present. The episode further states that the "Asura went away in a north-easterly direction...possessed himself of the whole of the great wealth which was guarded by Yakṣas and Rākṣasas". The Dānava architect collected his "rough materials" from the palace of the Asura king Vṛṣaparvā[21] which lay towards the north, of Mount Kailāsa. It is in vain to search for historical evidences in these legendary accounts, yet one feels inclined to imagine the existence of some remote tradition, which must have been responsible for such a context. Does the episode of Maya's fetching material from Asura Vṛṣaparvā has some distant affiliation with Aśoka's introducing foreign artists and foreign technique? Groups of foreign masons, artisans and architects working with large blocks of stones and huge shafts carried from far and wide must have aroused wonder amidst the common folks and looking to the gigantic monument thus erected, the later generation exclaimed that it was no work of mortal hands. To them the distant foreign engineers of bygone days became the genii or *asuras*.[22] It is quite likely that stories of the Asura Architect became current just after the great upsurge of building activity in the Mauryan epoch and was known till the time of Fa-hsien.

One of the reasons of the origin of this story might be this that after the degeneration of the Maurya dynasty, the usage of stone for building extensive personal palaces probably ceased. Stone, it seems, mainly if not exclusively, was used in religious construction while palaces, courts and dwelling houses were generally built of wood, brick and mixture of mud, clay and smaller blocks of stone and rubble. Thus, fanciful stories were concocted to account for the construction of these huge Maurayan edifices. The editors of the epic, to place Yudhiṣṭ hira, the ideal of Hindu sovereignty on a higher level than the Buddhist emperor, ascribed the former with a palace and court surpassing the grandeur of that of the latter.

Had stone been a very common medium of architecture, this supernatural *Dānava* would not have been introduced. A distinct echo of this tradition is found in the *Rāmāyaṇa*[23] which connects Maya with the beautiful grottos in the Vindhyas. It is said that this mysterious cave-dwelling was built by Maya *dānava*. This episode probably point to the fact that the cave-architecture, which we shall presently see, adopted from Achacmenid Iran by Aśoka, was later on thought to be Asura i.e., foreign in origin, and Maya, the builder of the court of Yudhiṣṭhira is, quite interestingly also the builder of the cave-dwellings in the Vindhyas.

Historians look for some more points connecting Indian traditions with the Persian art and architecture. The agreement between the epic, the accounts supplied by the classical authors and the archaeological finds is striking! Thus Maya *dānava*, also embellished the court of Yudhiṣṭhira with a "peerless tank"[24] or transparent water having artificial aquatic plants and flowers all made of bright gems. The court was also adorned with golden trees (*śātakumbha-maya-drumāḥ*). Artificial trees and vines were the fashion of the day in the luxury-loving court of the Achaemends. A large golden plane tree adorned the court of the Persian monarch, and a golden vine shaded the couch of Darius the great.[25] Curtius describes golden vines clasping the pillars at the Hall in Pāṭaliputra, silver birds sat on the golden creepers.[26] Remnants of golden leaves were unearthed at Kumrahar during the excavation.[27]

Symmetrical courses of water or artificial streams representing rivulets were an essential feature of Persian gardens and it is not unlikely that this characteristic decoration found it's way into India with other architectural plannings. Whatever Dr. Suniti Kumar Chatterji said about Chinese influences on the Indian garden art, can well be applied to Persian influence too; "India of course had her own garden art"...yet "that does not preclude foreign ideas from coming in and enriching it".[28] The *Māhavastu* in fact mentions golden palm-trees embellished with other precious metals and gems viz.,—coral, silver, ruby, beryl etc. in the palace of king Arcimat in the city of Dīpāvatī, and in the royal city of Indratapanā.[29] With the above evidences at hand, we think, it would not be totally wrong to ascribe that these legendary accounts of artificial trees and decorations originated after the Persianized court of Mauryas, and thus had a strong foreign influence working at the root of it.

That the epic really bespeaks of the Mauryan court, or at least adopts the idea from the latter, is probably attested by the fact that it mention in detail about the Sabhāgṛiha (i.e., the Court) comprised of columns which were the main characteristics of the Persian model, and was copied for the first time in India by the Mauryas.

i.c.: A few words may be said here regarding the *stambhas* or the free-standing columns. The installation of *dhvajas* was an ancient Indian practice.[30] But the design of the Asoka's monolithic columns were created directly inspired by the Persepolitan models[31] to serve a different purpose however. The capitals with animal figures on them originated in Assyrio-Persian art[32] and the so-called "bell" or "drooping sepal" ran its course of evolution, originating in Egypt and developing in Achaemenid Iran till culminating into perfect form in Maurya India. Coomaraswamy any how, thinks that the bell-capital was in reality the lotus capital and it is completely indigenous in character.[33] But most of the scholars perceiving the similarity with the Persian ones, believe that the design was copied from the columns at Persepolis. There remains great divergence of opinion regarding the probable date of the first introduction of this form in India. Rowland thinks that the importation was not earlier than the consolidation of the Mauryan empire.[34]

Rawlinson on the other hand says "It is so adapted and transformed, that we cannot help tracing its first introduction back for many years before the accession of Chandragupta Maurya".[35] This speculation of Rawlinson leaves a vacant gap in between the earlier and the purer type and the "adapted" and "transformed" Aśokan ones. Coomaraswamy thinks[36] that the earlier prototype was in wood. But in the absence of any plastic evidence in extant we would like to agree with Rowland that the first introduction of this bell motif was not much prior to the time of Chandragupta, but most probably later.

Rowland, moreover, thinks that those which adorned animals were actually executed by foreign sculptors while the case may be just the opposite; the Indian artists worked out the designs copying from the Persian models supplied by the foreign master-carvers and the former were responsible for the strong transformation or the Indianization of the composite Iranian forms. This change of "hands" and not the "time" was the probable cause of the transformation in form. It is now practically certain, that both Indian and foreign artists worked side by side in the guilds and workshops under Aśoka. Thus the bull of the Sarnath abacus with it's typified realistic treatment of deeply incised rib-bones and prominent dew-laps as well as the striding horses appear to be the work of some non-Indian hands. Bearing in mind, that the characteristic Indian motifs become more or less stiff and clumsy in the hands of the foreign craftsman, we cannot expect such forceful yet reposed bull of Rampurva (compared with the bull of the Sarnath abacus) from a foreign hand.[37] The Achaemenid artists, of course, showed dexterity in delineating animals but the heraldic beasts of the Persian reliefs and sculptures were more restrained, rigid[38] and aristocratic in comparison to their Indian brother's, full of natural grace and vitality. This opposite treatment of animal study most certainly point to the workmanship of mixed hands in Mauryan art. Scholars have deciphered certain stages of development of pillars and capitals[39] from a careful study of their component parts.

i.d.: The earliest example of cave-shrine or hill resort are those dedicated by Aśoka to the benefit to the Ājīvika sect in the Barabar Hill near Gaya, Bihar. There are three more caves on the Nagarjuni hill, and the best is the Lomaśa Risi cave "which though bearing no inscription may be taken to belong to the Maurya period".[40] It is certain that the idea of this type of rock-hewn sanctuary was derived from Achaemenid Iran, where Darius had introduced it.[41] Darius was inspired by the Egyptian grottos during his visit to Egypt with the army of Cambyses, when he had the chance to see it. It is quite likely, that Aśoka came to know of the rock-cut sanctuaries of Darius the Great from the Graeco-Iranian ambassadors and artists, and had undertaken the one on the Barabar hill. Once the practice was adopted and applied by Aśoka it served the religious zeal of the Indians for over a thousand years and created a long history of its own development. It has been shown previously that the foreign impetus at its origin was remembered and was shrouded in a legendary allegory.[42]

The city of Bhir Mound, Taxila yields no architecture which can be styled as foreign. The bearings of the sites of Sirkap and Sirsukh are dated by Marshall in post-Mauryan period.

(ii) The archaeological remains grouped under the Śuṅga period assert more or less a purely native tradition and is free from any foreign impacts. Thus a detailed discussion of them would be quite out of context here. The few sculptural reliefs representing foreign or semi-foreign subjects are "western" from the subjective point of view only, and are purely indigenous in the stylistic and technical treatment.

(iii) The next phase is marked by the dominance of the Bactrian Indo-Greeks, Scythio-Parthians and the Kushans in the northern and western India. The single city of Takṣaśilā with its three particular sites has yielded considerable materials for the study of art, architecture, socio-political and religious history of this period.

(iii. a) The Greek city of Sirkap was more planned, had parallel roads running and buildings grouped in blocks, unlike the Mauryan settlement unearthed at Bhir Mound.[43] This consequently point to the probable contribution of the Greeks to the development of city-planning.

The fortification of the second city at Sirkap gives us some distinct idea about the fortress building with stone and rubble masonry.[44] There were gates, guard's rooms, ramps for mounting on the wall and gradients at the gateway.[45] Sculpture reliefs from Lahore and Peshawar (see Plate No. 7)[46] serve the plastic delineation of the ancient fortification of the north-west. Though the artist was to depict the city-gate of the town of Kuśinagara, the Graeco-Iranian Orders of west, viz., the slightly diminishing concave curve of the bastion wall,[47] the triangular loop-holes, the entablature on the door, and the dentil moulding made themselves obvious, and distinguish the architectural style brought by the Scythio-Parthians. Another piece from Lahore (See Plate No. 8)[48] shows the city wall (most probably of the Kushan city Sirsukh) with two projecting bastions and five ledges showing the successive storeys with their triangular, oblong and cross openings, some of which were overhung with heavy cornices. This exactly tallies with Marshall's observations.[49] On the above ground the bas-reliefs can be easily taken as the realistic representations of the contemporary city-walls represented on the *Toraṇa* carvings of Bharhut[50] and Sanchi[51] clearly show off the difference and the marked western impact on the fortress and architectural designs adopted in north-western India. The vivid description of the siege of the city of Dvārakā by Śālva related in the epic has drawn the attention of scholars, who think that the nature of the fortification reminds one of the siege of Amida as described by Ammianus Marcellinus.[52]

The palace at Sirkap "bears a striking resemblance to the Assyrian palaces at Mesopotamia". It has been compared with the palace of Sargon at Khorasabad.[53] The Parthians introduced the method of the diaper masonry by the end of the first century A.D. The plan of the house remained based on the traditional "*catuḥśālā*" of Indian origin, in which the rooms were placed in rows around a square courtyard. But many a Graeco-Iranian mouldings such as the acanthai, rosettes, beed and reel, dentil and the stunted Corinthian pillar, Ionian capitals and triangular gable front etc., where introduced to ornament the outer facades of the buildings. The engaged Corinthian and

Romanesque pilasters were used in profuse to enhance the beauty of the royal courts, halls, and the drum of the *stūpas*. Contemporary reliefs testify these.[54]

That various types and styles were assimilated in the Gāndhāra region is best illustrated by the shrine of the double-headed eagle where the traditional Indian *toraṇa* and the ogee arch find their place side by side with the pedimental fronts of the Hellenistic facade. The double-headed eagle motif was introduced by the Scythians,[55] who probably adopted it from the Hittites and introduced it in both east and west. The shrine also illustrates how ornate motifs.of Hellenistic origin viz. "the mouldings, pilasters, dentil, cornice and the pedimental niches came to adorn a stupa". The only pure Greek building was the Zoroastrian temple at Jandial, which belonged to the Ionic Order, with its peristyle, proneos and noas. According to Marshall this temple, Ionic in plan, and Zoroastrian in purpose was built in the Scythio-Parthian epoch.[56] If this is the temple described by Appolonius of Tyana[57] as the temple of the Sun, then we find that the Indians must have been visitors to it, which sheltered the archives of Puru. This, moreover, point to the cosmopolitan nature of the population of Taxila and their liberal outlook.

The Kunala stupa is another piece of architecture which betrays a Greek influence. According to Tarn[58] it was built in an age when the rules of the Hellenistic Order were misunderstood and misrepresented in practice.

(iv. a): From the extant remains at the city of Sirsukh, it appears that the Kushans placed more reliance on the artificial defences than on natural barriers.[59] But the Indian view, as expressed in the *Manusaṃhitā*, prefers to take advantage of the natural barriers served by a mountain, a desert or a stream and strategic positions amidst the forest etc.[60] This new practice of fully relying on artificial defences of walls with bastions and gates "was probably the outcome of the developments of military engineering" of the Kushans. It may be mentioned here for a general interest that the epic[61] represents a fort and describes its defensive measures with greater detail than that offered in the *Arthaśāstra*.[62] The *Viṣṇupurāṇa* incidentally remarks that the castle at Dvārāvatī was so secured as to be defended even by women.[63] All these evidences probably indicate the fruitful results achieved by the Indians in the art of military defences through constant raids, conquests and political contacts with the Indo-Greeks, the Scythio-Parthians and the Kushans.

The Kushans moreover carried the art of diaper-rubble masonry from Gāndhāra, where it was introduced by the Parthians, to Harwan in Kashmir.[64] The art of different types of diaper-masonry, viz., the diaper-rubble and the diaper-pebble were invented by the Parthians to enhance the durability of the walls and was certainly an addition to the age-old rubble masonry of the Mauryan epoch.[65]

A reference to a peculiar military craft may be cited from the pages of the *Jatugṛihadāhaparvan* of the great epic. Here minister Kanika (evidently a non-Indian name with particular Kushan sound) advises Dhṛitarāṣṭra to destroy the Pāṇḍavas. The king then orders Purocana to build a house of inflammable materials consisting of lac, lud, ghṛita, hemp and other stuffs.[66] The episode is very interesting. It tells how Vidura, anticipating the conspiracy, warned Yudhiṣṭhira in *Mlecchabhāṣā* (i.e., foreign language) and helped the Pāṇḍava brothers into escape by sending a miner, who dug a sub-terranial passage (*suraṅga*). Tarn thinks that the term *suraṅga* in Sanskrit was derived from Greek 'syrinx'.[67] This together with the archaeological evidences furnished by the excavations at Taxila attest the contribution of the Graeco-Scythians in the field of military architecture. It might be that the craft of building inflammable houses was brought in by one of these western intruders.

(iv. b, c, d): Intact specimens of residential houses are extremely rare, and a complete study of foreign impacts on secular architecture is difficult without some assumptions made from a combined survey of the foundations of the secular buildings, monasteries, rock-cut caves and shrines. From a study of the monasteries at Jaulian and Mohra Moradu, the cave-shrines at Bamiyan, the later temples at Kashmir and the representation of the architecture in the Gāndhāra reliefs, it becomes apparent that foreign architectural orders and decorative mouldings like the Corinthian pilasters, the

Acanthus, the gable-shaped triangular pediments[68] the lantern ceiling,[69] the volutes, Hellenistic frets, spirals,[70] torus etc. appeared in works of stone, stucco and wood. They were used in profusion in the houses and temples of Gāndhāra, Kashmir, Sindhu-Sauvīra region. Some of these architectural motifs were copied in paintings which are found from the murals at Bamiyan[71] and added new items in the painter's repertory. These are repeatedly executed in Gupta reliefs and used as ornamental bands or oblongs in the Ajanta ceiling.[72] Goetz has patiently compared and listed the details of these classical Roman motifs on the carvings of Gupta and later period.[73]

It is difficult to assess how far these Graeco-Roman motifs were used in other parts of contemporary India, owing to the flimsyness of the structures made of wood, clay and sun-dried bricks. The pyramidal tiers alternating with half-closed blue lilies from Persepolitan Order or the dentils were quite common in the bas-reliefs of Bharhut and Sanchi[75] and not unknown to the sculptors of Mathura.[76] According to Coomaraswamy these motifs as well as the others, viz. the winged lion, the scroll and foliages of a palm like plant were not new additions due to Achaemenid or Hellenistic contacts but were reproduced from the 'Early Asiatic' stock.[76] But owing to the complete absence of any earlier specimen in wood it is impossible to know the earliest possible date when these were introduced or invented by the Indian artists.

Lastly, from the minute serutiny and comparisons made by Acharya[77] in between the *Mānasāra* and the Treatise on Architecture by Virtruvius, historians feel inclined to believe with Goetz that the Indian counterpart of this Roman treatise was composed indeed, inspired by the later. Though time has not yet come to give the final verdict regarding this influence and borrowing, and the supposed cultural importance of the conquest of Ujjaini by Chandragupta II has not yet been proved by strong corroborative evidences, and therefore it lies within the limited scope and speculation.[78] All the indications in art and development of architecture lend support to this direction.

A curious fact remains to be mentioned. Nagnajit, the king of Gāndhāra who is the recipient of the maxims of painting according to the *Citralakṣaṇa*, finds mention in the *Mānasāra*, the *Matsyapurāṇa* and the *Bṛihatsaṃhitā*.[79] The case is similar with *Mānasāra*, which is a generic name (like that of Nagnajit) with the connotation of a title of architectural treatise too, is represented as a king of Mālava in the *Daśakumārcarita* of Daṇḍin.[80] The interesting point is that, both Gāndhāra and Mālava were territories where strong Hellenistic and Scythio-Kushan influences were felt! These two were the lands from where "foreign" elements were constantly flowing into the vast stream of Indian art and architecture. Were these two names: 'Nagnajit' and '*Mānasāra*' were invented to absorb all that was 'foreign' and hide them in a shroud of legendary mystery under these vague appellation? This assumption seems quite acceptable in the light of the fact that it would appear rather strange if all the foreign items, discussed above, practised and applied in Indian architecture should have been adapted and absorbed without leaving least indication in the theoretical texts. The connection of the names of Nagnajit and *Mānasāra* with Gāndhāra and Mālava respectively trace the missing link and point to an age-old (the *Mānasāra* is dated in between the *Matsyap*. c. 450 A.D. and the *Bṛihatsaṃhitā* c. 550 A.D.)[81] tradition of affiliating these two regions with the history of architecture.

References

1. Spooner, A.S.I. 1912-13, pp. 53-81; N.R. Ray, Maurya & Sunga Art, p. 18.
2. Fergusson, p. 131-2; Brown, p. 12-13; the actual date depends on the date of the accession of Aśoka, see Thapar, pp. 15, 19.
3. Coomaraswamy, HIIA.
4. Brown, Pl. VIII Besnagar, 150 B.C.; curiously enough Rawlinson Bactria, supplies a different picture of the column which seems more authentic; N.R. Ray op. cit., pp. 60-61, "The lowest third of the shaft is octagonal, terminating by eight half lotus designs; the middle third is hexagonal which is terminated by an octagonal band being decorated by a stylized full and round lotus designs, the upper third is round and super-imposed by a bell-shaped capital that... is related ...with the typical Persepolitan ones with a ring of pointed lotus petals at the end of the lotus".

5. Marshall, A.S.I., 1912-13, pp. 23-25.
6. Marshall, Guide to Taxila, p. 109 ff.
7. Rowland, p. 102, Hackin, Begram,, Fig. 145 shows arched doorways in between Hellenistic Corinthian pilasters.
8. Hackin, CASII, ch. I; Rowland, p. 101 ff.
9. R.C. Kak, AMK, pp. 50, 110, 152.
10. Rawlinson, J.B.B.R.A.S., Vol. XXIII, 1911-12, p. 224, but there must have been some artistic communications prior to this, which are responsible for the 'Early Asiatic' motifs.
11. Coommaraswamy, HIIA, p. 22, Goetz, India, p. 41; but N.R. Ray prefers the view that the court was executed under Aśoka, See op. cit. p. 20.
12. Megasthenes' description, Arrian, x, CAI, p. 224.
13. Strabo xv. I. 36, CAI, p. 262; Aelian xiii, 18. CAI, p. 414.
14. *Arthśāstra*, Shamasastry, pp. 50-55; Basak, pp. 57-63.
15. Rowland, p. 43.
16. Olmstead, HPE, p. 168, "the ornamentation with which the hall was adorned was brought from Ionia...The artisans who dressed the stones were Ionians and Sardians".
17. Huart, APIC, pp. 88-89, Fig. 9, the addorsed are original but the side volutes are Ionian.
18. Rowland, p. 47, Fig. 3, "Although these elements are combined in a manner different from that of the Ionian capitals, they suggest not only this prototype but, largely through the profile of the side volutes also the Greek Ionic".
19. Ibid., p. 44.
20. P.C. Ray, Eng. tr.II; Mbh. 2.1.11 (B.O.R.I.),

    "*Yatra divyān-abhiprāyān paśyema vihitāṃstayā*

    Asurāṃ-manuṣāṃścaiva tam sabhāṃ kuru vai Maya".

    Spooner, J.R.A.S. 1915, vide for the use of the word '*abhiprāya*'.
21. Iranian affiliation of the King, Vide Davar, IA, pp. 47, 54.
22. The Travels of Fa-hsien, p. 45, "The kings palace in the city with it's various halls, all built by spirits who piled up stones, constructed walls and gates and carved designs, engraved and inlaid after *no human fashion* is still in existence". (emphais added) The mystery regarding the name of Maya is not solved yet. He is one of the chief architects in the *Mānasāra* (P.K. Acharya, IAMS,

pp. 34-35, 166-167) and is mentioned in the Matsyap. (255. 2-4) and the Bṛi. Saṃ. (LVI, 29). P. K. Acharya thinks they might not be the same personage, and *Maya* is generic name.

23. *Kiṣkindhyā-kāṇḍ*. ch. 50, 51; Matsya, chs. 130, 138 etc.
24. Mbh. 2.3.27-29 (B.O.R.I.).
25. Herod., vii. 27; Huart, op. cit., p. 90; N.R. Ray, op. cit. P. 20, "...the vine hanging over the couch of Darius, a gift of the Lydian Pythias and perhaps of Ionian workmanship".
26. Curtius, viii, IX, CAI, p. 105, "the palace is adorned with gilded pillars clasped all round by vine embossed with gold, while silver images of those birds which most charm the eye diversify the workmanship".
27. The *Kalpavṛikṣas* mentioned in the *Mānasāra* (P.K. Acharya, p. 64) might have developed from this practice.
28. S.K. Chatterji, India & China, p. 102-104; Rowland, p. 40, hints of the similarity in between the royal park in Pāṭilīputra and the Persian 'Paradise' of the days of Darius and Xerexes.
29. *Mahāvastu* I, p. 152-153; III,. p. 221 etc.
30. The Minor Rock Edicts of Rupnath and Sahsaram, Pilllar Edict VII, Basak, pp. 113, 140.
31. Rowland, p. 43.
32. Ibid., p. 46.
33. Coomaraswamy, op. cit., p. 11, p. 17, f.n. 6.
34. Rowland, p. 41.
35. Rawlinson, op. cit., p. 228.
36. Coomaraswamy, op. cit., pp. 13-14, "It must be however, constantly borne in mind, that a motif was not necessarily invented or borrowed at a date of it's first appearance in permanent material, indeed a first appearance in stone, almost tantamount to proof an earlier currency in wood".
37. N.R. Ray, op. cit., pp. 97-98; Pls. 9, 10.
38. Delaporte, Mesopotamia, p. 328-29 the Achaemenid art was influenced and evolved from the conventionalized prototypes of the Assyrian art forms.
39. N.R. Ray, op. cit., pp. 26-27.
40. Ibid., p. 57, according to Fergusson the Lamas Risi Cave with it's beautiful facade is the latest of the group.

41. Coomaraswamy, op. cit., p. 18, the idea was Iranian but the style of execution was typically Indian; Rowland, p. 42.
42. This is mainly assumed from the references in the classical Sanskrit literature about the activities of Maya.
43. Marshall, Guide, pp. 143-44, "In their general plan these buildings are much more irregular than those laid bare in the Parthian town of Sirkap, and they differ from them in other features also, particularly in the construction of their walls".
44. Ibid., p. 78 ff., "this new wall is constructed of rubble masonry throughout and varies in thickness from 15 ft to 21 ft 6 in. It is strengthened at intervals of the outside by solid rectangular bastions with a low berm between, intended specially to protect it's foundation..."
45. Ibid., p. 79.
46. Ingholt, Pls. 151, 152.
47. For a similar Sassanian palace vide Christensen, Fig. 12.
48. Ingholt, Pl. 464.
49. Marshall, op. cit., p. 110, "In the bastions these loop-holés widens towards the outside and are closed on the outer face of the wall with triangular arches which give them a singularly western appearance".
50. Rowland, Pl. 17 this paradise of Indra from Bharhut depicts a three-storeyed palace with railing and ogee-arched windows.
51. Ibid., p. 40, Pl. 26.
52. Am. Marc. xix. 1-8; Kramrisch, Indian Sculpture, Pl. 4 railing post from Mathura shows parts of a fort with battlements that are quite different from Sanchi.
53. Marshall, op. cit., pp. 83-84; Coomaraswamy, p. 54 for diaper masonry vide A.S.I,. 1912-13, Fig. 1; Guide p. 85.
54. Ghirshman, Iran, p. 36, "By the same token (usage of the vaulted roof) the column ceased to act as a support, engaged in the pier, (unless replaced by a pilaster) it served a purely ornamental purpose".
55. Guide, p. 88, A.S.I. 1912-13, Pl. XXVII a; Coomaraswamy, op. cit., p. 11, n. 1, "the double headed eagle is probably Hittite and earlier". p. 12; Breasted, p. 157, Fig. 94, p. 252 "the Hittite sculptors received the early Babylonian symbol of eagle with outspread wings and a lion's head or some times a double head".
56. Guide, p. 100 ff., Coomaraswamy, p. 55.

57. CAI, p. 388, "They saw the temple of the sun, and in it statues of Alexander and Porus, the one gold and the other of bronze; it's walls were of red marble, but glittering with gold; the image of the god was of pearls, having as in usual with the barbarians in sacred things a symbolical meaning". Guide pp. 105-6.
58. Tarn, GBI, p. 360 f., Guide p. 75 f.
59. Ibid., p. 111.
60. Manu. VIII.
61. Mbh. 3.14.5-23 (Haridas).
62. *Arthśāstra*, ch. III, IV.
63. Viṣṇup. V. 23.11; in the picturesque description of Dvārakā one is tempted to see an actual account of some sea-coast city of western India guarded by the Scythian Ksatrapas.
64. R.C. Kak, op. cit., p. 55.
65. Bhir site was purely made of rubble masonry.
66. Mbh. 1.133.8-11 (B.O.R.I.); 138. 11-12; 139. 22 ff. (Haridas)
67. Tarn, GBI, p. 360; *Śilappadikāram*, p. 201, f.n. 4; *Mahāummagga Jātaka*, however prove that the Indians were skilled in sub-terranial engineering from very early days.
68. The Martand Temple, Rowland, Pl. 67; Ibid., Pl. 68 Pandranthan; Marshall, Buddhist Art, Pls. 79, 86, 87, 88.
69. Rowland, p. 121, Fig. 14, Pl. 56 a.
70. Kak, op. cit., Pl. XXVIII, 13, 15.
71. Divinities are seen within pedimental niches. This triangular cut at top shape are seen in the houses of the trans-Himalayan regions especially in Central Asia.
72. Dey, Pls. XLII, XLIII of Cave I.
73. H. Goetz, Imperial Rome and the Genesis of Classic Indian Art, East & West, Vol. X, No. 3, 1959, pp. 153-181, Vol. X, No. 4.1949, pp. 261-268.
74. Rowland, Pl. 17; Zimmer, Pl. 19.
75. Agrawala, Handbook , p. 14, No. 99, –balcony faced with pyramidal tiers of the Persepolitan order. According to Agrawala there were Indo-Persepolitan capital embellished with human heads, vide MMC, part III, p. 79 No. 1599 and p. 82, No. 2564. If the assumption is true then these unique pillars must have added a marked singular feature in the city architecture of Mathura.

76. Coomaraswamy, op. cit., pp. 11-14.

77. Acharya, IAMS, pp. 134-59.

78. Goetz, op. cit., discusses them in detail. But T. Bhattacharya, A Study on Vāstu-vidyā, p. 198 ff. thinks in a different direction.

79. *Citralakṣaṇa*, p. 128 f.; T. Bhattacharya, pp. 96-97; Bṛi-Saṃ LVIII, 4, here, of course, Nagnajit is apparently connected with Drāviḍa.

80. Acharya, p. 171, "There are several works in the Sanskrit literature, which seemed to have been named after their patron..." Was it possible that this vague generic title consciously hid the name of some foreign ruler who patronized the art of architecture?

81. Acharya, p. 198, f.n. 1.

Section II

Schools of Sculpture

In this section I will discuss the foreign impacts upon the development of the contemporary Indian schools of sculpture.

1. **Gāndhāra School**: We are fortunate in getting access to a large number of more or less intact specimens of sculpture and relief belonging to this school. The enormous output of purely religious, socio-religious and secular art objects interest us with their hybrid style and techniques. But we are similarly unfortunate to be left in the dark regarding their history and a systematic survey, due to the absence of any inscription on them in a known era. As to the exact source of inspiration that gave impetus to this school, the scholars' personal preferences and discrepancies vary and we are to choose it's nomenclature from a vast and varied list.[1] In the following discussion we will designate the art movement as "Gāndhāra School" and try to estimate the origin of this exotic impetus and its contribution to the later Indian art-forms.

Of course, there is no room for doubt that the inspiration working under the current of this art was derived from the West and it was a foreign impact. But there are certain grave difficulties and problems regarding the systematic history and the source of origin of this school. They are as follows:

(i) What was the approximate period of rise and fall of this school; and to what direction either Hellenic, Iranian or to Roman West did it owe it's origin?[2]

(ii) Was Gāndhāra the creator of the first Buddha image?

(iii) What was the era used in the following effigies:

  (a) Headless Buddha from Loriyan Tangai, dated 318

  (b) Buddha from Hashtnagar, dated 384

  (c) Hāritī from Skarah Dheri, dated 399

  (d) What was the date of the two reliquaries from Bimaran and Shah-ji-ki-dheri?

It has been maintained by some scholars that as the Indo-Greeks of Bactria and north-west India did not leave behind them any monument or reliquaries of art, except the endeavour of "minting a series of magnificent coins", the art of Gandhāra wholly belongs to the Kushan times and looks to the Roman East viz., the workshops of Alexandria, Palmyra, Hatra and Dura Europos for its style and craftsmanship. There is truth in the above contention and scholars like Benjamin Rowland and Ingholt have tried to show the affinities by skilfully comparing similar art objects found from India and West.

But it seems that this belittles the endeavour of the Bactrians and the Scythio-Parthians before the chance comes to the Kushans to uphold the cause of art.

If we accept the date 78 A.D. for the accession of Kanishka, then the chronological table of Ghirshman,[3] becomes susceptible to certain changes. Moreover it condenses the period of the Scythio-Parthian rule in India. It was in Parthian period that the Iranian gods were fully anthropomorphized by the Greeks.[4] This tendency probably paved the way for the human representation of the Buddha in the art of north-western India. There is every possibility that the Indo-Greeks and the Parthians or any one of them, probably to secure and assert their position amongst their Indian subordinates, evolved out the Buddha image in a pose of reassurance and benediction. By doing so they sought for the admiration and support of their Indian Buddhist subjects.

The figures of Shami and Uthal (c. 2nd century B.C.)[5] must have had several copies of them made during the intervening time, before the post was manifested again in the Buddha from Hashtnagar, which, most of the scholars, ascribe not to Seleucidan era but to one of the later eras. Thus the time elapsed between the Parthian proto-type and their Indian copies (i.e., the Buddha of Hastnagar and others) was longer. It is quite probable that the Buddhas described by Marshall as the earliest cult statues (Marshall, Buddhist Art, figs. 85, 86) were made within this intervening period. It is presumed that the right hands of both were in the re-assuring pose.

However, if we are to assume that the Indo-Greeks and the Scythio-Parthians patronized the art-movement in the Gāndhāra region, we have to look for some more evidences to corroborate our assumption.

It seems rather absurd that the numismatic art would develop without any collateral sister art with it.[6] Skilful artists indeed, were there, who executed fine miniature reliefs for the coins of the Greeks in Bactria and India. It is only natural, that some of the groups of workers must have settled in Indian mint-cities like Kāpiśa, Puṣkalāvatī and Takṣaśilā. It would not be improbable to assume further, that bands of Indian craftsmen were also appointed together with the foreign engravers, as we find workmanship of pure Indian hands on the coins of Maues Azes and Azelises.[7]

A silver alloy plate which has been tentatively ascribed by Frye to belong to Bactrian workmanship[8] present some very interesting illustrations. In the center is a heraldic eagle facing right. This was probably borrowed from the Scythian repertory, or it may show that the plate was a Scythian creation with remarkable Hellenistic features. On the left top a nymph-like female figure, attired in a diaphenous high-belted Greek chiton and himation is represented. Her drapery reveals the body underneath clearly like that of the Indian *Yakṣiṇīs*. She is holding the hand of a bearded old man. In between them rises a full-bloomed lotus amidst leaves depicted in typical Indian style. In her left hand she holds a dish. On her left is a seated female holding a child, who is identical with Demeter. The next figure is an Amazon riding on a galloping winged-horse[9] The next male figure attacks a bear under an Aśvattha (Ficus religiosa) tree. The next four figures form a composition, a noble prince is sitting on a stool dressed in purely Greek costume. A lady wearing a short chiton and a pair of flared trousers like that of the Amazon, is looking her right. Curiously enough, the prince and his consort are both pointing their forefingers to a very robust page who is engaged in flogging a knelt man, wearing short locks and a shirt A female is standing fettered, obviously reduced to slavery. Two men, one with a jug and shield, and the other behind the bearded old man, stand holding a sword. This completes the roundel.

From a close study of the subjects delineated it seems that the dish was manufactured in a place where the Greek craftsmen well-versed in Scythian and Indian motifs were there. This points to Bāhlīka, i.e., Bactria. It possibly illustrates some legend[10] current amongst the Bactrians. The background is plain and the figures are related to each other with gestures, according to old Greek tradition. With future discoveries of similar art-objects the lost link may be found some day.

The Scythio-Parthians kept the fine numismatic tradition intact. The Parthians of Iran appreciated Hellenistic art and it is natural that their Indian kinsmen followed them. This is proved by the coins of Maues, Azes, Azelises as well as that of Vonones, Gondopharnes and others.[11] The style of the treatment of the subjects, i.e., the mounted king and the goddesses with palm (P.M.C. Pl. XI, 179, p. 117, Type 11, Azes), enthroned Demeter and Hermes (Ibid., Ol. XI. 217, p. 120, Azes, Type 14) are typically Hellenistic while the king seated cross-legged (Ibid., Pl. XI, 195, p. 118, Azes, Type 13) show pronounced Scythian influence. The Demeter of the coin served as the prototype of Ardoksho of the Scythio-Parthian pantheon and Hāritī of Buddhist lore. The Artemis and the Bull (Pl. X. 10, p. 99), the lunar deity and Nike (Pl. X. 13, p. 99), enthroned Zeus and the city-goddess (Pl. X. 15, p. 99), Poseidon and Bacchante amidst the vines (Pl. X. 20) and Herakles (Pl. XIII, 254), all represent the subject matter according to Hellenistic ideals. Nos. 334 and 335 of P.M.C. Pl. XIII, represented a pair of unidentified god and goddess. The limbs are clearly depicted under the Greek dresses. The posture of the hands and feet recall the figures from the "stair-riser" bas-reliefs.[12] These reliefs in stones which are "characterized by the isolation of the figures against a plain background"[13] are compared with the Augustan reliefs from Ara Pacis and belong to the earliest phase of the Gāndhāra School.

This is corroborated by the numismatic evidences. The "stair-riser" reliefs on the above ground may be placed sometime in the early Scythio-Parthian epoch (c.20, B.C.–78 A.D.)[14] Rowland admits that this style of isolated figures related to each other by gestures is based on the Greek style of fifth century B.C. and thus has a long tradition behind it. After the new light thrown by Ghirshman on Parthian art it can be well assumed that this style was probably kept alive by the Greek artists of Nysa and Bactria, wherefrom the remains of temple unearthed, presuppose a strong Hellenistic bearing.[15]

In the absence of any monument in India precisely belonging to the Graeco-Bactrian age, formerly it was surmised that the so-called "Hellenistic tradition" was a "mirage"; the only art-form was that trickling through the streamlet of engravings on coin-moulds. But the discoveries of Ghirshman has put the whole "theory" into question, and the plans are to be revised as more new materials would come to light.

The reliquary from Bimaran, generally placed in Azes' epoch has been taken by Lohuizen de Leeuw to be later, because

(i) It shows an oblong cut on the surface of the pillars, and

(ii)The eagle heralding the top of the pillars.[16]

Lohuizen de Leeuw puts the epoch of Azes in c. 50 B.C. but Indian scholars, D.C. Sircar and Raychaudhuri feel sure that Azes came to throne during c. 5 B.C.-30 A.D. i.e., after Maues and before Gondopharnes in c. 47 A.D.[17] The actual date of the reliquary cannot be ascertained but it would be the same (i.e., 1st century A.D.) at which Lohuizen de Leeuw arrives, though from a different point of argument.[18] We think that it actually belonged to the Scythio-Parthian epoch after Azes, and before the Kushans. The reasons are as follows:

The figures on the reliquary show the same graceful movement and treatment of drapery as on the coins of Maues and Azelises. The Scythio-Parthians were skilful workers in gold ornaments.[19] It was easier for them to impart grace and a feeling of movement on a repousee of gold.

The oblong cut on the pillars may not detain us unnecessarily; if we are to accept the Seleucidan era for the Buddhas of Loriyan Tangai and Hashtnagar, we find that the oblong-cut of the Bimaran reliquary supplies a link between the development:

(a) Loriyan Tangai, c. 6 A.D.

(b) Bimaran, Aze's Epoch

(c) Hashtnagar, c. 72 A.D.

If we do not accept the 'Seleucidan era' theory, still we find a gradual change of deterioration of the oblong recess starting from the age of Azes:

(a) On the Bimaran it is well executed and double recessed.

(b) On the pedestal of Loriyan Tangai.

(c) On Hashtnagar.

(d) Ingholt, Pl. 15, 90.

(e) Ingholt, Pl. 33, 76, 140, 158 (the pillars are staunted).

(f) Ingholt, Pl. 82, 92

(g) Ingholt, Pl. 465 (appears more straight)

(h) Jaulian Monastery, Pl. 521.

(i) Ingholt, Pl. 101, 300.

In the above classification under group (i) they are minimized and fall into a conventional practice, thus marking the last stage. Sometimes the recess is carelessly incised (as in Pls. 125, 433) or elongated disproportionately as in Pls. 127 and 303.[20] In this classification we may not take the round Corinthian pillar of the 'Stair-riser' series and 'Sikri' stupa earlier than the flat-surfaced ones of Bimaran. The two types could have been more or less contemporary, the former being borrowed from the Hellenistic repertory while the flat-surfaced were the outcome of the Graeco-Parthian combination.

Also, it may be pointed out that in the shrine of the double-headed eagle, belonging to Parthian city, flat-surfaced pillars are used in the corners and this feature need not be taken as of very late development.[21]

(ii) The Scythian and the Parthian princes of India were intimately connected with each other; there is no wonder if Azes (some take him as Parthian) had adopted the eagle. This typical Scythian motif was later on introduced in Europe to enjoy highest popularity as heraldry decoration.

(a) Loriyan Tangai, c. 6 A.D.

(b) Bimaran, Aze's Epoch

(c) Hashtnagar, c. 72 A.D.

(a) On the Bimaran it is well executed and double recessed.

(b) On the pedestal of Loriyan Tangai.

(c) On Hashtnagar.

(d) Ingholt, Pl. 15, 90.

(e) Ingholt, Pl. 33, 76, 140, 158 (the pillars are staunted).

(f) Ingholt, Pl. 82, 92

(g) Ingholt, Pl. 465 (appears more straight)

(h) Jaulian Monastery, Pl. 521.

(i) Ingholt, Pl. 101, 300.

Rowland prefers a late date for this gold repousse, he opines that the figure of the Buddha attended by Śakra and Brahmā was suggested by the figures of Christ with St. Peter and St. Paul in early Christian sarcophagi. According to him, combination of figures framed within architectural setting is first to be seen on the Sidarma Sarcophagi of the Second century A.D.[22] But now we know that the deified ancestors of the Parthian kings were kept into niches and the whole conception of this sort of placement developed from Zoroastrian ossuary.[23] So there is no grave doubt in placing the reliquary in Azes' epoch. Moreover, Rowland admits, "that the arches of the arcade are not in the least classical, but have the familiar ogee-form of the Chaitya window" found at double-headed Eagle Shrine of Sirkap and on the ornate frieze from the Dharmarajika Stupa, Taxila. Apart from the freshly minted coins of Azes, the latest date for the script of the steatite vase (c. 50-70 A.D.) also coincides with the date of Azes.[24]

The fact that Marshall did not find a single Buddha image or even a head from the Parthian stratification of Sirkap is indeed a strong support to the theory that Buddha was represented first under the Kushan monarch. Some heads of Bodhisattva only have been found from the Apsidal Temple of Sirkap. But there again, some points regarding the Buddha on the coin of Kanishka and the reliquary of Shah-ji-ki-dheri should be considered. The Buddha images however crude and reduced into miniature size present some characteristics:

(a) The Buddha on the coin[25] is delineated in the *Uttarāsaṅga* and a *Saṅghāṭi*. He is holding his *Saṅghāṭi* with his left hand and re-assuring with the right. There is a marked halo around his body. Signs of the *Uṣṇīsa* can be seen, and it seems that his feet are shod in coverings. These characteristics no doubt presuppose an earlier model, and show that already during Kanishka, the iconography was quite developed.

(b) The lotus-petalled auriole appear behind the head of the Buddha in the reliquary. This was no doubt borrowed from the repository of the images of Tīrthaṅkaras[26] from Mathura.

(c) The Buddha's body is covered with a thick robe; this was a deviation from the traditional Indian conception of representing Yakṣas and Tīrthaṅkaras in fine garments or in a bare-body. The thick robe developed in Gāndhāra country, because there the realistic mode of treatment of the foreign-artists, adopted the real *Uttarāsaṅga* and the *Saṅghāṭī*. It appears that the robe in Gāndhāra sculptures was the representation of the real dress of the contemporary Buddhist monks. Then it was adopted by the schools of Mathura and Amaravati, and gradually became conventionalized into fine transparent raiment, looking like thin muslin or silk typical for all Buddha images thereafter.

(d) The representation of the two worshippers viz., Śakra and Brahmā are more archaic. The craftsmen 'Agesilas' obviously, unaccustomed with the Indian style, just copied these figures from some earlier models, and was unable to impart grace or life in them.

(e) The caryatids are portrayed more freely in an easy movement. The 'foreign' artist was well-acquainted with these garland-bearing puttis, and the flying geese.

It is a pity that the lid of the Bimaran reliquary is lost. The base mouldings are nearly same in two reliquaries. On the whole the Bimaran has got a more composite and graceful appearance, while in the other the artist exerted some effort to put the different motifs together. There again, the Scythio-Parthian coins display a more graceful treatment than the Kushan coins bearing bold, rigid and heavier look; the faces too are larger in proportion to the body of the figures.

It seems quite unlikely that Kanishka immediately upheld the Buddhist cause, and ordered a statue of the Buddha to be made, just after his accession. There also remains serious doubt about placing the casket in his reignal year one,[27] but the 'Buddha' on his coin, proves however beyond doubt, that the human representation of the Master was current during his time. After that it developed rapidly. If we admit that the casket belongs to the reignal year one of Kanishka II, then we see that the Parthian element was stronger in the image on the coin, and the Indian elements were prominent on that on the casket.

The sudden deterioration or archaicness that marks the image of Hāritī from Skarah Dheri,[28] which, if dated in the Seleucidan era, would come just after Kanishka's accession. The stringed ridges on the fold of the *sāri* and the very stiff rendering of the top-knot with wreath show that the Kushan artist had some difficulty in handling these objects. Or it might be that, by that time the coiffure and the *sāri* had become conventionalized. The face assumed a mask-like appearance with sharp clear-cut lines for the eye-brows, evidently pointing to a late and decadent period. But curiously enough that full sleeved blouse is much analogous to that on the figure of the female deity and princess Washfari from Hatra.[29]

Various assumptions about the dates have been made, which lead us nowhere:

(i) If it is in the Seleucidan era i.e., 399-312=87 A.D.

(ii) If it is in the Vikrama era i.e., 399-58=341 A.D.

(iii) If it is in the Śaka era i.e., 399-78=477 A.D.

(iv) If it is in the Scythian era (Lohuizen) i.e., 399-129=270 A.D.

Bearing in mind the date of destruction of Hatra in 241 A.D. the date c. 270, for this statue of Hāritī seems most fitting as it places the statue nearest to it's Hatrene prototype.

The Buddhas from Loriyan Tangai and Hashtnagar then can be placed in c. 189 A.D. and c. 255 A.D. respectively. This once more emphasises that from the time of the statues of Shami and Uthal (2nd Century B.C.) the pose was repeated on and on till it became the most common pose for the deceased Souls or great Souls as well as the tutelary divinities of Graeco-Iranian pantheon, and manifested itself on the Bimaran reliquary.

For the greater part the chronology suggested by Lohuizen de Leeuw is reasonable and her theory of one gradual development seems to be more acceptance. The only change that we have made, is to place the Bimaran reliquary earlier in the Scythio-Parthian epoch.

A few words may be added lastly. It seems that the so-called "stair riser" reliefs[30] and others of similar character (Ingholt

IV, 1-3, Pls. 411-414; and Marshall, Buddhist Art, Figs. 40-46) had no connection with Buddhist iconography, but was used to serve some other purposes. The atmosphere of a banquet and Dionysia pervading the whole scene and the distinction of the dresses of it's participants i.e., Greek and Indian nobility, support the above contention. For a general interest, it may be pointed here, that the figures of the ladies draped in *sāri* and holding lotus in their raised hands from the pedestal bearing the inscription of the year 47 of Kanishka[31] (Lohuizen de Leeuw, Pl. 66) bear a strong resemblance to the female figures in the stair-riser reliefs.[32] (Ingholt, Pl. 413-414). The mode of draping the *sāri* in this way originated in Gāndhāra region and not in central or eastern India. Moreover, the relief from Mathura show that the artist was working with a set example, the crudity presented in the pedestal carving is not the outcome of archaicness, but of a general solidity and bluntness presented in many of the works of the Kushan epoch. The female participants in the stair riser reliefs are earlier because they still wear the '*adhovāsa*" and a separate '*uttarīya*' draped over the shoulders and around the arms, but their bosoms are left bare according to the Indian taste, while the Greek ladies are dressed in the high-belted chiton, and a himation that drapes over it. Whether these bas-reliefs were connected with some religious significance is not known, because of the obscure provonance of these reliefs. But in the Mathura pedestal the pose, it seems, as well as the dress, were copied from the Gāndhāra school of sculpture. This gradual change in the female-dress probably leads us to some clue regarding the chronology of the Gāndhāra sculptures.

The images of Hāritī and Pañcika also show certain stages of development:

(i) The first type developed from Demeter and holds the cornucopia. She is accompanied by Pañcika, who iconographically can be called the "Indianized Zeus". Here Hāritī is dressed in a *sari* which clings close to her body revealing the contour of the physique and the softness of the flesh.

The artists with utmost patience has curved out the typical Indian ornaments, viz. the ear-pendants, the necklaces, bangles and the heavy anklets. The figure is imparted with a feeling of animation and expresses the motherly affection. The realistic pose bespeaks of actual study of contemporary life and nature around. This is the Hellenistic contribution in technique and style but the concepts of beauty remained true to Indian ideals.[33] (Ingholt, Pls. 340, 342). The artificial 'swallow-tail' fold on Pañcika's left leg is a surer guide to its Roman inspiration and later age.

(ii) The next are analogous to the former, but the thriving liveliness has been reduced to conventionalism. The dress-details, and some peculiarities such as the Scythian leggings, the jar of wealth etc., are depicted with careful attention. The drapery folds and the gestures are somewhat stylized.[34] It is probably later than the previously discussed one.

(iii) The standing Hāritī[35] (Ingholt, pl. 341) is iconographically fully developed into all the rigid formality of a tutelary goddess, attributed with her symbols. The children here are not caressed with a motherly affection as in (i) but are placed as attributes showing that they were to be protected by her in safety and welfare. The face of the divinity has assumed a schematic hardness, being softened a little only by the curvature of the lips showing benevolence. The body is strong and well-built. The feet are covered with stuffed shoes.

(iv) The stunted quaint looking Hāritī from Sirkap of the first century A.D. presents a different tradition altogether.[36] (Ingholt, pl. 347). But this is the earliest of the four classes. The composite deity of Demeter-Ardoksho-Hāritī from Gāndhāra region exerted some influence on the iconography of Lakṣmī in the following period. The *śloka* from the Matsyapurāṇa which states:

"*Hāra-Keyūra-sampannā kṛikavākudharā tathā*
Vaiṣṇavī Viṣṇu-sadṛiśī garuḍe samupasthitā. 28
Caturvāhuśca varadā śaṃkha-cakra-gadā-dharā
Siṃhāsana-gatā vāpi bālekema samanvitā.29" (261)

This shows that the Demeter-Hāritī was the model for the Vaisnavi image in the Gupta period, or it is possible that the

Hāritī with children, and holding the mace (*gadā*) and the wheel (*cakra*) was worshipped as Vaiṣṇavī by the Hindu devotees of Gāndhāra country during fourth-fifth centuries A.D.

It is easier to classify the types but it is not so to arrange them in a chronological order. Even if we think out a believable scheme, the whole plan dilapidates when we try to fit the dated sculpture-pieces into it. Thus the scheme suggested by Ghirshman and Ingholt works out all right when Kanishka is dated in c. 144 A.D. But if we are to accept c. 78 A.D. as the beginning of the era of Kanishka, their scheme becomes susceptible to changes. This makes the Scythio-Parthian period too short, and marks a faster development of the school.

Another point should be borne in mind, that in a region where different types, and traditions reached within a very short space of time different modes of representation which existed side by side, and we are not in a position to attach strict adherence in the chronology of styles. This is particularly true about the later productions of the Gāndhāra school, when the artist's repertory became loaded with a medley of conventions. While one local branch of the School followed a particular tradition started by some master artist, the other ateliers followed a different one, but probably both worked in near proximity of time.

The contribution of the Gāndhāra School to the traditional Indian art of the following Gupta period may be classified as follows:

(i) The heavily draped Buddha figures. Had the Hellenistic influence not reached the north-west of India, the delineation of the robe of the Buddha probably would have remained confined into the fine and linear treatment of the garment. According to Marshall the *Uṣṇīṣa* was also the outcome of the Graeco-Pathian top-knot, a sign of aristocracy.

(ii)The cupids and the garland-bearing puttis (see Plate No. 9) were introduced into the Gupta art from the north-west. According to Goetz the "funny folk of playful but clumsy little beings busy in practically all human activities" as seen in the Gupta reliefs are the Indian counterparts of the Hellenistic Erotes.

(iii) The unspecified flora (in the scroll) of the Ajanta frescoes and Gupta reliefs[37] from Deogarh was probably an adaptation from the Greek Acanthus.

(iv) The typical Hellenistic fret and the Sassanian rosettes and lozenges,[38] and rosettes studded within alternate diamonds (rhomboid ornaments) were taken from the north-west.

(v) The iconography of Śri Lakṣmī in the Gupta period was influenced to some extent by the Ardoksho-Hāritī of Gāndhāra. The Matsya prescribed Lakṣmī to be "*Kañcukābaddhagātrī*" i.e., dressed in a *Kañcuka*. This was no doubt derived from the Hellenistic chiton seen in so many images from Gāndhāra. In Kashmir Lakṣmī was attributed with the cornucopia of Demeter, which again show the impact of the western influence.

2. **Mathura School**: Synchronous with the Art School of Gāndhāra in the north-west, two other Indian Schools of Sculpture were active—one in Mathura in the north, and the other at Amaravati in the south.

Mathura, the famous township which fell under the vicissitudes of the Yavanas invasion was the seat of the Satrapal House of Rājula, the Śaka. From the art products of Mathura, it appears that the city was inhabited by a group of foreign artists, or foreign-trained artisans, who worked side by side with the native sculptors in accordance with their foreign master's order. It seems that the Scythio-Kushans of Mathura adopted *Brāhmaṇya*, *Jaina* or *Bauddha* faiths and patronised both the religious and secular branches of art developing within it's environment.

The relief illustrations which show two Scythio-Kushan chiefs, or an aristocrat with his attendant proceeding towards a Śiva-linga with a fillet in his hand,[1] and the other with a Scythio-Kushan noble (No. 1454) "wearing collared coat and a belt" and holding lotus flowers[2] depict the religious fervour of these crude yet adaptable people.

Almost no art expression in India can be set aside as purely secular, because every little thing may be attributed to some religious practice one way or the other. Yet the statues of the highly fashionable belles of Mathura probably constitute an important item in the list of secular art.[3] That women, even courtesans participated in the religious and social life of the city is attested by inscriptions.[4] It has been discussed in the sections of Caste system[5] and Vaisnavism[6] how the women of Scythian nomadic stock played their role in contributing to those aspects of India's cultural life. The predominance and the high status enjoyed by the courtesans in Mathura may have some connection with the Scythio-Kushan predominance of that city, and the flourishing cults of Vāsudeva-Kṛṣṇa and Baladeva, whose rituals retained the Dionysiac aspect[7] of extravagant drinking. It is needless to say, that the beautiful courtesans enhanced the charm of this Indian "Dionysia", celebrated in Mathura in the days of the Śaka-Kushans, and had lent a permanent mark on the development of sculptural art in this region.

Moreover, the city was the venerated centre of Jaina faith; under the Scythians, especially under Kanishka it became a centre of Buddhism too. This School is credited with the installation of the first Buddha made in purely Indian tradition and style. In this respect the artists of Mathura owed the credit of being the pioneers.

Foreign impact is clearly discernible in the following products of the School:

(i) The portrait Statues:

- (a) the seated statue of Wima Kadphises
- (b) the standing effigy of Kanishka
- (c) the torso of Caṣṭana (Shaṣṭana)

(ii) The heads:

- (a) in stone (Nos. 157, 749, 1252, 1566, 1599, 2122, 2564)
- (b) in terracotta (Fig. 13 of the Handbook)

(iii) The statues dressed in foreign constumes;

- (a) Male figures:
    1. Seated in European fashion (No. 2514)
    2. Kushan noble man clad in tunic (G. 13)
- (b) Female figures:
    1. Women clad in Greek chiton (No. F. 27)

2. The Hāritī wearing *sāri* and wtrath (F. 42)

This was an import from Gāndhāra atelier.

(iv) The Bacchanalian Scenes:

(a) From Palikhera (No. C 2)

(b) From Maholi (No. 2800)

(c) Bacchus-Baladeva (No. 1580), this is taken to be of same characteristic with the (a) and (b). It probably depicts Bacchus-Baladeva "in a dancing attitude...wearing conspicuous *garland interwoven with leaves and flowers*". (emphasis added) This particularly points to a Hellenistic affinity of the deity, who is garlanded with a *wreath* and not *vanamālā* made up of flowers only.

(v) The sun icons:

(a) "Sitting squatting on a chariot" of four horses. It has traces of wings (No. D. 46)

(b) "Seated like a Kushan emperor" and dressed in the particular Scythian tunic and cap (No. 269).

There are other statuettes of this deity, which show that Mathura became a centre of the Scythian Mihira-cult introduced by the *Maga-Brāhmaṇa* during the reign of Kanishka. These Sun-images were represented in the typical '*udīcyaveśa*' consisting the colaka (tunic) and the *Saṃpuṭikā* (trousers) which covered the thighs. The fact, that gods were conceived in terms of royal personages, and the '*Devaputra*' kings in vice versa, is clear from this squatting figure of the sun-god garbed in short jacket and cap. His posture and facial expression are more humane than divine.

(i) The effigies of the Kushan monarchs found from Mat are something unique in ancient Indian artistic specimens and constitute a rare group by themselves. These Scythio-Kushan monarchs, [as we find Caṣṭana (Shaṣṭana) connected with them][8] had introduced the custom of installing images in the *devakula*.[9] We do not find any evidence of the continuity of this custom in later times, but it must have had exerted a considerable influence on the contemporary society, as we find Bhāsa in his *Pratimānāṭaka* applied the idea to enhance the dramatic situation of his plot. It is moreover mentioned in the drama that the '*pratimāgṛiha*', where the images of the deceased Iksvāku kings were installed was decorated with '*sthāsaka*' singns[10] which was believed to drive away the evil spirits.[11] Surely, Bhāsa did receive his inspiration from the Kushana *devakula* at Mathura.

It would not be unjustifiable to surmise that for some time at least the installation of images in a *devakula* was adopted as an Indian royal custom. So Bhāsa had no hesitation to apply this purely Scythio-Parthian custom on a scion of the family of Raghu. It might be that the *Pratimānāṭaka* was to be performed before a public who would have appreciated the *devakula* device. This indicate the fairly large number of foreigners amidst the general population.

The effigies are all portrayed in their typical costume of overcoat, tunic and heavy trousers or with the tunic and trouser. The rosettes, scale patterns and the designs on the plaques of Caṣṭana are typically Scythian in taste and are all curved with utmost care[12] and beauty.

(ii) A number of heads of different sizes have been collected from the sites around Mathura. According to Ghirshman, heads "cut short at chins" was an ancient Iranian device, and human heads were applied in ornamental mouldings in art under the Parthians and Sassanians. Some of the Mathura heads (like Nos. 1252, 1566 and 2122) are detached from the body.[13] The head-dresses show varieties of close-fitting skull-cap, Greek helmet and the Scythian Tigrakhauda (G. 32; See Plate No. 4). One of them (No. 1566) is ornamented with a lunar symbol. The high-tiaras with solar and lunar symbols are seen in the Gāndhāra sculptures too.[14] The head-gears with ram's horn (*śṛingiṇa*) also point to a foreign extraction. According to Agrawala some of the heads (Nos. 2564 and 1599) represent the capitals of some Indo-Persepolitan pillars.[15]

(iii) In these types of figures clad in foreign dress, the artists were to depict their foreign masters in different attitudes,—especially worshipping the divinities and offering their homage to the Buddhist or Jaina centres. Some might have been meant for decorative purposes, or were created out of the artists' whims to delineate the cosmopolitan population of his native town.

(iv) The Bacchanalian scene have been rightly observed by Agrawala as "adapted to Indian conception". He prefers[16] the identification of the male figure with Kubera or Jambhala, to Greek Silenus. I have tried to show, that the cult of Balabhadra influenced that of Kubera and both of them were amalgamated with Dionysus, whose worship was introduced by the Hellenistic Indo-Greeks and Scythians.

The prevalence of male and female figures engaged in drinking[17] evidently points out the Bacchanalian aspect of the social enjoyments.

The dancing man wearing a wreath[18] is most probably a delineation of intoxicated Bacchus-Baladeva. A composite deity like "Bacchus-Baladeva-Kubera", no doubt, satiated the socio-religious zeal of both the Graeco-Scythians and the Indians,—the Hindus and the Buddhists alike. The ideal of a synthesis, indeed, was most befitting with the spirit of the age and with the cosmopolitan environment of *Madhupurī-Mathura*.

In this aspect of blending the heterogeneous traditions, the art-history of Mathura is none the less interesting and important than that of Gāndhāra.

3. **Amaravati School**: The Southern School of relief and sculpture flourished mainly centering round the sites of Amaravati and Nagarjunikonda.. Though art was economically patronized here by the Indo-Roman trade,[1] it was free from any foreign influences in its theory and practices. Some isolated exotic motifs, however, like the one represented by the Kañcuki with the staff (from Nagarjunikonda) show how occasionally the artist came across a western subject. In general, the style was the development of the pure indigenous Indian tradition and served as a link between the earlier works from Central India belonging to the Śuṅga epoch and the later Schools of Ajanta and the art under the later Hindu dynasties of the south. Some of the motifs like the winged lion and the beed reel which appear to be of Hellenistic borrowing are really from the 'Earlier Asiatic' stock-motifs. The grouping of the figures in Amaravati might show "illusionist" composition of the Roman

work but it cannot be proved with certainty, because we do find a prototype of this type of crowded composition in the carvings of Sanchi and Bharhut.

4. **Kashmiri School**: For singular contribution of the Kushans in the field of terracotta art and the curious blending of heterogenous motifs one should look to the remains at Harwan in Kashmir (c. 300 A.D.).[2] Here the physiognomy of the people represented are noticeable; the high cheek-bones, the prominent nose, sunken eyes and the receding forehead, make these apparent as the life like "representation of the mysterious people, the Kushans". There are some foreign motifs like the deer looking at the moon, and the conventional roosters. The narrow skull of the men and women of Harwan terracotta and of the young monk from Ushkar[3] are marked with receding foreheads which were the result of the "lateral pressure" practised amongst certain tribes in Central Asia. Heads of Bodhisattva, Brāhmaṇa ascetic and of the "*Upāsikā*" show the realistic delicacy of the Gāndhāra School.[4] All these influences show the intimate connection of Kashmirian art schools with that of north-west and Central Asia under the rule of the Kushans. The impetus which Kashmir received under the Kushans, set a distinct type of artistic development at work here in this valley. The later products of Kashmir retained its peculiarities adapted from the Gāndhāra School of Afghanistan and north-west India.

References

1. Gandhara School

1. The ablest and prominent authorities designate the school in different names; Foucher: Graeco-Buddhist, Marshall: Hellenistic or Buddhist art of Gāndhāra, Coomaraswamy: Gāndhāra School, Rowland: Graeco-Roman art of Gāndhāra etc.
2. Ghirhsman, op. cit., p. 3, the fuller understanding of the Greek forms represented in the "Illusionist" type of the discovery of Surkh Kotal, probably the Parthian art did develop from a mixture of Bactrian (Hellenistic) and Iranian traditions.
3. Ibid., vide the chronological table supplied.

4. Ibid., p. 362, "It was perhaps due to the Greek influence that the god was later, treated anthropomophically".
5. Ibid., Pls. 99, 100.
6. This problem has been presented afresh by the discovery made at Surkh Kotal.
7. PMC, Maues, Pl. X, 32; Azes, Pl. XII, 308; Azelises Pl. XIII, 333.
8. Frye, Heritage of Persia, Pl. 111, a similar bowl from Kustani (Russia) has been dated by Ghirshman in the 1st-2nd centuries A.D. In this specimen too, the figures are related to one another by gesture of their hands.
9. Ghirshman, Pl. 119, –a terracotta relief of a horse-rider, Parthian craftsmanship, cf. with the figure of the Amazon, note the flowing himation at the back.
10. Ibid., pp. 219, 274-77, – the Iranians were very fond of marvelous stories.'
11. PMC. Vide the coins of the Indo-Scythians and the Parthians.
12. Ingholt, Pl. IV, 1, 2, 3, –cf., the figures of the PMC., Pl. XIII, 327, Marine gods, Ingholt, IV 2; the pose of the female deity PMC. XIII 334 is somewhat analogous to the Buddha of the Bimaran reliquary.
13. Rowland, pp. 82-83.
14. Raychaudhuri, PHAI, p. 439, -c.33 B.C.-c.47 A.D.; D.C. Sircar, c. 20 B.C.-79 A.D.
15. Ghirshman, p. 30, Pl. 41, – the rhytons from Nysa.
16. Lohuizen de Leeuw, p. 84 ff.
17. Raychaudhuri, op. cit., p. 440.
18. Lohuizen de Leeuw, p. 86, "We, can, therefore assume that the reliquary dates from the 1st century A.D. at the earliest but possibly from sometime afterwards, as it is not possible that the great emperor Kaniṣka had ordered a reliquary to be made which was far less beautiful in all respect".
19. Herod. iv.
20. The sketches here are made from the plates in Ingholt.
21. As taken to be by Lohuizen de Leeuw, vide pp. 84, 104; Marshall, Buddhist Art, p. 54 thinks the style was adopted from the 'Sanghao-Nathu' group; Ibid., Pls. 60, p. 80.
22. Rowland, p. 85.
23. Ghirshman, p. 29.

24. Lohuzen de Leeuw, p. 94; Ingholt, p. 26, thinks "The Bimaran reliquary (Pl. III, 1) seems to fit best in this group taking into consideration the drapery folds of Buddha. It recalls in several respects a Sassanian silver jug (Pl. XI, 1) on which a row of priestesses is standing within arches supported by columns". But on account of the striking similarity of the casket with the general design of the shrine of the double headed eagle I would prefer to place the casket in the Parthian epoch of 1st century A.D. The placement of the figures within niches developed from the Zoroastrian custom of keeping the body in the ossuaries, which were carved in the forms of niches along the rocky walls of the grottos. The idea of the spirit rising from the niches (or body, in art) expressed eternal life. What is a more be-fitting ornamentation for the reliquary of the Great Soul? This Zoroastrian idea was no doubt engrafted on Buddhism by the Scythio-Parthians, and so we need not look for a far western model from the Sidarma Sarcophagi as does Rowland.
25. Rowland, Pl. 30 H.
26. Lohuizen de Leeuw, Pls. XXX, 55; XXXII, 57.
27. Ingholt, p. 30.
28. Lohuizen, Pl. XII, 19.
29. Ghirshman, pp. 92-93, Pl. 103, 104.
30. Ingholt IV 1-3, Pls. 411-414.
31. Lohuizen, Pl. 66.
32. Ingholt Pl. 413-414.
33. Ibid., Pl. 340, 342.
34. Ibid., Pls. 343, 344, 345.
35. Ibid., Pls. 341.
36. Ibid., Pl. 347.
37. Zimmer, Pls, 110, 111, the first band of the decorative leaves are not any actual plant but the representation of highly stylized Acanthus, same is represented issuing out of the jars at the sides; Goetz, East & West, X, no. 3, p. 158, Fig. III 3.
38. Ibid., Pls. 110, 111 show the rosettes within the lozenge strewn garland.

2. The Mathura School

1. Handbook, No. 2661.
2. MMC III, p. 77, No. 1457.

3. Ibid., p. 62, Nos. 784, 785.
4. Ibid., p. 35, the *āyāga-paṭa* of Vasu the coutesan; there is another more well-known of Āmohinī, CHI, p. 574.
5. Vide supra, p. 103 f.
6. Vide infra, Chapter Five, Sect., on Vaisnavism.
7. Vide infra, Chapter Five, sect. On Baladeva.
8. Rowland, p. 92; Lohuizen p. 46,–the Scythian king must had some relation with the Tukhāra line if kings.
9. MMC III, p. 41.
10. *Pratimānāṭaka*, III.
11. This "*sthāsaka*" sign is used in Syria, vide Francis, Jataka Tales, p. 153, n. 1; it probably had the same significance with the Scythio-Kushans too.
12. MMC III, p. 38 f.
13. Ibid., pp. 44-45.
14. Ingholt, Pl. 287.
15. MMC III, p. 82.
16. CBIMA, p. 95.
17. MMC III, p. 57, Nos. F28, F29, females engaged in drinking both being to Kushan period; p. 79, No. 1609, standing male figure holding a cup. Probably a worshipper of Baladeva (?).
18. For Dionysus' wreath, staff and wine-cup, vide Marshall Buddhist Art, pp. 26, 39, cf., Mathura figures holding staff and cups.

3. Amaravati School & Kashmir School

1. Rowland, p. 126.
2. Kak, AMK, p. 110, but Rowland, p. 118 assigns a much later date (724-60 A.D.) to the remains of Harwan and Ushkar.
3. Ibid., p. 153 (d), Pl. LVIII, Pl. XXIII, 3.
4. Ibid., Pl. LVIII, a, b, c.

Section III

Painting

There remains very little to say something definitely regarding western influence on Indian painting of this period. There is no doubt about the fact that artists were engaged and employed in the art of painting simultaneously with other branches of art, and we may justifiably assume that Gāndhāra, Mathura, Vidiśā and Amaravati had their own Schools of painting side by side with that of sculpture and architecture. But the total effacement of the paintings due to the changes of nature leave us nothing but to build on hypothesis, on mere assumptions from the occasional references in literature.[1]

The only intact specimens that belong to the two early centuries before the Christian era are those seen in Cave X of Ajanta. The style and composition of this work totally belong to traditional native style stemming out from the sculptural School of Central India.[2] Scholars have also found striking similarities in between the figure compositions of Ajanta and Amaravati,[3] which prove that the School represented in the frescos of Ajanta was purely indigenous in character and owed little to Iran or farther west. Moreover, it has been found that the typical style of this School was transplanted to far away frontier regions of India in the institutions of Bāmiyān and diffused to Central Asia from Afghanistan.[4]

It is at Bāmiyān that we come across a hybrid style representing a mixture of Iranian and Indian motifs. From this it may be assumed that the contemporary houses in Kāpiśa, Puṣkalāvatī, Takṣaśilā and other large and small townships were decorated with this medley style. The Sun god[5] depicted on the vault of the niche at Bāmiyān is dressed in tunic, mantle and boots and the goddesses of the dawn are garbed like Athena Pallas. The applying of flat colours without shading recalls the Sassanian treatment.[6]

Same hybrid in character was the Bodhisattva of cave group E, seated on a rainbow. Rowland thinks that in this aspect he resembled the Pantokrator of the Romanesque art, and evidently drew it's inspiration from the Roman East.[7]

The Sassanian style of painting of the third and fourth centuries A.D. remained current at various places in Afghanistan and similar decorations have come to light from Fondukistan which show that the tradition was alive upto seventh century A.D.[8]

Same colout-scheme of Ajanta, which used lapis-lazuli, yellow, red-ochre and light-green is seen on the frescoes of Kuh-i-Khwaja in Seistan of the first century A.D. This probably asserts some relation in between the artist's pallettes used in Seistan, Afghanistan and India.[9] It is probable that the artists in India procured lapis-lazuli and other colours from the districts of Afghanistan and Iran that were famous for stone and mineral pigments. That all the mural decorations were not of religious character is attested by the painting at Dukhtar-i-Nushirwan which represent, "a Sasanian king or prince seated, with his legs slightly apart, upon a throne formed of the fore-parts of two horses in close juxtaposition".[10] We may take this pose as the model for the Buddha seated on *Siṃhāsana* depicted in Cave XVII of Ajanta.[11] From the environment of the scene with groups of foreigners wearing coats and distinguished by their helmets, peaked head-gears and flat caps, it seems that the artist intentionally used the Sassanian royal posture for Buddha. Here Buddha is sitting like the Sassanian king and preaching to the congregation of different peoples.[12] This pose was the symbol of sovereignty and authority over all.

The typical Sassanian ornamentation of string of pearls, animals with neck-bands and waving fillets are profusely used in the caves of Bāmiyān.[13] It is interesting to note that these neck-bands were absent on the geese depicted in Sanchi and Bharhut but appear in late Gupta works. According to Goetz the string of pearls was adopted from the Roman West.

A few words may be said about the "illusionist" composition found in Kuh-i-Khwaja, Ajanta, Amaravati and Bāmiyān. In the frescoes of Kuh-i-Khwaja the figures are placed slightly overlapped by the other and thus impart a feeling of depath.[14]

This style also adopted in Afghanistan "show clearly the influence of the Hellenistic East" on the early art of Bāmiyān.[15] Similar treatment in composition found from Ajanta might have had developed from Amaravati tradition and owed nothing to the *'Augustan* phase of the Western art. The similar technique[16] and treatment of applying flat colours within a dark contour seen at Kuh-i-Khwaja and some murals at Ajanta might have developed in these far off regions independently without any borrowing on either side.

The isolated exotic subjects delineated in Ajanta are the representations of Khusrau II with his attendants, his embassy to the court of Pulakeśin II, and the panel depicting the old Turanian.[17] The features, costumes as well as the composition of the first is so similar to the banquet scenes of Sassanian repertory that it is impossible to think of it other than the representation of the said Sassanian monarch. Even, if it had gained the different significance in the minds of the Buddhist artists as Kubera with his female attendants, the motif was, no doubt, directly taken from Iran.

The embassy scene most probably belong to the Chālukyan epoch but the Indian artists of Deccan and Western India were familiar with Scythian people prior to that, and the painting may be depict some other court scene as well.[18]

So there is every possibility that by Gupta and Chalukyan period these subjects already became the stock motifs in Indian artists repertory.

We are again left to assumptions regarding the transference of these motifs from one place to another. Fa-hsien tells that "he passed two years in the monastery at Tāmralipta copying the Buddhist texts and drawing pictures of images". This is actually the method by which motifs were transmitted from centre to centre. The artists copied the theme in tracings and transformed it by the process of stencil. We are evidently reminded of the expression "*Kvaciccitreṣu darśayet*" found in the *Matsyapurāṇa*. These *ādarśacitras* or the model-drawings were responsible for the exotic blendings in the art of painting. The Sassanian banquet "which with slight variation is repeated no less than four times" was reproduced no doubt with the help of tracing.

One could easily imagine that the ateliers were full of rolls of stencilled parchment that were used repeatedly. We would have been fortunate if some of these survived the vicissitudes of nature and came into light. In the paucity of available evidences we are to satisfy ourselves with these few sporadic specimens that betray foreign impact.

References

1. *Mahāummagga Jātaka* (546) describes how the artists decorated the walls with pictures of Śakra, Sumeru mountain and it's environs, the oceans, the dvīpas, the sun, the moon and the *caturmaharājikas* etc., it also relates the preparation for the mural painting, vide, I. Ghosh, Vol. VI, p. 299.
2. Rowland, p. 67, Dey, Pl. VII.
3. Rowland, p. 150.
4. Ibid., p. 108 ff.
5. According to Hackin, p. 5, Fig. 4, this is a representation of the moon god.
6. Rowland, p. 108.
7. Ibid., p. 109, cf., Tāranātha, Datta, p. 18, "He gave Siddhi to all men, and from animal to worms and disappeared in the rainbow-body".
8. Rowland, p. 110.
9. Ghirshman, p. 41 ff.
10. Hachin, p. 6.
11. Dey, Pl. XXIV.
12. *Mahāvastu*, I, p. 135.
13. Hackin, p. 5, Pl. II, Fig. 3, 3A.
14. Ghirshman, p. 41; Pls. 56, 57.
15. Hackin, p. 3.
16. Rowland, p. 146.
17. Ibid., pp. 148-49; Yazdani, p. 46-50; Pls. XXXVIII.
18. Apart from the Scythian houses of Ujjaini, contacts between western India and Iran was frequent. Mitrasena, the king of Bhṛgukaccha sent embassies to Varhran III. So did the Ābhīras and the Kṣatrapas of Avantī and Bhagadatta of Surāṣṭra.

Section IV

Miscellaneous Branches of Minor Arts

A few scattered references from the epic and later literature may be cited to show as to how far foreign influence was felt in the scope of the minor arts.

In the *Āśvamedhikaparvan* of the epic[1] a story has been related how Yudhiṣṭhira went to the Muñjavān mountain, that lay in the north-west of India, propitiated Mahādeva and obtained the golden vessels belonging to king Marutta. The Muñjavān parvata lay beyond Gāndhāra country. The story may faintly recall the fact, that in olden times various kinds of golden vessels were brought into India from Bactria or Iran, or from the lands of Central Asia. The rich courts of Indian monarchs were in constant need of the vessels, cups, cauldrons, rhytons and jugs and the workshops of Parthian Iran must have supplied India with the vessels of foreign make.

The other is the fanciful episode of "*Dvātriṃśatputtulikā*" which goes under the name of the poet-laureate Kālidāsa. The novel idea of the throne was no doubt suggested by the Caryatids or Atlantes of Hellenistic repertory,[2] who stand holding a throne or an entablature.[3] The provenance of the story is the kingdom of king Śālivāhana, and it was probably in the realm of these Andhra kings, or the Śakas of Western India, that an unique seat was made, whose pedestal was made up a thirty two caryatids. The seat was famous for its uncommon features[4] and folklores grew about it. It became famous like the peacock-throne of Shahjahan, and later on in Gupta India the stories were gleaned in the name of *Dvātriṃśatputtalika*. It is not unlikely that the Śaka satrap, who imported sweet wine, fair concubines and silver vessels for their court, probably ordered the novel seat, like the one suggested in the story, to be made and used it in the court of Ujjaini. Goetz thinks that the court of the Kṣatrapas in Ujjaini became that seat of the refugee literati, priests, astrologers and artists onwards from A.D. 226

till it was captured by Chandragupta II,[5] and they were responsible for the strong Roman impact on the development of Gupta Art. It is not unlikely then that '*āsanas*' with '*puṭtalikās*' (caryatids) were first introduced during the Śaka-Śātavāhana period.

References

1. Mbh. 14m Ch. 65 (B.R.M.), it is explicitly mentioned that the vessels were of vast and variegated shapes. The caravan of camels described remind inevitably of some desert tract across Central Asia. Central Asia was Famous for it's gold (vide Stein, Ruins of Desert Cathy, II, pp. 437, 444-447) also Tibet and Dardistan, and this had been the result for these wonderful tales. But probably the Hellenistic rhytons of fanciful shapes are alluded to here.
2. Breasted, Ancient Times, p. 455.
3. Huart, op. cit., p. 93, Fig. 11 throne of Darius at Persepolis.
4. *Mahāummagga Jataka*, mentions female statues like caryatids standing beside the throne. *Ramayana* mentions idols that fanned Ravana by mechanism. But these literary references are later than the Greek caryatids and there is every possibility that the idea was suggested by an exotic model.
5. Goetz, East & West, 1959, p. 262.

Section V

Music, Dance and Drama

Foreign elements contributed immensely to the growth and development of Indian performing arts. We will discuss the subject under following heads,—(i) the tunes and dances that were adopted from the incoming tribes, (ii) the foreign dress adopted by the musicians and the dancers, (iii) foreigners in ancient Indian drama, (iv) the possible foreign influence on the open-air theatre, and (v) the common musical instruments.

(i.a.) **Gāndhāra**: From the ample references in the Sanskrit literature it is attested that the Gāndhāra were celebrated for their aptitude in music and dancing. The very situation of their territory makes it highly suggestive that foreign influences first crept into the musical system through the artists of this land. The *Rāmayāṇa* states that the Gandharvas inhabited the land of Gāndhāra. The Gandharva tribe has been represented as semi-divine beings who kept themselves busy in the pursuit of music and dancing. They possessed such delicate musical instruments, and were the masters and such subtle techniques, which were beyond the human accomplishments and not known in India proper.[1] This evidently remind us of the artists of Kuchar who created tune from the sound of the gushing water-falls during the rainy season.[2] It is highly probable that the Gandharvas kept close contact with the eerie tribes of the Kinnaras (whose name really means "Kiṃ-nara" i.e., are they human?) and were experts in playing the *Kīcaka-veṇu*, i.e., a flute from the reed of Kīcaka bamboo that grew on the banks of the Śailodā river.[3] The story related in the *Kinnarī Jātaka*[4] show that the Kinnaras shunned the populace and retired to the deep quitude of trans-Himalayan rocky nooks and forests. But their skill in vocal and instrumental music was well-known to the Aryan society, who made them the musicians of the court of Devaraja Indra.

It is interesting to note in this connection that Śiva, who is primitive deity of the Himalayan and trans-Himalayan ranges is called Gāndhāra in the epic[5] and presides over the realm of music, dance and dramaturgy. The description of his ritual with a large number of musical instruments, no doubt, betrays a foreign affiliation.[6] It has been noted that Śiva and Kubera presided ever the Yakṣhas, Rakṣas, Kinnaras, Gandharvas, Piśācas and Guhyakas – many of whom were actual tribal folk residing in the valleys of the Hindukush and the Himalayas.[7] Their religious music then, no doubt, contributed a great deal to the Indian musical system. We are inclined to identify this type of musical ritual of Śiva with the reference to the procession of 'Dionysia' in the classical literature.[8] The contention that Dioysus taught the Indians to carry on Bacchanals with the beating of drums and cymbals, dance and music – indeed, indicate to the contribution of this trans-Himalayan peoples to the musical system of ancient India.

The *Vāyu-purāṇa* while relating the story of king Raivata, describes in detail the Indian musical system and gives the list of the component parts of the musical key-borad.[9]

The *Gāndhāra* is the name of the third note as well as the third scale. The notes and scales were called after the places of their provenance. So *Sauvīrī* tune was called after the Sauvīra country, and *Madraka* after the Madras. The *Gāndhāra-grāma* was specially studied by the Gandharvas. It had innate meaning and possessed magical charms that mesmerized beasts, serpents, human beings – even self-mortifying sages.[10] The abstruse technique of playing upon the music was kept in strictest secrecy. According to Mallinatha the *Gāndhāragrāma* is denoted in the *Meghadūta*.[11]

(i.b.) **Kāmboja**: Closely associated with the Gāndhāras were the Kāmbojas. P.C. Bagchi had pointed out that the similarity between Kāmbojā and Khāmboja is striking. If the raga Kāmboja of the *Bṛhaddeśī*[12] can be connected with the Kāmboja tribe of the Badakshan-Kafiristan and the later rāga Khāmbāja, then the contribution of the Gāndhāran artists seem to be attested once more. The rāga from Kāmboja country was most likely introduced by the Gāndhāras, who occupied the region between India and the land of the Kāmbojas.

(i.c.) **Other foreign tunes *Hariṇāsyā* and *Śuddhamadhyamā*:** The *Purāṇas* mention the original homeland of several tunes. Thus the *Vāyupurāṇa* mentions that *mūrcchanā Hariṇāsyā* was born in Harideśa and *mūrcchanā Śuddhamadhyamā* was born in Marudeśa. We do not know whether this Harideśa and Marudeśa are identical respectively with Harivarṣa and the desert (maru) of Central Asia or Seistan. The Harideśa may denote the region of the Hari-rud, or the Haraquaiti in the Hāra-hūra territory. The way the Vāyu explicitly mentions the provenance of these *mūrchanās*, connotes that these tunes originated outside India.

(i.d): Two other Scythian rāgas called *Śakamiśritā* and *Śakākhyā* were introduced by the Śakas during their political supremacy. We do not know as to what extent the 'fair maidens' and the 'singing boys' in the harem of the Śaka satrap Nahapāna contributed their shares in enriching the contemporary musical system. But this reference is a sure proof to the music loving nature of the Śakas. It can be safely surmised at least, that the Indians of this age, who lived in large metropolises like Ujjaini, Mathura and Takṣaśilā were not unfamiliar with exotic music. On the other hand, it is highly probable, that *Mahākṣatrapa* Rudradāman, who was a celebrated connoisseur of music, art and letters[13] might have had done much for the enquiry and advancement of the Indian musical system by introducing new items and patronizing a synthesis. The similarity in between South Indian (Carnatic) and Greek style of music may point to the result of the trade connection between South India and the Hellenistic West.[14]

It is interesting to note in this connection that the Śaka name Rebhila which is given to a musician in *Mṛicchakaṭika*, recalls immediately the nomenclature of Guptila and Musila, two other experts from Ujjaini (Guptila Jat. 243).

It is not unlikely that the sun-worship introduced by the Magis of Persia incorporated within its rituals a special role for music and dancing. We know[15] that the dancing girls appointed in the temples of the Sun delighted the deity with dance and music. Both the Chinese and the Indian references[16] attest the position of the temple-dancers in cites of Multan and Ujjaini, which witnessed the Śaka subjugation for a considerable period. Thus the custom betrays a strong foreign impetus. It would have been interesting to know how far these dance and music brought the age-old Babylonian tradition with it.

(i.e.): Synchronous with the Śakas, the Ābhiras, had gained power in Western India. Their contribution to the music and dance of India was considerable. The term Ābhīra later on denoted the gopas i.e., the cow-herds. *Ābhīrī* was a folk-music sung by these cow-herds which later on was standardized into a rāga.[17] Moreover the opening verse of the *Bṛhaddeśī* which runs thus:

"*Abalā-bāla-gopālaiḥ kṣitipālairnijecchayā*

Gīyate sānurāgeṇa svadeśe deśirucyate".

takes note of the song of the *gopālas*, who were no doubt mostly Ābhīras.

The group-dance during the harvest moon was very popular among these nomadic folks. The ballet was performed in a ring of male and female partners hand in hand. When the participants started to move in a circle the tinkling of the jewellery of the *gopis* enhanced the sweet note of songs sung by them. Obviously the women took a more active role in this group dance, they sang louder than Kṛṣṇa. The particular forward and backward movement of the dance has been noted too.[18]

A similar type of tribal dance in which the females encircle the male participant is described in the *Harivaṃśa* as *Hallīsaka*.[19] "Hallīsa" seems to be a non-Aryan word denoting folk-dances. In one of the *Purāṇas* the Bhil women are said to be delighting in *Hallīsaka* dance.

At present the word "*hallā*" dentoes boisterous revel. The modes of *Rāsa* and *Hallīsaka* have striking similarities with the *Garbā* dance of Gujarat, Kathiawar, and the folk dances of the Rajasthani Lambardi Banjaras. All these provincial variations seem to have traditionally come down from the *Rāsa* and the *Hallīsaka* of the *Viṣṇupurāṇa* and the *Harivaṃśa*.

The *Harivaṃṣa* presents another very interesting musical recital called "*Chālikya-krīḍanam*". A group of nymphs, i.e., *apsarās* dressed in the costume of the Yādava women[20] presented an opera show before Balabhadra, Revatī and other Yāvana scions. The songs related the activities of Vāsudeva-Kṛṣṇa in Vṛindāvana and Mathura. The rāgas of songs changed according to the moods expressed in the lyric. The Yādavas with ardent endeavour learnt the subtle technique of the *Chālikya* music. The vivid and lively description of the atmosphere that prevailed over the performance, indeed, show the *Chālikya* was highly appreciated in the contemporary society. A.N. Sanyal opines that this novel *Chālikya* was the precursor of more classical Rūpaka of the *Saṅgīta-ratnākara* and the mediaeval *Ṭhuṃrī* style of the Lucknow School.[21]

Thus we see tradition of the *Ṭhuṃrī* School goes back to the ancient days of the *Harivaṃśa* (third fourth centuries A.D.). The nymphs who performed the show were no doubt Ābhīra women who due to their inherent aptitude for music and dancing were often identified with the celestial dancers and were actually professional *narttakis* of ancient India.[22] They were probably affiliated to the moving bands of musicians who earned their livelihood by singing the songs of Vāsudeva-Kṛṣṇa.

(i.f.) **The Ṭakka and Varāṭi rāgas**: The *Ṭakkarāga* which finds numerous mention in Mataṅga's work as *Ṭaku*[23] (*Taṅki*) and *Ṭakka*[24] is mentioned along with another foreign melody the *Boṭṭrāga*.[25] *Ṭakka-raga* is said to be propitiating to Goddess Lakṣmī (*Kaśyapamatetu Ṭakkarāga eva mukhya Lakṣmī-prīti-karatvāt*). O.C. Ganguly thinks that it was sung by a tribe called Ṭakka who settled in Punjab, originally hailing from the Turanian kingdom of eastern Iran.[26]

Lastly, we may mention another rāga in which some foreign affiliation may be traced. This is rāga *Varāṭī*. Scholars are not definite about the origin of its appellation.[27] O.C. Ganguly thinks that the name was derived from Virāṭanagara, and it was a "*nagarākhyā rāgiṇī*". But Svami Prajñanānda draws our attention to Nānyadeva's statement, "*Varāṭī Lāṭadeśajā*" which proves its connection with Gujarat region.

Previously we have seen that the Varāṭas or Varuḍas might have been identical with the Pāratas[28] who were the Paratacenae of the Medes. If this assumption is attested by some corroborative evidences in future, then it will prove that the Varāṭī rāga of Mataṅga is the tune introduced by the Varāṭas or Varuḍas, a so-called low-caste from the western coast of India.

(ii) **Foreign dress of the Musicians**: We have taken notice of the panel from Sanchi which presents a group of drummers and musicians in western costume.[29] A comparison between this and the description of the Indian musicians to China, which runs as follows, "The Indian musicians use a cap of black cloth, they put on a silken white tunic, violet coloured breeches of brocade and a red mantle"...etc., show that the dress of the Indians were not "Indian" at all, and some radical change must have taken place in the realm of musicians just before the panel of Sanchi was curved (early first century A.D.; the red 'mantle' is no doubt the Chlamys seen on the figures) and the tradition remained intact uptill c. 581 A.D. when the Chinese emperor invited all the musicians to attend the international musical conference in China. The dress just described was the uniform worn by the Indian orchestra party. Thus it is evident that the Indian musicians had not only adopted foreign notes and tunes, but also the Graeco-Scythian dress, which became the traditional garb of some group of musicians. The Chinese description continues thus "the dancers are two in number. They have their hairs plaited and they put on a *Kāṣāya* of ch'ao-hia, similar to the dress of the monks. They walk with shoes made of ropes and green hemp".[30]

Let us compare this dress with that of the dancers portrayed in the Bagh Cave (6th-7th centuries A.D.). The male dancers are dressed in tight-fitting full sleeved tunics and wore their hair in the '*alaka*' style, in which the coiffure was arranged in short locks around the forehead and fell upon the shoulders resembling the wig. This style was very popular amongst the young students, poets and the literati in Roman West. Though chronologically the Bagh Cave is beyond the scope of our present study, it is considered necessary for attention.

The female dancers with the drum (*dholak* and *marddala*) depicted on a terracotta panel from Harwan, Kashmir[31] wear a sleeved tunic and a pair of loose trousers. The fact that this became the traditional costume of the court-dancers is attested by the paintings of Ajanta and bas-reliefs from Deogarh, both belonging to the Gupta-Vākāṭaka period. In the fresco of Ajanta the *Naṭī* is dressed in a suit, the upper part of which comprises a multi-coloured full-sleeved tunie with long side-openings. The lower part of the body was covered with a striped sari won in lungi style. In the sculptural piece, the accessory consists of a full-sleeved *Kāmiz* and a *curidār paijāmā*. The peculiar long side openings (See Plate 3a) no doubt came from the Scythians of Central Asia and is still found in the shirts worn by Chinese and Punjabi women folk. Thus the literary as well as the archaeological evidence point to the fact that the Scythian costume of tunic and trousers was much appreciated and adopted by the musicians, the *naṭas* and *naṭīs* of ancient India.

(iii) **Foreign tribes in Indian Theatre**: The theory of the origin of Indian drama from the Greek has long been discarded[32] since the true derivation of the term "*Yamanikā*" and not "*Yavanikā*"[33] (from the Yavanas). But the foreign characters were not totally alienated from the theatrical performances. Thus Bharata lays injunctions for the dress and complexion of the Ābhīras, Śakas, Yavanas, Pahlavas, Bāhlīkas and those from *Bhadrāśva-varṣa* and *Uttarakuru*.[34]

From Bharata's reference to the costume of the *Ābhīra-Yuvatīs* it becomes evident that they were well-known characters in drama. The blue apparel ("*nīlaprāyamathāmbaram*" Nāṭ ya, xxi. 69a;

"*nīlapītāmbarābhiśca taruṇībhiralaṃkritam*" Hari, II. 5.28

"*nīlapītāruṇaistāsāṃ vastvairagrastanocchṛitaiḥ*", Ibid. II. 9. 16) and especially the "*dviveṇīdhara*" coiffure recall the Iranian dancers represented with two plaits of hair[35] on Sassanian vases. This once more attest the connection of the Ābhīras with Iran, and consequent extra-Indian impact.

(iv) **The Open-air Theatre**: If the readings of Bloch of the inscriptions of Jogimārā and Sitābengā caves on Ramgarh are accepted, then it appears that the Sītābengā cave was used as an open-air theatre and was visited by dancers, musicians and poets, especially during the full moon of spring. Kālidāsa in the *Meghadūta* and Bāṇa in his *Harṣacarita* refer to the dancing girls in the caves of the western hills. Some has taken the term '*Leṇaśobhikā*,[36] as denoting courtesans and connects them with the dancing girls of the caves. Kālidāsa however, refer to the courtesans who entertained the *nāgarakas* in the rocky taverns of the Niraiḥ hill which stood in the vicinity of the township of Vidiśā. The reference to the Astagiri "the hollows of whose cave resounded with the tinkling anklets of Varuṇa's intoxicated and tripling women" in the *Harṣacarita*, however fantastic in character, simplifies the problem of "Śūtanuka nama devadaśI". Whether she was a "*devadāsī*" or a "*devadarśinī*" *Vāruṇī* woman[37] as propounded by Jayaswal, there is no doubt about the fact that she was a dancer. The reference of Bāṇa clearly shows that these female adopts use to dance and drink to appease Varuṇa, or Baladeva (Viṣṇu, v. 25). So there remains no objection to take Śutanuka as a professional dancer even if not a *devadāsī* proper. We know of similar female prophets who predicted under the influence of gods and bacchantes who used to dance and drink to propitiate Dionysus. In the present state of knowledge it cannot be stated whether these Indian Vāruṇī women had any connection with the maenads of Dionysus. But the striking similarity in between the cults of Dionysus and Baladeva-Varuṇa are to be noted especially.

It cannot be stated finally whether the open-air theatre of the Greeks had influenced the Indian systems of performances to certain extent. It seems, that the innate love for nature of Indian character made them choose the natural rocky resorts for theatrical performances.

(v) **The Musical Instruments**: Some reciprocal must had taken place in the field of musical instruments too. The Chinese description seem to refer to the same sort of instrument seen on the Sanchi panel,—probably the "sphinx-headed lute called K'ong-hou" and the "transversal flute called heng-ti" respectively denote the *vīṇā* curved with animals head and the double reed pipe. The last mentioned is seen on paintings from ancient Iran, and Egypt.[38] It seems that the trumpets with animals heads and the double reed pipe depicted on the Sanchi panel were introduced from outside India. Scholars have drawn our attention to the similarity of names of a lyre-type string instrument called *citra-vīṇā* in sanskrit and '*cithara*' in Arabic. The modern forms of the names are *Sitar* in Hindi and *Zithar* in Greek and Latin.[39]

The above discussion makes it clear that foreign influences were active in this aspects of Indian culture, too, and the spirit of absorption paved the way for future synthesis and enrichment.

References

1. Mbh. 3. 49. 39-43 (Haridas).
2. P.C. Bagchi, India and China, p. 165.
3. *Kumārasambhavam*, I.8.
   Mbh. 2.50.2 (Haridas).
4. *Mahavastu*, II, p. 191 ff.
5. Sorensen, p. 231.
6. Vayup. 40, 18-25.
7. This assumption is corroborated by the reference to the Yakṣalipi, Gāndhārva-lipi, Kinnara-lipi with Daradalipi, Ṛiṣya-lipi, Cīna-lipi, Hūṇa-lipi etc. in the *Lalitavistara*, p. 125; had they not been actual tribal people their scripts would not have been mentioned along with other scripts of different peoples.
8. Vide infra, Chapter Five, Section on Śiva.
9. Vayup. Chaps. 86-87.
10. Ibid., 86, 59-66.
11. *Meghaduta*, *Uttara*, 25.
12. Bṛihad, p. 106.
13. Ep. Ind. Vol. VIII, p. 44.
14. Rāga O Rūpa, p. 47.
15. Vide supra, p. 108, n.57.
16. Vide supra, p. 142, n. 87.
17. Bṛihad., p. 107.
18. Viṣṇup. V. 13, 49-56.

19. Hari, II, 20; Bhāratīya Saṅgīer Ittihāsa, II, p. 135.
20. Vide supra, p. 75, n. 162.
21. Prācīna Bhārate Saṅgit Cintā;
    Rāga O Rūpa, pp. 65-66.
22. Vide supra, pp. 133-134.
23. Bṛihad, p. 84, vs. 314; taku-rāga.
24. Ibid., p. 143, vs. 391 (Dheṅki), p. 98 etc.
25. Ibid., p. 96.
26. BSI, p. 20.
27. Rāga O Rūpa, p. 230 f.
28. Vide supra, 59-60 ff.
29. Vide supra, pp. 162-163.
30. India & China, pp. 166-67.
31. Vide supra, p. 172, n. 70.
32. BSI, II, p. 315, n. 174.
33. Manomohan Ghosh, *Prācīna Bhārater Nāṭyakalā*, p. 64.
34. Nāṭya, XXI, 102, 111.
35. Ghirshman, p. 214, Pl. 256; p. 215; Pl. 268, the plaits and the close fitting bandana on their head, make them conspicuously similar to the modern 'Irāṇī' gipsy women.
36. It might be *loṇaśobhikā* as well, vide Agrawala, Meghādūta, Purva, 26; Harsa, VI, Cowell, p. 187.
37. K.P. Jawaswal, I.A. 1919, p. 131; Vessantara Jat (547), Ghosh, pp. 351, 422; In Vidurapaṇḍita Jat (545) Varuṇa is the name of the Nāgarāja. Some tradition must have had connected Varuṇa with Baladeva the incarnation of Śeṣanāga, Mbh. II. 9.6ff. (Haridas).
38. Pritchard, p. 65, Pls. 208, 209.
39. For a detailed discussion, see BSI. P. 35 ff.

Five

Religion

In this chapter will be discussed the foreign elements that exerted some influence on the realm of Indian religion on the Hindu way of life. The chapter has been divided into seven sections dealing with the worship of Śakti, Śiva, Kṛṣṇa-Viṣṇu, Sūrya, Lakṣmī, Baladeva and Kāttikeya.

Section I

The Cult of Śakti Durgā

It is needless to elaborate here that the worship of a 'Great Mother Goddess' was carried on in the pre-historic days throughout the regions extending from Indus Valley to Iran, Syria and Asia Minor and spread as far as the Caucasus. It was prevalent in Egypt and Crete.[1] The universal idea of conceiving the earth as a mother, the common attributes of which were the fertility and sustenance of beings served as the link in between. The earth was conceived in the female form of a mother, the Great Goddess, progenitor of all life.

The cult was flouring in the Indus Valley and it was inherent to the pre-Aryan inhabitants of India. The great goddess is mentioned as Vāk in the *Ṛigveda*[2] as Śakti in the *Taittiriya Āraṇyaka*[3] and in the *Kena Upaniṣad*.[4] Her personality developed rapidly and she is often found invoked in the *Mahābhārata*[5] and in the *Rāmāyaṇa*. In the period under discussion, the foreign traits in this cult become obvious from the study of the contemporary literature, coins and cult images.

In the *Durgāstotras* of the *Mahābhārata* Durgā is described as the sister of Vāsudeva Kṛṣṇa and possesses the virtue of bestowing victory in war. This aspect is also prominent in the

Rāmāyaṇa. She is explicitly mentioned as "*Raṇapriyā*" and is attributed with various kinds of weapons. In this aspect she resembles the Ishtar-Nanā of Babylon and Cybele of Phrygia and Rome.[6] These common attributes led to her common worship by the foreign merchants, sailors as well as warriors. The attributes of course, were not foreign, they developed out of the indigenous Vedic idea. The verses in the epic describes her composite character:

"*Durgāttarāyase Durge tattvam Durgā smṛtajanaih*

Kāntāreṣva-Vasannānāṃ bhagnānāñca mahārṇve 21".

(i) The Goddess of the desolate regions:

"*Kāntāravāsinī*" Durgā was actually the primitive goddess of many wild regions and mountainous valleys[7] where she did receive the homage of native wild tribes and travelers that passed by her abode in the forelorn spots. Such a deity presided over Hinglaj which lay hidden within the fold of a rocky cliff in South Baluchistan by the side of a very ancient track of communication.[8] This deity was identified with the Indo-Iranian goddess Nana who later on was amalgamated by the Brahmanical Hindus with Umā or Durgā. This sacred spot received the status of the one of the most prominent *Pīṭhas* of Śākta cult.[9] The goddess is still called Nānī, reminiscent of her old name and the priests belong to Mohammedan faith. It is said, that images of the Sun and the Moon are carved over the entrance of the cave, which possibly indicate a Sassanian affinity. The Arabitai and the Oreitai who inhabited the surrounding territories were probably the earlier worshippers of this goddess who was also connected with the Dahae Scythians and the Lohas.[10] It undoubtedly received a new impetus under the Sassanians in whose reign goddess Anahita was raised to a higher status together with the Sun and the Moon deities. As the portraits of these two gods are carved on the facade of her shrine,[11] it seems, that here in Hinglaj, Nanā or Umā was worshipped as Anāhita. Moreover, these parts of South Baluchistan together with Drangiana in Seistan, was subjugated by Varhran III[12] and were kept into intimate connection with Sassanid Iran, in the third century A.D.

(ii) Śaktis of different regions:

Another holy seat of Bhīmadevī has been mentioned in the epic and drawn the attention of Hiuen-Tsang.[13] This Bhīmādevī was the spouse of the Lord of Gāndhāra region which we have seen earlier came under profound foreign impacts. It is difficult to determine how far the foreign trends had influenced the ritualistic aspects of the cult, but this much can be safely surmised that both Indians and the Western immignants tried to identify their traditional goddesses with the Indian Śakti and vice versa. Thus the epic takes notice of one goddess Śāṇḍilī who guarded the Śṛṅgavān Parvata beyond the ranges of Jambudvīpa (India). She was identical with some native divinities of the trans-Himalayan region. Thus we come across more names of foreign goddesses viz., Auṣadhī and Kuśodakā who were conceived as 'Sākti's of Uttarakuru and Kuśadvīpa. We know from the accounts of Herodotus that the Scythians worshipped a goddess called Tabiti.[14] The Indians must have had known some such foreign divinities and tried to identify them as 'Śaktis' presiding over different regions of the world around. One is reminded of the goddess Śākambharī, whose very name is reminiscent of the Śakas or as the divinity presiding over the vegetation. However, the tale that has been related to account for the peculiar nomenclature[15] seems to be a forced attempt on the part of the *Purāṇakāras* to adjust this foreign divinity within the fold of Hindu pantheon. That the goddess Kātyāyanī was worshipped by the nomadic Gopas is attested by a reference in the *Bhāgavatapurāṇa*.[16] The foreign extraction and affiliation of the Gopas have already been discussed, and the above reference then proves that they also took to the worship of Śakti.

(iii) The Kumārī, or the Virgin Mother:

We shall now discuss another manifestation of the goddess that was especially connected with the concept of "Virgin Mother" who presided over the coastal regions and harbours. The Periplus mentions a virgin goddess of the Cape of Comari in the extreme southern point of the Indian Peninsula. It describes, "Beyond this (Balitae=modern Varkkallai, 842 n,

76.43 C) there is another place called Comari and a harbour; hither come those who wish to consecrate themselves for the rest of their lives and bathe and dwell in celibacy and women also do the same; for it is told that a goddess dwelt here and bathed".[17] The Comari or Kumārī is a name of Durgā.[18] There is every possibility that the worship of this virgin mother goddess Kumārī was not confined only to the South Indian port, but was known in north-western India too. The reference to the "*Kumārikāṇāṃ tīrtham*" in the epic points to a direction where Ammianus Marcellinus places the "Gynaecon limen" or the Woman's Haven.[19] This recalls the observation on the cult of a supreme female deity prevalent in the southern parts of Baluchistan.[20]

However, in the South, "Kumārī" was one of the seven sisters of the South Indian pantheon and she probably received her special virgin mother attribute, or, that aspect was heightened up by the Graeco-Roman traders who frequently visited her place during the early centuries around the beginning of the Christian era.

The stories about virgin mothers were very popular in Lydia and Phrygia. The cult of the Virgin Mother Nanā or the Great Mother Cybele and Attis was introduced in Rome in about 204 B.C. To remain celibate is one of the important features of this cult and the priests of Cybele practised castration.[21]

It resembled in some respect with the cult of Isis in Egypt, the mother of Herus. She received devout homage from the Egyptians and her worship permeated to the sea-faring Greeks who lovingly called her "Stella Maris" i.e., the Star of the Sea.[22] When they reached the shores of India after crossing the tempest tormented ocean they might have come to pay their grateful thanks to this "Kumārī" mother, to them who appeared as an incarnation of the Virgin Isis. With them probably came the legends of western mythology not only of the Graeco-Romans or the Egyptian Greeks but also the Indians probably took active role in amalgamating these similar ideas. The Indians who frequented the city of Alexandria must have had been inspired by following the cult of "Stella Maris" Isis, whose Indian counterpart was the goddess Diśā, an aspect of Durgā and the ocean-deity Manimekhalai; the saviour of the sea.[23] It seems, from the Tamil epic that the worship of the goddess was popularized during the period of the Graeco-Roman trade. This shows the foreign impetus that invigorated the cult of the "Saviour Mother of the Seas".

It would be interesting to note in this connection that a similar shrine of Bhagavatī (Great Mother) is mentioned in the *Dvātriṃśat Puttalikā*. The shrine was visited by a merchant while going to Dvārakā from Ujjainī. It is not explained why he took this sea-route to his pilgrimage to Dvāraka. However, in his voyage, he came across a rock amidst the waters and after disembarking he found the temple of the Devī. On the left side of the image lay two torsos, one male and the other of a female. The story goes on relating how the dead bodies were rejuvinated by the benevolence of king Vikramāditya. Now, we know, from the Periplus that the western coast of India was infested by pirates. The Meds and Koris who inhabited these coastal haunts were given to piracy. It is not improbable to assume that this heinous way of worshipping the Devi was conducted by these banditti people. Brigands and burglers have been traditionally associated with the cult of Kali. It is curious to note that the merchant was accompanied by many "*Videśīs*" i.e., foreigners and "*anāthas*" i.e., parentless persons,[24] in his pilgrimage.

(iv) The Iconography of Śakti:

The earliest cult images represent the Mother in nude state bejewelled with prominent ornaments. These terracotta figurines were most probably kept in every household and worshipped. During our period of study, terracotta figurines of this type, have been found influenced by some foreign traits. In the Parthian city of Sirkap, Taxila Marshall came across several small figurines, which he connected with the worship of the Mother-Goddess. They are similar to the Mathura sculptures in regard to their highly prominent limbs, on the other hand they exhibit Graeco-Parthian modelling. It seems that they were highly popular, otherwise the foreign or native artists trained under the Gāndhāra School of craftsmanship would not have manufactured them.

Some of these ex-voto plaques and one figure represent the divinity dressed, more or less in a skirt like costume. In one of the specimens the costume appears to be a pair of trousers worn like the modern Pathan or Hazara women. According to Marshall none of these figures are later than the second century B.C.[25] Figures Nos. 16, 17 and 18 of Marshall's Taxila II probably depict Aphrodite as these resemble the same from Naukratis and Cyprus. The arms retain the particular Ionian attitude and 'possibly go back to an Ionian tradition introduced into the Punjab during Achaemenid times'. Nos. 20, 21 and 22 have been described as 'Draped female deities seated, with bird on folded arms' the posture is European. Hrozný points to the fact that, "Shakush, shakuntash may be a goddess representing the Babylonian Ishtar. The sacred animal of the Babylonian goddess of love and mother goddess Ishtar's was the dove or perhaps the swallow"[26] Nos. 23 to 25 represent votive terracotta plaques with a mother holding a child on her left hip; the drapery is free flowing the both are ornamented heavily. In the Babylonian religion Ishtar, Aphrodite and Nanā became amalgamated together and they were thought to be the different aspects of the same Great Mother.[27] From the archaeological facts given above it appears that these deities held a composite influence on the Śakti cult in Gāndhāra region.

The archaeological data is corroborated by the numismatic evidence, which show clearly Bhaveśa and Nanā in a Duality. Nanā here takes the place of Śiva's consort Umā or Durgā.[28] The earliest coin, which tentatively suggests a Simhavahini form of Durgā is the coin, type No. 30 of Azes.[29] Whitehead and Coomaraswamy have taken it to be Lakṣmī, holding a lotus in her raised right hand, but Gardner has suggested she might be Durgā as well, as a lion is seen, under her left elbow. But the presence of the animal is not discernible.

According to J. N. Banerjea the mode of representing the goddess in akin to the device of the reverse of Chandra Gupta Kumāradevi coins and the "lion slayer" type of Chandragupta II, and not so much like the Kushan coins or seals representing the Iranian goddess Nanā riding on a lion. Both Śiva and his consort Ambikā were predominant over the north western region of Gāndhāra. So if the coin under consideration bears the image of Ambikā on it, it shows that the style of representation was not yet influenced by the iconography of Nanā though its issuer was a foreigner himself.

The influence makes it obvious enough under the rule of Huvishka. In his gold coins Nanā is depicted accompanying the god 'Oeso' who is identical with Bhaveśa Śiva. On the other gold coins of the same ruler Śiva appears with Ommo i.e., Umā, who is attributed not with the Indian lotus but with the cornucopia. This evidently shows that Iranian Nanā and Indian Umā was one and same to her worshippers, who must have paid their homage to a composite deity Nanā-Durgā in the Kushan epoch. The cornucopia of Hellenistic origin was attributed to Lakṣmī, Ardoksho, Durgā and Nanā indiscriminately, but the Lion of Nanā was only associated to Umā or Durgā alone. It is interesting to mark that nowhere in the *Durgāstotras* in the epic she is called "*Siṃhavāhinī*", an epithet which predominates the later works. Vidyanidhi, however, thinks that the great hound which accompanied Śiva was later on associated to his wife,[29] but in the light of the impacts from the cult of Nanā, it is certain that the lion of the latter became the vehicle of Durgā.

(v) The northern cults of Dākinīs and Śākinīs:

The earliest hint to the cults of female deities called the Ḍākinīs and Śākinīs is probably to be found from the *Anuśāsanaparvan* of the epic. The narratives related the adventures of Aṣṭāvakra in the trans-Himalayan region. He having crossed the ranges of the Kailāsa, Mandara, Haima and Kirātadeśa reached an Āśrama, where there was a golden palace. Hither came out seven beautiful damsels and ushered him in to an old lady. After having tested his power of self-control (*brahmacarya*) she transformed herself into a beautiful young woman and revealed her identification; she was the personification of the Northern Region (*uttarāṃ māṃ diśam viddhi*) i.e., the presiding deity of the north.[30] The companions of this goddess are the precursors of the later "Rūpikạ-Lākinīs, Dākinī's and Śākinis" of later Tantric literature,[31] while the goddess herself is identical with Lha-mo of western Tibet.

According to P.C. Bagchi, the Ḍākinīs were the witches of the Dags and the Śākinīs were the sorceress of the Śaka people.

In this period of increasing foreign aggression and immigration and tribal movements, informative stories about the exotic cults became quite current and popular amongst the Indians. From a similar reference in the *Rāmāyaṇa* to the female sorceress having magical powers, it appears that this was the period when the cult of the Ḍākinīs and Śākinīs were introduced into the Śakti cult in India.

(vi) Mātṛkā:

Goddess Lohitāyanī is depicted as one of the nurses of Kārttikeya. This goddess, it appears from her name, was connected with the mountain Loha where resided the war-like people, the Lohas.

She is also known as Kiṃśulakā of the ruddy-hue. This goddess, or the group of goddess in similar names derived their titles no doubt, from the red arsenic obtained from these mountains, and presided over the caves of Hiṅgula (literally, realgar or an important ore of arsenic).

It seems that once upon a time the worship of a "Red-goddess" was prevalent in many parts of Afghanistan and Baluchistan, where the goddess was called "*Hingulā*". But in later times the northern Lohitāyanī was forgotten and only her southern manifestation at the shrine of Hinglaj remained. From the reference in the epic we are to assume that the war-god was considered as the son of this "Red-Goddess" of the hills. Later on she became one of the more obscure "Mātṛkā".

References

1. Hrozmý, WAIC, pp. 26, 186 (Fig. 106), 193.
2. Ṛigveda, x, 125, Devīsūkta.
3. X. i. 7.
4. Kena Upaniṣad, III, refer to Uma Haimavati.
5. Mbh. 4.6.1-13; 6.23.4-16 (Haridas).
6. ERE. IV, p. 377b; Przyluski, I.H.Q. X.
7. Matsya. 13.50 gives the names of the Śaktis of Uttarakuru and Kuśadvīpa.

8. Holdich, p. 162.
9. S.K. Chatterji, India and China, p. 114; Tarn, Alexander the Great, p. 106 f.; D.C. Sircar, Sakta Pithas, p. 85.
10. Agrawala, IKP, p. 40; Mbh. 3. 192.40; Ibid., 3.93.10 (haridas).
11. Marutīrtha Hiṅglāj, pp. 279-80, it seems from the reference that these carvings were the symbolic representation of the sun and moon deities.
12. Besides this Gāndhāra, Oḍḍiyāna, Jalandhara and Kashmir were the famous centers of Tantricism. Vide D.C. Sircar, op. cit., p. 89, it would be rather fer-fetched to connect goddess Kusodaka with some goddess in Ethiopia (Kusha); Kuśodakā was probably some goddess residing on the Hindu Kush ranges. Cf. The Greek goddesses mentioned in the Aṅga-vijjā, Chatterji, India & China, p. 114.
13. Mbh. 3.67.102-3 (Haridas); Watters, I, p. 221.
14. Herod. iv.59; McGovern, p. 57.
15. 3.69.13-17 (Haridas).
16. Bhag. XII.22.1-5.
17. Periplus, 58.
18. ERE, II, p. 813.
19. Mbh.3.63.100 (Haridas); Am, Marc. xxiii, 6.73.
20. A. Stein, MASI, 1931, No. 43, pp. 26-27.
21. ERE, II, p. 218 on Attis; Frazer, I, ch. XXXIX, p. 457.
22. Frazer II, p. 505; Goetz, India, p. 60, calls the ivory Lakṣmī the "Indian form of Venus Stella Maris".
23. Mahāvastu, III, p.71, n. 4, p. 81; cf. *Sankha Jātaka* (442). *Manimekhalai*; there is every possibility that the cult of this goddess of the sea received a new impetus after the Graeco-Roman trade with south India.
24. Upākhyāna, VII.
25. Marshall, Taxila II, p. 443, Class II, Nos. 9-16; p. 447, Class III Nos. 17-19; p. 448, Class V, Nos. 23-25, the last one "comes from the Greeks Stratum referable to the second century B.C."; p. 451, Class XIII, Nos. 45-53, these show the Greek influence on them.
26. Hrozný, op. cit., pp. 26, 178.
27. Przyluski, op. cit.

28. Tarn, GBI, p. 29.
29. PMC. P. 129.
30. Mbh. 13.19.31 (Haridas).
31. Bagchi, I.H.Q., Vol. VII, 1931 on foreign elements in Tantra.

Section II

The Cult of Śiva

It is not easy to determine the impact of foreign influence on the cult of Rudra-Śiva, as the available facts are vague and meagre for the purpose of a complete study. For the earlier development of the cult we are dependent on the literary data which throw some light on the sect by their occasional references. The coins of the foreign rulers supply information regarding the iconography during the centuries around the beginning of the Christian era. But regarding a detailed knowledge of the ritualistic worship one is left in the dark. We have discussed the subject in separate divisions, and have tried to show certain possible foreign affiliations.

(i) Śiva, the god of the northern mountains:

From the references to Śiva and his devotees made by Pāṇini and Patañjali,[1] it is evident that by their time a sect flourished around the cult of the old Vedic divinity Rudra-Śiva. But his non-Aryan affinity was never lost sight of and he was repeatedly connected with northern India and the mountains. Patañjali mentions the northern town of Śivapura, this was the capital of the Śibis or Śivis who were devoted to Śiva. But his worship was not limited to Śibi and Gāndhāra territories but was known to the lands bordering on India and beyond. Thus he is connected with the Muñjavān mountain, the Śaravana range and even with Śākadvīpa.[2] He was obviously affiliated to foreign and semi-foreign tribes of the trans-Himalayan regions who were occupied in the procuration of fragrant aromatics, of gold and were the cutters of the wood. These are evident from his epithets: *Gandhadhari, Bhūtacaṛī, Girirūha, Madhukalocana* (brown-eyed, i.e., ethnologically different from the Indians, cf. with the *piṅgalākṣa* defining the Sun), *Kanaka*, *Kāñcana* (he who presides over the gold), *Bhūtālaya*, *Vaṇij* (traders), *Varddhakī* (carpenter), *Gāndhāra*, *Sugandhāra*, etc., mentioned in the epic.[3] Notwithstanding the facts, that, the later authorities have ascribed these appellations with allegorical and philosophical significance, they were most probably derived due to some practical reasons as suggested above.

(ii) Śiva and Dionysus:

There are some interesting reference about Śiva in the classical accounts, in which he is identified with Dionysus. Megasthenes found, "a particular race of people called "Nyssians" and their city called Nysa (in modern Koh-i-Mor Valley, vide. Holdich, pp. 123-124) which Dionysus had founded, and the mountain which rose above the city, Meros they farther called Oxydrakai the descendants of Dionysus". Here Megasthenes refers to the people of Nysa, who were a group of Greek settlers, inhabiting the land from earlier times than Alexander. About the same people Arrian states, "In the country on Alexander's route between the river Cophen and the Indus lay the city of Nysa, supposed to have been founded by Dionysus, at the time of his conquest of the Indians". The Nyssians were no doubt Greeks who sent their chief Ocuphis to Alexander.[4] Both the writers refer to the abundance of ivy growing in that region and the pomp and grandeur of the Bacchic mode of worship, complete with Dionysia and phalloi. Evidently Megasthenes and others refer to the tradition which connects the Nysians with Greece and Dionysus. But actually, it appears, that Śiva was worshipped from remote antiquity by the inhabitants of the Koh-i-Mor Valley as well as the Kṣudrikas, and when the Hellenistic Nyssians reached that place they identified their Dionysus with Śiva who was the god par excellence in that region. This is a possibility which needs further corroboration by archeological evidence.

Megasthenes was however, occasionally confused between the Indian/Dionysus (Śiva) and Herakles. Thus he states, "They said also that the Sibae were descendant's from those who accompanied Herakles on his expedition, and that they preserved badges of the descent, for they wore skins like Herakles, and carried clubs and branded the mark of a cudgel on their oxen and mules". This reference is undoubtedly made about the *Śiva-bhāgavatas* of Patañjali who carried the iron lances in their hands.

Although it is difficult to understand Megasthenes' distinction between the worshippers of Dionysus and Herakles and the whole account relating these gods is extremely confused one, it certainty throws light on the fact, that Śiva was worshipped in the mountains and forests while Kṛṣṇa was revered by the more civilized inhabitants of the cultivated plains. He is again confused regarding the account of the daughter of Herakles. It seems that the epithet *Kanyākumārī* caused some confusion in his mind and due to the term '*Kanyā*', he made Pandaea the 'daughter' of Heracles. This Pandaea, was probably a Śakti presiding over the extreme south and was the consort of Śiva. Thus she was to be connected with Dionysus and not with Herakles. The Indian legends of Kṛṣṇa (Herakles) knew no Pandaea.

(iii) The Dionysiac philosophy and the Pāśupata system:

As early as seventh century B.C. the Orphic brothers preached a new message to the Greeks. Their dogma presents some similarity with the main philosophy of the *Pāśupatas* in India. The Orphic Brothers proclaimed, "the soul of a man is divine and of divine origin; that the body is it's impure prison-house, where it is in danger of contracting stains; that by elaborate purification and abstinences the soul might retain it's purity, and by sacramental and magic methods, the pure soul might enjoy in this life and the next full communion with god".[5] One is tempted to connect this system with the *Pāśupatavidhi* of India. It is not absolutely impossible that the preaching of the Orphic Brothers might have influenced the Saiva cult in India through the Greek immigrants to Nysa, but in the absence of more profound evidences nothing can be assumed further. However, the whole idea is literally applicable to the main dogma of the *Pāśupatāvidhi* which contemplate the body as impure paśu, but the Soul within is pure and divine. Another noteworthy fact is that both sects prescribed modes of worship which involved the evocation of a particular mood and a kind of emotional music, accompanying the Dionysiac hymn known as the dithyramb, or the mantra. Both the systems lay stress on magical formulae and presented somewhat frantic observances.

Lākulīśa, the originator of the *Pāśupata* system resided in western India in a country called *Kāyārihaṇa* and there is no evidence to show that the system in its rudimentary form was not known to the *Siva-bhāgavatas* of the north and north-west earlier to Lākulīśa. His name, which means the bearer of a cudgel evidently reminds of the club of the Śibis and the staff carried by the worshippers of Dionysus.

(iv) Śiva and the Foreign Rulers:

That Śiva was the most important divinity in north-western India is attested by the observation of the Greek writer Hesychius who says, "the bull was the god of Gāndhāra". Śiva was obviously well-known in this region in both his anthropomorphic and theriomorphic forms. Tarn has shown that though Puṣ kalāvatī (present Charsadda) was partially Buddhist, Śiva was the god par excellence and his humped bull became the coin-type of the Greek mint.[7] Although, the Greeks paid their homage to Artemis as Anitis, the native and the semi-foreign population of the city revered Śiva, "It is possible therefore that he appealed special force to the half foreign people of the north-west".[8] Apollodatus' round silver coins show on one side Śiva's humped bull, with the foot-print of Nandī on its hump.

The earliest representation of Śiva with considerable foreign look is the figure supposed to be of Poseidon, found on the coins of Maues. He carried a trident in his hand, and tramples over a dwarfish figure. He is almost identical with Poseidon, represented on the coins of Antemachus Theos. But the composition is reminiscent of being purely Indian and its similarity with the Indian representation of Śiva trampling over the *Apasmāra Puruṣa* makes it highly probable that actually it is the image of Śiva but with a strong influence of Poseidon.

Banerjea tentatively points out that the Herakles and the bull-shaped Dragon of Bronze Seal 12 of Sirkap, Taxila may be identified with Siva as Visvamitra and is not actually Herakles as supposed to be.

Śiva as he appears on the round copper seal discovered at Sirkap (1914-15) is noteworthy because of his resemblance with

Herakles. He holds a trident in his left hand and a club in his right. His pose is slightly different from the pose of the same god found on the coins of Gondopharnes and Wima Kadphises. Banerjea draws our attention to the club held in the right hand of the deity for it greatly resembles the knotted club of Herakles on some of the Indo-Greek coins. It is evident that though club was an age-old symbol of the god, it found a new and foreign orientation in the hands of the Taxilan artists.

The similarities and influence of Herakles on Śiva reminds us once again about the confusion made by Megasthenes between the two deities.

The special feature which marks the similarity between the coin types of Wima Kadphises and the coins of Demetrius and other Indo-Greek rulers, is the fashion of wearing the upper garment. It is slung round the forearm in the mode of Herakles' wearing the same.

It is evident that the Scythians and Kushans were well-acquainted with Śiva's phallic form and offered homage to this divine symbol. The scene portrayed on a fragmentary relief belonging to first century B.C. depicts two Scythian potentates dressed in long coat, tall headgear and heavy Scythian boots, approaching the phallic emblem with fillets in their hands. The vine-carved on the side reveals the connection of the worshippers with the north-west specially with Dionysus while the costume marks them as the intruders from Central Asia. It is well-known that ivy and vine were sacred to Dionysus, and while vine was present in other parts of India ivy could not be found elsewhere other than Nysa under Mount Meros, which made the Macedonians "home sick". So the presence of this foliage indicate to the fact that by Scythio-Kushan period the identification of Śiva with Dionysus was complete. Or else, the whole scene has to be identified as the Scythio-Kushan depiction of a Greek Dionysia procession complete with phalloi, as mentioned earlier.

From all the above information it becomes clear that the Śaiva sect was increasingly flourishing in north India from Pāṇini's period onwards, and had been able to attract groups of worshippers, both native and foreign.

It has been stated earlier that foreign elements were active in the development of this faith but with regard to certain aspects, the necessary details are lacking. In the field of iconic representation of the cult-deity the foreign elements undoubtedly played a greater role. Likewise Buddha represented by the Bodhi-tree, the foot-print, the alter or the wheel in the Śuṅga art, Śiva in the earlier indigenous coins was represented by the bull, shrine, trident or mountain symbols. When the need for anthropomorphic representation became pressing, the artists looked for a similar conception and the model was served by the image of the Greek god Poseidon, whose certain characteristics were similar to the attributes of Śiva. Of course, Śiva in his anthropomorphic form first made his appearance in the coins found in Ujjaini region. The coins of Audumbara chief Śivadāsa, Rudradāsa and Dhārāghoṣa represent Śaiva shrines with trident-battleaxe standards. These coins belong to the first and second centuries B.C. The copper coins of an anonymous Kuninda chief belonging to second century A.D. present standing figure of Śiva. These prove that side by side both the indigenous and the foreign traditions were working in modelling the icon of Śiva.

Poseidon, the Greek god of Sea and waters had some similar trends in his character with that of Śiva. His epithet "consort of the Earth", his trident or the three-pronged fish-spear, sacrifice of bulls, and bull as his symbol made him closest to Śiva.[9] So it is only natural that when the foreign rules like Gondopharnes and Wima Kadphises issued coins with the image of Mahādeva on them it resembled the slightly bent posture of Poseidon. Gondopharnes was an ardent devotee of Śiva, which has been presumed from his epithet "*Deva-Vrata*" or "*Sudevavrata*" inscribed on some of his coins. On certain bullion coins of Gondopharnes "he (Śiva) stands facing with his left leg slightly advanced and head bent a little towards the left, clasping a long trident in his right hand and a palm-branch in his left which rests in the approved Indian iconographic manner on the hip (*Kaṭihasta*)". The foreign touch introduced by the placing of palm-branch which is undoubtedly a Greek insignia, is absent in the second variety of Gondopharnes' coins, but the slightly bent pose or *Dvibhaṅga* is very important as it shows that Poseidon made a deep impression on the iconic representation of Śiva.

On some copper coins of the great Kushan monarch Śiva appears as holding a spear or a staff in his right hand and the left hand rests on the club. There is a set of coins of Kanişhka on which elephant-goad along with water-vassel are crowded in one hand. "This mode of crowding two attributes in one hand" is thoroughly un-Indian. On Kushan gold coins Śiva is typically Indian (See Plate No. 3).[10]

(v) Kirātaveśī Śiva:

An interesting information is supplied in the epic. Here Arjuna is seen entering into a combat with the *Kirātaveśī* Mahādeva (Śiva clad in a Kirāta's dress). The Kirātas, often referred to in the epics and the *Purāṇas* are the aboriginal Mongoloid tribes inhabiting the forests and the mountainous regions of north and north eastern India. In the epic Śiva was accompanied by his consort Umā-devī and her numerous female attendants, – all attired in the same aboriginal manner. From this reference it is clear that Śiva was worshipped among these tribal folks in the form of a Kirāta chief. Mention should be made here of Śiva on the famous Guḍimallam Liṅga of Madras, which shows a district Mongoloid facial character "with a somewhat snub nose, high check bones, narrow forehead and oblique eyes".[11] In the list of the sixty-eight *Svayambhūva Liṅgas*, the name of the presiding deity of *Kailāsācala*, is given as Kirāta.[12] The Guḍimallam Liṅga has got no *Yajñopavīta* or "the Brahmanical sacred thread, insisted upon in all Agamas". The Mathura Linga belonging to the second century A.D.[13] marks the same facial feature i.e. the snub nose, high broad check bones, broad lips with less chin and narrow and small eyes.

These evidences indicate that a Kirāta-Mongoloid influence together with the western impacts permeated through the cult of Śiva in the period under discussion, and contributed to the growth of the sectarian worship and its iconography.

References

1. Pāṇini, IV.1.112; Agrawala, p. 360 ff; Puri, ITP, pp. 188-189. The *Āyaḥ-śūlikas* were the Śiva-bhāgavatas, the Siboi (Śibi) tribe inhabiting the "lowere part of the Rachna Doab".
2. Vayu. chs. 39-41,the Gāndhārvas, Yakṣas, Rakṣas, and the horse-faced Kinnaras worship Śiva in the various parts of the northern and western mountains.
3. Mbh. 14. Ch. 65 (B.R.M.).
4. Arr. V. p. 163.
5. ERE, Vol. VI, p. 408.
6. Ibid., Vol. XI, p. 93.
7. GBI, p. 135.
8. Ibid., pp. 172-73.
9. *Mahāvastu*, III, p. 71, merchants in distress called out Śiva and Varuna, cf., Alexander worshipped "to please the god of water courses and to find a pleasant voyage".
10. For all the coin types discussed vide J.N. Banarjea, DHI, ch. On Brahmanical Divinities on Coins.
11. G. Rao, p. 66.
12. Ibid., p.84.
13. Coomaraswamy, HIIA, Pl. XVIII, 68.

Section III

The Cult of Kṛṣṇa-Viṣṇu

Vaiṣnavism afforded the easiest way to attend salvation, i.e., to communicate with the Supreme. Being by the institution of '*bhakti*' or loving faith. This was indeed, a unique and original contribution which made *Vaiṣṇavadharma* acceptable and accessible to all. Consequently foreign tribes that were eager to accept Indian mode of life found a refuge under the cult of Kṛṣṇa-Viṣṇu and enriched it with their own contributions. Uptill now considerable amount of study have been made on the foreign impacts that helped the growth and development of this sect.

Before going into its detail it is appropriate to take a view of the characteristics of the *Bhāgavata* or the *Vaiṣṇava dharma*. Though it was mainly continuation of the ancient worship of the Sun-God or Viṣṇu of the Ṛigvedas,[1] it developed immensely under the patronage of the Vṛṣṇi prince Vāsudeva-Kṛṣṇa who became the personification of God and was the central figure of worship. That the Vṛṣṇi hero took an ante-Vedic stand and did not find a general celebration is clear from the references in the *Jātakas*,[2] and the *Arthaśāstra* of Kauṭilya[3] where it has been stated that the Vṛṣṇi family was not as dignified as the other contemporary *Kṣatriya* families, and Śiśupāla insulted Vāsudeva-Kṛṣṇa saying that he was a *Gopa*.[4] Again in the epic it has been stated that the Vṛṣṇi and the Andhaka dynasties were *Vrātya-Kṣatriya* and naturally censurable.[5] The stand of the Vasudevaism is more clearly marked by the expressions like: "*Arihantā vā, Chakkavaṭṭi vā, Baladeva vā, Vāsudeva vā,...*" etc. found in the Jaina canons which explicitly mentions that these are not born in miser, poor or *Brāhmaṇa* families but are born in royal *Kṣatriya* clans.[6]

Inscriptions[7] as well as literary date prove that casteless foreigners were admitted into the fold of Vaisnavism. Thus the *Bhāgavatapurāṇa* states:

"*Kirāta-Hūṇāndhra-Pulinda-Pukkuśā*

Ābhīra-Suhmā-Yavanāḥ Khaśādayaḥ

Ye' nye ca pāpā yad-upāśrāyaśrayāḥ

Śudhyanti tasmai prabhaviṣṇave namaḥ" (II, 4. 18).

This lenient outlook towards the so-called degraded tribes made Vaisnavism open to foreign adepts.[8]

(i) Bhakti:

Grierson thinks that though "bhakti" propounded explicitly for the first time in *Gītā*, little before c. 300 A.D., it was free from any Christian influence. But its later development show traces of Christianity.[9] According to Garbe, McNicol[10] and others *bhakti* in *Gītā* was purely Indian in its origin, and was not borrowed from Christianity. It was this feeling of the loving faith that attracted the foreigners towards Bhagavatism.

Yet, the Indians of this period were aware of a purer type of *bhakti*. The story related in the *Nārāyaṇīya* section of the *Śāntiparvan*[11] should not be brushed aside as a mere 'fancy flight' of legend. It relates the visit paid by Nārada to '*Svetadvīpa*' and describes the worshippers of Viṣṇu-Nārāyaṇa as well as the mode of worship.

This portion, probably a later addition to the body of the epic has been proved to be the baffling problem for many. Some think that truth lies in it garbed in the allusion of legend.[12] According to Grierson the *Śvetadvīpa* was to be sought in somewhere Bactria or Central Asia, which had many Christian as well as Manichaean settlements. He also draws our attention to the tradition that Apostle Thomas visited the court of Gondopharnes in Taxila.[13] He consequently thinks that the *Śvetadvīpa* was a community of Christians.

B. N. Seal thinks that an actual journey was undertaken to the coasts of Egypt and the Eucharist is described here.[14] Facts are not wanting to prove that India held intimate commercial connection with the ports of Egypt in second and third centuries A.D.

According the others[15] the *Śvetadvīpa* refer to the Mahāyānī centers in Central Asia. Raychaudhuri, however, after reviewing the available data comes to the conclusion with the opinion of Barth, Hopkins and Bhandarkar that *Svetadvipa* and its inhabitants are of highly imaginable character, and it gives nothing but the description of Nārāyaṇa's heaven, and not of any actual place.[16]

There remains of course every possibility to believe that a fact lies at the base of the narrative which later developed into a legendary tale. This becomes obvious if we take the words not too literally, and try to explain them in a new way. For instance "*anindriya-nirāhārā*" have been taken by Raychaudhuri to mean persons, "who have no organs of senses. They do not take any food",[17] Is there any difficulty to take the terms as really meaning men, who practiced severe austerities, and shunned from sensual pleasures? The term "*nirāhāra*" may as well imply—those who practiced penance by fasting hard. Of course, we admit, that descriptive passages like "*sama-muṣka-catuṣkā-rajīpacchadapādāḥ*"... or "*ṣaṣṭhya-dantair*" etc., cannot be explained in the above-said manner, but this much is true possibly, that once certain accounts of the austere devotees reached India from the West through the sailors and merchants, the *Bhāgavata* claimants touched it up with colourful additions of many a 'fairy-tale' like tints before it was engrafted into the body of *Śāntiparvan*.

We know for certain that there were settlements of anchorites in the desolate tracts of the Lybian desert in the third century A.D.[18] These anchorites practiced rigorous self-mortifications in deserts and forelorn places. They often continued fasting for several days. They gazed towards the blazing sun and refrained from all pleasures of life. The expressions like "*anispandāḥ*", i.e., 'winkless' may well refer to this tireless gazing at the sun.

The *bhakti* is no doubt, a pure Indian development, this journey of Nārada to *Śvetadvīpa* shows that the Indians at least had some knowledge about the anchorites who were aspiring for the faith through stages of severe self-mortifications, and the Indians had identified this faith with their own towards Nārāyaṇa to some extent. This happened because, it is a natural instinct in human mind to identify all the common traits found amongst the other people with one's own. Nārada, the divine messenger would naturally receive instructions from the God himself and not from any mortal beings.[19] The compiler of the narrative obviously had this idea in his mind and knew that Nārada's direct contact with the "Invisible God" would attract much more admiration of the common folk and evidently tried to create an episode out of the accounts received from the traveler-merchants who had seen the Christian Anchorites of Syria, Egypt and North Africa.

That the Indian merchants, and through them the Puraṇakāras knew something about the foreign lands, people and cities, and identified their mode of worship with Bhagavatism is probably alluded to in the *Kūrmapurāṇa*. It describes the city of Harivarṣa embellished with archways, pillars, gates and elevated courts with flight of stair cases. There the Yogīs contemplate on Viṣṇu.[20] It faintly recalls the fame of Alexandria for its museums, libraries, halls and luxurious living.[21] Near Alexandria were beautiful pleasure-resorts of delightful climate.[22] The accounts of the foreign lands probably supplied the basic idea of the fairy-tales related in the *Purāṇas*. Stray references in the *Purāṇas* show that India, like Iran imported legends from western centers of art, religion and philosophy, and was not so isolated from the rest of the world, as often thought to have been, and many a marvelous story must have reached India from Alexandria.

*** *** ***

Next comes the question of Ābhīra contribution to the cult of Vāsudeva-Kṛṣṇa. Their contributions have been discussed under the following heads:

(i) the stories of infant Kṛṣṇa in a cow settlement

(ii)the nature of the *Gopas* (cow-herds) identical with the Ābhīras, a non-Aryan tribe, probably of nomadic Iranian or Scythian origin.

(iii) The association of *gopinīs* and the sixteen thousand wives of the Vṛṣṇi prince Vāsudeva.

(i) The boy-god:

The Sanskrit works which deal with the episodes of the infant Kṛṣṇa are the *Harivaṃśa*, the *Vāyu*, *Matsya Viṣṇu* and the

Bhāgavat purāṇas. The *Harivaṃśa* seems to be the earliest of these, and as it contains the word "*dināra*" Bhandarkar and others thick that it was compiled sometime in third century A.D.[23] On the other hand, we have seen that the Ābhīras had entered India sometime after Alexander, and established themselves in the lower Sind by the first century A.D.[24] Formerly it was believed that the Ābhīras brought the story of the massacre of the infant from Christian legends, but as Patānjali refers to the enmity between Kaṃsa and Vāsudeva and the Ābhīras entered India, prior to the birth of Christ, the theories have been discarded.[25]

But surely the other popular episodes of the valour of the child-god such as the turning of the wagon, the killing of the demoness, Putanā, and the destroying of the ass called Dhenukāsura, are brought in by the Ābhīras. The chapter in the epic which mentions these acts[26] is rightly thought to be interpolated later.[27] It seems possible that the Ābhīras, who settled near Śūrasena (Mathura-Vṛndāvana region) came to know about the stories of the migration of Vṛṣṇi race from there to Dvāraka (in Kathiawar) where also dwelt groups of Ābhīra cow-herds. They evidently adopted the Vṛṣṇi prince, as their hero and to lend a more intimate colouring associated some typical nomadic stories with his early life; by this the character of Kṛṣṇa became more particularly a '*gopa*'.

The reason for their particular liking to Vāsudeva cult may be as follows:

(a) The Andhaka-Vṛṣṇis had a large number of livestock, and was renowned for their "*go-dhana*" (literally, cattle-wealth);

(b) The nomadic Ābhīras must have liked the shifting of the Andhaka-Vṛṣṇi from Mathura to Dvārakā,[28] this being particularly suited to a nomadic taste. Moreover both the regions had Ābhīra population, and this must have had proved an inspiring miraculous co-incidence.

(c) As Viṣṇu was called '*gopā*' in the *Vedas*, and was associated with the cows,[29] it once more helped his new-identification with the child cow-herd.

(ii) The Ābhīras:

So after reviewing the reasons for the special liking of the Ābhīras to Vāsudeva-cult, we will now see the particular stories:

(a) The turning of the *Śakaṭa*[30] relates how child Kṛṣṇa upturned an wagon with his feet. The story found popularity and plastic representation of it found expression on the reliefs at Deogarh (See Pl. No. 6). The panels show that Ābhīras were closely associated with the cult, as Yaśoda is depicted here in a typical Scythian costume and not in an Indian dress. This is evidently the '*Gopālikāvapuḥ*' mentioned in the epic.[31]

(b) The episode of Dhenukāsura,[32] may point to the fact that tales of wild asses which caused great disturbance amongst the live-stock in the pasture regions, were brought by the nomads from northern grasslands, and was engrafted on Kṛṣṇa legends. This is also reminiscent of the account of Strabo who relate that the Carmanians sacrifised ass to Ares.[33]

(c) The story of Putanā[34] likewise proves the existence of a '*bālagraha*' amongst the Ābhīras who caused infantile diseases. Belief in malevolent spirits in the form of demoness or female divinity is existent among all primitive folks, settled or nomadic.

The over-powering of the Kāliyanāga[35] seems to point out, gradual diminishing of the Nāga-cult of Mathura region by the Saṃkarṣaṇa-Vāsudeva cult. All these episodes are essentially coloured with a foreign and nomadic tinge. The wagons, the cows and other aspects of a typical cowherd-settlement point to the Scythian way of life. McNicol thinks that the Ābhīras worshipped a deity of the spring, and the renewed life of nature, as Dionysus... The Maenads are Dionysus' nurses, and we see them paralleled in '*Gopīs*'.[36] This Dionysiac aspect was marked more by the foreigners to due Baladeva's similarity with Bacchus.

In the *Ṭīkā* of *Harivaṃśa* a *Ghoṣa* (i.e., settlement) is explained as *Ābhīrapalli*.[37] The term Ābhīra originally did not mean cow-herd, but later on as most of them followed this pursuit of tending cows, it became synonymous with the term *gopa*.

They lived in temporary encampments and moved from place to place in search of good pasture. Thus they moved from Vraja to Vṛndāvana.[38] They suffered a good deal if a torrential rain broke out.[39] The *Viṣṇupurāṇa* mentions that they placed their wagons in a semi-circular plan.[40] Their women were strong and sturdy, and arrayed in a colourful row carrying the load of milk-jars on their heads: –

"The milk-women, with jars on their heads, and being arranged in rows, like stars coming out of the sky, issued out of Vraja (15). Having their breasts covered with blue, yellow and shining jackets (Aruṇa=reddish) those milk-women, while going on the road appeared like a rain-bow" (16).[41]

The description in the *Viṣṇuparva* of the *Harivaṃśa* and in the *Bhāgavatapurāṇa* are so lively and vivid that as if the writer had witnessed the actual journey of this nomadic folks and the encampment from Vraja to Vrindāvana. This immediately recalls the Scythio-Iranian nomads, who moved from place to place in search of pasture, putting all their belongings, the women and the children in the wagons.

It has been mentioned that in Kathiawar region the Andhaka-Vṛṣṇis, and the Ābhīras dwelt in close association. There remains a blank in the details of the social life they enjoyed there. We have no other preferences but to assume that before second century A.D. the Ābhīras probably inter-married in the Andhakavṛṣṇi clan, which still occupied in Gujarat-Kathiawar, and in between first century B.C. to third century A.D., the Andhaka-Vṛṣṇis got totally mixed up with the foreigners, so as to represent many a common traditions and customs in their socio-religious behaviour.[42]

It is exactly in the same region the Gujars gained supremacy in the following age, Kennedy thinks that the *muralī*, a special type of reed-pipe played on by the Gujars gave rise to the "*Muralīdhara*" aspect of Kṛṣṇa.[43] These evidences show that the foreign influences crept into the cult from western coast of India and not from the Śurasena country.

(iii) The introduction of Gopinīs:

The introduction of the *Gopinīs* in the Kṛṣṇa-legends embellished the cult with a romantic grace. This aspect though stamped as "inconsistent with the advanced morality of the Vāsudeva religion" is certainly the most vital and charming phase of the cult, which had imparted inspiration to all devotees, an artist, or a musician, a poet or the faithful worshipper repeatedly through the ages, since its origin in the days of the Ābhīras. They were the simple, youthful tribal maidens occupied in the rearing of live-stocks. It has been stated that women enjoyed a more carefree life in a tribal society. It is quite natural to find their dalliances with Kṛṣṇa as he grew up amongst them. Rādhā, the predominant figure among the *gopinīs*, is not mentioned in the earlier literature, that fall within this period of study. We find only a stray reference to her name in a passage stating "*Rādhā Vṛndā vane vane*".[44] Interestingly enough the passage quoted above gives the list of the place-names, and Śaktis worshipped therein.

We are tempted to assume that it is because of the supremacy of the Ābhīras in Deccan that the stories of the *Vrajavadhūs* (i.e., *Gopīs*) and Kṛṣṇa became current amongst the rural population quite early. According to R.D. Basak the Gāthā of Hāla which mentions the name of Rādhā, and other dalliances of the *gopīs* with Kṛṣṇa, is a work which carries the picture of the rustic life during the Andhra supremacy in Deccan. It would be not improbable to assume that the stories became current before the Gupta ascendancy in 320 A.D.[45]

The *Hallīsaka* dance mentioned in the *Harivaṃśa*, and the *Rasa* described in *Viṣṇupurāṇa* are essentially the same, being performed at the Harvest Moon of the Autumn nights. Quite early these dances became associated with the names of Kṛṣṇa and the *gopinīs*. The rustic folks of Gujarat-Kathiawar must have participated in this dance singing the songs of Vṛndāvana.[46]

But the *gopinīs* are lost sifht of when Kṛṣṇa, with his family moves to Dvārakā. However, a huge band of 16,000 women become Kṛṣṇa's wife besides the eight queens. It is related that these women were brought from the '*Avarodha*' i.e., seraglio of

Narakāsura, and were wedded by Kṛṣṇa. Kṛṣṇa appeared before all of them simultaneously by multiplying his form, as he did at the night of the *Rāsa* dance.[47] After his death his eight queens entered the funeral pyre.[48] The others were guided by Arjuna towards Hastināpura. In Punjab, the Ābhīra *Dasyus* joined in a conspiracy to ransack the seraglio of Arjuna[49] and carried off the women to sea-shore.[50] This evidently show that the *Kṛṣṇa-Kāminīs* were of questionable character, and possibly had some affinity with the Ābhīra banditti, whom they followed out of their own will. In the Vṛndāvana region Vāsudeva is associated with the *Gopīs* while in Dvārakā he is associated with these sixteen thousand women from Narakāsura's seraglio. Evidently, he is not free from the association of women and is connected with them in some way or the other. It is quite possible that in Śūrasena region the Ābhīra women followed of pursuit of cow-herdesses but in Dvārakā, the concubines and courtesans were recruited from the Ābhīra stock.[51] Repeated references to these multitude of women, their artifices shown at the pleasure trip to sea-shore, and drinking make it evident that they were the concubines of Vāsudeva's harem. The culpable act, according to Hindu Śiṣṭacāra, of their yielding voluntarily to the Ābhīra highway-men though disheartening, seems quite natural for women having racial affinities with the *dasyus*.

The evidence of the *Mastyapurāṇa* show that the women took '*Anaṅgavrata*' by the fulfillment of which they could be delivered to *Viṣṇuloka*. This and other references[52] prove that the courtesans took the worship of Vāsudeva. Vaisnavism with its tenet of bhakti was thus more yielding than any other sectarian religions of India. It gave a shelter to everybody who aspired for God, and Vāsudeva became the great refuge (*paramāśraya, paramāgati*) of the longing soul.

The foregoing discussion shows that Vaisnavism had accepted the foreigners, as well as their contributions in ideas and legends which enriched it's repertory through the ages. It was this tendency of acceptance that made the Christian contribution possible on the growth and development of the sect of Āḷwārs in the following age.

References

1. Vedic Index, p. 465 f., Vol. II; p. 238, Vol. I, Vedic Mythology, p. 30.
2. Cowell, Vol. iv, pp. 55-56; Vol. v, p. 138.
3. Shamasastry, p. 11.
4. Mbh. 2.39.6-15 (B.O.R.I.).
5. Ibid., 7.124.15 (Haridas).
6. *Kalpa-sūtra*, IV. 16, repeated.
7. Raychaudhuri, EHVS, p. 99 ff.
8. Hazra, PRHRS, pp. 193-200.
9. ERE, Vol. II, p. 538.

   J.R.A.S., 1907, p. 315.
10. McNicol, Indian Theism, App. C. pp. 272 ff.
11. Mbh.12.335 (B.R.M.); 12.231. 8-13 (Haridas); ibid., 331.19-35 (B.O.R.I.) states the same with certain changes in terma.
12. Raychaudhuri, EHVS, p. 134; McNicol, op. cit., p. 274.
13. ERE, vol. II, pp. 548-550.
14. B.N. Seal, as quoted by Raychaudhury, op. cit., p. 135ff.
15. De la Vallee Poussin, as referred to by Chattopadhyaya, Early Theistic Sects of Ancient India, p. 93.
16. Raychaudhuri, op. cit., pp. 134-40.
17. Ibid., p. 136.
18. ERE. Vol. II, pp. 67, 74-76; Encyclopaedia of Region, p. 21.
19. This aspect has been taken by Telang as an objection to the trustworthiness of the story, vide EHVS, p. 136.
20. *Kūrmapurāṇa, Pūrva*, chs. 46-47.
21. Am. Marc. xxii.,16.13 and f.n. 1; Kennedy, J.R.A.S., 1907, pp. 953-957 for Indian contact with Alexandria.
22. Am. Marc. xxii. 16.14; Rawlinson, IIW, p. 176, "...This is just the period (Paul of Alexandria fled in 251 A.D. and his followers St. Antony died in 356 A.D.) when Indian influence in Alexandrian literature is most in evidence".
23. R.G. Bhandarkar, Vaisnavism etc., p. 51.
24. Vide supra, pp. 44-45 ff.
25. Raychaudhuri, op. cit., p. 144 ff.
26. Mbh. 2. Ch. 41.

27. R.G. Bhandarkar, op. cit., p. 50.
28. Viṣṇup. V. chs. 22-23.
29. Vedic Index, I, p. 238.
30. Viṣṇup. V. 6.1-7.
31. Vide supra, pp. 44-45.
32. Hari, M.N. Datta, p. 285-287.
33. Strabo, xv. 2.14.
34. Viṣṇup, V. 8.7-10; Hari, M.N. Datta, p. 277-87.
35. Viṣṇu, V. ch. 7.
36. Indian Theism, App. p. 274.
37. *Amarakoṣa*, II, 633.
38. Hari, M.N. Datta, p. 270-73; Viṣṇup. V. ch. 22-27.
39. Ibid., V.11.1-12.
40. Ibid., V.6.31.
41. Translated by M.N. Datta.
42. Vide supra, p. 43 ff; 131 ff; pp. 168-169.
43. Kennedy, op. cit., p.981 ff.
44. Matsyap. 13.38.
45. R.G. Basak, Beng. tr.of *Gāthā Saptaśatī*, Inroduction.
46. It is still current as the Garba. A varient of Garbā in which the participants hold the colourful scarfs that are hung from the top is reminiscent of the European Maypole. The portion of the *Bhāgavata-purāṇa* (X.11.33) which describe the journey on wagons states that the women sang the songs of *Kṛṣṇalīlā*. These '*niṣka-kaṇṭī*' '(a golden ornament for the neck or breast', Monier-Williams, p. 562) women were the Ābhīra cowherdesses.
47. Viṣṇup. V. 31.14-16.
48. Ibid., V. 38.2.
49. Ibid., V. 38.12-18.
50. Ibid., V. 38.26.
51. *Purāṇapraveśa*, p. 70 f.
52. Matsyap. 82.29; ch. 100.

Section IV

The Cult of Śūrya

The Sun, one of the most prominent members of the Indo-European pantheon[1] was worshipped by the Indo-Iranian as well as by the Indo-Aryans of the Vedic age. In the Vedas the sun has been eulogised and referred to by numerous names.[2] He was conceived both in his animate and inanimate symbolical forms, and was praised for his friendly (i.e., *Mitra*) benevolent aspect. The *cakra* (i.e., wheel) or the lotus symbols on the early punch-marked coins of India[3] are the symbolic representations of the sun-deity.[4] A considerable amount of progress was made from the time of these early coins, to the anthropomorphic representations of the divinity in the Gupta period; it has been proved that all was not due to indigenous development but owed much to foreign inspirations. In the current section an attempt has been made to decipher these exotic traditions that contributed to the growth of the cult of the Sun.

Sun has been one of the more popular deities of Achaemenid Iran, the supremacy being given to Almighty Ahura Mazda. From a study of the Persian Inscriptions of the Achaemenid dynasty, it appears the Mitra gained more importance after the time of Darius, and onwards from Arta Xerexes,[5] in whose inscriptions he is invoked with Ahura Mazda and Anītis (Goddess Anāhita).

While Taxila with parts of Gāndhāra and Sindhu came under the jurisdiction of Darius, a band of Magian priests must have came and settled in the city of Taxila, where they erected a temple to the Fire or the Sun.[6] This is moreover corroborated by the introduction of the Magian custom, which prescribed disposal of the human corpses by the birds. Stray references in the classical writings show *Brāhmaṇa* sects of Sun worshippers were extant at that time.[7]

The earliest literary references to the icon of the Sun and his temple are supplied by Curtius and Plutarch. Curtius observed that the Indian solidiers of Porus carried an image of

Herakles, while advancing against Alexander.[8] As Heralkes has often been identified with Indian Viṣṇu, an aspect of the Sūrya,[9] it seems that the image of Herakles was actually that of *Sūryarūpī Viṣṇu*. This assumption is moreover corroborated by the account of Plutarch that the Indian soldiers with their elephants ascended on a ridge on which probably stood a temple or an alter of the Sun.[10] Cunningham has identified this spot with the ruins on Balnāth-ka-Ṭilā on Hydaspes (Jhelum).[11] These references show that at the time of Alexander (327-326 B.C.) the Sun-cult was flourishing due to Achaemenid influences in parts of Gāndhāra and Punjab,[12] but as to the details of the modes of worship or the iconography of the deity we have to remain contented with these accounts in absence of a more exhaustive history.

Apollonius of Tyana visited the "Temple of the Sun" in the vicinity of the city of Taxila. Moreover Phraotes the king of Taxila, said, "he drank out little wine, as he usually poured out in libation to the Sun".[13] All this show that the Sun-cult was well-established in the Taxila region in the first century A.D. But the earliest Sun icons found in India except the "northern Sun-god" at Bharhut show little traces of foreign influence.

Mention should be made about four sculpture pieces, all ranging from the first century B.C. to second century A.D. in date. They are found in (a) the Buddhist cave at Bhaja; (b) in Ananta Gumpha, Udaigiri, Orissa; (c) on the upright pillar of Bodh Gaya; and (d) at Lala Bhagat, Kanpur, U.P. A somewhat detailed description of at least two of these sculpture pieces is necessary, because a comparison between these and the Sun icons of the Gupta and post-Gupta period would show the different changes that took place due to the foreign impact on the cult.

In the Bodh Gaya upright pillar of first century B.C. the Sun-god is depicted as driving a four-horsed chariot (quadriga), with Uṣā and Pratyuṣā on his either sides shooting arrows. Iconographically this figure is quite analogous to the Greek god Helios but the treatment is purely Indian. Rowland observes, "the representation of Sun-god in quadriga is sometimes interpreted as an influence of Hellenistic art, although stylistically there is nothing beyond the iconography to remind us of the characteristic representations of Helios in classical art, in which the solar chariot is invariably represented in a fore-shortened side view". He is of opinion that as the conception of Sun-god on chariot originated in Babylonia and Iran, wherefrom it spread to Greece and India, "the representation is simply an interpretation of the iconography, and not the borrowing of a pre-existing stylistic motif".[14] Sūrya's horse-drawn chariot is known in the Vedas, but in the absence of a earlier plastic representation of Sun in chariot, the observation of Tarn cannot be brushed aside altogether. Plato's coin[15] represent Sun in a quadriga, the himation flowing at the back and rays issuing out of his head. Tarn, keeping in view the theories of Herzfeld of Rostovtzeff, says, "The Sun's quadriga appeared in the Greek East on the coins of Andragoras and Vakshuvar (? Oxyartes). These coins and especially that of Plato, supply one of the few definite instances (as opposed to assumption) of a Greek artistic motive passing into Indian art through Bactria;... It still remains to be ascertained whether the original Greek and Iranian conceptions of that quadriga were independent of each other or, if not, how they were related. But however that may be, the coin type of unimportant Plato, constitutes a most important point in the travels of this artistic motive".[16]

The panel at Bhaja shows Śūrya on the four-horsed chariot, driving over a crouching demon. He is accompanied by two female attendants carrying chowrie and umbrella respectively. The deity may represent Savitṛi whose anthropomorphical characteristics were more developed than Śūrya, and who is explicitly invoked to remove evil dreams and the demons and sorcerers of the dark.[17]

These reliefs are important from the point, that they show, though Śaka influences had probably reached India in the fifth century B.C.[18] the sculpture pieces were obviously free from any exotic influences, and approves indirectly the contention of Banerjea "that the Iranian themselves are not in the habit of worshipping images and our search for an image of Mithra would be in vain; i.e., before Mithraism itself was to a great extent Hellenized".

The coins of Philoxenus and Telephus which represent the Sun as "facing, radiate, clad in chiton, himation and boots; holds in l. hand long scepter; r. extended". These coin types stand in between the time of Plato and Kaniṣhka, and the deity in the coins of Kaniṣhka, is more akin to the type of Philoxenus, than on Platos' discussed earlier.[19]

Before the Scythio Kushan epoch the Persian Magi or the Maga priests immigrated to India, and occupied the position of the chief priests of the Sun-worship.[20] The great epic together with the *Purāṇas* viz. *Viṣṇu*, *Matsya* and the *Bṛhat Saṃhitā*, main bodies of which were compiled and composed finally under the Guptas have numerous references to the Magas of *Śākadvīpa* (i.e., Magis of Persia and Seistan). The Maga priests imparted strong influence on the dynasty of the Vardhanas of Kanauj and of the *Bhaviṣyapurāṇa*, a late work, yet possessing particular historical value, which contents accounts of the Magis and their mode of Sun-worship.[21]

The Geography of Ptolemy[22] refers to Brakhmanio Magi i.e., the *Maga Brāhmaṇas* who had colonies in South India, but nothing is known about their contribution to the Solar cult in South.

The evidence of *Viṣṇupurāṇa* which states:–

"*Sākadvīpe tutair Viṣṇu Sūryarūpo dharo-mune*".

And other references in *Matsyapurāṇa*, *Bṛhatsaṃhitā* and lastly in the *Bhaviṣyapurāṇa* clearly prove the Iranian influence on the cult and Scythian impact on its iconography.

The Scythians originally possessing a barbaric type of culture, became imbibed with Iranian traditions before entering into India. For this, it is necessary to describe the sun icons of ancient Iran to a certain extent before discussing the Indian images. In ancient Persian monuments Mithra was represented by a symbol;[23] in the sepulcher of Darius in Ishtakhr, near Naqsh-i-Rustam, Mithra is represented by a bull.[24] But we cannot take these busts within circles as the prototype of fully anthropomorphic Indian sun-images. The actual re-modelling was done by the near Eastern royal families who sprang after the wreckage of Alexander's empire and who were "fervent worshippers of Mithra".

The Greeks found in Iranian Mithra a very close counterpart to their Apollo-Hellios and they soon attributed Mithra with a full anthropomorphic form. This took place near about 69-38 B.C. when Antiochus I of Commagene set up the monument of Nimrud Dagh.[25] But the sun-god from Bharhut tends to show that the anthropomorpism was done earlier.

One figure among the pantheon of the four divinities has got the inscription 'Apollo-Mithras-Helios-Hermes'. On the relief Antiochus is depicted holding a hand of Mithra, wearing a Persian dress like the king and distinguished by a radiating nimbus round his head, and holding a bunch of 'barsam' in his hand. This may be called the actual proto-type which served as the model for the later north-Indian sun-icons.

In the coins of the Kushan monarch Kaniṣhka[26] Mithra or Mihira was depicted wearing a heavy cloak and boots with "his extended right hand holding something" (was it 'Barsam'?) his left hand clasping a sword hanging down from his waist and his head encircled by a radiate numbus. These coin-types strikingly resemble the coins of Apollodotus with figures of Apollo on them, the only difference being in the delineation of the upper garment and attributes.[27] One deity in biga wearing rayed crown, and holding lance appear on the coin of Maues[28] and recalls Plato's. This is the representation of Sun no doubt. The idea of the investiture by the Sun-god developed out of the conception of Nimrud-Dagh and we find a gradual development in the idea.[29] From the coin of Wima Kadphises[30] and the statue of the squatted king found from Mathura[31] it appears that sometime the king himself with his peaked cap, club, beard, heavy cloak and high boots is represented on a 'bigha'.[32] Again the statue from Mathura has caused discrepancies amongst the scholars about its identity. It seems that it was too a representation of the Scythian monarch in a deified state of Sun-god.

Stein observes,[33] "Mithra the god of heavenly light may well claim precendence from the important position he occupies in the Avestic mythology, as well as in the eastern cult generally.

The Iranian Mithra has been recognized long ago in the very characteristic type of the sun-god, that on the rare coins of Kaniṣka bears the name of HELIOS. Not less varied are the forms in which his Iranian names appear. MIOPO and MIIPO (fig. i & ii) are the most frequent readings and represent but slightly varied pronunciations of the same form Mihr, which Avestic name must have assumed at a comparatively early date through the regular phonetic change of the "th" into 'h'".

The fully anthropomorphic form of the Sun God in Parthian and Sassanian art[34] and the standing figures of the deity from India show some common peculiarities, because they evolved out of the same Hellenistic, or Graeco-Iranian model.

The foreign features introduced into this land are the armour, or a tunic, the *Avyaṅga* the high leggings and the tall Scythian headgear known as "*Kirīṭamukuṭa*". One of the ancient authorities on Iconography of images, the *Matsyapurāṇa* states[35] about Sūrya image:

"*Colakācchanna-vapuṣam kvacitcitreṣudarśayet*
Vastrayugmasamopetam caraṇau tajasā-Vṛtau".

Another authority, the *Bṛhat Saṃhitā* states the injunctions that the body should be represented in "*Udīcyaveśam*" the feet are "*guḍhaṃ pādāduro-yāvat*" and the body is concealed in cloak i.e., "*Kañcukagupta*".[36] The coat-of-mail (*kavaca, colaka* or *Kañcuka*) which covered the upper part of the body was nothing but the Graeco-Iranian tunic or chiton. It become more heavier cloak due to that taste of the Scythian-Parthians and was understood by the Indians as *Colaka*, which they were used to see during war of the belligerent soldiers from the north.[37] The headless effigy of Kaniṣka and the heads from Mathura with high helmets and the soldiers costume from the Gāndhāra relief show this *udīcyaveśa* in full. One of the tall helmet in Mathura is moreover decorated with Sun and Moon symbols.

The *Avyaṅga* has been identified with the '*aivyaonghen*' of the Avesta. The *Maga Brāhmaṇas*, ushered in by Sāṃba from *Śākadvīpa* had the '*Avyaṅga*'—with them.[38] In the Kushan coins the cloak is heavier, and conceal the '*Avyaṅga*' but as the upper tunic becomes finer in later sculptural representations, the artists find the chance to depict it markedly.

The pair of high boots taken from the Scythio-Iranian repertory causes some confusion to the artists as well as to the ancient iconographists. The legs of the icon are not described as covered in *pādukā* (leggings) but as "*guḍhaṃ pādāduro yāvat*" (legs hidden upto the thighs). But what did conceal the legs? According to *Matsyapurāṇa* it was the '*tejasa*' i.e., effulgence. The deities feet were invisible to mortal eyes. It seems, that to keep the iconographic tradition intact, the Purāṇakāras prescribed that it was ominous to leave Sūrya's feet uncovered.

It seems from the reference of the *Viṣṇupurāṇa* that the icons were painted with colours.

Tatastamātāmro-jjvalahraṣva-bapuṣam

Iṣadā-piṅgalanayana-mādityam-adrākṣīt. (IV. 13. 10).

i.e., the complexion of Sun God was coppery-red and the eyes were yellowish brown. This also point to his northern and foreign affinity.

A few words might be said here about the expression "*kvaciccitreṣu darśayet*" Banerjea thinks that '*citra*' is sculpture in round and not painting.[39] But drawings and paintings of cult images were used in general in ancient India, and '*citra*' here obviously mean actual painting or drawing which the Magi priests possessed or were supplied by the Graeco-Iranian master-artists to their Indian counterparts to serve as models. Fa-hsien took back with him some model-drawings of Buddha images while returning from India in a similar manner, and at a later date.

The reference to '*citra*' in connection to Sun, moreover recall the painting of the god from the Bamiyan ceiling. Here he is represented exactly according to the *Matsyapurāṇa*.

But soon the Indian artists got over the western impact, and the traditional style seen in the four earlier images succeeded the surge of foreign conceptions. The genius of the native artists permeated a graceful dignity and vital consciousness in the icons; the faces radiated with the benevolent smile, and in comparison to the Indian types, that from Hatra and Palmyra look schematic, idol-like and vapid.

Scholars think that those sculptures (except the four earlier ones) in which Scythio-Iranian elements are best noticeable are later than those having conspicuous and prominent 'foreign' traits.

Both the *Bhaviṣyapurāṇa* and the *Padmapurāṇa* refer to the consecration of *devadāsīs* in the temple of the sun.

The close connection between the Sun (Mehar) and Verethragna (Vṛtrahana or Behram) was probably extolled by the *Maga Brāhmaṇas* of India so that a name like "*Varāhamihira*" become famous of a *Maga Brāhmaṇa* scion.[40]

Boar's head was a very favourite symbol and oft-used motif in Sassanian art; from a verse in the *Droṇaparvan* it appears that the Boar and the Sun (*Arka*) symbols became quite well-known in the Sindhu-Sauvīra country. Jayadratha the ruler of Lower Indus Valley thus attributed with a symbol of *Varāha* and *Arka* on his chariot *dhvaja* (flag).[41] This seems a later addition to the epic during the Sassanian contacts.

References

1. The record mentions Mitra, Varuṇa, Indra and the Nāsatyas, vide, Vedic Age, p. 204.
2. Vedic Mythology, p. 29 ff; Ṛigveda, I.35. 2-11; VI. 71.1-16; VII. 45.1.
3. C.J. Brown, Pl. I.
4. J.N. Banerjea, I.A., 1925, p. 161 ff.
5. S. Sen, Persian inscriptions, pp. 164, Hamadan ins; p. 166 f., Susa ins; p. 170 f., Persepolis ins.
6. Marshall, Taxila, III, Pl. 44; Guide, p. 105.
7. ICGW, p. 91 f.
8. CAI, p. 119, "An image of Hercules was borne in front of the line of infantry".
9. Vedic Mythology, p. 30 ff.
10. CAGI, pp. 189-190; Diodorus, CAI, p. 168, "He (Alexander) then sacrificed to the sun ...".
11. CAGI, p. 189.
12. McGovern, Indika of Ctesias, p. 12, "He mentions the sacred spot in the midst of an uninhabited region which the venerate in the name of the sun and moon". n. 26.

13. CAI, pp. 388-89.
14. Rowland, p. 60.
15. PMC, Pl. IX, No. v, p. 87, "Deity in Quadriga".
16. Tarn, GBI, p. 110 f.
17. *Ṛigveda*, i.35, 2-11.
18. Przyluski, I.A. 1926, p. 13, n. 8.

    Ibid., 1929, pp. 315-17.
19. Banerjea, DHI, p. 140.
20. Rowland, Pl. 30, I, from the effigy of Mihira on Kanişhika's coin it is clear that the Magis brought them before the Kushan epoch, D.R. Bhandarkar, I.A., 1911, p. 18 ff. thinks that they entered India sometime after 78 A.D. and before c. 450 A.D.; Davar, pp. 65-66.
21. Saṃba episode in the Bhavişyap. I. 129, show the sanctity of Mitravana and lies stress on the beneficent (curing of leprosy, cf. Herod.i.138) aspect of the deity.
22. Ptolemy, 74, CAI, p. 375.
23. McGovern, p. 83, "...hence the sun, the chief source of perceptible light was chosen as the best symbol of the supreme being".
24. ERE, Vol. VIII, p. 753.
25. Ghirshman, Pl. 80, Apollo-Mithras, 69-34 B.C. in situ.
26. PMC, Pl. XVII, 53, 63; Smith, CCIM, Vol. I, pp. 70, 73, Kaniş hka's pp. 82, 83, Huvishka's.
27. J.N. Banerjea, op. cit.
28. PMC, Pl. XV, i, Maues, "deity on biga" cf.

    Pl. IX, v, Plato, "deity on quadriga".
29. Ghirshman, Pl. 233, p. 190, investiture of Ardashia II (4th century A.D.) by Mithra and Ahura Mazda. Mithra is standing on an "Indian" lotus having drooping petals and prominent capsules.
30. PMC, XX. iii, Stater of the 'biga' type.
31. Zimmer, Pl. 60, states it as a statue of a Kushan king (2nd century A.D.) but the mark of the fire alter at the base of the pedestal marks the divine character of the image. He holds a club and a short dagger.
32. PMC, Pl. XX. iii.
33. A. Stein, I.A. 1888, Vol. XVII, p. 89 ff.

34. Ghirshman, Pl. 2, Sun-god, bust from Hatra, Pl. 71 the Palmyrene triad dressed in Roman costume; Pl. 233, Sun-god in full Sassanian royal dress; cf. Christensen, P. 171, Pl. 8, it recalls the deity represented on the Bamiyan vault.

35. Matsyap. 261. 4.

36. Bṛ. Saṃ., LVIII, 46-48, –details about the features and dress; 49-52, details abut the auspicious signs and measurements.

37. Nāṭya, XXI, 135, "*Vicitra-śastra-kavaco*"; Harṣa, VII, *colakas* and *kañcukas* on the kings while setting out for campaign. The Scythian dress was no doubt the "*udīcyaveśa*".

38. Bhaviṣyap. I. 141-142.

39. I.A. 1925, p. 165.

40. Davar, p. 66.

41. Mbh.7.90.20 (Haridas).

Section V

The Cult of Lakṣmīdevī

A careful study will disclose that the cult of goddess Śrī-Lakṣmī, though mainly indigenous in character imbibed many extra-Indian traits with it's pre-Aryan and Aryan elements.

The old *Ṛigvedic* idea of Śrī i.e., the beautiful and bountiful was gradually anthropomorphized as a goddess and gained position in the popular pantheon.[1]

Lakṣmī first made her plastic appearance on the medallions and *toraṇa* decorations at Bharhut and Sanchi. She is depicted as sitting or standing amidst the waving stalks of lotus which is an emblem of life and water. Sometimes she is seen bathed by two elephants. She was the popular deity of Śuṅga period and was represented in terracotta figurines too. Lakṣmī, from the very beginning, is intimately connected with the fecundity rituals and was essentially a goddess of fertility. A terracotta idol which has been described thus, "the figurine (106) is certainly religious in character is understood from it's motif. The important point by which we can arrive at this is that in the place of the head there is the fully blossomed lotus with petals falling over the shoulders".[2]

This fecundity goddess represented by lotus, indeed had close connection with water, the sap of life. When the abstract idea of '*Śrī*' became personified she was modelled after these ancient earth goddesses. Her worship, which was of simple *vrata* type was undoubtedly performed by the womenfolk for the prosperity of the household. This worship probably come within the '*Māṅgalika*' group of rituals known in the Maurya times.[3]

But soon she was extolled as a great goddess bestowing health, riches and prosperity to all and was worshipped by the traders as well as agriculturists. She was also connected with the Yakṣas who guarded over the wealth.

Mention should be made of two terracotta pieces, one found from ancient Tāmralipta and the other from Basarh.[3] The pose of the female deity found from Basarh site is similar to that of Śrī from Sanchi and the meandering lotus and other aquatic plants depicted are similar. The other terracotta from Tāmralipta (present Tumluk) is quite akin to the former but the goddess is replaced by a standing Yakṣa. The most remarkable feature of these plaques is that in both of them pairs of wings have been attached to the shoulders of these two deities.[4] According to Coomaraswamy "these types have behind them a long history; they may have been votive tablets or auspicious representations of mother goddess and bestowers of fertility and prototype of Māyādevī or Lakṣmī". U.P. Shah connects Vedic Ilā or Irā with Greek Iris.[5] In classical literature, painting and sculpture Iris has been described and depicted as golden winged.[6] If this terracotta plaques do represent the Vedic goddess, then we find that the Greek idea of the winged deity Iris has a parallel Indian counterpart. As Lakṣmī was intimately connected with water, there seems every possibility of her being worshipped as Irā with wings.

One comes to more sure ground about this parallel developments of iconography by examining the numismatic evidences. On the coins of the Indo-Greek rulers Agathocles and Pantaleon the figure of the "Dancing girl with long hanging ear-rings and Oriental trousers"[7] has been taken as to represent Lakṣmī.[8] But Banerjea thinks that it was a representation of Yakṣī, probably Yakṣinī Aśvamukhī. The posture of the figure is remarkable. A similar female has been represented on a Sassanian jug from Kalar-Dasht. It seems that the Sassanian artist copied the pose from the Indo-Greek coin motif. Lakṣmī was quite well-known in the north-west and is represented in the typical Indian pose on the coins of foreign rulers like Azes and Azelises.[9]

In Gāndhāra her iconic representations were influenced to some extent by foreign ideas. They city goddess of Puṣkalāvatī, who was no doubt Lakṣmī (the Puṣkara i.e., lotus goddess) was a mixed personality. The Greek idea of Fortuna-Nike was akin to the Indian conception of 'luck' and 'happiness' personified as Śrī. Thus Nike was identified with Śrī-Lakṣmī and some of her attributes were attached to the latter. Lakṣmī of Puṣkalāvatī, thus took the mural crown of Artemis and hold in her hand the Indian lotus. The mural crown was adopted by Artemis from water-goddess Anitis of Bactria. This Anāhita again absorbed some of the traits of Artemis and became associated with 'Victory'. On the coins of Maues and Azes Lakṣ mī is depicted wearing Greek robe and standing amidst the vines.[10]

The Iranian Ardoksho has made a more lasting impression upon the iconography of Lakṣmī than the city-goddess Anitis of Bactra. Ardoksho was the Iranian goddess presiding over wealth. She arrived with the Scythio-Parthian invaders and was worshipped in the north-west.[11] She was accompanied by her consort Farro. This tutelary couple has been represented in art with bags and cornucopia, emblems of bounty, and jars of coins indicating riches. (See Plate No. 10).

This deity soon came to be worshipped as Hāritī, the spouse of Vaiśravana-Kubera, the lord and guardian of wealth. It is interesting to note that in Japanese Buddhist mythology Hāritī is said to be the mother of Lakṣmī.[12] This association of the deity of childcare with the goddess of prosperity indicate that the legend was originally current in some region where Lakṣ mī and Hāritī were to be seen in close connection.

The exotic style of depicting the coins flowing out from an upturned jar, was adopted by the Indian artists. On the seals found from Bhita, Lakṣmī is seen standing between a pair of dwarf goblins, who are busy in pouring out loads of coins under the feet of the goddess.[13]

The cornucopia of Demeter (from whom it was attributed to Ardoksho) remained the symbol of Lakṣmī till quite late. The Gupta coins as well as sculpture in Kashmir bear evidence to this fact.[14]

The divinity, who is represented by an image from the Mohmand frontier and similar others from Peshawar Valley, is probably Hāritī. The loose tunic, the mace, wheel, cup, *truśūla* and the *kamandulu* are to be noted. It the Hindu codes of iconography she is described as Vaiṣṇavī.[15] Banerjea thinks that she represented a Hellenized Vaiṣṇavi. She was undoubtedly one of the Māṭrikas who substituted Hāritī in Hindu pantheon.

Curiously enough, Lakṣmī has been invoked for the bestowal of victory in the *Harṣacarita*.[16] In this aspect she represented Anāhita or Nike. Her description is also strikingly reminiscent of Anāhita on a Sassanian sculpture.[17] This evidently shows that from the time of the Indo-Greeks Lakṣmī was associated with the idea of royal fortune and victory in battle. Her foreign attributes remained intact during the Gupta period and she was worshipped by the rulers as late as the time of Bāṇabhaṭṭa, especially for the bestowal of victory. But, it seems that soon after that epoch the Graeco-Iranian attributes were lost sight of and the idea of 'Rājya-śrī' (fortuna) only remained confined within the scope of poetic conventions.

From the foregoing discussion on the Brahmanical cults, it becomes apparent that foreign ideas were accepted freely wherever it appealed the Indians. The iconographic aspect of religion was more enriched by the exotic modes than the ritualistic side. The Indian authorities on art, iconography and religion never admit what they have received from the foreign contacts. The casual references are the only available evidences that have to be gleaned from extant literature and used in reconstructing the history. Fortunately contemporary works of art corroborate the literary evidences to a great extent, and help one to study the fuller history of foreign influences on Indian religion.

References

1. Coomarswamy, East. Art. Vol. I, p. 175 ff.
2. C.C. Dasgupta, Indian Clay Sculpture, Śrī-sūkta, 13; Matsyap. Ch. 169; Viṣṇup. II, 2.9.
3. P.C. Dasgupta, The Early Terracottas from Tamralipta, Indian Folklore, Jan-March. 1958, pp. 33 ff; Coomarswamy thinks that the figurine belongs to Maurya period, vide IIA. p. 21; But C.C. Dasgupta, Ind. Clay. Sculpl. p. 177, Fig. 98, thinks that it belongs to Sunga epoch.
4. Stein, Ind. Ant. 1888, Vol. XVII, p. 91 ff. connects the winged goddess with the Avestic *Vanaiñti uparatāṭ* i.e., "Victorious Superiority".

5. U.P. Shah, I.H.Q. Vol. XXXIX, p. 260 ff. Ilā is the goddess of nourishment, Vedic Myth, p. 124.
6. E.R.E. Vol. XII, p. 741b. She is very same to Nike in this aspect, and is hardly distinguishable from the latter. P.M.C. p. 197, 132, "Winged goddess to left, with palm in L. hand and wreath in outstretched R. hand". Pl. XVIII. She is probably the Anitis of Bactria, conceived as Nike or 'Victory'. The pose of Anitis in No. 133 is somewhat analogous with that of Anāhita from Naqsh-i-Rustam (Ghirshman, p. 176, Pl. 218) and with the goddess on Azilises (P.M.C. Pl. XIII, 334). That the personality of this goddess symbolizing victory became a composite-one becomes clear from Pl. XVI, 82 of Zeionises, p. 157, where the deity is seen with the cornucopia of Demeter and the diadem which she is handing over to the king. The diadem (or the wreath) of Nike or Anāhita.
7. P.M.C. Pl. II, 35; p. 16; Compare with the Dancing Girl on the Sessanian Jug from Kalar-Dasht, Ghirshman Pl. 256.
8. J.N. Banerjea, DHI, p. 111.
9. P.M.C. Pl. XII. No. 308; Pl. XIII, No. 332, 333.
10. P.M.C. Hippostratos, pp. 74-77; Peukolaus, p. 80. nos 642, and 606; also 631, "represent the city goddess with Mural crown" and palm. Pl. VIII. P.M.C. p. 99, type: Poseidon and Bacchante, Pl. X. 20 "Female figure standing to front between trees".
11. Stein, In. Ant. Vol. XVII, p. 97; the name Ardoksho was probably derived from "Ashis-vaṇuhi", the Avestic goddess of wealth and fortune, Vide Fig. XV and XVI of Kaniṣhka and Huvishka.
12. Coomaraswamy, East. Art. Vol. I, p. 177, n. 27; Matsyap. 261, 47-49; describes Rākṣasas and Vetālas attending Lakṣmī, this was no doubt added due to the cult of Ardoksho-Hāritī.
13. Motichandra, Padmaśrī, Fig. 24.
14. Smith, C.C.M. Pl XV, 1,2,4,6,8 (p. 103); R.C. Kak, p. 122, Fig. L.
15. Smith, History of Fine Arts, p. 78; Ingholt, Pl. 341. *Matsyapurāṇa* calls her Vaiṣṇavī, 261, 29-30a. J.N. Banerjea, DHI, p. 137; *Bṛhatsaṃhitā* LVIII, 37-39 describes goddess Ekanaṃsā, who has some common attributes with Vārāhī, and this Hellenized Hāritī.
16. *Harṣacarita*, III, Cowell, p. 96 "out of a dazzling white silken robe, embroidered with hundreds of diverse flowers and birds, and gently rippled by the motion of the breeze, her form rose up as from an ocean's water"...

17. Ghirshman, p. 176, Pl. 218: – "Falling in long parallel fold her robe fans out in a billowing mass around her feet, clearly intended to remind us of the movement of waves of her function of the goddess of the water". The Jaina work *Aṅga-vijjā* refer to Anāhita as Anāditā, see Chatterji, India and China, p. 114.

Section VI

The Cult of Baladeva-Saṃkaṣaṇa

According to Megasthenes, "those who inhabited the mountains hymn the praises of Dionysus,...but the philosophers in the plain worship Herakles".[1] This he told about the religious attitude of his contemporary Indians. Dionysus as mentioned by Megasthenes has been identified with Śiva, while Herakles has been thought to be Kṛṣṇa.

Arrian, however, has placed little credence on the fact that really did Greek Dionysus and Heralkes come to India. He thought that the Greeks had invented stories of Dionysus' conquest and in the surge of devotion they tried to identify some of their native gods with deities found in India and ẹlsewhere.[2] Yet, it would not be improper to judge from the account of Megasthenes that there was a dual gọd who had resemblances with both Dionysus and Herakkes. While Dionysus was of more divine type, Herakles was actually a mortal hero, later on deified for his marvellous acts, just like Balarāma and Vāsudeva-Kṛṣṇa of the Andhaka-Vṛṣṇi family residing in Mathura.[3]

It is quite possible that in pre-Aryan India, a very ancient fertility deity was worshipped, his symbols were the *liṃga* (phallus) and the *lāṇgala* (plough). Later on the conception gave rise to the separate and distinct personalities, one Śiva and the other Baladeva-Saṃkarṣaṇa. The liṇga was the symbol of the former while the lāṇgala was attributed to the latter. Sylvain Levi has shown that the words 'liṇga' and 'lāṅgala' were derived from the same Drāviḍian root.[4]

The above assumption has been corroborated by the fact that both Śiva and Baladeva are given some common attributes. They were of white complexion and sturdy physique. The snakes (i.e., the spirits of the water) ornamented their body. In fact, Baladeva has been identified with Śeṣa-nāga the lord of the snakes.[5] Further, they were notorious for their intemperance. Baladeva was addicted to wine while Śiva indulged in other intoxicating drugs. These common traits indicate that they might have been one and same in the remote days of pre-Aryan antiquity.

The Greek god Dionysus had identical similarities with the characteristics of Śiva-Baladeva who was the god par-excellence of Mathurā region, as found from the references in the *Viṣṇupurāṇa*.[6] He has also been connected with the Raivata-parvata of Dvārakā. The Greeks were well-acquainted with the Mathurā region as well as western India, and hence it is possible that by Herakles they meant Baladeva and Kṛṣṇa both. The nearness of relation between Baladeva and Kṛṣṇa must be held responsible for the confusion of the Greek writers.

It is to be noted further that by third-second centuries B.C. the old Vedic god Varuṇa lost his earlier magnanimity and was identified with Baladeva-Saṃkarṣaṇa the lord of the sub-terranial waters,[7] and his Śakti was called Vāruṇī.

There is every possibility that Bacchanalian festivals were held by the devotees of this god and his spouse. A causal reference to the *Jaṭila* (i.e., who wore matted locks of hair) and *Muṇḍa* (i.e., shaven-headed) worshippers offering drinks in the *Arthaśāstra* indicate the prevalence of Saṃkarṣaṇa cult among the Gopas.[8] The intoxicant offerings to this deity were considered sacred.

Kauṭilya, while stating the shrines within the fort, mentions, "*Śrī-Madirā-gṛham*", i.e., the abode of goddess Madirā. Basak thinks Madira was a name of Durgā.[9] But it appears to be the common appellation of Vāruṇī or Sūrā-devī, the consort of Baladeva-Varuṇa. It is interesting to note that while Lakṣmī was coupled with Kṛṣṇa-Viṣṇu, Madirā or Surā was regarded as the Śakti of Balarāma. Both Lakṣmī and Sūrā came out of the ocean which is reminiscent of the aquatic origin of Aphrodite.

Who was this Madirā? In the *Viṣṇupurāṇa* she is said to be appearing before Balabhadra from a Kadamba tree in the vicinity of Nanda-gokula in Vṛndāvana. This region was noted for the worship of Vṛkṣakās (wood-nymphs) who were the guardians of the vegetation. Tarn has drawn our attention to the fact that Mathura has been called the 'daughter of the gods'.[10] The name Mathura was probably derived from Madhu-pura or Madirā, who was the tutelary divinity of this place. It also attests that the Greeks had known the legend of this goddess. Innumerable statues of Yakṣiṇīs found from the environs of Mathura corroborate the literary evidences. This Yakṣiṇī Madirā was connected with Baladeva-Saṇkarṣaṇa before the advent of the Greeks. Under the successive foreign rules, an attempt no doubt was made, to identify and adapt the rituals centering round Saṃkarṣaṇa-Madirā, with the needs of the new-comers.

The synthesis was rendered by Dionysus-Bacchus who closely resembled Baladeva in his drunken aspect. The swooing lady depicted on the Maholi sculpture is to be identified as Vāruṇīdevī Madirā. The other relief from Palikhera depicting a pot-bellied deity accompanied by females is generally identified with Kubera in a Bacchanalian scene. It is probably a delineation of the composite deity Bacchus-Baladeva and the attendants, dressed in sleeved tunics, skirts and shoes seem to be a crude Scythian representation of the Maenads of Bacchus. In the *purāṇas*, Balabhadra is described enjoying beverage in accompany of his wife Revati and other females. He is compared to Kubera (*Kubera iva Mandare*). In all possibility this type of Puranic conceptions grew out of the mode of worship extant in Mathura in the Scythio-Kushan period, which amalgamated the cults of Bachhus-Baladeva with that of Buddhist Vaiśravaṇa-Kubera. The art and iconography no doubt drew their inspiration from the same common source.

The cult had obviously, gained a high popularity as it's idea was most suited to the needs of the Hellenistic, Buddhist or Hindu worshippers paying their respect to Dionysus, Vaiśravana or Baladeva.

References

1. Strabo, XV, 1, 58.
2. Diodorus, ii. 38, 39; Arr. v. p. 165.
3. Detailed account of these two divine hero brothers are told in the *Mahābhārata, Harivaṃśa, Viṣṇu* and *Matsya-purāṇas*. The dates of compilation of greater parts of these books come within the period under discussion, and surely they had been given the final shape before c. 600 A.D. During the Indo-Greek and the Indo-Scythian period, these heroes became quite popular.

4. Pre-Aryan and Pre-Dravidian in India, pp. 8-15.
5. Viṣṇup. II, 5, Verse-13-18.
6. Viṣṇup. V. 36.12-13.

   Harivaṃśa, II, he is the constant companion of Kṛiṣṇa throughout the narrative.
7. DHI, p. 504, Vāruṇī later became a Matṛikā.
8. Shamasastry, p. 432, "Spies disguised as ascetics with shaved head or braided hair and pretending to be the worshippers of god Saṇkarshana, may mix their sacrificial beverage with the juice of the madana plant (and give it to the cow-herds) and carry off the cattle".
9. Shamasastry, p. 54; Basak, Vol. I, p. 62.
10. Tarn, GBI, pp. 251-253.

Section VII

The Cult of Skanda-Karttikeya, the God of War

From the references in the *Aṣṭādhyāyī*, the *Mahābhāṣya* and the *Arthaśāstra* it become apparent that the worship of Skanda-Kārttikeya was popularly known during the earlier part of this period.[1] The images of Śiva and Skanda "were a source of living to their keepers".

The epic furnishes numerous stories about the origin of this war-god and his valourous deeds.[2] The western tribes of the Yaudheyas and the Mālavas adopted the worship of Skanda about first-second centuries A.D. It is from their coins that one comes to know that this deity was invoked during war and was asked to bestow victory.

Scholars have come to the conclusion that this god was an amalgamation of different tutelary spirits that used to preside over different parts of India. In the epic his martial aspect has been focussed more than any other characteristics. From some sporadic references, there seems, every reason to believe that a strong foreign influence acted in shaping and developing the cult during this period. It was because of this exotic inspiration that the diffused earlier cults were united and formed the Kārttikeya-legends, so popular in the Gupta epoch.

(i) Kārttikeya was intimately connected with the mountains of the north. Different parts of the Hindu Kush and the Himalayas have been designated as his favourite resort. The *Kukkuṭa* or the *Mayūra* were his emblems.[3] This *Kukkuṭa* might have some connection with the Kukkuṭa-giri (Falcon's Perch-"Uparisaena") of Afghanistan near Herat.[4] This was exactly the region referred to in the *Vāyu-purāṇa* where dwelth the Ulaṃghī Rākṣasas on the Niṣadha mountain. One is tempted to connect these Ulaṃghīs with the tribes inhabiting the Lamghan Valley, who were also known as the Lampākaṣ. There is no doubt that these Ulaṃghīs together with the Guhas or

Guhyakas worshipped Karttikeya. All these tribes of the Lohas, Guhas, and Ulaṃghīs lived by martial pursuits.

(ii) Kārttikeya has been attributed with a host of malevolent spirits who serve him as his attendants. They are known as '*bāla-grahas*' and '*apasmāras*'. A pair of names that attracts attention is that of two divinities called '*Miñjikā-Miñjika*'. Holdich has reported that in Badakshan, a hymn was sung in honour of a war-god, the language of which resembled the Paiśācī dialect. This war-god evidently reminds one of Kumāra-Kārttikeya worshipped in the hills. Curiously enough there is a mountain called Añjumān in Badakshan. A stream known as the Miñjān flows by. This Añjumān was probably known as Muñjāyana in the days of tha Atharvaveda and the Aṣṭadhyāyī, which mentions the Mauñjāyana people who spoke in Mauñjāyanī speech. The epic also refers to the Muñjavān mountain.[5] The term Muñja in Sanskrit denote a kind of sedge like grass grown in the hilly regions and marsh lands. This is again reminiscent of the legend that Kumāra was born in the tuft of Śara-grass and Śara-vana was his favourite retreat. The Scythians, among whom the name Miñja or Munja were common enough,[6] probably brought theses stories as well as the tutelary couple *Miñjikā-Miñjika* with them to India.

(iii) It seems that primitive worship of demons like Kailung, who presides over diseases and child-birth and is worshipped by the Gaddis, became fused with the cult of the war-god. It is natural that the rude tribes of north-west[7] whose life was constantly disturbed by the turmoils and the hardships of severe climatic condition could only think of spirits that guided them in war and saved them in the dangers of child-birth, deathly diseases and mishaps causing from unknown reasons. At first, it seems rather absurd, that the war-god should be accompanied by a galaxy of demons that caused infantile diseases (*Skandāpasmāras*), but by a study of it's foreign origin, the discrepancy disappears.

(iv) But how did theses elements reach India? The description of the myriad of soldiers that followed Kumāra on his march probably give an answer to this question. Some names of the followers of Skanda, viz., Śveta-kalinda, Śveta-siddha, Javana, etc. inevitably remind one of Alexander who reached the plains of India with his thousands. The epic states that all these followers of Kumāra were girt in leather armours with swords and were conversing in various *Mleccha* dialects.[8] It is not unlikely that this is a allegorical reference to the phalanx of the Macedonian conqurer which steadily advanced surviving the tremendous hardships met oh the ridges and ravines of Afghanistan (*Lohita-giri* and *Kukkuṭa-giri*, the haunts of Mahāsena's attendants). It is not improbable, that the moving army of Alexander had came across the native stories about the war-god of these hills. Though the classical authors are silent on this point, it seems, from the references in the epic, that Alexander was identified with Skanda-Kārttikeya. A comparison of the activities of the Macedonian hero, with that of the war-god will show the possibility of the above assumption.

The epic relates that Kārttikeya was anointed as *Senāpati* of the gods in *Samanta-pañcaka tīrtha* on the Sarasvatī. The *Taijasa tīrtha* of Varuṇa was also sacred to him. This evidently reminds of the oblation made by Alexander to Poseidon, the lord of the waters. Alters were erected by Alexander at the bank of Vipāśā, at which Chandragupta sacrificed. The name 'Taijasa', indeed remind one of Nicaea 'the city of victory' where "the sacrifices of thanks giving for victory" were conducted. It is to be noted that Punjab is the region, connected both with Alexander and Kārttikeya.[9]

Tarn thinks that the name of Alexander was remembered in India as 'Skanda' the bogey who frighten children. In the light of the above references it seems that he was remembered in the stories of the marvellous deeds of the war-god. Sylvain Levi has shown that Alexander was called '*Caṇḍakośa*' or '*Alasascaṇḍakośa*' in ancient Indian romances. It is quite possible that there were certain variations of the same story known to the editors of the epic as well as Bāṇabhaṭṭa.

It was then, due to the Macedonian invasion that the war-god of the obscure frontier regions[10] was suddenly elevated to the position of a national deity and was largely represented in the numismatic and sculptural art of Gupta India.

References

1. Agrawala, IKP, pp. 362-63; Puri, ITP, pp. 182-183; Shamashastry, p. 54.
2. Vide Mbh. 3. Ch. 187 ff; 9 Ch. 41 ff. (Haridas).
3. Mbh. 9.42.58.
4. Agrawala, pp. 40-41.
5. Mbh. 3.193.10; 3. 193. 15 (Haridas); Agrawala, IKP, p. 447, for Muñja grass, Vide Monier-Williams, p. 821.
6. A. Stein. Ind. Cult. Vol. I, p. 353 ff.
7. ERE, Vol. I, pp. 233-34.
8. Vide Mbh. 9.42 (Haridas).
9. Mbh. 9. 43. 88-97 (Haridas), – the destruction of Vana; 9.43. 111-112 – Taijasa tīrtha; cf. CHI, p.334, f.n. 2.
10. Holdich, pp. 131-133, the Kafiri hymn to their war-god Gish invariably reminds one of Śiva as the lord of "Gir Nysa", but more of Kārttikeya in his war-like aspect. From the references of Holdich, "Katan Chirak is explained to be an ancient town in the Minjan Valley of Badakshan now in ruins; but it was the first large place that the Kafirs captured, and is apparently held to be the symbolical of victory. This reference connects the Kamdesh Kafirs with Badakshan, and shows this people to have been more widespread than they are at present". ..."According to Grierson the language of the hymn was derived from the Piśāca" who are probably identical with the Pashai tribe inhabiting the Langhan Valley. This is again corroborated by the evidence of the epic that the war-god was followed by innumerable Piśācas, Bhūtas etc. It moreover shows that these legends were actually brought in by the invasion of Alexander who passed by those Valleys. Popular imagination, no doubt connected this ancient war god with Alexander himself.

Conclusion

On the basis of the study that we have made in this book, it would be clear the that the foreign influence on the three important aspects of Indian culture viz. social life, fine arts and religion is not insignificant. The Indian sources do not specifically admit what they had received or accepted from the foreigners, but it has been found, that the foreign influence had been indirectly permeated in the ancient Indian cultural life. The foreigners who settled in or along the natural borders of India and came into contact either as immigrants or invaders or as commercial people were considered somewhat low in position on account of different religious observances and social customs, but were not treated unsympathetically. This general softness, sobreity and tolerance of Indian character made both the parties, the proper inhabitants of the land and the immigrants to meet on friendly terms of mutual understanding. It was not until the end of the ancient period and the beginning of the mediaeval, i.e., the time of the Mohammedan conquest, that the rigidity solidified into a complete disagreement and debarred the foreigners totally from infilterating into the Hindu system.

Abbreviations

Acharya	Indian Architecture according to Manasara Silpa-sastra by P.K. Acharya
Agrawala	India as known to Panini by V.S. Agrawala
AII	The History of Indian & Indonesian Art by A.K. Coomaraswamy
Altekar	The Position of Women in Hindu Civilization by A.S. Altekar
AMK	The Ancient Monuments of Kashmir by R.C. Kak
Am. Marc.	Ammianus Marcillinus
ANEP	Ancient Near East in Pictures by Pritchard
Bau.	Baudhāyaya Dharma-sūtra
Bhavisyap	Bhaviṣya-purana
B.O.R.I.	Bhandarkar Oriental Research Institute
Bṛi-Saṃ.	Bṛihat Saṃhita.
BSI	Bharatiya Sangiter Itihasa by Prajñānānanda
CAGI	Cunningham's Ancient Geography of India
CAI	Classical Accounts of India ed. By R.C. Majumdar
CASII	Studies in the Chinese Art and some Indian influences by J. Hackin & others
CBIMA	Catalogue of the Brahmanical Images in the Mathura Art by V.S. Agrawala

DCA	Dictionary of Classical Antiquities
DHI	Development of Hindu Iconography by J.N. Banerjea
Dharmasutras	Dharma Sutras, A study in their Origin and Development by S.C. Banerjee
Dey	My Pilgrimages to Ajanta and Bagh by M.C. Dey
EHNI	Early History of North India by S. Chattopadhyaya
EHVS	Eary History of the Vaisnava Sect by H.C. Raychaudhuri
Ep. Ind.	Epigraphia Indica
ERE	Encyclopaedia of Religion and Ethics
ESAI	Ethnic Settlements in Ancient India by S.B. Chaudhuri
Fergusson	History of Indian and Eastern Architecture by J. Fergusson
GAP	Gandharan Art in Pakistan by H. Ingholt
GBI	The Greeks in Bactria and India by Tarn
Ghirshman	Iran
GI	Gates of India by T. Holdich
Goetz	India, Five Thousand Years of Indian Art (Art of the World Series) by H. Goetz
Guide	Guide to Taxila by Sir J. Marshall
Hackin	Studies in Chinese Art and Some Indian Influences by J. Hackin and others
Hari	Harivaṃśa
Haridas	Haridas Siddhantavāgīśa, ed. The Beng. Ed. of the Mahābhārata
Handbook	Handbook to the Sculptures in the Curzon Museum of Archaeology,

	Muttra by V.S. Agrawala
Hazra	Studies in the Puranic Records on Hindu Rites and Customs by R.C. Hazra
Herod	Herodotus
HIIA	History of Indian and Indonesian art by A.K. Coormarasway
Holdich	Gates of India by T. Holdich
HOS	Harvard Oriental Series
HPE	History of Persian Empire by Olmstead
Huart	Ancient Persian and Iranian Civilization by C. Huart
I.A.	Indian Antiquary
IAMS	Indian Architecture according to Mānasara Śilpaśāstra by P.K. Acharya
ICGW	India in the Classical Greek Writings by B.N. Puri
I.H.Q.	Indian Historical Quarterly
IIW	Intercourse between India and the Western World by H.G. Rawlinson
IKP	India as Known to Pāṇini by V.S. Agrawala
Ind. Cul.	Indian Culture
Ingholt	The Gāndhāran Art in Pakistan by I. Lyons and Harold Ingholt
ITP	India in the Time of Patañjali by B.N. Puri
J.B.B.R.A.S.	Journal of the Bombay Branch of the Royal Asiatic Society
Jain or J.C. Jain	Life of Ancient India as Depicted in the Jain Canons by J.C. Jain
JISOA	Journal of the Indian Society of Oriental Art
J.R.A.S.	Journal of the Royal Asiatic Society of Great Britain and Ireland

Kak	Ancient Monuments of Kashmir by R.C. Kak
L.C.L.	Loeb Classical Library, Lohuizen de Leew. The 'Scythian' Period
Mārkaṇḍeyap.	Mārkaṇḍeya-purāṇa
MASI	Memoirs of the Archaelogical Survey of India
Matsyap	Matsya-purāṇa
Mbh	Mahabharata
Mbh. Samaj	Mahabharater Samaj by Sukhamaya Śāstri
McGovern	The Early Empires of Central Asia by W.M. McGovern
MMC III	Mathura Museum Catalogue Part III by V.S. Agrawala
M.N. Dutt	The Dharma-śāstras, Eng. tr. By M.N. Dutt
Nāṭya	Nāṭyaśāstra by Bhrata
Naya or Nayadh	Nāyādhammakahāo
PBVB	Pracina Bharatiya Veśa-Bhūṣā by Motichandra
PHAI	Political History of Ancient India by H.C. Raychaudhuri
PMC	Catalogue of the Coins in the Punjab Museum, Lahore, by R.B. Whitehead
PW	Position of Women in the Hindu Civilization by A.S. Altekar
Ram	Rāmāyaṇa
RBIF	Rome Beyond the Imperial Frontiers by M. Wheeler
Rowland	The Art and Architecture of India by Benjamin Rowland
RSHC	Racial Synthesis in Hindu Culture by S.V. Viswanatha

SSB	Sacred Books of the Buddhists
SBE	Sacred Books of the East
SCAII	Studies in Chinese Art and some Indian Influences by J. Hackin
Schoff	Periplus Maris Erythraei by W.H. Schoff
Shamasastry	Kautilya's Arthaśāstra Eng. tr. by R. Shamasastry
Shipping	Shipping in Ancient India by R.K. Mookerji
Suryavanshi	The Abhiras: Their History and Culture by B. Suryavanshi
TAI	Tribes in Ancient India by B.C. Law.
T. Bhattacharya	A Study on Vastu-vidya or Canons of Indian Architecture by Tarapada Bhattacharya
Tamara Talbot	The Scythians by Tamara Talbot
Saletore or IDW	India's Diplomatic Relations with the West by B.A. Saletore
Upadhyaya	India in Kalidasa by B.S. Upadhyaya
Vāyu or Vāyup	Vayu-Purāṇa
Viṣṇu or Viṣṇup	Visnu-Purāṇa
Viswanatha	Racial Syntheses in Hindu Culture by S.V. Viswanatha
WAIC	Ancient History of Western Asia India and Crete by B. Hrozny
Yazdani	Ajanta by G. Yazdani
Zimmer	The Art of Indian Asia by H. Zimmer

Bibliography

Original Sources

(i) **Vedic Works**: –

1. Ṛigveda Samhita — Vedic Research Society, Poona, 1933-51
2. Devī Sūkta — ed. K.C. Chatterji, Calcutta University, 1945
3. Śrī Sūkta — ed. Kasi Sanskrit Series, Varanasi, 1949
4. Atharva-veda Samhita ed. W.D. Whitney, H.O.S. 1905
5. Aittareya Brāhmaṇa Vol. 25, H.O.S. 1920
6. Satapatha Brāhmaṇa S.B.E. Vol. XLIII, Oxford, 1897
   S.B.E. Vol. XXVI, Oxford, 1885
7. A compilation of well-known 120 Upanishads, Nirnaya Sagara Press, Bombay, 1948.
8. Niruktam of Yāska — Anandasrama Sanskrit Series, Poona, 1921

(ii) **Epics**: –

1. Rāmāyaṇa (Gauḍīya Pāṭha) ed. with Beng. tr. Amareśvara Thakur, Calcutta, 1338-1349 B.S.
   Rāmāyaṇa (Yuddha-kāṇḍa) ed. Narendrachandra Vedāntatirtha, Nirnaya Sagara Press, Bombay
2. Mahābhārata — ed. with Beng. tr. Haridas Siddhantavāgīśa, Calcutta, 1338 B.S.
   Mahābhārata — Bhandarkar Oriental Research Inst. Poona, started from 1933.
   Śāntiparva to the end ed. with Beng. tr. Bardhamān Rajbāti Mahābhārata Kāryālaya, B.S. 1291.
3. Khila Harivaṃśa — ed. Kinjawadekar, Poona 1936.
   Khila Harivamsa — Eng. tr. M.N. Datta, Calcutta

(iii) **Sastras**: –

1. Dharmasūtras of Āpastamba, Gautama, Vaśiṣṭha and Baudhāyana,...S.B.E. Vols. II & XIV, Eng. tr. G. Buhler.

Baudhāyana Dharma-sūtra — ed. Govindasvamin, Mysore 1907.

Gautama Dharmasūtra — Sanskrit Text Society, 1876.

Also, Dharmaśāstras — Eng. tr. M.N. Datta, Calcutta, 1908

2. Manu Saṃhitā — ed. with Beng. tr. Yogendranath Vidyaratna, Calcutta, B.S. 1292.

Manu Saṃhitā — Eng. tr. M.N. Datta, Calcutta, 1909.

3. Arthaśāstra of Kauṭilya — ed. Drs. J. Jolly & R. Schmidt, Varanasi, 1923.

Arthaśāstra of Kauṭilya — Eng. tr. R. Shamasastry, Mysore, 1960

Arthaśāstra of Kauṭilya — Beng. tr. R.D. Basak,

4. Nāṭyaśāstra of Bharata — G.O.S., Baroda, 1954.

5. Kāma-śāstra of Vātsyāyaṇa — Eng. tr. B.N. Basu, Calcutta, 1954

6. Bṛhat-saṃhitā of Varāhamihira — ed. with Eng. tr. V.S. Shastri, Banglore, 1947.

7. Bṛhaddeśī of Mataṅga, Trivandrum, 1928.

(iv) **Grammatical Works**: –

1. Aṣṭādhāyayī of Pāṇini — ed. S.C. Vasu, Motilal Banarasidas, 1962.

2. Vyakarana Mahābhāsya of Patanjali — Nirnaya Sagara Press,

Word Index to Patanjali's Vyakaraṇa — Bombay, 1935-1945.

Mahābhāsya — B.O.R.I. Poona, 1927.

(v)**the Puranas**: –

1. Mārkaṇḍeya-purāṇa	ed. With Beng. tr. Pañcānana Tarkaratna, Calcutta B.S. 1316.
2. Vāyu-purāṇa	ed. With Beng. tr. Pañcānana Tarkaratna, Calcutta B.S. 1317.
3. Matsya-purāṇa	ed. With Beng. tr. Pañcānana Tarkaratna, Calcutta B.S. 1316.
4. Viṣṇu-purāṇa	ed. With Beng. tr. Pañcānana Tarkaratna, Calcutta B.S. 1314.
5. Kūrma-purāṇa	ed. With Beng. tr. Pañcānana Tarkaratna, Calcutta B.S. 1311.
6. Bhaviṣya-purāṇa	Venkatesvar Press, Bombay, 1959.

(vi) **the Kāvyas, Nāṭakas and Tales**: –

1. Pratimā-naṭaka of Bhāsa	ed. T. Ganapati Sastri, 1915.
2. Raghu-vaṃśm of Kālidāsa	ed. With Beng. tr. Upendranath Mukhapadhyaya, Calcutta, B.S. 1323.
3. Abhijñana Śakuntalam	ed. With Beng. tr. Upendranath Mukhapadhyaya, Calcutta, B.S. 1323.
4. Dvātṛmśat Puttalikā	ed. With Beng. tr. Upendranath Mukhapadhyaya, Calcutta, B.S. 1323.
5. Daśakumāra-caritam	ed. N.R. Acharya, Bombay, 1951.
6. Mṛcchakaṭikam of Śūdraka	ed. N.R. Acharya, Bombay, 1950.
7. Harṣa-carita of Baṇabhaṭṭa	Eng. tr. Cowell & Thomas, Varanasi 1961. Beng. tr. Prabodhendunath Thakur, Calcutta, B.S. 1359.
9. Ratnāvalī of Śrī Harṣa	ed. S.R. Ray, Calcutta, 1919.

(vii) **the Tibetan Works**: –

1. Citralakṣaṇa	ed. With German tr. Leipzig, 1913.

2. Mystic Tales of Lāmā
Tāranath — Eng. tr. B.N. Dutta, Cal, 1957.

(viii) **the Buddhist Works**: –

1. Mahāvagga — Eng. tr. I.B. Horner, S.B.B. Vol. XIV, London, 1951.
2. Majjhima Nikāya — ed. Chalmers, London 1951.
3. Anguttara Nikāya — ed. E. Hardy, London, 1885-1900.
4. Digha Nikāya (Brahmajāla Sutta) — Eng. tr. Rhys. Davids, S.B.B. London, 1956.
5. Jātaka — Eng. tr. Cowell, Cambridge, 1895-1905.
   Jātaka — Beng. tr. Isanachandra Ghosh, Calcutta, B.S. 1323-1337.
6. Mahāvastu — Eng. tr. J.J. Jones, London, 1949-52.
7. Divyāvadāna — ed. P.L. Vaidya, Darbhanga, 1959.
8. Laitavistara — ed. Lafmann, 1902.

(ix) **the Jaina Works**: –

1. Nāyādhammakahāo ed. N.V. Vaidya, Poona, 1940.

(x)**the Tamil Works**: –

1. the Śilappadikāram — Eng. tr. V.R. Ramachandra Dikshitar, Oxford, 1939.
2. the Manimekhalai — Eng. tr. Krishnaswami Aiyangar, London 1927.

(xi) **the Cinese Texts**: –

1. The Travels of Fa-hsien (399-414 A.D.) or the Record of the Buddhistic Kingdoms
   H.A. Giles, London, 1959.
2. Si-Yu-Ki — Buddhist Records of the Western World, S. Beal, London, 1906.
3. On Yuan Chwang's Travels in India
   T. Watters, reprinted in Pecking, China 1941.

(xii) **the Classical Works: Greek & Roman**: –

1. Herodotus — Eng. tr. H. Cary, London & New York, 1847.
   Herodotus — Eng. tr. A.H. Godley, L.C.L. 1946.
2. Diodorus Siculus — C.H. Oldfather, L.C.L. 1946.
3. Strabo's Geographica — Eng. tr. H.L. Jones, L.C.L., 1949.
4. Pliny's Natural History — Eng. tr. H. Rakham, L.C.L. 1947.
5. Periplus Maris Erythraei — Eng. tr. W.H. Schoff.
6. Arrian's Anabis — Eng. tr. Aubrey Selincourt, The Penguin classics, 1958.
7. McCridle's;
   (a) Ancient India as described by Ptolemy, Calcutta 1927.
   (b) Ancient India 2 described by Ktesias, Calcutta 1881.
   (c) Ancient India 2 described by Megasthenes & Arrian, Calcutta, 1926.
8. Amminus Marcellinus — Eng. tr. J.C. Rolfe, L.C.L. 1950-52.
9. The Classical Accounts of India — ed. R.C. Majumdar, Calcutta, 1960.
10. India in the Classical Greek Writings — ed. by Puri

(xiii) **Archaeology & Epigraphy**: –

1. Memoirs of the Archaeological Survey of India.
2. Archaeological Survey of India, Annual Reports.
3. Epigraphia Indica.
4. Old Persian Inscriptions of the Achaemenid Emperors ed. with Eng. tr. S. Sen, Calcutta University, 1941.
5. Aśokan Inscriptions — ed. with notes, Sanskrit & Eng. tr. R. Basak, Calcutta, 1959.

(xiv) **Catalogues of Coins, Sculptures etc**: –

1. Catalogue of Coins in the Punjab Museum, Vol. I., R.B. Whitehead, Oxford 1914.
2. Catalogue of Coins in the Indian Museum, Vol. I, V.A. Smith, Oxford, 1906.
3. Catalogue of the Gupta Gold Coins in the Bayana Hoard A.S. Altekar, The Numismatic Society of India, Bombay 1954.
4. Summary Guide to the antiquities of Western Asia, British Museum, London 1952.
5. Handbook to the Sculptures in the Curzom Museum of Archaeology Muttra, V.S. Agrawala, Allahabad, 1939.
6. A. Catalogue of the Brahmanical Images in Mathura Art, V.S. Agrawala, Lucknow, 1951.
7. Mathura Museum Catalogue, Part III, Jaina Tirthankaras & Other Miscellaneous Figures, V.S. Agrawala, Lucknow, 1952.

Secondary Sources

(i) **Lexicons, Dictionaries, Encyclopaedia etc:** –

1. Encyclopaedia of Religion and Ethics, ed. James Hastings Charles Scribner's Sons, New York, 1955.
2. Encyclopaedia of Religion, ed. V. Ferm, Philosophical Library, New York, 1945.
3. Dictionary of the Arts, ed. Martin L. Wolf, Philosophical Library, New York, 1951.
4. A Dictionary of Classical Antiquities, ed. Oskar Seyffert London, 1957.
5. Vedic Index of Names and Subjects, ed. Macdonell & Keith London 1912.
6. An Index to the Names in the Mahabharatas, ed. S. Sorensen London, 1904
7. The Puranic Index, ed. V.R.R. Dikshitar, Madras University, 1951-55.

8. Sanskrit-English Dictionary, ed. Monier Williams. Oxford 1956.

(ii) **Modern Books:** –

Acharya, P.K. Indian Architecture according to Mānasāra Silpa-śāstra, London 1927

Agrawala, V.S. Matsya-purāṇa, a study Varanasi 1963

Agrawala, V.S. India as known to Pāṇini, Lucknow 1953

Altekar, A.S. The Position of Women in Hindu Civilization Varanasi 1956

Bagchi, P.C. Pre-Aryan & Pre-Dravidian in India Eng. tr. Of Sylvain Levi, Calcutta, 1929.

Bagchi, P.C. India and China, Bombay (Second Ed.)

Bagchi, P.C. India and Central Asia, Calcutta, 1955.

Barua, B. Barhut, III, 1937.

Basu, G.S. Purāṇa-praveśa (Beng.), Calcutta, B.S. 1341.

Banejea, J.N. Development of Hindu Iconography, Calcutta.ed's 1941 and 1956.

Banerjee, G.N. Hellenism in Ancient India, Cal. 1921.

Bhandarkar, D.R. Some Aspects of Ancient Indian Culture, Sir William Meyer Lectures 1938-39, published Madras, 1940.

Bhandarkar, R.G. Vaisnavism, Savism and Minor Religious Systems, Strassburg, 1913.

Bhushan, J.B. The Costumes and Textiles of India, Bombay, 1958.

Bhushan J.B. Indian Jewellery Ornamental and Decorative Designs, Bombay, (First Ed.).

Brown, Percy Indian Architecture, Buddhist & Hindu, Bombay, 1956.

Breasted, J.H. — Ancient Times, a history of the Early World, Ginn & Company, 1944.

Caroll, M. — Woman in all ages and All Countries, Greek Women, Philadelphia, 1907-8.

Cary & Warmington — The Ancient Explorers, London, 1925.

Chakladar, H.C. — Social Life in Vatsyāyana.

Chatterji, S.K. — India and China: Ancient Contacts, What India received from China, Calcutta, 1961.

Chattopadhyaya,S. — Achaemenids in India, Calcutta, 1950.

Chattopadhyaya, S. — The Śakas in India, Santiniketan, 1955.

Chattopadhyaya, S. — Early History of North India, Calcutta.

Chaudhuri, S.B. — Ethnic Settlements in Ancient India, Cal. 1955.

Christensen, A. L'Iran — Sous Les Sassanides, Paris, 1936.

Commaraswamy, A.K. — History of Indian and Indonesian Art, New York, 1927.

Cunningham — Ancient Geography of India ed. Surendranath Majumdar Sastri, Calcutta, 1924.

Das Gupta, C.C. — Origin and Evolution of Indian Clay Sculpture, University of Calcutta, 1961.

Davar — Iran and India Through the Ages, Bombay, 1962.

Delaporte, L. — Mesopotamia: The Babylonian and Assyrian Civilization, London, 1925.

Dey, M.C. — My Pilgrimages to Ajanta and Bagh, Oxford, 1950.

Fergusson, J. — History of Indian & Eastern Architecture, London, 1910.

Francis, H.T., Thomas, E.J. — Jataka Tales, Cambridge, 1916.

Frazer — The Golden Bough (Abridged Ed.), London, 1927.

Ghirshman — Iran, London, 1962.

Ghurye, G.S. — Indian Costumes, Bombay, 1951.

Goetz, H — India: Art of the World, Bombay, 1959.

Gupta, C.B. — The Indian Theatre, Varanasi, 1954.

Hackin, J. & others — Studies in Chinese Art and Some Indian Influences, London, 1938.

Hazra, R.C. — Studies in the Puranic Records on Hindu Rites and Customs, Dacca 1940.

Herzfeld, E. — Zoroaster and His World, New York, 1947.

Holdich, T. — Gates of India, London 1910.

Hrozny, B. — Ancient History of Western Asia, India and Crete, New York, 1953.

Huart, Clement — Ancient Persian and Iranian Civilization London, 1927.

Huntington, E.B. — The Pulse of Asia, New York, Ed. 1919.

Indra, Prof. — The Status of Women in Ancient India, Varanasi, 1955.

Ingholt, H.& Lyons, Islay — Gandharan Art in Pakistan, New York, 1957.

Jain, J.C. — Life in the Ancient India as depicted in the Jain Canons, Bombay, 1947.

Kak, R.C. — Ancient Monuments of Kashmir, London, 1933.

Kramrisch, Stella — The Art of India, London 1954.

Law, B.C. — Tribes in Ancient India, Poona, 1943.

Le Coq — Buried treasures of Chinese Turkestan, London, 1928.

Lohuizen de Leeuw — The 'Scythian' Period, Leiden, 1949.

McGovern, W.M — The Early Empires of Central Asia, University of North Carolina Press, 1939.

MacNicol, Nicol — Indian, Theism, Oxford, 1915.

Majumdar, R.C. & Altekar, A.S. ed. — The Vākāṭaka Gupta Age (c. 200-550 A.D.), Varanasi, 1954.

Marshall, Sir J. — Guide to Taxila, 1936.

Marshall, Sir J. — Taxila, Vols. I, II, III, Cambridge University Press, 1951.

Marshall, J. — The Buddhist Art of Gandhara, Cambridge 1960.

Motichandra — Prācīṇa Bhāratiya Veśa-Bhūṣā (Hindi), Allahabad Vi. Sam. 2007.

Motichandra — Sārthavāha: Prācīna Bhārat ka Patha-paddhati (Hindi), Patna, 1953.

Mookerji, R.K. — A Historyof Indian Shipping, Calcutta, 1957.

Munshi, K.M. — Saga of Indian Sculpture, Bombay, 1957.

Narian, A.K. — The Indo-Greeks, Oxford, 1957.

Olmstead — History of the Persian Empire (Achaemenid Period) University of Chicago, 1948.

Puri, B.N. — India in the Time of Patañjali, Bombay, 1957.

Pollard, E.B. — Woman in all Ages and All Countries, Oriental Women, Philadelphia, 1907-8.

Prajnanananda, Svami — Rāga O Rūpa (Beng.), Vols. I, II; Bharatiya Sangiter Itihas (Saṅgīta O Saṃskriti) (Beng.), Sri Ramakrishna Vedanta Math, Calcutta, 1961.

Przyluski, J. — Ancient Peoples of the Punjab, Eng. tr. C. Sen Calcutta, 1960.

Rao, Gopinath,	Elements of Hindu Iconography, Madras, 1916.
Rapson, E.J. ed.	Cambridge History of India, Vol. I, Delhi, 1955.
Rawlinson, H.G.	Bactria, London, 1912.
Rawlinson, H.G.	Intercourse between India and the Western World, Cambridge, 1926.
Ray, N.R.	Maurya and Sunga Art, Calcutta University, 1949.
Raychaudhuri	Political History of Ancient India, Calcutta University, 1953.
Raychaudhuri	Early History of the Vaishnava Sect, Calcutta.
Rowland, Benjamin	The Art and Architecture of India, London, 1953.
Sircar, D.C.	The 'Śākta-piṭhas', J.R.A.S.B. Letters, Vol. XIV, No. 1, 1948.
Saletore, B.K.	India's Diplomatic Relations with the West, Bombay, 1958.
Shastri, Sukhamaya	Mahabharater Samaj (Beng.) Visva-Bharati B.S. 1353.
Shastri, S.R.	Women in the Sacred Laws, Bombay 1953.
Shastri, N.K.	Foreign Notices of South India, ed. Age of the Nandas and the Mauryas, Varanasi, 1952.
Stein, M.A.	Ruins of Desert Cathay, London, 1912
Suryavanshi, B.	The Abhiras: Their History and Culture, Baroda, 1962.
Talbot, Tamara,	The Scythians, London, 1958.
Tarn, W.W.	The Greeks in Bactria and India, Cambridge, 1951.
Tarn W.W.	Alexander the Great (narrative), Cambridge, 1951.

Thapar, R. Aśoka and the Decline of the Mauryas, Oxford, 1961.

Upadhyaya, B.S. India in Kalidas, Allahabad, 1947.

Vidyanidhi, J.C. Ray Pujaparvan (Beng.) Visva-Bharati, B.S. 1358.

Viswanatha, S.V. Racial Synthesis in Hindu Culture, London, 1928,

Wheeler, R.E.M. Rome Beyond the Imperial Frontiers, Pelican Books, 1955.

Yazdani, G. Ajanta, Oxford, 1930-1955.

Zimmer, H. The Art of Indian Asia, Bollington Books, New York, 1955.

Index

H

T

X

Y

Z